Cretin Family

Cretin Family

A History of the Ramones Through
Their Tribute Bands Worldwide

Mark Leadon

First paperback edition: 2024

ISBN:
Paperback: 978-1-80541-615-9
eBook: 978-1-80541-614-2

The author has made every reasonable effort to trace the photographers in this book. If there are any omissions of credits, please accept my apologies.

Front Cover Illustration by Charly Fuller
Back Cover Illustration by Alessandro Sacco

To Mum, Dad, brother Steve,
Maddie, Alice, Ben and Tom.

Dedicated to Joey, Johnny, Dee Dee,
Tommy, Marky, Richie, C.J and Elvis.
Thank you for the memories.

Special thanks to Agnes Likus for her help, advice
and continued support in the writing of this book.

To all those musicians who shared their recollections,
experiences and love of The Ramones, helping to keep
their name alive, my sincere thanks and gratitude.

Contents

Contents

Foreword

Something to believe in

The Ramones are one of those bands that come around once in a generation. A band that changed the pulse and sound of music. They influenced so many kids to grab a guitar, pick up some drum sticks and start paving their own path to success!

What makes them so special is that they were innovators! They didn't play by the rules, they played from the heart. That is what I believe makes their music so timeless and not sound dated.

Photograph by Daniel Noble

There was nothing pretentious about them. No fancy outfits, just street clothes that all the kids could relate to. They never wanted to make themselves feel more important than their fans. They saved many kids from drowning because the Ramones gave them hope and made them feel that it was OK to be different than everybody else. Their lyrics and songs gave them something to believe in,

That's the Ramones I knew.

That's the Ramones I loved.

Richie Ramone
6/6/24

Introduction: The Good, The Bad & The Ugly

That was the year that was: 1977

I was just 15 years of age when I heard The Ramones for the first time. It was 1977 and I was in the fourth year at school with the somewhat scary prospect of "O" levels exams in the not too distant future. Looking back now, it seems a different world. Internationally, Jimmy Carter, the peanut farmer, had been sworn in as the 39th President of the United States whilst who cannot forget the footage of the NASA Space Shuttle, Enterprise, hopping a lift off the back of a Boeing 747. It was also the year of the deadliest accident in aviation history when two planes collided on the runway at Tenerife airport killing 583 people but maybe even more shocking is that in September the last legal beheading in the western world took place in France by guillotine. Across the border in Spain, 1977 also heralded a new era, with the nation's first democratic elections for 41 years whilst thankfully the year was also the last occasion that a naturally occurring case of the killer disease smallpox was diagnosed throughout the world.

Back home, we had a Labour government in power. James Callaghan was the premier and the only 20th century politician to have held all four major offices of state: Chancellor of the Exchequer, Home Secretary, Foreign Secretary and Prime Minister. His tenure coincided with a national strike undertaken by firefighters with potentially the armed services and their so-called "Green Goddess" fire engines, on stand-by in case of emergencies. It was an age when 56% of Britons owned one car or more and the Ford Fiesta went on sale for the first time in the UK. Think about this, in 1977, a couple with two children had an average net income of £363 a week but a pint of beer was just 38p and a can of coke for us youngsters a mere 11p. There were no such things as DVD or CD players. For your music, you used a stereo or listened to your favourite tunes on a cassette recorder. Oh the joy, if your much-loved tape got tangled or came out of place and who recalls the usually unsuccessful rigmarole of using a pencil to attempt to wind it back in place? Maybe in Britain, 1977 was best known as Queen Elizabeth's silver Jubilee year, with the popularity of the Royal Family surging as the celebrations across the country took hold. This would of course herald a collision course with punk upstarts the *Sex Pistols* but more about that later.

In terms of sport, I adored it and it was truly a memorable year - the Century Test between Australia and England was played at the Melbourne Cricket Ground but let's not dwell on that result. More pleasurable was observing an English cricketing milestone when dependable Geoff Boycott scored the 100th century of his career against the Aussies at his home ground at Headingley in Leeds. Red Rum won a record third Grand National at Aintree whilst the Embassy World Snooker Championship moved to the Crucible Theatre in Sheffield for the ever first time. In tennis, Virginia Wade was crowned Queen of Wimbledon in its centenary year – she is still the last British lady to claim the single's title. Talking of Wimbledon, my beloved football club was elected to the league in place of Workington on June 17th. It's a date that is etched in my memory with the expectation and hopes of Division 4 football at Plough Lane rather than constraints of the Southern League. Continuing with the beautiful game, there was the almost universal disbelief of a Tommy Smith's headed goal as Liverpool claimed their first European Cup by defeating the West German league champions Borussia Mönchengladbach in Rome. It was also the year when Don Revie was vilified as he blotted his copybook by resigning as England's national manager only to accept the higher paid role of United Arab Emirates national football team coach, 24 hours later. Sport was my life as a teenager – *I ate, breathed and slept it.*

As for television, there were only three channels – BBC1, BBC2 and ITV – but somehow there was always something worth watching. On ITV, *the New Avengers*, was the flavour of the day, a revival of the Sixties series - it starred Patrick Macnee, Joanna Lumley and Gareth Hunt as John Steed, Purdey and Mike Gambit respectively. The National Institution of *Coronation Street*, was the number one soap with the likes of Annie Walker, Ena Sharples, Ken Barlow and his Uncle Albert, the larger than life characters. Mike Yarwood and his wonderful impersonations along with *The Morecambe & Wise Show* attracted audiences of more than 28 million, one of the highest ever in UK. television history over the Christmas period. There was no live T.V football in those days apart from those celebrative matches such as the F.A Cup final and that year Manchester United sneaked past old rivals Liverpool by the odd goal in three. Soccer highlights was our staple diet and nourished by either Saturday's BBC's *Match Of The Day* or a Sunday helping of Brian Moore's *The Big Match* on the *other channel.* In the summer, there was ball to ball coverage of all five days of each and every test match with Richie

Benaud and Jim Laker at the helm with the analysis. Invariably, I would be glued not just to these but to all sporting programmes on *the box*.

If you prefer the big screen, then the big attraction was *Star Wars*, where humans, aliens and robots cohabited in "a galaxy far, far away" and where interstellar travel between planets was common due to the light speed hyperspace technology. Sticking with the space theme also saw Steven Spielberg's *Close Encounters of the Third Kind* receive positive reviews when an everyday blue-collar worker life changing encounter with a UFO. Another blockbuster was *Saturday Night Fever* – not my cup of tea for sure, bringing the discotheque out of the clubs and dumping it into your living room. No doubt, if you liked your disco beat, white suits or indeed John Travolta, *you would be dancing* to this.

Of course, there were a number of well-known celebrities who passed that year with undoubtedly the most famed being Elvis Presley, *the King of rock 'n' roll*. Aged just 42 years old when he died in Memphis, Tennessee on August 16th he was unquestionably one of the most significant cultural figures of the 20th century. Another famed singer and actor who lost their life in 1977 was crooner, Bing Crosby, perhaps best known for his song "White Christmas" or his smash hit comedy films, *"Road To"* in partnership with Bob Hope. Sir Charlie Chaplin, English comic actor who rose to fame in the era of silent film, passed away on Christmas Day of that year. His acting career spanned for more than 75 years and is considered one of the movie industry's most important figures. Other notable deaths included actress Joan Crawford and the master of quick wit, comedian and actor Groucho Marx. It was also the year of the execution, by firing squad, of the American killer, Gary Gilmore which would be the inspiration of a punk song by *The Adverts*, the following year.

Looking at the 1977 number one hits, is a real stroll down memory lane. The year started with Johnny Mathis' "When A Child Is Born" at the top of the tree after his successful sales at Christmas time in 1976. *Starsky and Hutch*, actor, turned singer David Soul bagged two number ones that year with "Dont Give Up On Us" and "Silver Lady" as did Swedish super group Abba with "Knowing Me Knowing You Abba" and "The Name of the Game". A further number one was "Way Down" by Elvis Presley which reached the top spot posthumously and was Elvis' first for seven years. Indeed, the cut was stagnating at number 42 the week before his death before suddenly climbing and hitting pole position in early September, staying there for five weeks. Is there anyone who can fail to remember the corny international hit "Chanson d'Amour" by *Manhattan Transfer* or the equally cringeworthy "Yes Sir, I Can Boogie" hit single by the Spanish duo *Baccara?* It was the same with the bland triumphs such as Leo Sayer's "When I Need You" or Julie Covington's "Don't Cry For Me Argentina". *Lovely, nice, pleasant, agreeable, fine....* All adjectives you could use for these songs but for an adolescent, not something which would get the pulse pumping. Then there was the kilted, *Campbeltown Pipe Band* accompanying Paul McCartney and his *Wings* as they marched to a Christmas Day number one. Do me a favour please, top of the hit parade? To cap it all, the rumour was going around that Rod's Stewart's double A-side single of "I Dont Want To Talk About It" and "The First Cut Is The Deepest", which was officially number one in May, was being artificially placed as top dog. The accusation was that the singles charts, as used by the BBC was being rigged to prevent *The Sex Pistols'* "God Save The Queen" from reaching number one… [1]

The Sex Pistols had already made a mark in England in 1976 signing for EMI and releasing their debut single "Anarchy In The UK". On December 1st, the band caused havoc on prime time live TV on Bill Grundy's Thames Television show *Today*, which was broadcast in the London and south-east regions. With host Bill Grundy goading the lads into swearing, the band found themselves banned from playing live in the UK due to the media furore in the aftermath. 1977 continued with headline after headline for the act which became synonymous with British punk. After just one release, record company EMI sacked the controversial *Pistols* after reports the band had vomited and spat their way on to a flight at Heathrow Airport, whilst the *Today* programme incident effectively ended Grundy's career to all intents and purposes. Soon after, bassist and chief song-writer Glen Matlock left the group, with his replacement being the compelling but flawed punk icon and undoubtedly less talented, Sid Vicious. More controversy was to follow as A&M Records signed the band in a ceremony in front of Buckingham Palace only for the contract to be swiftly terminated as a result of the band vandalising property and verbally abusing employees during a visit to the record company's office. Not to rest on their laurels, the group signed for Virgin and it was at this point that they released their second single "God Save The Queen". Never to miss an opportunity for a publicity stunt, *The Sex Pistols* attempted to interrupt the Queen's Silver Jubilee celebrations as the lads performed on a boat on the River Thames – an event which witnessed a scuffle taking place and the police making several arrests including their manager, Malcolm McLaren. In

October, the band release their controversial L.P "Never Mind the Bollocks, Here's the Sex Pistols", and despite refusal by major retailers in the UK to stock it, it entered the album charts at number one, the week after its release.

So it was during this musical hotchpotch that I spent my formative years – a real case of *The Good, The Bad & The Ugly*. The pop world had fragmented. On the one hand, there was conformity – led by disco and an array of bland pop music which I just couldn't relate to. On the other hand, there was punk fronted by the snarling, grimacing, anarchistic, *Sex Pistols*. Although, unquestionably I leaned towards those nihilistic boys from London, there was something missing, something which I still needed to search for. A few years earlier, I had enjoyed a taste of *glam*. Yes, some of the songs were undeniably *naff* and some of the outrageous clothes, platform-soled boots, gaudy make-up was also pretty gross, but within all of it, there were glimpses of a new dawning. Many would point to the hippy-like Marc Bolan as the ultimate in glam whose *T. Rex* produced a string of classic, catchy, wonderful hits with simple but appealing riffs and strange lyrics to boot. Possibly the pick of the bunch was "Solid Gold Easy Action", "20th Century Boy", "Get It On", "Telegram Sam", "Children Of The Revolution" and "Jeepster" - all delivered spectacularly. Similarly, I make no apologies, when stating that many felt that the King of glam was Gary Glitter and his support musicians *The Glitter Band*. Nowadays the man who was born Paul Gadd is ridiculed - rightly disgraced for a series of sex offences. However, before these facts were known, in his heyday he did create that instantly identifiable trademark sound, *The Glitter Beat* - a thumping sub tribal rhythm coordinated by two drummers, crunchy guitar riffs with sporadic terrace chanting. "I'm The Leader Of The Gang (I am)" is probably his most famous hit but there were so many others too. "I Love You Love Me Love", "Hello, Hello, I'm Back Again", "I Didn't Know I Loved You (Till I Saw You Rock 'n' Roll)" and "Do You Wanna Touch Me There (Oh Yeah)" are just a few tongue twisters which reminds us of Glitter's glory days. However, for me, "Rock And Roll Parts One and Two" takes some beating with the more instrumental version (Part 2), complete with its heavy drum beat, "heys" and timely "grunts" an absolutely gem. Glitter, just like Iggy Pop, has been hailed as a "godfather of punk" and there is no doubt that some punk groups were influenced by his band. *The UK Subs,* for instance, at their peak even entered on to the stage to the tune of "I'm The Leader Of The Gang (I am)" whilst the chanting vocals and dual relentless drumming style of *Adam And The Ants* coined as the *Burundi* beat very much is reminiscent of Glitter at his best.

As well as *The Sex Pistols*, punk *threw up* a multitude of bands that year and it would be impossible to go through each and every one. Undoubtedly, three groups are cited more than any others and all fashioned records which sit in my collection. Firstly, *The Damned* who undeniably wrote some absolute corkers including "New Rose" which was the first British punk single to be released the previous year. The group also provided a charismatic edge with the band members having their own distinctive individual identity but maybe the fact that they didn't seem to take it quite as seriously as they should have, got up people's noses. Secondly, *The Clash,* a torrent of pure energy with the self-titled debut album release a universally acclaimed masterpiece. They even had a song titled "1977" with the line *No Elvis, Beatles or the Rolling Stones"* beautifully summing up the change in the music status quo. Thirdly, *The Stranglers* - For many would-be punks, this bunch were the first group that they could enthuse about. Easier to listen to then *The Damned, Sex Pistols* or *The Clash* but still with the attitude needed during that era for street credibility, for countless teenagers this was the group of preference. *The Stranglers* also provided the punk world with musical integrity. These guys could actually play their instruments and not just rely on a three chord thrash. Indeed, it was *The Stranglers* which I initially turned to but there was still a quality that cannot be easily described as missing – *a certain je ne sais quoi.*

At school, we used to weigh up the calibre of these bands. I remember I wasn't really into political rantings or anti-establishment sentiments which was driven by *The Pistols* and *The Clash* whilst *The Damned* were a little too hit or miss for my liking. *The Stranglers*, on the other hand, certainly had those great melodies but were too mid-paced. It seemed like they needed a jump-start with even "London Lady", probably their punkiest and speediest effort from their debut album "Rattus Norvegicus", hardly getting out of third gear and not the tempo I expected from this genre of music. It must have been around October, 1977, when I heard The Ramones for the first time. I admit that I had little idea who they were or what they were about. At this time, I was a *Little Englander* in splendid isolation and, of course, more into my sporting fixation rather than any deep musical interest. Alex, a friend at my school in Battersea, lent me a tape of their debut album, the self-titled "The Ramones" and said to me "I reckon you will like these, they are pretty fast." He was right! At first, I thought they were funny. Each song was over so quickly and oh my god, "Now I wanna sniff some glue" were virtually the only words to this song! Who were these geeks? Are they for real? However, after three or four plays, I soon realised that this was different. This was the *real deal*. Fast, hard-edged short songs, stripped-down to the bare bones. The louder I played it, the better it sounded. I simply had to buy this album for myself and quickly went down to the local record shop to purchase one. I then gazed at that album cover for the first time. I was right, they were geeks! I stood there as if transfixed with the album in my hands. Who was that gangly *creature*? Did that man really comb his fringe like that all the time? Was this a band or a bunch of street fighting junkies ready to mug any person who dared look at them in the eye? Then it struck me. Blimey, I was wearing torn jeans, had plimsolls on my feet and had that straight brown hair. I just needed a leather jacket and I too could be one of them, part of that *extended family*. Next day, I went down to the Portobello Road Market in Notting Hill and bought myself one ensuring I made the first step in joining their clan.

Gabba Gabba
We accept you, we accept you, one of us
Gabba Gabba
We accept you, we accept you, one of us

Up until that time, I had had two loves – football and cricket. The Ramones were certainly going to be a third. Within a couple of weeks, a month at tops, "Leave Home" and "Rocket To Russia" were also purchased. From then or in, I became a Ramones geek and it's fair to say that once you truly love The Ramones, you will be hooked - there will be no other band for you. As soon as I was old enough, I went to my first Ramones gig. This was at London's *Rainbow Theatre* in Finsbury Park on

February 9th, 1980. They quite simply blew my mind. It wasn't their best concert, however. That was saved for 18 months later - the *Midnight Madness* concert at the *Victoria Apollo* on 19th November, 1981. The group never got on stage until around 1 o'clock in the morning. I managed to get right in front of Johnny, leaning on the stage in front of the spread-eagled maestro. He gave me one his plectrums which added to the experience and fuelled my love of the band. During that concert, I can confirm that Dee Dee presented his bass to someone in the crowd. According to one friend, the bass was not won easily and fights took place in order to earn the right of that four-stringed guitar. In August 2017, I also had the privilege to be invited on stage to sing "I Wanna Be Well" along-side Richie Ramone at *The Flag* in Watford on one of his individual tours. It may have been a small venue, with an audience of probably no more than 40 or so people watching and not The Ramones as such but that evening certainly was a dream come true for this old timer.

The Ramones would thankfully come back to England frequently and would always take in one of the large venues of my home town in London. Venues such as the *Electric Ballroom, Hammersmith Odeon, Hammersmith Palais, The Venue, Lyceum Ballroom, the Town and Country Club, London Astoria* and *Brixton Academy* were always rammed but I would somehow ensure that I managed to get a ticket. London audiences consisted of a variety of cohorts – it was not unusual to see old school punks with their spikey dyed hair, side to side moshing with skinheads, Mohicans, headbangers or simply Ramones clones with their bowl-like basin cut, T-shirts, leathers, ripped jeans and sneakers. The memory plays tricks but from what I recall, by the end of their career, there were both the old generation of enthusiasts and more than a sprinkling of a younger fan base as well. Although there were always more males in the crowd, there were also a good proportion of females with some of the *punkettes* often the most-crazed, hyped, loudest and wired of them all. What was for certain, is that at any gig there was a bond of togetherness, the feeling of being part of that Ramones *Happy Family,* just like the famous tune. Indeed, all across the world, the fan base might be made up of outcasts, oddities, loners or misfits who feel frustration, isolation, alienation or being misunderstood but one thing is for sure there's a knowledge that other Ramones fans will feel those same feelings. You will be part of that extended **Cretin Family** – "Cretin Family" was not just one of my favourite songs but for me perfectly encapsulated the spirit of The Ramones fan base. I had no hesitation naming this piece of literature on Ramones tributes under that designation.

Oh and what happened to that 15-year old boy who loved sport back in the day? Well, I became a PE teacher, what else? Oh yeah, I am also part of that extended Ramones family. I became one of those *cretins* in a tribute act.

Sitting Here in Queens:
The Fast Four

The Ramones were formed in 1974 in Forest Hills, Queens, New York. One of the early misconceptions was that the band members were related but this was not the case. Tamás Erdélyi and John Cummings had already been in a high-school band in the late '60s called *The Tangerine Puppets* and made friends with Douglas Colvin who moved into the area. The fourth member of the group was Jeffrey Hyman who had played in the early 1970s glam rock band called *Sniper*.

The early line-up of the group only featured Cummings on his recognisable instrument on lead guitar. Richard Stern was on bass, Hyman was on drums whilst Colvin played rhythm guitar and sang lead vocals. Changes were soon made however. Stern quickly left, Colvin moved to bass, as he found it difficult to sing and perform simultaneously and because he would become hoarse if he sang for too long whilst Hyman switched roles to become vocalist. This left a space for a drummer which would be taken up by Erdélyi. Tamás, who had assumed the role as manager, would often teach potential replacement drummers the required technique. Soon it was realised, that he performed better than those auditioned and instead moved full time onto the drummer's stool.

During this period, Colvin allegedly was inspired by *The Beatles'* Paul McCartney use of the pseudonym Paul Ramon. Colvin assumed the name Dee Dee Ramone (this forename was often used when he was a child and short for Douglas). The rest of the band took the collective name also and thus Erdélyi (Tommy), Cummings (Johnny) and Hyman (Joey) all adopted the Ramone pseudonym.

In March 1974, The Ramones played their first show in front of an audience at *Performance Studios* in New York. Within another month, they were playing at the now legendry Manhattan club *CBGBs*. In the book, the essential celebrated punk account of that era *Please Kill Me* written by Legs McNeil and Gillian McCain, the early Ramones style was succinctly captured by Richard Hell, ex member of bands such as *Television, The Heartbreakers* and *The Voidoids*. "All their songs were two minutes long" he stated. "They had maybe five or six at the time. 'I Don't Wanna Go Down To The Basement', 'I Don't Wanna Walk Around With You', 'I Don't Wanna Be Learned, I Don't Wanna Be Tamed' and 'I Don't Wanna" something else'." [2] Rather ironically Hell went on to add that according to Dee Dee, The Ramones "didn't write a positive song until 'Now I Wanna Sniff Some Glue'." [3] Right from the outset Dee Dee would start to count in each song with his famous "one, two, three, four" simply because the group could not figure out how to do a silent count. Indeed, the count-off, signature rapid-fire cry of "1, 2, 3, 4" would not only be a trademark of the band but synonymous with punk in general too. Similarly, even early on, the guitarists both adopted that imposing, distinctive stance when they played. Johnny's description of how he eventually drilled the incoming C.J Ramone years later showed how much importance The Ramones placed on appearance at their shows. "We had a mirror in front of us in the rehearsal room. I'd say, C.J, face there. Don't look at Mark. Look in the mirror. When you see me go forward, you go forward. Get your bass down below your waist. Get your legs spread apart. Look forward and play forward." [4]

According to writer Alan Kozzin, it was the journalist and publicist Tony Barrow who played a crucial role in shaping the public's perception of *The Beatles* during the early '60s coining the phrase the *'Fab Four'* in a timely news release. [5] Well, if the lads from Merseyside earned the right for that nickname, then there is no doubt in my mind that a rightful moniker for the boys from Queens should be the *'Fast Four'*. With their characteristic stripped down songs at lightning speeds one critic stated that "The Ramones may or may not have invented punk rock, but they were inarguably the most important band in punk history, creating the stylistic prototype that would be followed by countless bands who emerged in their wake. They were informed by the thunder and flash of the *Who* and the *MC5*, the speed and primitivism of Iggy and the *Stooges*, and the alternately sullen and goofy musings of '60s garage rock, but The Ramones synthesized their influences into something raw and revolutionary, a fury of pounding rhythms and downstroked guitars married to rudimentary melodies and comically absurd lyrics that both mocked and celebrated popular culture and teenage life." [6] Throughout this book I will refer the band as the *'fast four'* which *perfectly* encapsulates their wondrously simple but oh so effective *modus operandi*.

By this time, The Ramones had featured on the front cover of the renowned *Punk magazine* and were spearheading this new punk movement. As the co-founder of this magazine, McNeil, stated "they were all wearing these black leather jackets. And they counted off this song…and it was just this wall of noise… they looked so striking. These guys were not hippies. This was something completely new." [7] The group also now had a manager – Danny Fields. The band accepted his offer to come on board, under the condition that he provided them $3,000 for some new equipment. By late 1975, they came to the attention of Seymour Stein, who was president of Sire records and a contract was signed. In January 1976, The Ramones started recording their debut self-titled album at *Plaza Sound Studio*. The iconic first L.P cover was taken by Roberta Bayley, shot in the neighbourhood of East Second Street, between Bowery and Second Avenue, a stone's throw from *CBGB's*. It was the ideal venue for the shoot and undoubtedly set the tone for hundreds of snapshots for future punk wannabes with leather clad and ripped jeans band members aligned up against a wall. Johnny Ramone, in his autobiography *Commando,* succinctly described the setting stating that "it was bedraggled, with lots of black brick walls which was perfect for us. That's why we took most of those early photos around there. It was perfect for black and white, since there was little colour in the neighbourhood." [8]

That first album was undoubtedly a game-changer. Described as "flawless", "untouched by the rust of time", "a brilliant recording from front to back" and "not only one of the most important albums in the history of Punk/Punk-Rock; it might be one of the most influential and important albums ever." Clocking in at just under half an hour in length, driven by ferocious guitars, The Ramones committed 13 original tracks and one cover to their debut. In one review by *AllMusic*, it sums up the L.P perfectly. "With the three-chord assault of 'Blitzkrieg Bop', "Ramones" begins at a blinding speed and never once over the course of its 14 songs does it let up. The Ramones is all about speed, hooks, stupidity, and simplicity. The songs are imaginative reductions of early rock & roll, girl group pop, and surf rock. Not only is the music boiled down to its essentials, but The Ramones offer a twisted, comical take on pop culture with their lyrics, whether it's the horror schlock of 'I Don't Wanna Go Down to the Basement', the gleeful violence of 'Beat on the Brat' or the maniacal stupidity of 'Now I Wanna Sniff Some Glue'. And the cover of Chris Montez's 'Let's Dance' isn't a throwaway -- with its single-minded beat and lyrics, it encapsulates everything the group loves about pre-*Beatles* rock & roll. They don't alter the structure, or the intent, of the song, they simply make it louder and faster. And that's the key to all of The Ramones' music -- it's simple rock & roll, played simply, loud, and very, very fast. None of the songs clock in at any longer than two and half minutes, and most are considerably shorter." Despite the lack of popularity in its era, the importance of the album for the development of punk rock music was incredible, influencing many of the most well-known names in punk rock, including *The Damned, The Clash, Black Flag, Misfits, and Green Day*. Billie Joe Armstrong, singer for *Green Day*, explained his reasoning for listening to the band: "they had songs that just stuck in your head, just like a hammer they banged right into your brain." The album also had a great impact on the English punk scene as well, with the bassist for *Generation X*, Tony James, saying that the album caused English bands to change their style. "When their album came out," commented James, "all the English groups tripled speed overnight. Two-minute-long songs, very fast." In another interview, James stated that "everybody went up three gears the day they got that first Ramones album. Punk rock—that rama-lama super- fast stuff—is totally down to The Ramones. Bands were just playing in an *MC5* groove until then." There have been "few albums as seismic" and for many "it's considered to be the first true punk rock album" inspiring a generation; "its shockwaves and influence is still being felt and heard to this day." [9]

Their first appearance in England was ironically on Independence Day July 4th, 1976 at the Roundhouse, London, where they supported the *Flamin Groovies*. The following night, the band met members of *The Sex Pistols, The Clash* and *The Damned* at Dingwall's Club which helped kick start the punk scene in the UK. Johnny Ramone understood the significance of the British tour. "When we got to England, we saw that something was really happening there", he observed. "They were all cool-looking kids, which was what we needed for the movement. We were aware that we were changing music by this point, and that we were at the forefront of something new, but we couldn't do it alone. These were people and bands who could help us. We knew that we needed this British invasion." [10]

1977 saw two albums. "Leave Home" had a rather more "tinny" and more polished sound but continued with the break-neck pace and stripped down minimalist methodology. Drummer Tommy felt that their second 33 was "heavier, more melodic, with more bite. It has more of a pop feel. That was our mood – insane pop songs with lyrics inspired by cheesy slasher and horror flicks, with a happy-go-lucky feel to it" going on to add that "while the first album is more conceptual", the second is "happy pop, less arty with more real musicianship." [11] One fact which often gets overlooked is that The Ramones had now released two albums before the likes of *The Saints, The Damned, The Clash* and *The Sex Pistols* had even fashioned one.

This was quickly followed by their third album which was released in November. Never one to worry about protocol, the aggressively titled "Rocket to Russia" had a slightly more commercial inclinationl whilst retaining its punk roots and roller coaster speed. John Holmstrom, editor of *Punk* magazine" gets it spot on when he describes The Ramones during this period liking them to "heavy metal bubblegum." [12] "Rocket To Russia" eventually peaked at number 49 on the Billboard pop albums in the States and although it was one of the band's most successful releases, it still did not result in that all important breakthrough. According to John Doran of the BBC, "their third album, is perhaps their most critically acclaimed, mixing an obvious yearning for rock 'n' roll's past with a minimalist punk attack which made them sound fresh." [13]

1978 saw the first change in the line-up of the band when Tommy, who was tired of the constant touring, quit the group to concentrate on producing. It would not be the last time he would collaborate with the band, however, as he would help in the production of their next album and 1984's "Too Tough To Die". The drumming position was filled by Marc Bell who had played in Richard Hell's The *Voidoids* along with *Dust,* a heavy metal band. The biggest compliment that can be bestowed on Marky is that despite him not being the original drummer, many fans still think of him as arguably *the best drummer.*

The first album with Marky was "Road to Ruin", a rather more pessimistic titled release then the previous L.Ps. Although this had some typical speedy tracks, it also had a few more medium paced and lengthier songs too. Legs McNeil felt that it was "their bravest album" going on to add that "it was at this point in their career, after releasing three great rock 'n' roll records, that they realised they weren't going to catch any breaks. The rock 'n' roll fantasy of instant superstardom was quickly evaporating: no jet with their name on it, no screaming hordes of girls waiting at the airport." [14] Despite this realisation, Marky and the others soon became movie stars. The Ramones made their film debut in the largely unforgettable *Rock 'n' Roll High School* released in 1979. Dee Dee played the "fall guy" with his continued quest for pizza throughout the motion picture.

Although the illustrious producer Phil Spector's "End Of The Century" helped them achieve their greatest commercial success of their career with the fifth studio album peaking at number 44 in the Billboard charts, the late '70s and early '80s arguably witnessed their weakest phase. More emphasis on the slower, over produced ballads and less on Johnny's favoured rawer, raucous guitar was evident with the net effect of a dumbing down from the traditional Ramones sound. Despite this lull, there were still some quality tracks although one surely can't help thinking that a more basic production sound would have made these into classics – "All The Way", "All's Quiet On The Eastern Front", "You Sound Like You're Sick", "Outsider", "Time Bomb" and the rest all just needed a little bit less commercialism and a little bit more power. As Johnny said about the subsequent album "Pleasant Dreams", "I knew I was in trouble immediately when Gouldman (the producer) said, 'your amp is buzzing too much, you have to turn it down'." The guitarist went on to point out that "I knew going in, that this was not going to be the type of album I wanted. It really could have used another two or three punk songs." [15] Interestingly enough, the digitally re-mastered CD recent re-releases indicate that there were some excellent *'heavier'* demos which somehow did not make the cut onto the original L.Ps. Tracks such as "I'm Not An Answer", "Stares In This Town", "No One To Blame", "Unhappy Girl", "Kicks To

Try" and "Sleeping Troubles", if included undoubtedly would have made for a stronger period for the band.

At the end of their next album, "Subterranean Jungle", the band needed their third drummer. Marky was sacked due to his alcoholism in early 1983 and ex-*Velveteen*, Richard Reinhardt aka Richie Beau, stepped onto the drummer's seat as Richie Ramone. "Subterranean Jungle", according to freelance journalist and *MTV* senior writer Gil Kaufman, also "officially marked the end of The Ramones' flirtation with the mainstream. From then on the boys did what they wanted, charts and label hacks be damned and they were better for it." [16] Richie's first album with the group was "Too Tough To Die". Back to basics and back to top form, the album in my opinion was without doubt their best since 1978. With the tried and trusted Tommy Erdélyi and Ed Stasium returning to the production team, the minimalist approach worked again. Indeed, Dee Dee commented that Tommy was a great part of "the whole 'less is more' thing," [17] and this slant coupled with a better relationship between the two guitarists led to a more natural sound. Archetypal tracks such as "Danger Zone", "Humankind" and "Daytime Dilemma" were a breath of fresh air. The album also saw the only instrumental track, "Durango 45" which would thereafter start all Ramones gigs as well as seeing Dee Dee's hair looking more like Sid Vicious than a 1960's Beatle or Monkee. Richie featured in two more albums "Animal Boy" and "Halfway To Sanity", before he left the band, quitting after Johnny refused to give a larger chunk of the merchandise sales. Nonetheless Richie played an important role in revitalising the group not just with his talented drumming but also with his backing vocals. Additionally, the new stick man had a song writing talent of his own penning, for example "Somebody Put Something In My Drink" and "Smash You".

Richie's replacement was none other than Clem Burke – the celebrated drummer of *Blondie*. It was not a match made in heaven, however and Elvis Ramone, as he was dubbed, could not drum at the required speed and was quickly replaced after just two gigs. With Marky now clean, he returned to the fold, joining the band for a second time. After the 1989 release of "Brain Drain", the unthinkable happened. Dee Dee, founder member, chief songwriter and the punk image of the band, left the group. Quickly, the pragmatic Johnny organised auditions and a Dee Dee clone emerged. Christopher Joseph Ward took up the challenge and would go on to complete seven years with the band. During that time, C.J Ramone, would perform in "Mondo Bizarro", the somewhat tame "Acid Eaters", (an album completely of cover songs) and their final album, the aptly named "¡Adios Amigos!" The new member would not only play bass but act as secondary vocalist and of course count the group in with the usual "1, 2, 3, 4s". Without a shadow of doubt, C.J deserves so much praise; filling the iconic bassist's plimsolls was an impossible task but he sure did give it a go. With Dee Dee still writing for the group, there was minimal disruption and although there's no doubt that fans missed Dee Dee's individuality and nuances, C.J's youthful energy gave the group a new lease of life.

Old Father Time, however, catches up with us all and band members knew they were ready to hang up the leathers. Johnny, for instance, felt that "near the end, our albums had long since gotten weak, and I was very protective of how we were looking and how the fans would see us. On the last studio album, "¡Adios

Amigos!" we went for the cover photo shoot, and I told them that we were keeping our backs to the cameras." [18] With the implication that a firing squad had them lined up against a wall to have them executed, this was the perfect way to bow out, bearing in mind their first L.P started with that symbolic wall photograph back in '76.

After a farewell tour, the band played their 2263rd and last gig on August 6th 1996, at the Palace in Hollywood, Los Angeles. Guest appearances from Pearl Jam's Eddie Vedder, *Soundgarden's* Chris Cornell, and *Rancid's* Tim Armstrong and Lars Frederiksen seemed to suggest that The Ramones were leaving their punk legacy to some of the youngsters to carry on their work. Maybe the highlights of the show, however, were *Motörhead's* Lemmy playing the classic "R.A.M.O.N.E.S" and Dee Dee back on stage singing along-side C.J on "Love Kills".

There was to be no comeback gig with Joey sadly dying of lymphoma in 2001. The following year, the singer was posthumously inducted into the "Rock and Roll Hall of Fame" along with Johnny, Dee Dee, Tommy and Marky. On November 30th, 2003, a further honour occurred when a block of East 2nd Street in New York City was officially renamed Joey Ramone Place. It is in the area where the singer once lived with bandmate Dee Dee and is near the former site of the music club *CBGB*, where The Ramones began their career. By June 2002, Dee Dee had died of a heroin overdose whilst in September 2004, Johnny passed away from prostate cancer and Tommy succumbed of bile duct cancer in July 2014. It seems quite surreal that all four of the original group are now all no longer with us and maybe highlights not only the toil of constant touring but also their express train *loco Lifestyle*. Indeed, this hectic schedule will be highlighted as the various tribute bands across the world are analysed. Taking 1980, as an example, The Ramones played 150 times in that calendar year equating to a gig roughly every two and a half days. That, however, does not paint a true picture of the frenetic rota – As well as nearly 60 gigs in the United States, the band visited Britain, Canada, France, the Netherlands, Belgium, Italy, Spain, Portugal, Germany, Norway, Sweden, Denmark, Switzerland, the Republic of Ireland, Japan, Australia and New Zealand. It seems crazy in hindsight, but in that year alone, the *'fast four'* toured England on no less than three occasions. Maybe, once one starts to take into consideration this draining touring roster then it becomes more understandable why the dynamics of the band members become so strained. What is also apparent, is how many places The Ramones touched. This is highlighted below which shows the various countries the New Yorkers performed in and the first date which they played in that nation. Once our tribute bands are viewed, the book will broadly follow this chronology.

- United States of America - March 30th 1974
- England - July 4th 1976
- Canada - September 24th 1976
- Switzerland - April 24th 1977
- France - April 28th 1977
- Belgium - May 5th 1977
- The Netherlands - May 6th 1977
- Denmark - May 12th 1977
- Sweden - May 15th 1977

- Finland - May 16th 1977
- Scotland – May 21st 1977
- Germany - September 11th 1978
- Northern Ireland - September 23rd 1978
- Republic of Ireland - September 24th 1978
- Wales - October 3rd 1978
- Italy - February 14th 1980
- Japan - June 27th 1980
- Australia - July 8th 1980
- New Zealand - July 21st 1980
- Norway - August 30th 1980
- Spain - September 19th 1980
- Portugal - September 22nd 1980
- Brazil - January 31st 1987
- Argentina - February 4th 1987
- Puerto Rico - February 19th 1988
- Greece - May 12th 1989
- Mexico - June 23rd 1989
- Austria - November 21st 1990
- Yugoslavia - November 24th 1990
- Chile - September 13th 1992
- Slovenia - October 10th 1994
- Croatia - October 11th 1994
- Czech Republic - October 13th 1994
- Uruguay - November 14th 1994

A more visual representation can be seen below in the map entitled "Touring, Touring". It depicts *The Ramones World*, highlighting the countries where they played in red.

GREENLAND
CANADA
UNITED STATES
MEXICO
CUBA
VENEZUELA
COLOMBIA
ECUADOR
PERU
BOLIVIA
BRAZIL
CHILE
ARGENTINA
URUGUAY
RUSSIA
KAZAKHSTAN
MONGOLIA
CHINA
UKRAINE
BELARUS
POLAND
TÜRKIYE
IRAN
PAKISTAN
INDIA
SAUDI ARABIA
YEMEN
OMAN
IRAQ
WESTERN SAHARA
MAURITANIA
MALI
NIGER
CHAD
SUDAN
ALGERIA
LIBYA
EGYPT
NIGERIA
ETHIOPIA
SOMALIA
DR CONGO
KENYA
TANZANIA
ANGOLA
ZAMBIA
NAMIBIA
SOUTH AFRICA
MADAGASCAR
JAPAN
PHILIPPINES
MALAYSIA
INDONESIA
AUSTRALIA
NEW ZEALAND
"Touring Touring"
The Ramones World
Created with mapchart.net

The pace of a Ramones concert is now legendary with the boys able to perform 30 or so songs at break neck speed without the need to come up for air. Yet, I have heard some people even question whether they can be classed as a punk band. Yes, admittedly, some of their songs or photographs were commercial. I still cringe at the coloured T-shirts on the cover of "End Of The Century" - an act which Johnny Ramone vehemently was against and confessed in his autobiography *Commando* that he made a mistake in allowing anyone to take a photo shoot without the trademark leather jackets on. [19] Similarly, the violin accompaniment on Phil Spector's "Baby I Love You" during the same period was an embarrassment. Indeed, I remember to this day, having to justify my love of the group to my mates at my sixth form after their performance of the single on BBC's *"Top of the Pops"*. Some of their singles may also be a little melodic for your archetypical 1977 punk or skinhead. "Sheena is a punk rocker" had the title but did not portray the aggression of an expectant English audience. However, The Ramones needed that big hit and tried everything to smash the *airwaves*. Unfortunately, they never got it although they did finally make it big in South America playing to packed, frenzied audiences.

Other people have classed their music as too *headbangy*. Again, certainly a handful of their songs such as the guitar break in "Havana Affair" or the brilliant "Chinese Rock" or "Cabbies On Crack" wavered towards that genre. Indeed, the classic "Suzy Is A Headbanger" openly invites Lemmy and his crew to join The Ramones happy family. However, not punk? Come on, be serious. "Chainsaw", "Loudmouth", "Commando", "Judy Is A Punk" and "I Don't Wanna Go Down To The Basement"? These are punk classics and if you cannot see that then you certainly need a "Lobotomy" or a dose of "Psycho Therapy". In fact, as if to prove a point, some of The Ramones' later material was quite hardcore. "Wart Hog", for instance, from the album "Too Tough To Die" with Dee Dee's *satanic* vocals, pounding drumming and guitars sounding more akin to a hatchet than a musical instrument almost seemed to state to new punk bands "if you want some hard stuff, this is how to do it." Other tracks such as "Endless Vacation, "The Crusher", "Cretin Family", "I Lost My Mind" and "Animal Boy" continued in the same vein and certainly should have pleased the "punkier punks" out there. As Eddie Vedder stated, when inducting the band into the "Rock and Roll Hall of Fame" back in 2002, "The Ramones didn't need Mohawks to be punk." [20] Eventually, their pioneering work within punk rock was more and more recognised – the group, for example, received Grammy Awards for lifetime achievement on February 12th, 2011. This was long overdue - after all they were a band that had liberated the spirit of rock 'n' roll with their aggressive, quick fire, simplistic and often twisted form of melodic punk rock music.

Yet it was not just the music that made them the greatest punks. It was the attitude, the style, the energy, the conflicts, the lyrics…Let me expand. There was always an edge about the group. The locomotive pace, the clothes, the wall of noise they created was different – way ahead of their time. Even the band themselves had arguments on stage. As they grew older, it is now well documented that these arguments turned even sourer. Not only were there musical differences but political differences too. Johnny was a disciplinarian and conservative whilst Joey was a liberal Jew. When Johnny "stole" Joey's girlfriend, the two band members did not talk to each other. Indeed, although Mickey

Leigh disputes the idea [21], legend now has it that Joey's song "The KKK Took My Baby Away" has nothing to do with the Klu Klux Klan but is about Johnny and Linda. When you add Joey's OCD and other health problems, Marky and his alcoholic addiction, and Dee Dee's drug abuse and bipolar disorder then there was undoubtedly a volatile mix to the group. All these tales and many more will be drawn out within the stories of our tribute bands but what is crystal clear, is that these idiosyncrasies and frailties made The Ramones what they were. What is also apparent is that we cannot under-state their effect on punk or music in general and this will also be highlighted by musicians, analysts and fans throughout the book. Their legacy is huge. Who can argue with one review by the BBC when discussing the band, for instance? "Dumb, crude, three-chord thrash? Yes. Fast, exhilarating and brand new? Yes. Intelligent, boundary smashing and woefully underrated? Definitely. The Ramones were all of these things and more." [22] Brian Cogan states that the Americans were "one of the two most important bands in punk history" and "created or at least articulated, the 1970s version of punk." [23] Music historian Jon Savage writes of their debut album that "it remains one of the few records that changed pop forever." As described by *AllMusic* critic Stephen Thomas Erlewine, "The band's first four albums set the blueprint for punk, especially American punk and hardcore, for the next two decades." Douglas Wolk, writing for *Slate* in 2001, pointed out that they were "easily the most influential group of the last 30 years." [24] Marco Pirroni of *Siouxsie and The Banshees* so eloquently also stated "The Ramones were just brilliant. They really did invent their own punk style and gave punk its speed… It was The Ramones who took everything one step further and simplified it even more." [25] The list of admirers goes on and on. Indeed, every time you see ripped jeans, leather jackets, a photograph of a group up against a wall or the call of "1, 2, 3, 4" remember the '*fast four*' and those boys from Queens. These were not just the first true punk rockers but quite simple the best too.

Discography

Studio Albums

- Ramones - Released: April 23, 1976 – Label: Sire
- Leave Home - Released: January 10, 1977 - Label: Sire
- Rocket To Russia - Released: November 4, 1977 – Label: Sire
- Road To Ruin – Released September 22, 1978 – Label: Sire
- End Of The Century - Released: February 4, 1980 – Label: Sire
- Pleasant Dreams – Released July 20, 1981 – Label: Sire
- Subterranean Jungle - Released February 23, 1983 – Label: Sire
- Too Tough To Die – Released October 1, 1984 - Labels: Sire, Beggars Banquet, Ariola, RCA, Closer
- Animal Boy – Released May 19, 1986 – Labels: Sire, Beggars Banquet, Ariola, RCA, Barclay
- Halfway To Sanity – Released September 15, 1987 – Labels: Sire, Beggars Banquet, Ariola, RCA, Barclay
- Brain Drain - Released March 23, 1989 – Labels: Sire, Chrysalis
- Mondo Bizarro - Released September 1, 1992 – Labels: Radioactive, Chrysalis
- Acid Eaters - Released December 1, 1993 – Labels: Radioactive, Chrysalis

- *¡Adios Amigos! – Released July 18*th, 1995 - Labels: Radioactive, Chrysalis

Live Albums

- Its Alive - Released: April 1979 – Label: Sire
- Loco Live - Released: March 1992 - Label: Sire
- We're Outta Here - Released: November 1997 – Label: MCA

Singles

- "Blitzkrieg Bop" b/w "Havana Affair" – Released 1976
- "I Wanna Be Your Boyfriend" b/w "California Sun/I Don't Wanna Walk Around With You" (recorded live at The Roxy, Los Angeles) – Released 1976
- "Swallow My Pride" b/w "Pinhead" - – Released 1977
- "Sheena Is a Punk Rocker" b/w "I Don't Care"– Released 1977
- "Rockaway Beach" b/w "Locket Love"– Released 1977
- "Do You Wanna Dance?" b/w "Babysitter"– Released 1978
- "Don't Come Close" b/w "I Don't Want You"– Released 1978
- "Needles and Pins" b/w "I Wanted Everything"– Released 1978
- "She's the One" b/w "I Wanna Be Sedated"– Released 1979
- "Rock 'n' Roll High School" b/w "Do You Wanna Dance? (Live Version)" – Released 1979

- "Baby, I Love You" b/w "High Risk Insurance" – Released 1980
- "Do You Remember Rock 'n' Roll Radio?" b/w "Let's Go" – Released 1980
- "I Wanna Be Sedated" b/w "The Return of Jackie and Judy" – Released 1980
- "We Want the Airwaves" b/w "You Sound Like You're Sick" – Released 1981
- "She's a Sensation" b/w "All's Quiet on the Eastern Front" – Released 1981
- "The KKK Took My Baby Away" b/w "Don't Go" – Released 1981
- "Time Has Come Today" b/w "Psycho Therapy"V– Released 1983
- "Howling at the Moon (Sha-La-La)" b/w "Smash You"/"Street Fighting Man" – Released 1984
- "Chasing the Night" b/w "Howling At the Moon (Sha-La-La)"/"Smash You"/"Street Fighting Man" – Released 1985
- "Bonzo Goes to Bitburg" b/w "Go Home Ann"/"Daytime Dilemma (Dangers of Love)" – Released 1985
- "Something to Believe In" b/w "Somebody Put Something in My Drink"/"(You) Can't Say Anything Nice" – Released 1986
- "Crummy Stuff" b/w "Something to Believe In"/"(And) I Don't Wanna Live This Life" – Released 1986
- "A Real Cool Time" b/w "Life Goes On"/"Indian Giver" – Released 1987
- "I Wanna Live" b/w "Merry Christmas (I Don't Want to Fight Tonight)" – Released 1987

- "Pet Sematary" b/w "Sheena Is A Punk Rocker"/"Life Goes On" – Released 1989
- "I Believe in Miracles" b/w "All Screwed Up" – Released 1989
- "Poison Heart" b/w "Chinese Rocks"/"Sheena Is A Punk Rocker"/"Rockaway Beach"– Released 1992
- Strength to Endure" b/w "The Ballad of Tipper Gore" – Released 1992
- "Journey to the Center of the Mind" – Released 1993
- "Substitute" b/w "7 And 7 Is"/"Out Of Time" – Released 1993
- "7 and 7 Is" - Released 1994
- "I Don't Want to Grow Up" b/w "She Talks To Rainbows" – Released 1995
- "R.A.M.O.N.E.S." – Released 1996

All The Stuff and More
Volume 1: The Ramones in Brief

- The Ramones formed in Forest Hills, Queens, New York in 1974.
- Their first gig was at *Performance Studios* on March 30th, 1974. This was performed as a trio rather than a four-piece.
- The group made their first appearance at *CBGBs* in New York on August 16th, 1974.
- Their self-titled debut album was released on April 23rd, 1976
- The band made their first appearance in England on July 4th, 1976 at *The Roundhouse Theatre* in London. Many feel that this helped kick-start the punk movement in Great Britain
- They recorded 14 studio albums and three official live albums.
- The Ramones performed 2,263 concerts.
- The group played in over 30 countries spanning five different continents.
- They played their final show on August 6th, 1996 at *The Palace* in Los Angeles.
- In 2001, The Ramones received a Grammy Lifetime Achievement Award.
- In 2002, the band were inducted into the "Rock and Roll Hall of Fame".

- In 2003, a block near *CBGBs* was renamed Joey Ramone Place.

Eight *Freaks of Nature* performed in The Ramones – one singer, one guitarist, two bassists and four drummers. Only two, played in every concert – Johnny and Joey. Here is a brief biography of each of those eight musicians who made up *the 'fast four'*.

Freaks of Nature

Joey Ramone

BIRTH NAME: Jeffrey Ross Hyman
DATE OF BIRTH: 19/5/1951
PLACE OF BIRTH: New York City, USA
DIED: 15/4/2001 (aged 49) - New York City, USA
YEARS IN THE RAMONES: 1974-1996

Jeffrey Hyman was born in Queens, in New York City to a Jewish family. As a youngster, he grew up with his parents and brother Mickey Leigh and went to Forest Hill High School but family life was not plain sailing. His mother, Charlotte Lesher, divorced her first husband, Noel Hyman when he was eight years old and her subsequent marriage ended in tragedy after a car accident killed her second spouse. Described as a misfit, an outcast, a loner, Jeffrey was shy although not a recluse or a hermit. [26] His health was also, at times, a cause for concern - at 18 years old, for example, he was diagnosed with obsessive-compulsive disorder and schizophrenia. Growing up he was a fan of Little Richard, Chuck Berry, *The Ronettes, Beach Boys, The Beatles, The Who,* David Bowie and *The Stooges* and music was always a major part of his life. He took up the drums at 13 but in 1972, joined the Glam Rock band, *Sniper* as a singer calling himself Jeff Starship, which he performed in until early 1974, when he was replaced. In 1974, he co-founded

The Ramones and for a fleeting period was on drums until re-organisation gave him the opportunity as front-man. As with all the band members, he took a pseudonym, assuming the stage name of Joey Ramone which he would eventually be famed for. At around 6 foot, 6 inches, he became one of punk's easiest recognisable characters with his ultra-thin build, long hair and round tinted glasses. Left foot forward, leaning over his mic stand swaying gently, the towering singer's "signature bleat was the voice of punk rock in America." [27] Joey, along with Johnny Ramone, were the only two founding members who stayed in the band until it disbanded in 1996. Despite this, for much of the band's existence, there was much conflict between the two, ranging from their differences in personalities and political leanings to the complete break-down in their relationship after the singer's ex-girlfriend fell in love and married the guitarist. Joey was involved in a couple of small side projects – in 1983, he sang along-side his brother Mickey in the band *The Seclusions* whilst in 1999 he co-produced Ronnie Spector's EP "She Talks to Rainbows". By 1995, he diagnosed with lymphoma which he kept private until it was revealed in March 2001. He died in the April, a month before his 50th birthday. Two solo albums were released posthumously – In 2002, "Don't Worry About Me" which featured the track "What A Wonderful World" and in 2012, "Ya Know". Part of his legacy saw a block near *CBGB* officially named after him – Joey Ramone Place in 2003, whilst a year earlier, he was posthumously inducted, along with other band members into the "Rock and Roll Hall of Fame".

Johnny Ramone

BIRTH NAME: John William Cummings
DATE OF BIRTH: 8/10/1948
PLACE OF BIRTH: New York City, USA
DIED: 15/9/2004 (aged 55) – Los Angeles, USA
YEARS IN THE RAMONES: 1974-1996

John Cummings was born in Queens, in New York City and was the only child of Francis, a construction worker of Irish descent and Estelle, a waitress of Polish-Ukrainian origin. The family were Catholics and he made his first Communion when he was six although was not a regular church goer. John was a huge baseball enthusiast supporting the New York Yankees and as a child was a pitcher in the Little League. He also developed a love for the movies and particularly enjoyed science fiction films. John was a big Elvis Presley fan and also listened to Ricky Nelson, the Everly Brothers, Little Richard and Jerry Lee Lewis. John's father was a loving but strict disciplinarian and was sent him for two years to military school – first to Staunton Military Academy and then to Peekskill near West Point in New York. As a teenager, Cummings played along-side Tamás Erdélyi (Tommy Ramone) in a band called *The Tangerine Puppets* and after leaving Forest Hills High School in 1966, became a self-confessed delinquent involved in both drugs and crime. Johnny was a great concert goer and went to many shows including *The Rolling Stones, The Who, The Beatles* (where he claims to have to have taken rocks to throw at them), *Black Sabbath,* Alice Cooper, *The Doors, MC5* and *The Stooges* which he particularly loved. John got a job in construction and struck up a friendship with Douglas Colvin (Dee Dee Ramone), who worked nearby and eventually the pair would buy guitars together with Cummings' purchase being a blue Mosrite for $50. [28] By 1974, he co-founded The Ramones and took up the pen name of Johnny Ramone. Visually he was renowned for his spread-eagle stance and snarling grimaces and famed for his fast, downstroking technique which combined with his characteristic tone from his guitar amp, produced an aggressive sound, heavily influencing the punk rock genre. He was also known for being the grouchy, tough, *sergeant major* and many feel that his no-nonsense authoritarian approach kept the band together. In 1983, Johnny was severely injured in a street brawl and needed emergency brain surgery to save his life whilst he was also involved in one of the major sources of animosity when he began dating and later married Linda Daniele, who had previously gone out with singer, Joey. This was Johnny's second marriage after marrying Rosana in 1972. Johnny was obsessed with money, a staunch supporter of the Republic party, and even mentioned President Bush, when being inducted in the "Rock and Roll Hall of Fame". He died in his Los Angeles home, following a five-year battle with prostate cancer whilst in 2012, Johnny's autobiography, *"Commando"*, was posthumously released. In 2009, he appeared on *Time's* list of the 10 Greatest electric guitar players and ranked number eight and number 28 on *Spin's* and *Rolling Stone's* 2012 and 2015 respectively lists of the "100 greatest guitarists of all time."

Dee Dee Ramone

<u>BIRTH NAME:</u> Douglas Glenn Colvin
<u>DATE OF BIRTH:</u> 18/9/1951
<u>PLACE OF BIRTH:</u> Fort Gregg-Adams, Virginia, USA
<u>DIED:</u> 5/6/2002 (aged 50) – Los Angeles, USA
<u>YEARS IN THE RAMONES:</u> 1974-1989

Douglas Colvin was the son of an American soldier and a German woman. As a child he was relocated to West Berlin due to his father's military service and as a result of these frequent moves, he had a lonely childhood. His parents separated during his early teens and when he was 15, he and his mother and sister Beverley moved to Forest Hills, Queens to escape his alcoholic father. After an unsuccessful guitar audition for *Television,* he was convinced by John Cummings to form their own band. Initially on lead vocals and rhythm guitar, he quickly moved to bass duties as his voice would become shredded. It was the bassist who first suggested the moniker "The Ramones" after reading that Paul McCartney used the alias of Paul Ramon with Douglas becoming Dee Dee which he first used as a youngster back in Germany. [29] The bass player wrote or co-wrote the majority of the band's material including 53rd and 3rd, a story about male prostitution which was allegedly self-biographical and "Chinese Rock" which had a heroin theme and was first recorded by *The Heartbreakers.* Indeed, Dee Dee was a prolific song writer and according to Johnny Ramone "the most influential punk rock bassist. He set the standard that all punk rock bassists look to." [30] On his white Fender Precision bass, with his legs apart and bass slung low, he defined punk with his breakneck bass lines, bundles of hyped energy and signature "1, 2, 3, 4" introduction. Dee Dee married his first wife Vera Boldis but separated in 1990 and divorced in 1995 with his ex-spouse citing mental illness and drug abuse as the main reason that the relationship was strained. By 1989, he had had enough of The Ramones and to all fans astonishment, quit the band. Dee Dee, however, continued to write songs for the group even after his departure with the band paying for the rights of various tunes. The iconic bassist embarked on a number of projects which even featured an attempt as a hip hop rapper as Dee Dee King in 1987. After this embarrassing failure, he returned to his punk roots in various short-lived projects such as *Sprocket, Spikey Tops*, GG Allin's, *The Murder Junkins* and *Dee Dee Ramone and the Chinese Dragons*. Probably his most famed post Ramones outfit, however, was Dee Dee Ramone I.C.L.C (Inter-Celestrial Light Commune) which lasted from 1994-1996 and included the notable album "I Hate Freaks Like You". Dee Dee formed a Ramones tribute called *The Ramainz* along with drummer Marky Ramone, second wife Barbara Zampini, C.J Ramone as well as also recording several solo albums such as "Zonked". He was present when The Ramones were inducted into the "Rock and Roll Hall of Fame" and humorously thanked himself in his acceptance speech. In 1998, he wrote his autobiography *"Poison Heart: Surviving The Ramones"*. Dee Dee was found dead in his Los Angeles home on June 5th, 2002 with a heroin overdose as the official cause of death.

Tommy Ramone

<u>BIRTH NAME:</u> Tamás Erdélyi
<u>DATE OF BIRTH:</u> 29/1/1949
<u>PLACE OF BIRTH:</u> Budapest, Hungary
<u>DIED:</u> 11/7/2014 (aged 65) – New York City, USA
<u>YEARS IN THE RAMONES:</u> 1974-1978

Tamás Erdélyi was born in Hungary to Jewish parents who survived the Holocaust by being hidden by neighbours. The family left the country for the United States in 1957 due to the Hungarian revolution and after initially locating in the South Bronx, they eventually settled in Forest Hills in Queens. He changed his name to the more Anglicised designation of Thomas Erdelyi [31] and attended Forest Hill High School in the mid-1960s. It was here where he met school mate John Cummings (aka Johnny Ramone) and they both performed in *The Tangerine Puppets* with Thomas playing lead guitar and John on the bass. During his school days, Thomas also became good friends with Monte Melnick who would eventually become The Ramones tour manager and the pair would go to concerts together seeing acts such as *Cream,* Janis Joplin, Chuck Berry and *The Stooges*. After leaving school at 18, he started working as an assistant engineer at the *Record Plant* studio. Soon, Tommy, as he was better known and Monte had built and managed *Performance Studios* and they allowed the fledging Ramones to practice free of charge at the suite. Erdelyi originally intended to be the band's manager and record producer, but he found himself as percussionist once the original drummer, Joey was shifted to singer. When Tommy auditioned new stick men, he would demonstrate what he wanted them to do, but found that nobody could do it better than he did. He remained as drummer for the first three studio albums and also performed on the much heralded "It's Alive" L.P. Tommy is credited to have written "I Wanna Be Your Boyfriend" and the vast majority of the punk anthem "Blitzkrieg Bop". He is also attributed for creating the high hat 1/8th note rhythm that typifies most Ramones drum sections with a light and smooth style and is acclaimed by many as the major person responsible for creating the overall sound and image. By 1978, however, he was not only tired of the constant touring and wanted to concentrate on his real passion of producing but also felt that he was becoming clinically depressed. Despite leaving, Tommy handled band management and co-produced the fourth album, "Road To Ruin" whilst also later returned as producer for their eighth L.P, "Too Tough To Die". Post Ramones he went on to produce the *Replacements* album, "Tim", *Redd Kross's* "Neurotica" and oversaw the reunion of Marky and C.J' s recording of Jed Davis' Joey Ramone tribute "The Bowery Electric". He also performed on guitar as a bluegrass-based folk duo *Uncle Monk*, along-side long-time partner, Claudia Tienan. He was inducted into the "Rock and Roll Hall of Fame" and as part of his acceptance speech mentioned the late vocalist, Joey. Tommy died at his home in Ridgewood Queens after unsuccessful treatment for bile duct cancer. He was the longest-surviving original member of The Ramones.

Marky Ramone

<u>BIRTH NAME:</u> Marc Steven Bell
<u>DATE OF BIRTH:</u> 15/7/1952
<u>PLACE OF BIRTH:</u> New York City, USA
<u>YEARS IN THE RAMONES:</u> 1978-1983 & 1987-1996

Marc and his twin brother Fred were born in a New York Hospital in 1952. Influenced by Ringo Starr of *The Beatles*, he got his first snare drum at the age of 12, received some rudimentary drumming lessons and not long after his parents purchased his first basic drum set. Marc attended Erasmus Hall High School in Flatbush in the state of New York although did not get on too well, often cutting classes in the afternoons. [32] By 1971, he was playing drums with the hard rock/heavy metal band *Dust* which would go on to record two L.Ps. Bell auditioned for the *New York Dolls* after original drummer Billy Murcia's death but was unsuccessful, missing out to Jerry Nolan. In 1973, Marc joined *Estus* and recorded an album with them whilst he also played *for Wayne County & The Backstreet Boys* before moving onto *Richard Hell and the Voidoids*, playing on their first L.P "Blank Generation". In 1978, after Tommy left The Ramones, he joined the band taking up the moniker of Marky with his first gig on June 29th in Poughkeepsie and his first cut, their fourth album "Road To Ruin". The drummer performed with the group for the next five years which included starring in the movie "Rock 'n' Roll High School" and working with legendary producer Phil Spector on the "End Of The Century" album. In

1983, however, he was asked to leave the band due to his alcohol problems with his last performance on November 27th in West Islip, which is situated on Long Island. This was not to be his swansong, as he was asked to return to the band in 1987 after his replacement, Richie fell out with the band over merchandise money and the initial standby Elvis Ramone did not work out. His first gig, second time around, was on September 4th at Oyster Bay. Marky continued to play for the band until their last concert on August 6th, 1996 and took part in more shows and performed in more albums than any other drummer, widely acknowledged as an extremely skilled exponent of his trade. When he was inducted into the "Rock and Roll Hall of Fame" in 2002, part of his acceptance speech was to humbly acknowledge the work of founder member and first stick man, Tommy Ramone. Post Ramones, he teamed up with Dee Dee to form the tribute band the *Ramainz* in 1996 and also helped Joey in his solo album "Don't Worry About Me" in 2000. The drummer recorded two albums for his solo project *"Marky Ramone and the Intruders"* and another with *"The Speed Kings"* and in 2001, was presented with a lifetime achievement award from MTV by *U2* singer Bono. In 2004, The Ramones released a DVD entitled "Ramones Raw" which featured extensive footage courtesy of Mark's personal videoing. In 2015, he published his autobiography *"Punk Rock Blitzkrieg Bop: My Life as a Ramone"* and he continues to keep the legacy of the band alive by touring the world with his band "Marky Ramone's Blitzkrieg". He lives in Brooklyn Heights with his wife Marion Flynn.

Richie Ramone

<u>BIRTH NAME:</u> Richard Reinhardt
<u>DATE OF BIRTH:</u> 11/8/1957
<u>PLACE OF BIRTH:</u> Paissaic, New Jersey, USA
<u>YEARS IN THE RAMONES:</u> 1983-1987

Richard Reinhardt was brought up in a middle class family, the son of Leonard and Mary and went to the rather strange sounding named school of Franklin No. 3 in Paissaic. As a youngster he became obsessed with drums at an early age, getting his first snare at the age of eight [33] and eventually playing percussion in his high school band. Before he joined The Ramones in 1883, Richie had performed drums for *Velveteen* and *The Shirts* and when Marky was fired for his alcoholism, Richard went through two auditions to get the job, quickly learning some of The Ramones' most well-known songs. His first gig for the group was on February 13th in Utica in the state of New York. Although, he did not perform on the album "Subterranean Jungle", he did appear in the videos "Pyscho Therapy" and "Time Has Come Today" to promote songs from that L.P. In his first months in the band, he performed under the pseudonym of Richie Beau although by the time of his first recordings, in line with time honour tradition he was known as Richie Ramone. His first album was the much acclaimed "Too Tough To Die" which was released in October, 1984 – back to their best and back to their punk roots, there is no doubt that the hard hitting, cymbal bashing, Richie had a significant influence in recreating the minimalism of previous years. The drummer also featured on backing vocals on tracks such as the hard core "Wart Hog" and later on, would be the only Ramones stick man to sing lead vocals including "You Can't Say Anything Nice" or the unreleased demo "Elevator Operator". Richie also wrote a number of songs with probably the most famous being fans' favourite, "Somebody Put Something In My Drink". After two more albums, "Animal Boy" and "Halfway To Sanity", Richie left the band abruptly due to a financial conflict with Johnny over an increase in the share of merchandise money. After performing over 500 shows across the world, his last concert was in East Hampton in New York on August 12th, 1987. In 2011, The Ramones were awarded a Grammy Lifetime Achievement Award and Richie gave a short speech noting that it was the first time in history that all three long-serving Ramones drummers were gathered together. Post Ramones, Richie featured on Joey's posthumous album "Ya Know" and formed his own band, releasing two albums named "Entitled" and "Cellophane". He still regularly tours the world performing both self-penned material and Ramones classics with his group which include Clare Misstake, Ronnie Simmons and Chris Moye. He has also played with C.J Ramone with their first gig together in Buenos Aires in 2017. One year later, Ritchie's autobiography, *I Know Better Now: My life before, during and after The Ramones*", was published.

C.J Ramone

<u>BIRTH NAME:</u> Christopher Joseph Ward
<u>DATE OF BIRTH:</u> 8/10/1965
<u>PLACE OF BIRTH:</u> New York City, USA
<u>YEARS IN THE RAMONES:</u> 1989-1996

Chris was born in Queens but lived in Deer Park on Long Island in New York for most of his early life. He attended the elementary school of SS. Cyril and Methodius and thereafter graduated from Deer Park High School in 1983. Prior to joining The Ramones, he had played in a heavy metal group called *Guitar Pete's Axe Attack* and was also a big fan of *Da Brudders* before eventually joining the iconic band. He served in the United States Marine Corps but lost the title of Marine due to going absent without leave and was eventually discharged. When he heard about The Ramones audition after Dee Dee's departure, he initially went along simply for an opportunity to meet the band but did well enough to be offered a second try-out. He was in military custody when he heard the news that he had secured the position of bass player with Johnny advising him to do his time and get ready for his new job. Johnny who was a big advocate of C.J, as he would be known, gave the new member a number of tapes to emulate Dee Dee's movements in order to seamlessly slot into the role. He also quickly learned to adapt by lowering his bass and use a pic with the customary famed downstroking technique. His first gig was in Leicester in England on September 30th, 1989 and he would not only play the four-string but also blast out the accustomed "1, 2, 3, 4s", join in on the backing vocals and also lead on a number of appropriate songs. Indeed, as the band ended their career, C.J was given more and more responsibility for lead vocals. C.J would perform on three studio albums – "Mondo Bizarro", "Acid Eaters" and "¡Adios Amigos!", continuing to play right up to the last concert at *the Palace,* Los Angeles in 1996. During that last Ramones performance, he shared the stage with is hero, Dee Dee, who was invited back for one tune to sing "Love Kills". He also would later play with him in the tribute, *The Ramainz* which also featured Marky and Barbara Zampini. Whilst still performing in The Ramones, he started the hard rock outfit, *Los Gusanos* and post Ramones formed *Bad Chopper* which both released albums. Additionally, he has played with Richie and toured with his own band performing new and old material including his solo project, the album "Last Chance To Dance". C.J is rightly credited for briefing new life into the group and when The Ramones was inducted into the "Rock and Roll Hall of Fame", Tommy Ramone credited the "non-stated" Ward with "keeping the band young." Ward was married to Marky Ramone's niece with whom they had two children and has another daughter with his second wife, the lawyer Denise Barton.[8]

Elvis Ramone

<u>BIRTH NAME:</u> CLEMENT ANTHONY BOZEWSKI
<u>DATE OF BIRTH:</u> 24/11/1954
<u>PLACE OF BIRTH:</u> BAYONNE, NEW JERSEY, USA
<u>IN THE RAMONES:</u> 2 GIGS: These were performed on 28/8/1987 & 29/8/1987

Clem Burke performed just two concerts for The Ramones in August 1987 after Richie sensationally quit the band. Playing drums under the penname Elvis Ramone, the legendary ex-*Blondie* stick man played shows in Providence, Rhode Island and Trenton, New Jersey. After the two gigs, it was quickly realised that Elvis' freer, less rigid style did not suit the needs of The Ramones and it was essential for someone more akin to the faster pace to be brought it. With ex-drummer Marky now alcohol free, it seems that Clem was also happy to step aside. [34]

Born Clement Anthony Bozewski in Bayonne, he followed in the footsteps of his father with a love of percussion. Clem is left-handed but plays the drums with a right-handed kit and first took to the stage at New York's *Carnegie Hall* with his high school band. [35]

Although Debbie Harry may be the voice and face of *Blondie* and Chris Stein the main creative force, Burke will always be the heartbeat of the group which he joined in 1975, shortly after their formation. Whilst he will always be remembered for his time in the famed *Blondie,* he has also performed with many other artists over the years including *The Romantics* and *Eurythmics* along with playing along-side such luminaries as Pete Townsend, Bob Dylan, Iggy Pop and Joan Jett. Clem was inducted into the "Rock and Roll Hall of Fame" in 2006 as a member of *Blondie.*

We're A Happy Family: The Tribute

Little has been written about the origins of the tribute band and even less on trying to catalogue the thousands which have sprung up across the world. However, what does seem clear is that audiences were initially treated to acts played by solo artists and it may not surprise many that the first impersonators were Elvis Presley entertainers. For example, in the late 1950s, Buddy Ocha is often credited with being the "original Elvis tribute artist" performing at the Southern Methodist Church in Dallas. Indeed, upon hearing of Buddy's routine, *the King* befriended the youngster after meeting him in Killeen in 1958. [36] We are not certain who the first tribute group were, but it is fair to say that *The Beatles* had a significant impact on the development of these bands. One name that stands out was *The Buggs*, arguably the first recognised tribute who started performing in the mid-60s and sounded very much like the originals from Merseyside. The band went on to release an album titled "The Beetle Beat" with original compositions, as well as cover versions of "She Loves You" and "I Want To Hold Your Hand".[37]

One person who has made a living from the tribute is David Victor. He not only runs a promotion platform for bands to showcase their talents but has also performed in his own tribute band which culminated in an offer to join the original group, *Boston*. David has also distinguished himself with his work on the subject, who in 2023 penned an article entitled

The Complete History Of Tribute Bands. He initially ensured a clarity between a cover and a tribute band suggesting that the former would perform songs by many popular artists whilst the latter typically focuses on only one group, often presenting an act that mimics the original's look, costumes and set designs. Interestingly, however, some of the groups discussed in this book have specifically stated that they should be known as a Ramones *cover* band and have distanced themselves away from the term *tribute.* This may be because of the composition of the group – for instance some outfits have included three or five musicians and therefore immediately lend themselves to being different than The Ramones' structure of four. It may also be due to the fact that some of our groups do not try to imitate the original band either in looks or in sound and instead play the songs in their own unique style.

Within his commentary, Victor broke down the development of these performers into each decade. In the 1970s, he recognised that Presley was still very much at the forefront of these acts noting "that at the time of Elvis' death, he had over 170 artists emulating his greatness" and citing some of the more well-known impersonators, Bill Haney and Alan Meyer. Fascinatingly, Elvis appears to have enjoyed the former's act, inviting him to visit *Graceland* whilst the latter stopped performing after Elvis had died in 1977 seemingly as a mark of respect to his hero. Victor also states that many people "believe the Broadway *rockumentary Beatlemania* from 1977 to 1979 is responsible for the popularity of the tribute band idea." Here the show "swept the theatrical landscape of America" – rather than one music tour performing in various cities, the producers cut production costs by hiring local Beatles performers at each venue. This inexplicably led to small *Beatles'* tribute bands popping up all over the country. The '70s also saw the emergence of iconic rock bands such as *Led Zeppelin* and *Pink Floyd* and additionally the introduction of concept albums, music festivals and musicians with "larger-than-life attitudes and controversial lifestyles" which soon led to them becoming household names. This in turn impelled musicians to form more bands who wanted to honour their favourite artists. Victor points out that "tribute bands in the 1970s were still low-key, performing regionally" and also states that "they did not face too much flack, either from the audiences or the original artists." One has to concur with his comments when he felt that "the 1970s, in the history of tribute bands, is an essential decade as it cemented the concept and gave it a solid footing."

The '80s witnessed some tribute bands gain international recognition with *Aussie Floyd* cited as a prime example. "No longer content with playing in clubs or home grown festivals", David Victor remarks that "instead, they began the tradition of holding concerts that included concept albums played in their entirety, attracting die-hard *Pink Floyd* fans. The writer also describes how *MTV* encouraged more music lovers to wish to see live music. Since many original bands had either disbanded or were no longer touring, gigs by cover entertainers provided "this new breed of music enthusiasts a chance to experience emulated live performances."[38] Some of the more renown performers of the decade were undoubtedly *The Bootleg Beatles,* who since their creation in 1980 have performed over 4,500 shows around the globe. Maybe, even more famed are *Björn Again,* the top Australian Abba tribute act, founded in 1988 by Rod Stephen. Rod's production company for *Björn Again* is now based in

North London and employs first rate professional performers, having appeared in excess of 5,000 shows in over 70 countries. The personnel come from a pool of performers from throughout the northern hemisphere and have even been acknowledged by *Abba's* Bjorn Ulvaeus as being the show that single-handedly initiated the *Abba* revival in the late 1980s and early 1990s.[39]

The 1990s saw the continuation of the cover band scene and the origin of acts for newer artists, such as Californian punk group *Green Day* and Seattle's *Pearl Jam.* These tributes comprised of younger musicians, eager to play the music of their icons. One noteworthy side story in the '90s was the tale of Tim Owens who fronted the *Judas Priest* tribute band *British Steel* with the heavy metal singer making headlines in 1996 when he replaced Rob Halford. This is not the only example of a cover band member ending up in the original outfit. Arnel Pineda and indeed, David Victor, for instance, would eventually join the groups *Journey* and *Boston* respectively. Victor points out that in the 1990s, there were some "more-gimmicky" bands created. *Minikiss*, a *Kiss* tribute, for example, gained famed for being the shortest band on the planet and were recorded in the *Guinness Book of Records.* [40] Another stunt, came from when William Smith-Eccles and his singing partner Mark Moore, part of the *UK Blues Brothers,* when they officially changed their names by deed poll to Elwood and Joliet Jake Blues and Elwood J Blues. [41] The new found stature of the tribute was highlighted in 1997 when *No Way Sis,* an *Oasis* tribute, achieved a UK top 20 hit single with their rendition of "I'd Like to Teach the World to Sing". Furthermore, the band were asked to step in for *Oasis* and play to a sell-out audience in Paris after the Manchester outfit cancelled their own show. In the same year, journalist Tony

Barrell wrote a major feature for The Sunday Times about the UK tribute scene, which mentioned bands including *Pink Fraud, the Pretend Pretenders* and *Clouded House.* In the piece, Barrell asserted that "the main cradle of the tribute band…is Australia. Starved of big names, owing to their reluctance to put Oz on their tour itineraries, Australians were quite unembarrassed about creating home-grown versions." Other acts such as *The Beatnix, Zeppelin Live*, and *The Australian Pink Floyd Show* have experienced continued popularity. [42]

By the turn of the century, tribute bands were an integral part of the live music industry. This period also featured the development of more all-encompassing musical/historical variety shows with some cover acts having the versatility and ability to include multiple artists. According to Victor, the most successful of the multi-tribute performers are Minnesota-based *Hairball.* The group diversifies and plays a convincing impersonation of hard rock artists including Alice Cooper, *AC/DC, Van Halen, Queen, Metallica, Guns n' Roses* and Ozzy Osbourne. With production arguably as big as some internationally touring stadium acts, *Hairball* include a number of frontmen, who would change clothes between acts, while another singer was performing, in order to ensure there were no breaks and keep up the breakneck pace. The *noughties* were also a period which saw the tribute gain widespread acceptance on television. For instance, in 2000, this part of pop culture was featured in an episode of *"The Simpsons"* whilst in 2008 American TV host David Letterman highlighted tribute bands for a whole week on his late night talk show. In 2000, filmmakers Jeff Economy and Darren Hacker produced the documentary film *"An Incredible Simulation"*, which examined the tribute band phenomenon.

Similarly, in 2001 the documentary *"Tribute"* by directors Kris Curry and Rich Fox, which also covered the movement, was released. In 2007, producers Allison Grace and Michelle Metivier produced a four-part documentary series called *"Tribute Bands"* for Global TV which features covers to *The Police, Queen, Rush* and *The Tragically Hip.* [43] Other developments saw homage festivals becoming popular with the American *Tribute Fest,* for example beginning in 2009. Indeed, in the UK, the Milton Keynes Festival was held at Campbell Park in August 2023 featuring, amongst others, *Dire Streets, Rolling Stoned, Guns Or Roses* and *Dizzy Lizzy.* In May 2024, *Glastonbudget,* was billed as "the World's Biggest and best tribute band music festival" which included the amusingly named Young Elton who of course pays homage to the *Rocket Man,* Elton John. [44]

Further growths in the industry now include tribute cruise holidays where holiday and party goers can enjoy the sun on board ship listening to a variety of artists. One American vacation, for instance, offers an eight-day voyage and the chance to sail from Galveston, Texas with ports of call in Roatan in Honduras, Puerto Costa Maya and Cozumel in Mexico whilst listening to acts which amongst others features an Elvis impressionist. Additionally, David Victor points to the fact that a greater variety of genres in the 21st century were on offer ranging "from contemporary and jazz to blues, bluegrass, and soft rock" whilst at this time a little more originality started to emerge from the performers. This took the form in several ways such as all-female groups who honoured male bands – *Iron Maidens* being a classic example. Conversely in 2003, Mandonna, an all-male tribute to Madonna, was formed in response to the rise of these all-female tributes. Additionally, 'hybrid' groups sprung up – *Beatallica,* for instance, play a unique "mash up" of *The Beatles* and *Metallica* whilst originating in 2004, *The Red Hot Chili Pipers* give a unique blend of bagpipes, guitars, keyboards, and drums. Dressed in kilts, their brand of fusion music is famously known as "bagrock." [45] Another interesting breakthrough came in 2002 when the first biography of a tribute band was published. Entitled "Being John Lennon", the book is a humorous account of life on the road in *The Beatles'* tribute *Sgt. Pepper's Only Dart Board Band,* written by the group's founder, Martin Dimery. [46]

As the *noughties* ended and the *tenties* began, tributes became common at private events such as weddings, birthday celebrations or corporate functions. It also saw the true globalisation of these acts with groups including *Aussie Floyd* selling out all over the world. In fact, the widespread use of the internet allowed these type of bands to market themselves globally and with competition growing, those with a well-planned digital marketing strategy were able to amass a more extensive fan base. Not surprisingly, with these world tours came more intensive preparations and improved productions with many acts incorporating visuals, such as projections and light shows to provide a better experience for fans. This has included the controversial use of holograms by some highly successful tribute acts where past performers can be portrayed on stage by a light-beam process in a three-dimensional image. For example, Roy Orbison, dead for over 30 years, 'appeared' to perform at a Boston theatre in front of 1,000 paying customers. "The whole thing is a travesty of epic proportions," said Kevin Patey, a Boston-based singer/guitarist who plays roots rock and rockabilly. "There are tribute acts, but this is something entirely different, a violation of all that is pure. Let the dead be dead. Honour their memory, but not in this manner. Pay tribute, but with a shred of decency." [47] Although these events lack the intensity of real people singing and audience interaction, hologram concerts of Buddy Holly, Frank Zappa, Whitney Huston, and Amy Winehouse have been highly successful over the past few years. The popularity of the tribute was helped by the launch in Australia in 2012 of *The Tribute Show*. Initially criticised, the TV programme featured the best tribute bands from right across the world and provided artists with a chance to display their talent to the broader public. Another television series which ran from 2013 to 2017 in America was *The World's Greatest Tribute Bands*. Hosted by Katy Daryl, the series included tribute band concerts at famous venues across Los Angeles. Some prevalent acts featured in the series were *The Fab Four, Led Zepagain, The Police Experience, Purple Reign* and *Almost Queen*. One clever marketing ploy occurred at the 2010 Superbowl when a Dr Pepper advertisement not only featured the legendary *Kiss* but also another one of their tributes - *LittleKiss*. This development again showed how the concept of tribute bands was now playing a significant role within popular culture. The decade also saw younger audiences attending concerts with David Victor feeling that "this shift was a significant stamp of approval for tribute bands, who were clearly starting to attract music lovers beyond the initial nostalgic factor." He also went on to specify that "it wasn't uncommon for tribute bands to have their groupies. These fans wore customised shirts and attended concerts religiously." Indeed, some of The Ramones covers in this book sell their own merchandise or have produced their own C.Ds to supplement their income from live performances.

As Georgina Gregory states in her book *Send in the Clones: A Cultural Study of the Tribute Band,* "critical opinion on this type of entertainment remains divided." [48] Opponents have argued that tribute bands copied established artists' work and lacked natural talent. Purists also stated that acts which concentrated on musical nostalgia stifled creativity and innovation. Indeed, some feel that these performers take away both attention and revenue from newer artists and have contributed to the "homogenization of popular music" [49] resulting in too much standardisation. Moreover, critics feel that tribute acts were merely cashing in on other people's previous work. Indeed, one interview in the *Repeat Fanzine* made his views crystal clear regarding tribute acts stating that "I've commented before that being in a tribute band must be an odd existence. By and large their members are frustrated musicians who have not had the good fortune (or ability) to have made it in a "proper" band. However, they continue on performing effectively as a doppelganger for someone else."[50]

In fact, over the years there have been litigations against tribute bands with varying outcomes. For example, in 1979, *Beatlemania* was probably the first tribute to face legal action when Apple Corporation sued and won due to the use of various *Beatles'* trademarks. [51] Another case in 2005 was that of *Beatallica* who received attention when they were threatened with a lawsuit by Sony Music Entertainment over their unique interpretation of *Beatles'* songs done in a *Metallica* style. With the help of *Metallica* drummer and co-founder Lars Ulrich, the tribute won their legal battle, and still record and tour today. In addition, in 2009, another legal battle took place between *Bon Jovi* and the all-female tribute band *Blonde Jovi*. The case rested upon copyright infringement and the unlawful use of the trademarked logo. Indeed, a letter from the law firm Blakely Sokoloff Taylor & Zafman to *Blonde Jovi* stated:

"It has recently come to our attention that your band is using the mark and name *Blonde Jovi* in connection with live musical performances; more specifically, a *Bon Jovi* tribute band. Our investigation also uncovered that you are using BJP's Heart and Dagger› Logo trademark prominently on your website. Unfortunately, and despite the fact that our client appreciates the reverence that your band pays tribute to *Bon Jovi*, as a tribute band, our client nevertheless is charged with the duty of enforcing its trademark rights. In this regard, BJP cannot allow your band to use the mark and name Blonde Jovi (or any other BJP trademarks), as such use creates a likelihood of confusion with our client, and capitalizes on the goodwill and reputation of its well-known marks."

The end result was that the tribute act initially changed their name to *Blonde Jersey* but eventually stopped performing in 2010. [52] What this seem to highlight is that whilst some original artists like to be honoured by having musicians try to emulate them, others do not and this does raise the question about how bands can play so many songs without copyright issues. David Victor made the point that in the United States "most bars and clubs pay a licensing fee that allows them to play various songs. This includes live performances by tribute bands on their property. In the UK, the bands share a list of songs and get distributors' licenses before they can perform at various venues" although from experience this does appear to not always carried out. The promotor goes on to add that "even though a tribute band might have a license to sing certain songs, original artists can still prosecute them for copyright infringement based on appearance and idiosyncrasies. However, the process is lengthy and expensive. And it requires a new case for each tribute band, which is why, generally speaking, original bands do not bother with legal action."[53]

Those supporters of the idea of these type of groups have argued that far from being "fake or phony", tribute, cover and 'ghost' bands[54] provide a vital cog within the music industry and have delivered an excellent service in many ways. Possibly, the greatest argument of supporters of the tribute is that paying homage to a favourite artist by imitating their persona helps keep the musical legacy of these legendary artists alive. Not only that but many fans found comfort in the familiar sounds of the past, and tribute bands allowed them to relive the music of their youth. John Paul Meyers, an ethnomusicologist who studies music as a reflection of culture, believes that people listening to artists who play 'note-for-note' versions of the songs of previous bands, is "an unlikely way to celebrate history." He also argues that the bands and those who love them are "a community for whom an intense awareness of and respect for the past is an important part of their lives." Meyers feels that "these groups also provide a way to be a part of a musical heritage that neither the performers nor the listeners may have been able to be a part of in real time." Researchers Cristyn Magnus, P.D. Magnus, and Christy Mag Uidhir write that "the original band may no longer exist, may not perform locally, and will not be performing all the time, yet cover bands provide a surrogate for seeing a live performance by the canonical band." John Paul Meyers feels that "the tribute also serves as a way to recapture the presence of members who have died" citing the love of both their music and "their accents and stage mannerisms." The experience of seeing tributes", he claims, "has become its own phenomenon and the music, functions not just as a way to remember history, but to remember your place in it. To recall the feelings, memories, and emotions of a moment…But what tribute bands are doing isn't replicating the time, they're replicating the feelings."[55]

From a musician's point of view, cover bands are a way to live out a dream, playing songs of artists that shaped the way to their passion. Being in a tribute also allowed budding artists to showcase their skills and enter the music business. From a fans' viewpoint then maybe they offered the chance to connect with their favourite music in a way which was not possible before. For instance, specialisation allowed tribute bands to cater to specific audiences and still provide an authentic experience. At the same time, musicians are not afraid to also give the original songs a distinct appeal. These groups push the boundaries and often create a new sound that is both familiar and unique at the same time. Additionally, another reason for the rise of these type of acts is that these bands can perform in lesser known towns or cities where more renown groups would not visit. Furthermore, perhaps getting tickets to see the original artists in concert was often tricky, some tribute bands offered a nearly identical experience in a more intimate setting and of course at a much lower financial cost. Music lovers could even book these acts for their own private functions with the knowledge that trusted performers share their commitment to the originals and will attempt to stimulate every minor detail of their favourite music group. As well as keeping the music of disbanded greats alive for those past fans, what has also occurred is that it has simultaneously introduced new generations of fans to those legendary artists. A new batch of enthusiasts have had the chance to experience the live sets of the likes of *Abba, Led Zeppelin, The Beatles* and so many more. According to Victor "another sign of the increasing tribute band fandom is that more and more original artists are associating themselves with tribute acts in one way or another." [56] Original *Deep Purple* drummer Ian Paice, for instance, has played with members of *Deep Purple* tribute band *Purpendicular* on a number of occasions. [57] Indeed, throughout this book we shall see that Marky, C.J and Richie, to their credit, have all been extremely supportive of those bands who honour The Ramones.

According to one ticket sales promotion website, "the good tribute bands are doing very well. They are in high demand, and tickets to their shows often sell out. Over the last handful of years, there has been a surge in demand, and listing agents have watched as bookings grow to a flood. Popular demand is such, that you can now book just about any type of tribute band you want, ranging from the *Rolling Stones, Adele* and even Justin Bieber." [58] Naturally, the success of any tribute band depends on how well they reproduce the sound and the performance of the original artists or how they can market any particular nuance or distinction compared to other groups. What is now apparent is that although initially merely created to honour the original bands, many tribute bands have grown to now have their own fan base. Indeed, those bands and artists that have inspired a cult following in their fan base tend to have a significant tribute band presence as well. [59] Many have already been mentioned but other performers who are covered include the likes of *Status Quo, Black Sabbath, Genesis, The Misfits, Grateful Dead and Steely Dan.*

The Ramones certainly fit cosily into this *cult* category and as we will see throughout this book numerous tributes for the '*fast four*' have sprung up all over the world. Indeed, as we shall examine, it has often been said that everywhere they went, new bands and imitators formed. Johnny Ramone once stated that "a lot of kids bought guitars and started playing rock 'n' roll because of us" whilst Tommy Ramone proudly pointed out that "it wasn't just hip places like LA and England where bands would form in our wake. It was every town we hit." [60] Of course, at that time, the two musicians were not talking about tributes per say but discussing the development of the punk movement in general. What is also clear, however, is that a similar pattern has occurred in terms of the development of Ramones cover and tribute groups. This detail is certainly highlighted within this piece of research and will be emphasised by the fact that tribute acts have emerged from every country in which The Ramones toured and some even which were not on their touring rota, accentuating the truly international flavour of the band's legacy. Furthermore, it has been observed that Ramones tribute bands have been founded at regular intervals over the course of the last 30 years or so – indeed some were even coexisting whilst The Ramones were still active. It has also been noted that new acts are even still springing up over the course of the last year which will keep the memories of the band going way into the future. Similarly, what has been apparent is that those musicians who have formed these tributes have not merely been first generation punks. Yes, we have had some who witnessed The Ramones at their peak in the '70s and '80s but we have also seen younger artists who have been so touched by the band that they have been enthused enough to get out there and start a tribute. There is no doubt that The Ramones left a unique musical legacy which has continued to influence performers to this day right across the world and spanning different generations.

According to the American entertainment and pop culture journalist, Troy L. Smith, there is one criteria that "should be held above all others" when judging bands – the *influence* that they have had. There have, of course, been countless groups who have graced the various stages across the world. The majority, have come and gone, leaving little or no trace on the overall impact on the music industry or culture in general. Some, however, have had a major impression and Troy L. Smith had the unenviable task of attempting to rank the top 100 bands since the milestone of the release of the first *Beatles'* album. His task, is of course subjective and open to debate but his conclusion was that The Ramones ranked as the twelfth most influential band over the course of the last 60 years. His one-sentence summary of the New Yorkers impact is short and sweet but who can argue with his sentiments when he described The Ramones as "the first punk rock band; influenced not just that genre but the overall direction of popular music with a primal sound and groove still copied today." [61] As we shall see throughout this book, not only did they shape the punk movement, not only have countless musicians taken up an instrument throughout the world because of them but their influence goes even way beyond just music. Just look at their style – the plimsolls, the T-Shirts, the leathers, the jeans. Writer Andrew Luecke believes "The Ramones were the first to make ripped jeans a thing" going on to add that the band left you with that feeling "we're lower than low, take it or leave it." On the *Denim Dudes* website, Samuel Trotman agrees and adds that "it's safe to say that The Ramones really pioneered that distressed attitude with their iconic ripped at the knee and the pro Keds sneakers that were beaten and dirtied." [62] Indeed, Mickey Leigh, brother of Joey Ramone once reflected on the band's legacy after the sad passing of his sibling. "I saw him all over the place", he lamented. "I saw him in the thousands of kids on the streets who wore holes in the knees of their jeans." [63]

As we shall establish, not all of our tributes attempt to be Ramones *copycats* and even when these performers do take on *'operation clone'*, there are still many variations. Japanese group *Uramones* and the Brazilians *Acid Eaters*, for instance, are two examples of bands who wanted to reproduce the visual and audio experience as close to the originals as possible. Both, however, chose different routes with the Asian outfit selecting to imitate the original members of Johnny, Joey, Dee Dee and Tommy whilst the South American quartet deciding to pick up The Ramones' latter years which included impersonations of C.J and Marky. Whilst many of the bands have gone for the *full monty*, which has included wigs or hair-cuts to mirror the New Yorkers along with the obligatory ripped jeans, leathers, sneakers and T-shirts some of the bands have tried to stamp their own personality by not completely copying The Ramones' fashion approach. Of course, for some bands wearing hair pieces to imitate The Ramones would be pointless because of the make-up of the band. Three-piece groups such as *Too Tough 2 Die* or the quintet *GabbaGabbahey*, would simply never be able to look like the originals. Similarly, it would be futile for the all-female bands including The *Ramonas* or *Rockaway Bitch* or the mixed gender group from Holland, *The Hormones,* to attempt to impersonate the New Yorkers. As stated earlier, some of the groups in this study specifically asked to be known as cover bands rather than tribute acts presumably for these kind of reasons.

As well as those groups who wish to truly duplicate The Ramones experience, others have wished to give a touch of their own uniqueness. In fact, it was a pleasure to watch and listen to the various takes on the classic songs – some acts concentrated on a more melodic panache, some took on a more thrash metal style, a few added a hardcore element whilst some had a '70s British street punk feel. When I first set out on this project, it was of course fuelled by my love of the *'fast four'* and by the fact that over the years I had seen five different Ramones tributes which had all offered something slightly distinctive. Throughout this book, I urge readers to check out the various bands as it really does encompass the differing elements of The Ramones' tunes too. As well as the style of the various bands it was always insightful to look at the set list which the tributes produce. Those classic songs such as "Blitzkrieg Bop", "Sheena Is A Punk Rocker", "I Wanna Be Sedated" and "Rockaway Beach" were unsurprisingly covered by virtually every band but it was also pleasing to see the variations which were on offer. Some were clearly personal preferences with tracks, which The Ramones had discarded as live picks over the course of time, still cherished and honoured. "All The Way", "Loudmouth" and "Carbona Not Glue" were great examples of much loved songs which continued to get exposure. One observation, was that South American bands tended to give more coverage to those songs off the later albums than their European and North

American counterparts. Maybe the logical explanation for this is that the New Yorkers were taking countries such as Argentina and Brazil by storm when "Monzo Bizarro", Acid Eaters" and "Adios Amigos" were released. The Ramones have also received a *hybrid tribute blending* with the London-based band *Gabba* performing Abba songs in a stripped down punk style, typical of the boys from Queens. Tongue in cheek it may well be but some of the tracks are worth investigating such as "The Pinhead Take It All", "Super Shock Treatment" and of course "Hej Ho Disco"! Another original artist is the Frenchman, Bobby Ramone, whose album "Rocket To Kingston" combined the pleasures of The Ramones and incredibly, Bob Marley with ten *rasta* tracks such as "Glad To See You Cry", "Stirring In My Room", "I Don't Wanna Stand Up" and "Jamming Affairs" all on offer. There have also been other unique forms of Ramones tributes which this book will explore. Look out for the one-man tribute show from Texas, an all-female parody band from Pennsylvania and the multinational virtual group, all displaying distinctive slants to those familiar songs.

Tribute band names are often a pun on the original title or the names of band members, or are derived from a famous track or record album released by the original band. This has been a common theme seen throughout the book with either plays on the word Ramones or the use of album or single titles. Examples include the *Animal Boys* or *53rd and 3rd* who originate from Switzerland and England respectively. Likewise, when playing the part of a Ramone, many of the musicians will be seen to have taken up pennames just like *Da Brudders* did in the early stages of their career. A sense of unity, maybe back in 1974 but certainly a little bit of fun for our tribute performers nowadays. Undoubtedly, part of the pleasure of compiling this book was finding out some of the more humorous designations. It is also quite reassuring to find the famous Ramones eagle logo, one of the shrewdest and recognisable marketing creations, adapted by some many of our bands. Of course, subtle changes would be used with the band's own name on display along with the various musicians dotted around the outside. Many of the bands have also used this emblem for their own backdrop either as a physical hard copy or some form of electronic visual image.

What is abundantly clear throughout this research is the sheer joy tribute members get from playing the songs which in many cases have shaped their life. Although on some occasions, they have performed to large four figure audiences, in most instances this will not be the case and there is no doubt that our performers are in this for *love not the money*. When I first set out on this venture, I was quickly amazed by how many cover groups there were doing this kind of thing. I had seen five but it got me thinking… How many Ramones tribute bands actually were there currently playing or indeed had performed in the past? After just a couple of days, I realised that there were far more outfits dotted around the globe paying homage to the '*fast four*' than I could have imagined. The more I delved, the more I became intrigued and the more I wanted to find out about the performers who covered The Ramones and what motivated them to do what they were doing. It also coincided with the formation of my own cover band, *The Ramoanz,* so I could certainly empathise with many of the feelings that was shared by members of this *extended family* – the delights of playing those songs with like-minded friends but the constant difficulties such as getting decent venues, line-up changes, the on-going costs and so on and so forth. I quickly realised also, that it would be an impossibility to write about every Ramones tribute band that had ever existed. There were just too many – some have vanished with little trace – as Joey once penned '*here today gone tomorrow*' and with only a smidgeon of their activities on record, it would be futile to attempt to write constructively about them. Additionally, tracking down many of the musicians was an extremely difficult task and on occasions, some of the artists sadly did not respond to the correspondence which was sent. Maybe email addresses have changed, bands disbanded or they just simply did not want to be part of this venture. Thankfully, once contact was established, the overwhelming majority of the performers were fully behind this endeavour and I thank each and every one who has helped in the making of this book. Your drive to keep The Ramones legacy alive is truly magnificent and I salute your efforts to continue to play those cherished songs, in the majority of cases for the pure fun of it. It was also extremely humbling to hear the comments about this piece of work and your positivity was heart-warming. Thank you again.

The book sets out to accomplish a number of objectives. The first is to draw information from those grassroots musicians who perform in the tributes and cover bands and write their **individual narratives** referencing facts about The Ramones in each of their respective countries. This will be **a celebration** and I am delighted to have spoken to artists from **seventy-four** bands within this piece of literature. The fact that 74 accounts were selected was not a matter of chance – the writing of this book coincided with the 50th anniversary of The Ramones' first ever gig at *Performance Studios* on 30th March, 1974 and therefore this numeral was chosen for its symbolic nature – a historic milestone. By using interviews and first hand observations of Ramones tribute performers, **this book will be for the fans, by the fans**. The second objective will be to highlight these tributes in **every country** The Ramones performed within and I am thrilled that this was also accomplished - a local fan from each group from each nation has contributed to the narratives within this piece of literature bringing insight from right across the world. Some nations' groups were more difficult to track down then others but pleasingly every country was eventually covered. Gratifyingly, I even managed to speak to a handful of musicians from countries where The Ramones never toured such as Estonia and Poland which seemed to emphasise their influence on a global scale. As a bi-product of this, my third objective will also be evident – this is to highlight The Ramones' work in the various nations, plot their hefty touring schedule, unearth many of the venues they played in and write a unique form of **biography** of The Ramones' career using first-hand observations from the locals – facts that have not been assembled and lost to most Ramones fans. As the stories unfold, the group's legacy will also be revealed. Their influence has been colossal and this will be discussed using examples from a host of countries. Lastly, I wished to **catalogue** as many Ramones tributes as I could, acknowledging those bands which were not covered in the main text for those reasons already discussed. I do not claim that the following list is complete and there is no doubt that there have been other groups who would have covered The Ramones in some shape or form. What I do believe, however, is that this is the most comprehensive catalogue ever put together and probably the first attempt to pay homage to the

New York punk icons by discussions with working musicians in the 'bargain basement' end of the live music industry. Indeed, I have also been told that this piece of literature is quite possibly, the first book that catalogues tributes for any band but I will leave others to make that judgement call.

When Dee Dee drafted his famous song "Today Your Love, Tomorrow The World" it certainly had nothing to with the love of the fans. However, I think it aptly summarises the esteem the band is held in. Once The Ramones won our love, with their fire breathing, super-charged, untamed three chords of two-minute punk manifestos, they really did conquer the world.

Here is a list of those Ramones tributes unearthed. I have purposely not included acts like *Yee Loi* from Liverpool in England who although have extensively performed Ramones' songs on social media, play a variety of other band's music and not as such a cover band of the *'fast four'*. Those with an asterisk shows bands covered in the main part of the text. Those also listed are other known Ramones tributes – past and present. There have undoubtedly been more and I look forward to any additions.

- 53rd and 3rd: England *
- 53rd and 3rd: France
- 53rd and 3rd: United States of America
- Acid Eaters: Brazil *
- Acid Eaters: Chile *
- AmigosUnited: Poland *
- Animal Boys: Switzerland *
- Banda Lira Itapirense e Ramones Cover: Brazil
- Beat-On Brats: United States of America

- Black Jackets: Canada *
- Blitzburgh: United States of America
- Blitzkrieg Boppers: Norway
- Bobby Ramone: France
- Brain Drain: Greece *
- Bratters: Argentina
- Caponez: Belgium
- Carbona Not Glue: Scotland *
- Cavrones: Italy *
- CB Ramones: Wales *
- Chainsaw Eaters: Bosnia and Herzegovina * (originally Acid Eaters and Chainsaw Bop)
- Commando: Mexico *
- Commando Berlin: Germany *
- Commando (NYC): United States of America
- Cretins: United States of America
- Cretinz: United States of America
- Curse Of The Ramones: Northern Ireland
- Dee Dees: United States of America
- Der Ramoans: New Zealand *
- Don Ramone: Chile
- Don Ramones: Puerto Rico * (originally Surfing Bird and Psycho Therapy)
- Dumbs: Poland
- Durango 95: Croatia
- Durangos: Japan
- Gabba: England *
- Gabba Sweden: Sweden
- Gabba Gabba Hey: Italy
- Gabba Gabba Hey: United States of America *

- GabbaGabbaHey – Helsinki Tribute: Finland *
- Gabba Gabba Heys: United States of America
- Glue Sniffers: Switzerland
- Gramones: Spain
- Half Way To Sanity: Canada *
- Hamburg Ramones: Germany *
- Havana Affair: United States of America
- Hey! Ho! Lets Go!: United States of America *
- Hormones: Netherlands *
- Hormones: United States of America
- I Wanna Be Sedated: England *
- Les Ramons: France *
- Lobotomen: United States of America *
- Lobotomies: Germany
- Los Jamones: France
- Los Ramouns: Mexico
- Los Ramoyes: Netherlands
- Loudmouth Menorca: Spain
- Loudmouth USA: United States of America *
- Mamonez: Mexico
- Manny Lobotomies Rigo: Italy
- Maroons NYC: United States of America
- Melones: Germany *
- Mondo Bizarre: Brazil *
- Mondos Bizarros – Ramones and Blondie Revival: United States of America *
- Mormones: Norway
- Morones: United States of America *
- Nitrones: Germany
- No Matter: Northern Ireland *

- Original Sedated (formally known as Sedated – The World's Greatest Tribute to the Ramones and then shortened to Sedated – a celebration): United States of America
- Osaka Ramones (Shonen Knife): Japan
- Outsiders: Italy *
- Outsiders: Sweden
- Pinheads – Ramones Tribute – Italy
- Pinheads Ramones Rio: Brazil
- Pinheads tributo a Ramones: Brazil
- Poison Heart: Brazil
- Poison Heart Tribute: Croatia
- Project Ramones: Canada
- Radio Ramones: Italy
- Ramånes: Sweden *
- Ramines: France *
- Ramoaning: United States of America
- Ramona: United States of America
- Ramonas: England/Scotland *
- Ramoanz: England *
- Ramonada: Portugal *
- Ramoncs: Brazil *
- Ramoned: England *
- Ramonekes: Chile
- Ramonera: Brazil *
- Ramoaners: Scotland *
- Ramones Bratislava: Slovakia
- Ramones Clones: England
- Ramones Mania: Peru
- Ramones Not Dead: France

- Ramones Plzeň: The Czech Republic
- Ramones Revival: The Czech Republic *
- Ramonettes: Australia
- Ramonetures: United States of America
- Ramonez: England/Wales
- Ramonix: France
- Ramones Mania: Australia
- Ramonos: Argentina *
- Ramons: Spain *
- Ramoones: United States of America *
- Ramores: Canada
- Rämouns: Germany
- Rangones: Brazil
- Ranomes: Malaysia
- Rawones: Belgium *
- Rawones: Estonia *
- Rawmones: United States of America *
- Raymonds: A Ramones Experience: Canada
- Razones: Argentina
- Remones: Australia
- Remones: England *
- Remones USA: United States of America
- Renonc: The Czech Republic
- Road to Ruin: Australia *
- Rockaway Beach: United States of America
- Rockaway Beach Boys: United States of America *
- Rockaway Bitch: United States of America *
- Rockaways: Italy
- Romaines: United States of America
- Rocket To Russia: United States of America

- Rockit To Russia: United States of America *
- Ruhrmones: Germany
- Rumbones: Netherlands *
- Runarounds: Germany
- Sedated – A Tribute To The Ramones: United States of America
- Sedated – The Ultimate Ramones Experience: United States of America *
- Shamones: Wales *
- Sheena Punk Rocker: Portugal
- Shock Treatment: United States of America *
- Stalin: Uruguay *
- Take It Dee Dee: United States of America *
- The Brats: Netherlands *
- The Cretins: Austria *
- The Cretins: Sweden *
- The Exploding Mice: United States of America
- The Joeys: Brazil
- The Marones: England *
- The Ramone – A One Man Tribute: United States of America *
- The Ramones Denmark: Denmark *
- The Ramoms: United States of America *
- The Rockaways: United States of America
- Tip Toppers: Norway
- Tommy And The Rockets: Denmark *
- Too tough 2 Die: United States of America *
- Too tough To Die: MultiNational *
- Tributo A Ramones: Peru
- UK Ramones: England *

- Uramones: Japan *
- Wardogs: Italy *
- Wart Hog: United States of America *
- Weasal Face: United States of America
- We Need Cash: Norway *
- We're A Happy Family: United States of America
- Whoremones: United States of America

Rockaway Bitch:
United States of America

It seems appropriate that any review of Ramones tribute bands should commence with a group originating from New York. Even more fitting would be for this band to have an association with Queens, the borough of New York City and a place which has become synonymous with The Ramones. Fortunately, our first tribute, *Rockaway Bitch,* not only heralds from *The Big Apple* but also has strong links with that Borough and it will be here that our story unfolds.

Queens is located on Long Island and with 2.4 million inhabitants, the second most populous of the five New York City Boroughs. It is bordered by Brooklyn and shares 'water borders' with the boroughs of Manhattan, the Bronx and Staten Island as well as the state of New Jersey. Queens, was the site of the 1939 and 1964-65 *World's Fairs* with the latter event holding over 140 pavilions, building exhibitions and attractions representing 80 nations. In terms of sport, Queens is the home of a professional baseball team, the New York Mets who play their matches at Citi Field but is possibly even more renown for holding the U.S Open, the fourth and final Grand Slam tennis tournament of the year. Since 1978, this prestigious hardcourt competition has been played in the northern part of Queens at *Flushing Meadows* although at the time of The Ramones' formation would have been located at *West Side Tennis Club* three miles away in Forest Hills. This area is a mostly residential neighbourhood in the central portion of Queens and it was in Forest Hills that the fledging Ramones initially met. When Tommy Ramone gave his first press release he amusingly talked about the area the lads were brought up in. *"The Ramones all originate from Forest Hills and kids who grew up there either became musicians, degenerates or dentists", he laughed. The Ramones are a little of each. The sound is not unlike a fast drill on a real molar."* [64]

The first relationship and link can be traced back to Forest Hills High School and it was here that students Tamás Erdélyi, John Cummins, Jeffrey Hyman and Douglas Colvin all attended although Doug would eventually 'drop out' of school. [65] Tamás or Tommy as he was known, remembers that he first met Johnny in the cafeteria during his first year of high school and their connection was music. By 1966, Tommy and John were in a band called the *Tangerine Puppets* with Tom on lead guitar and John on bass. Indeed, one of Tommy's closest friends, Monte A Melnick, who would later take a pivotal role for the group, remembers that "it was a basic rock 'n' roll band, but they were good." [66] After they had left school, John had been in trouble with the law – he had got into fights, took drugs, sniffed glue, threw television sets off apartment buildings and was involved in robberies. By his own admission stated that "I was just bad, every minute of the day." Eventually, he "decided to get his life into order" and by 1972, stated to plan for the future. During this period, he really got to know Douglas Colvin. John started to work at 51st and Broadway in construction whilst Doug was employed in the mailroom of the same building. They would go to a topless place across the street named *Mardi Gras*, have a beer at lunch and talk about music. [67] Doug also recalls that he first met John at the top of a hill on 66th Road in Forest Hills when John was delivering dry cleaning from the cleaners where he worked before his construction employment. Once they got to know each other better they would talk about guitars, amplifiers and their shared a love of music such as *The Stooges* and Jimi Hendrix. [68] John recollects that soon he would go to clubs with Tommy and Doug. Tommy would encourage the other two to start their own band and eventually by January 1974 they took the plunge. John met Jeffrey Hyman through the initial friendship with Jeff's brother Mickey Leigh [69] who was known on the music scene as Jeff Starship, the vocalist in the glam band rock *Sniper*. Both John and Doug, however, recognised that he had also dabbled on the drums and asked him to take on this role for their new potential group. Doug, Jeff and a would-be bass player named Richie Stern initially got together at Johnny's Forest Hill's apartment but when Rich failed to impress, it was cut to a trio. By this time, Tommy and his friend Monte had built a rehearsal building known as *Performance Studios,* and the pair allowed them to practice at the venue. Of course, as the narrative unravels, we will see that Tommy Erdélyi, John Cummins, Jeffrey Hyman and Douglas Colvin will all eventually take the collective name of Ramone and play under the pseudonyms of Tommy, Johnny, Joey and Dee Dee respectively and go on to influence countless people.

One musician, Rockelle Cakes, who also originates from New York City was so inspired by The Ramones that she wanted to form her own tribute particularly after boyfriend and local musician Bruce Edwards was hired by C.J Ramone to play guitar at a gig at the *Continental* in 2013. "It was a wild night and packed with people wall to wall - they had to turn people away" she recalls. The next year, Marky Ramone and Andrew W.K. played a Ramones set at *Irving Plaza* in NYC and again it was a packed house. Being there and feeling the love of the music made me see that the demand for The Ramones is alive and well. I love the music. I wanted to give people access to hearing their favourite songs, in a live setting, and in the city that it all started. Being friends with members of Lez Zepplin and Judas Priestess and seeing the enthusiastic reaction of the fans digging all girl bands, I decided to form a top notch band for The Ramones." Rockelle or

Bassist Cakey of Rockaway Bitch: Photograph courtesy of Richard Carroll

"Cakey" as she is known goes on to elaborate about the start of her group which stemmed from Bruce suggesting to Cakey that she should form an all-girl Ramones band and call it *Rockaway Bitch*. After working previously with Marky, Edwards knew the required standards. "If there were any mistakes, the song would be cut from the set", going on to add that they "ran a tight rehearsal", and that Bruce "likened the music to a train, get on board, or get out of the way."

Since its formation in 2015, *Rockaway Bitch*, have had several female NYC musicians recruited over the years. The initial line-up saw Cakey on bass, Tanzi as vocalist, Jenny on guitar and Hana "Messy" Ramone on drums. After a couple of shows, Tanzi left and for about a year, the band played as a three piece with Cakey also singing until singer Patti joined the girls. The most recent line-up has seen Hitomi "Tomi" Ramone on the drummer's stool and Jo "Sette" Ramone on guitar. The choice of name for the band is a *corker* which is a play on words from The Ramones' classic tune "Rockaway Beach" whilst also implying that this all-girl group are an uncompromising bunch of *badasses*. All the members are seasoned musicians, participating in multiple bands and having experience on tours and TV shows. Cakey, for instance, has had an endorsement with both a guitar and bass guitar manufacturer whilst her original band *The Drive* was featured on *TLC* television show *The Good, The Bad and The Ugly*. Patty Rothberg's solo album went gold in the 1990s, and has toured nationally, appeared on the *David Letterman show*, and performed with singer and songwriter Chris Isaac. Guitarist Jo Sette also plays in the tribute band *Judas Priestess* and has toured across the United States of America with her group.

Photograph courtesy of Smoking Eel Photography

Rockaway Bitch have coincidentally played in many of the old haunts that the '*fast four*' patronised. Examples are numerous but highlights include performing at Richie Ramone's birthday party at *The Delancy* in New York City and at *The Chance* in Poughkeepsie in the state of New York – a venue which The Ramones themselves frequented. Other notable achievements saw them take stage at *Café 9* in New Haven Connecticut and the *Continental* in New York City which had not only seen *The Remainz* play there, a post Ramones group which featured Dee Dee, C.J and Marky but also Joey and C.J with their solo projects. All of the girls have also participated at some time or another with bands at *CBGBs,* probably the most identifiable venue connected with The Ramones. Maybe, most poignantly *Rockaway Bitch* were asked to play at the *Queens Museum* for the opening of a Ramones exhibit at Flushing Meadow in Corona Park. Here they got to meet Joey's brother Mickey Leigh and Monte Melnick who were part of that *extended Ramones family.* I would strongly recommend all fans to check out the information on this exhibition entitled *"Hey! Ho! Let's Go: Ramones and the Birth of Punk"* which can be found online. Cakey thoughtfully reflects that living in New York City she "was fortunate to see and hear about Joey Ramone in various East Village clubs" and of course was deeply moved when East 2nd Street and Bowery was re-named *Joey Ramone Place.*

A look at the girls' set-list shows a catalogue of nearly three score songs. Cakey expands stating that "the set changes every show, but we always keep the classics." By classics she is no doubt referring to the likes of "Blitzkrieg Bop", "Gimme Gimme Shock Treatment" and "Pinhead". However, there is so much more on offer than just those deemed favourites with an extended list covering the band's full history. Some of the more interesting picks include "Strength To Endure", "She's The One", "Merry Christmas (I Don't Wanna Fight Tonight)", "She's A Sensation" and "I Wanna Be Your Boyfriend." When asked about the reception the girls get after their live performances the bassist has great satisfaction when she states that "the best is when we get to play for Ramones fans that have seen The Ramones. We've gotten great feedback and that we capture the feeling and the vibe of The Ramones, there's no better compliment than that."

A look on to the social networking platform *Youtube* gives viewers a number of choices from the *Rockaway Bitch* collection and probably as good a starting point as any is their promotional video. Within this you will not only find some snippets of "Teenage Lobotomy", "Commando", "Psycho Therapy" and "Cretin Hop" but also general chitchat about the band and even advice on practising downstrokes and the use of the high hat. If you wish to hear some full songs, then check out their studio release of "I Wanna Be Sedated" which was featured on the *Amazon* prime show *Gen V*. Alternatively look up "The KKK Took My Baby Away", performed at the *Queens Museum* in the summer of 2016. For those who have rather more time, then there is a full concert on offer from 2019, live at the *Stanhope House* in New Jersey which contains my personal favourites of "Loudmouth" and "Wart Hog". Indeed, the superb vocal performance by the bassist Cakey on "Wart Hog" does not sound dissimilar to C.J as she blasts out those twisted lyrics – go check it out, you will not be disappointed. During all the tunes, you will find great energy and an unrelenting *in your face* music and although the softer female vocals do need acclimatising to, it is well worth a screening.

Cakey is not slow to come forward when asked about The Ramones' impact stating that they "influenced all of the punk bands of today. Tommy's back beat changed the way that punk rock sounded, and made it fun. The Ramones took songs of their day such as "Sheena Is A Punk Rocker" and updated the style into something upbeat and fun. Many people believe that The Ramones spearheaded the punk movement. The first tour of England was attended by members of *The Sex Pistols, The Clash, The Damned,* and many other future punk icons, their influence cannot be understated."

The future promises to be extremely bright for *Rockaway Bitch* and Cakey is excited. "We're taking this band to a whole new level" she says. "This timeless music renews itself as the heartbeat of rock 'n' roll and we hope that new generations coming into rock will be thrilled to discover the music as initial fans did in the 1970s."

The Ramoones:
United States of America

Although the band are synonymous with the venue *CBGBs*, their first fledging public show was not at the iconic club but at another establishment in New York - *Performance Studios,* a location where they had already practiced. The Ramones opened their doors to their rehearsal space on March 30th, 1974 not as a four-piece but as a trio with the build up to this historical event now passed down into punk folk-law and mythical status.

Specifically, the early make-up of The Ramones was far different to the line-up which we all know and love with only John Cummings performing his recognisable role on lead guitar. Jeffrey Hyman was on the drums whilst Douglas Colvin played rhythm guitar and sang lead vocals. Another friend, Richard Stern started out as the bass player but after a few days practising in Johnny's Forest Hills' living room, it was soon realised that Richie wasn't going to make the grade and Doug was moved to the four string. A further pal, Tamás Erdélyi or Tommy as he was better known and his colleague, Monte A Melnick had built and managed *Performance Studios,* a rehearsal workshop at 23 East Twentieth Street between Broadway and Park Avenue South and it was here that Tommy allowed them to practice free of charge with their first session on Sunday, January 27th. According to Johnny this was just four days after he had bought his 'baby blue' Mosrite guitar for $50 [70] whilst Dee Dee also states that he took the plunge buying his first bass, a Dan Electro at the same retailer, *Manny's Guitar Store* on 48th Street. (71)

Other developments saw the lads take on stage-names. Whilst John Cummins would naturally be Johnny, Douglas Colvin was now Dee Dee (a name he used as a boy) (72) and Jeffrey Hyman, despite Tommy Erdélyi advising him to become Sandy, was now calling himself Joey. Dee Dee allegedly was inspired by *The Beatles'* Paul McCartney's use of the allias Paul Ramon when he checked into hotels and all of group started taking the collective surname of *Ramone*, because it was "just a fun thing to do." (73) It also gave them "a sense of unity, a bond of sorts" (74) and made it much easier for people to remember their name. The fellas were not related of course, but some people assumed they were siblings with the band acquiring the nickname of *Da Brudders* in the early stages of their career. Whatever you think about the name, it stuck and the rest, to coin a phrase, is history.

Two months after they started practising, they invited a handful of friends and associates to their rehearsal space. The show at the end of March would turn out to be the only time the group performed as a threesome. As Eduardo Rivadavia suggests "under these retroactively curious and clearly short-lived circumstances, the brand new ensemble was only capable of cranking out seven, one-minute-long song-blasts bearing conspicuous titles like "I Don't Wanna Go Down to the Basement", "I Don't Wanna Walk Around With You", "Now I Wanna Sniff Some Glue", "I Don't Wanna Be Learned / I Don't Wanna Be Tamed", "I Don't Wanna Get Involved With You", "I Don't Like Nobody That Don't Like Me" and "Succubus". (75) As die-hard Ramones fans will know, three of these tunes would make it on to their debut L.P, one would see the light of day as a demo eventually on the re-mastered album in 2001 whilst the lesser known "I Don't Wanna Get Involved With You" would ultimately be released in 1994 on the "I Hate Freaks Like You" album under the guidance of Dee Dee Ramone's group *I. C. L. C.* Sadly, the last two on that list would be lost for ever with no recordings made of the tunes. A couple of people who saw the band at this early stage were Debbie Harry who went on to find fame in super group *Blondie* and David Johansen, former lead singer of *The New York Dolls*. Debbie claims that the performance was "hilarious" going on to add that "Joey kept falling over. He's just so tall and ungainly" whilst David recalls that he thought that they should "forget it, give up!" [76] Even Johnny Ramone described that first concert as "awful" going on to add that "our friends didn't even want to talk to us anymore after that." [77]

Dee Dee could not easily sing and play at the same time whilst his voice on occasions was "thrashed" if he sang for too long. Hyman was also struggling in the drummer's seat and with their limitations starting to show, changes were needed to be made. Johnny reminiscences that "Tommy suggested making Joey the singer, which didn't fit my image of a singer, but Tommy convinced me that he would look right between Dee Dee and I. Tommy was right. It worked." [78] The re-organisation therefore led to Johnny remaining on the guitar, Dee Dee on the bass, and Joey on lead vocals leaving a position on percussion. Erdélyi, who had taken up the role as manager, would often teach potential replacement drummers the necessary style. Soon it was realised, that he performed better than the "would be hopefuls" and instead joined the band on drums giving the sound a lighter, smoother, less choppy sound than previously. We now had our fourth Ramone with Tamás Erdélyi taking up the mantle of Tommy Ramone.

Johnny recalls that after Tommy joined the band, they went from practising once or twice a week to almost every day [79] and on August 16th 1974, they made their inaugural performance at *CBGBs*. Purchased by former Marine Hilly Kristal in December 1973, *'CBGB - OMFUG'* had maybe the most unwieldy name imaginable equating to *'Country, Bluegrass and Blues - Other Music For Uplifting Gourmandizers'*. It was located at 315 Bowery at Bleecker Street and was described as being "in the heart of Manhattan's danger zone, where biker gangs unleashed cruel forms of street justice and even the bums carried switchblades." [80] New inexperienced rock bands were looking for a site to play in the city with few alternative venues to perform especially with the collapse of the *Mercer Arts Centre* in the summer of 1973. Indeed, one of the earliest fixtures at the club were the band *Television*

who convinced Hilly and his wife Karen to let them play on Sundays. Although the owners had intended that the club would have poetry readings performed at the site coupled with country, bluegrass and blues music, the potential of larger audiences was not lost on the Kristals. Other artists that would soon perform there would be *Blondie, Talking Heads*, Patti Smith as well as The Ramones.

Dee Dee paints the picture of a notorious, seedy club. "When we loaded in for the soundcheck", the bass man suggested, "we had to watch out for rat, mice and dog shit on the floor. It was the pits." He also claimed that due to the poor sanitary facilities "the audience just pissed where they stood." [81] Initially crowds were minimal. Leee Childers photographer and former manager of *The Heartbreakers* remembers that the first time he went to *CBGBs* "there were literally six people in the audience." He also backs up Dee Dee's recollections of the quality of the venue stating that "the whole place stunk of urine. The whole place smelled like a bathroom." Leee, however, points out that there was something about the band that made them standout. "And then The Ramones went onstage and I went 'oh my God' he commented. "And I knew it, in a minute. The first song." [82] Johnny recalls a similar story about when they played one of the first shows at *CBGBs*. "Alan Vega from *Suicide* came over to me and Dee Dee" the guitarist recollects, 'this is great, this is what I've been waiting for.' I told Dee Dee, 'This guy's nuts. If we could fool this guy, maybe we could fool a lot more people.' When we got bigger, I kept saying to Dee Dee, 'I can't believe we're fooling all these people." [83] Johnny also felt that it was about the summer of 1975 when everything was really clicking into place with the band building up a big following at *CBGBs*.

They were the first group to raise ticket prices to three, four and eventually five dollars. [84]

Thankfully a theatre group who were opening for the group had the insight to record The Ramones early in their development with the first footage of the band at *CBGBs* on September 15th. Three songs are on offer - "Now I Wanna Sniff Some Glue", "I Don't Wanna Go Down To The Basement" and "Judy Is A Punk". If you have never seen this reel, then this should be an utter necessity for any devotee. On the one hand, there are oddities and humorous quirks about the performance which to the unsuspecting will leave you gobsmacked. As a starter, you will immediately see Dee Dee on Joey's right rather than to the familiarised left plus an unaccustomed cock-up in the mid-section of "Glue". More shockingly though is the singer's camp posturing, high kicks and knee crouching which fortunately was soon assigned to the trash bin. Additionally, the antics of both Dee Dee and Tommy are amusing. The bassist at one stage, crashes into his mic stand leaving it wobbling like a jelly mould whilst Tommy picks an argument at the end of one song, unsuccessfully demanding they switch the running order to include "Loudmouth" next. Drill Sergeant, Johnny, isn't free from the ridicule either as he is dressed to kill in black spandex trousers, looking like he is more akin to a glam rock star as opposed to a future punk rock icon. However, on the other hand, there is so much that you can pick from the video which is typical Ramones and the shape of things to come. Above all, there is that back-to-basis, no nonsense hammer-headed aggression waiting to smack you in your face if you just dare to turn away for a split second. Johnny's grimaces and snarling expressions are there, as is the wide-legged stance of both guitarists. Add Joey's recognisable youthful but tough delivery, Tommy's original intense 1/8th note drumming rhythm and Dee Dee's fidgety, agitated mannerisms along with his signature count-off cries of "1, 2, 3, 4s" (which they introduced simply because they could not master a silent start), you can see that you have the basis of something special.

By the time The Ramones played their last show at *CBGBs*, according to Monte Melnick, they had racked over 80 gigs at the famous place [85] with well-established routines encompassing their own unique brand of punk rock – basin hair, sneakers, T-shirts, leather jackets and knee-hole jeans all a must not only for the band but also for their devoted audience. Their last concert at the Bowery venue was on April 10th, 1979 which now featured Marky on drums. Interestingly, the gig was a benefit for the New York State Police in order to raise money so they could help purchase bulletproof vests. One person who saw the band not only at *CBGBs* but also at other New York venues such as *Max's Kansas City* was drummer Neil Richter who would eventually be part of the tribute band *The Ramoones*. His narrative about those initial times is so vivid, the story needs to be told in its entirety:

"I consider myself extremely lucky", Neil recalls. "It was 1976, I was 20 years old. I lived in the suburbs of New Jersey and had easy access to NYC and I got witness the beginnings of the New York Punk scene first hand, at places like *CBGB's* and *Max's Kansas City*, with The Ramones leading the way. One thing to remember about all this: The bands, like The Ramones and the venues like *CBGB's* and *Max's*, are now referred to in hushed reverential tones, and preceded with words like "legendary" and "iconic"… but it didn't feel that way in the moment. History, as they say, had yet to be made. My friends and I were just kids having fun. In fact, the whole scene wasn't as popular as it would later become. I was scorned by many of my peers for listening to punk bands, and laughed at for going to theses dumpy bars to see them. I heard The Ramones debut L.P on a small radio station in the suburbs of NY when it came out, and obtained my copy shortly afterwards. A few months later, I heard that The Ramones were playing at *Max's*. I had never been there before and was determined to go. I managed to twist another friend's arm into going with me. And it blew my mind! I was stunned! I loved the record, but to hear it live was incredible. I felt like I'd been hit by a panzer tank! The look, the sound, the volume, and the attitude crystalised what had been going on in my mind for some time. I felt validated! And I was hooked for life. In all, I probably saw The Ramones at *Max's* and *CBGB's* about four times at each venue, before their popularity grew and they started playing larger venues. In those days, they played two sets a night. At *CBGB's*, they let you stay for both shows, which was great... but at *Max's* they charged a separate admission for the early and late shows. To get around this, after the first show was over, we would hide in the bathroom stalls and come out after the crowd for the late show started filing in. This worked a few times, but one time we got caught! But the bouncer said "Look, just stand in the back and let the paying customers sit up front and you can stay." We had no problem with that! At *CBGB's*, the band could be seen milling around the bar with the patrons, and they were easy to approach and chat with... which I had no problem doing. As you might imagine, I was pretty inebriated in those days, and most of those conversations consisted of a lot of drunken babbling on my part, and are mostly lost in the haze of time. But I do remember a specific conversation I had with Dee Dee one time. It was when they still played on the original stage, and the infamous bathrooms were still upstairs (not in the basement where they would become legend.) As we spoke, every so often Dee Dee would lean forward, as if looking for something. Puzzled by this, I asked "What are you doing?" And his response was classic! He

said something like this: "Well, you see, we are right across from the ladies' bathroom... so every time the door opens, I look in to see if I can see anything!" After I stopped laughing, I did the only logical thing... I started looking with him! For the record, we didn't see anything. Somehow, I discovered the dressing rooms at *Max's* were up a flight of stairs from the main room. Again, being inebriated and having no fear, I simply walked up and entered like I belonged there and no one seemed to mind. In addition to speaking with Joey, I ended up talking with *Punk* magazine's John Holstrom, as well and had a photo taken of myself with Joey. One of my favourite shows from that era didn't happen at *Max's* or *CB's*, but at a small club about 25 miles north of Manhattan called The *Fore 'n' Aft in White Plains*, NY. While the band were popular in Lower Manhattan, they weren't so much outside of the city. There were literally only about 20 people in the audience. In between sets I hung out and played pinball with Joey! Tommy came over and said to him "Hurry up, let's play the next set so we can get out of here!" It was like they were playing just for me in my living room. The last time I saw them at *Max's* was probably late in 1976. The opening band were

Talking Heads. In closing, I just want to say that I am extremely blessed to have been able, at one point on another, to have met every member of the band (including Elvis/Clem Burke)."

Neil, would be part of the final line-up in 2013 of the group which also saw Mike Schimmelman as guitarist, Bill Poulos playing bass and Mike Laukaitis on lead vocals. As with time-honoured tradition, the musicians all took the sir names of Ramoone with Neil transforming into Rickey, Mike Schimmelman gaining the penname of Freshy, Bill naturally becoming Billy and Mike Laukaitis morphing into Doughy. Both Mikes were founding members of the group in 2002 which was based in Long Island, New York along with Ed "Eddie Ramoone" Hug on bass and Robert "Robbie Ramoone" Olmstead on the drummer's seat. Other stickmen included Herbie Walsh who had a spell between 2004-2006 and Justin and Danny who both played intermittently for multiple gigs. The musicians have performed for numerous other bands including *Moon, Moonshiners, Ice-9, Blueberry Jam, Filthy Two Lips, Slow Children at Play.* However, they wanted to bring the music of The Ramones to fans who were too young to have seen the original band, as well as giving the older fans the glorious memories of these legendary Ramones shows of yesteryear.

The band can boast over 170 shows mainly in the New York area but also branching out to Bristol in Rhode Island, Leetonia in Ohio, Hagerstown in Maryland, Pompton Lakes in New Jersey and Allentown in Pennsylvania. When pressed if he had any highlights from the impressive catalogue, singer Michael picked out a number of personal favourites. Not surprisingly, top pick was back where it all began for The Ramones on the main stage at *CBGBs* in May 2006, for a benefit for George Tabb of the punk rock band *Furious George. The Ramoones* vocalist exclaims "what a treat it was to play on that legendary stage. Full on rock n roll fantasy day for us. Before the show we did an interview with a punk rock magazine. After the show there was a bag of weed sold to a friend backstage. Dee Dee would have been proud of us!!" Also of note was the concert out of town at *Gillary's* in Bristol, Rhode Island in February 2008 with *Another State of Mind, Mustache Ride and the Ramoniacs*. At the concert, a little bit of friendly competition took place with the tribute band from Boston challenging the New Yorkers' to a *"Ramones-off"* with the boys from Long Island coming out on top in this *Battle of the Bands*. Satisfyingly, in December 2003 at the *Kings Club,* in Centereach in New York, the group performed with C.J Ramone's *Bad Chopper*. Strangely C.J chose to play first and needless to say, the band had a huge job in front of them following his set. "Glad to say, it went well" Michael reflects. "C.J was moshing in the pit in front of the stage, high fives for me and huge smiles from him. Great to see him enjoying our efforts to play the music that made him famous. After the show, we spoke with him at length. It turned out that I lived five houses away from one of his best friends. The following day, my wife and I were unloading groceries in our driveway when a red pickup truck pulled. It was C.J stopping by to say hello!" Impressively, the group also appeared on Connecticut Cable TV, *CT Concert Connections*, for a Ramones Christmas special in December 2007 ensuring that the memories of the band is not forgotten. On December 30th, 2005 the group also played the final Joey Ramone Holiday Bash at the *Continental* in NYC. It was a show of 20+ bands, each scheduled to play three or four Ramones songs. Frontman Michael describes that it was "a real head trip for me, putting on my Joey Ramone costume in the dressing room that night and seeing Joey's Mom and brother Mickey across the room from me. We didn't write up a set list that night as we waited to hear what everyone else was playing. We were going on last, and didn't want to play any repeat songs. We finally went on stage and tore through our four song allotment. The packed crowd was raging! They wanted more! So, we did another four song blast. By the time we finished, we'd played around two dozen songs, and clearly stole the show! It was a memorable highlight of a night for sure."

Their set list contained all our favourites with a catalogue of over 60 songs which varied somewhat from night to night in order to keep it as stimulating as possible. I make no apologies for citing some of the more unusual, often unheeded little pearls which include "You Should Never Have Opened That Door", "Locket Love", "Needles And Pins", "Slug", "I Can't Make It On Time", "The Crusher", "Endless Vacation", "Surf City", "Have You Ever Seen The Rain?", "My Back Pages" and that overlooked track played back in 1974 at *Performance Studios*, "I Don't Wanna Be Learned / I Don't Wanna Be Tamed". A probe onto social media shows a profusion of treats to review for yourself with the obvious starting point their concert in 2006 at *CBGBs* where they are witnessed performing "Cretin Hop" and "Do You Wanna Dance?" Wearing the obligatory blue jeans, sneakers, wigs, and black leather jackets, the boys from Long Island have their gestures inch perfect. Freshy, legs astride, head upwards, scowling menacingly with his guitar angled to strike periodically as only Johnny could, stands refreshingly to the singers right – *CBGBs* early style. Dee Dee, or should I say Billy, is maybe even more impressive. Head shaking, head nodding, shoulders twitching and a bundle of restless energy, is completely on the money, flawlessly impersonating the bassist's gestures. Doughy, fitted out in tinted glasses and gloved hands, leans over his stage, left foot forward Joey style with that perfect New York drawl. Herbie, at the rear, may not be visible but he certainly can be heard, keeping time to perfection like master Tommy all those years ago. If you wish for your tributes to emulate the prototype, then you will simply love *The Ramoones*. Other notable videos on *Youtube* include "Rockaway Beach" and "Merry Christmas (I Don't Wanna Fight Tonight)" from their TV special. Even better search for *"Loud, Hard and Fast"* where you will find two excellent renditions of "Beat On The Brat" and "We're A Happy Family" or their version of "Teenage Lobotomy" at the outside gig at *Tompkins Square Park*. Indeed, this is well worth a viewing just to witness the crowd's wild slam dancing in the pit!

It is probably fitting for a New Yorker to have the final words on New York's finest. Singer Michael pulls no punches when he describes the bands legacy. "The Ramones changed pop music forever. Period."

Rawmones
United States Of America

"Punk is coming! Punk is coming!" Without a title or a designation, the new bands that had started to frequent *CBGBs* and *Max's Kansas City* would have no doubt remained as isolated groups exposed to their five minutes or fame without being part of something much bigger. In January 1976, however, a new magazine was published entitled *Punk* which would see 15 issues printed between 1976 and 1979 and was the first publication to popularise the *CBGB* music scene. Founded by cartoonist John Holmstrom, businessman Ged Dunn and amusingly the 'resident punk' Legs McNeil, it used the term punk rock which

had been coined a few years earlier in *Creem* magazine. Legs picks up the story stating that in late 1975 Holmstrom initially wanted a magazine "to be a combination of everything they were into – television, reruns, drinking beer, getting laid, cheeseburgers, comics, Grade-B movies and this weird rock & roll that nobody but us seemed to like: *The Velvets, The*

Image by John Holmstrom

Stooges, The New York Dolls, and now *The Dictators*." After firstly toying with the title for the magazine as *Teenage News,* Legs came up with the moniker of *Punk.* It "seemed to sum up the thread that connected everything we liked", he said – "drunk, obnoxious, smart but not pretentious, absurd, funny, ironic, and things that appealed to the darker side." [86] Mickey Leigh, brother of Joey Ramone remembers that "the word was starting to get out about *CBGB.* Now at a Ramones show, when you turned around after the band had finished, there might actually be someone standing behind you." [87] Indeed, Holmstrom and McNeil managed to get an interview with musician and song-writer Lou Reed at *CBGBs* who was watching The Ramones and Lou would be the first feature in issue one of the magazine. Legs illuminates stating that "the next thing we did was go out and plaster the city with these little posters that said "Watch out, PUNK is coming! Everyone who saw them said, 'Punk? What's a punk? John and I were laughing. We were like, 'Ohhh, you'll find out." [88] *Punk* would now be a vehicle for promoting the underground music scene in New York and rather than faltering, the movement started to flourish. Patti Smith, for example featured in the second issue and The Ramones, for a mere 85 cents could be seen in the third in April 1976.

John Holmstrom is in no doubt that "*Punk* magazine really started punk rock and got the whole thing going back in 1975. And, while I may have started *Punk* magazine, our writer Legs McNeil started the punk movement." He also dismisses the argument, often cited from some in the UK, that questions the American's punk credentials. "The Ramones were punk rock" he unequivocally states. "They were genuine. Johnny was a violent punk. Dee Dee was worse. Joey was in a mental institution, from what I understand, as a kid. But they never talked about this in the media. That would have made good copy back in the day. People thought that New York bands were not authentic punks, but that they were intellectuals, artists and poofters." [89]

By this time, things were already falling into place for The Ramones. In the February and September of 1975 they recorded some demos at the *Dick Charles Recording inc.* and *914 Sound Studios* respectively. These are now available to listen to on *Youtube* and arguably even better than the album which was soon to follow. Powerful, raw, electrifying but simplistic and if anyone needed evidence that these were true originators then tune in to these tracks. The Ramones were now gaining more followers at *CBGBs* and also received a positive review from the *Rolling Stone* magazine at the *Summer of Rock Festival*. The band were not only putting up flyers to advertise the shows but also using the name *Loudmouth Productions* for the business side of things to appear more professional. Organised by Tommy, he would send out correspondence under the name Erdelyi to avoid people realising he was doubling up as the drummer. The next logical step was getting a manager with experience who could take them to the next level. Up steps Danny Fields who had been responsible for the signing of *The Stooges* and *MC5*. [90] Danny recalls that the group had been bugging him and a fellow journalist, Lisa Robinson, to see the band. "We made a deal that she'd go see them to get them off our backs and I'd go see some other band", he claimed. "The next day she said, 'You'll love this band. They're wonderful; they're so funny, every song is two minutes long. The whole set's over in 15 minutes.'" Danny quickly went to see the group at *CBGBs* and loved them. He asked the band if he could manage them after the set and The

Ramones agreed on the condition that he came up with $3,000 for a new drum kit. Fields visited his mother in Florida for a loan and she promptly wrote him out a cheque. [91] Interestingly, in the book *On The Road With The Ramones*, Danny's story is somewhat contradicted as the band state that they did buy gear with the money but it was spent on Marshall and Ampeg stacks and their own PA, another Mosrite guitar for Johnny and an additional Fender Precision bass for Dee Dee. [92] To be honest, this minutia is pretty irrelevant but what was vital was that by November 1975, Danny was managing the band. A record deal was now the goal and Johnny remembers that the first label audition was with Richard Gottehrer who was with Sire records. Although he offered the band a deal for a single "You're Going To Kill That Girl", "we turned it down" the guitarist said. "We didn't want a single; we wanted our own album." [93] Craig Leon, an Artists and Repertoire man from Sire who had already heard the demo tapes from earlier in the year was paramount at securing a contract. He and Linda Stein (who saw them at CBGBs and would eventually co-manage them with Danny Fields) then presented the band to Seymour Stein who was president of the company who had them play an audition. Fittingly and maybe symbolically, the contract was signed in Arturo Vega's loft, the man who would be instrumental in the designing of the famous Ramones logo and also the location of an early video of the band which is fundamental watching for all fans.

In the same month that the first edition of *Punk* was released – January 1976 - The Ramones started recording their debut self-titled album at *Plaza Sound Studio*. Produced by Craig Leon and aided by Tamás Erdélyi, aka Tommy Ramone as associative producer, the record remarkably needed just seven days and an outlay of only $6,400 to record the L.P. The recording process was similar to early *Beatles'* recordings which found the guitars and bass being heard separately on the stereo channels with the drums and vocals mixed in the middle. This was a masterstroke which enabled listeners, if they were so inclined, to turn down one speaker and just listen to Dee Dee or Johnny as they saw fit. Indeed, I know of more than one muiscian who learned their instrument by carrying out this technique. The band recorded the songs in the same order as they played them at the time and although they captured that live sound there was use of layered and structured technology of its time including some overdubbing and doubling of the vocals. Leon was "so happy with the recording that at one point, he wanted to record 'Ramones' as one single track with no breaks between songs. Eventually he opted otherwise but employed this technique in a more diminutive setting between the album's last two songs." [94]

The album is perfection and is 29 minutes of unadulterated pure punk paradise. From start to finish, I just cannot criticise. After the initial introduction of the first song with their anthem "Blitzkrieg bop" to the last song "Today Your Love, Tomorrow The World" they set the precedent that all punks would follow – fast tempo, minimalism, chainsaw guitars but still with those catchy hooks and melodies. Jon Savage in his critically acclaimed book *"England's Dreaming"* sums up the album perfectly when he states "The Ramones now sounds laughably simple: at that time, it was brutal and divisive. After hearing it everything else sounded impossibly slow." [95] Peter Aaron, gives further insight stating that nowadays "it may be tough to grasp just how revolutionary The Ramones' self-titled debut was when it hit the racks in 1976. Believe it or not, many naysayers wrote the band's music off as being simply too fast even to be considered rock 'n' roll. By the mid-1970s, though, what was passing for rock 'n' roll to the ears and wallets was questionable. There were a few bright sparks...but rock, overall, had lost the plot and moved far away from the adventure and liberating fun of the 1950s and 60s." [96] Nils Stevenson, Sex Pistols' tour manager and later manager of *Siousxie And The Banshees*, just about sums it up when he recounts their influence: "I was trying to do a compilation of all-time punk classics and when I finished I saw I had the whole of The Ramones' first album, every bloody song." [97] The album has everything - attitude, intrigue, controversy and humour. The L.P dares to tackle topics such as violence, drug abuse, male prostitution and Nazism but does it in such a way that you still go away humming the tunes. 53rd and 3rd is supposedly Dee Dee's autobiographical story of hustlers turning tricks at the notorious Manhattan interchange whilst controversy was avoided when the band reluctantly agreed to Seymour Stein's demands that they changed the words on "Today Your Love, Tomorrow The World". Much to the annoyance of the band "I'm a shock trooper in a stupor" replaced "I'm a Nazi Baby" which was still heard at live performances. [98] It is hard to pick out highlights because each song is so good but my personal favourites of "Loudmouth", "I Don't Wanna Go Down To The Basement" and "Listen To My Heart" – a smash hit waiting to happen for any *boy band* willing to re-make this classic – take some beating.

Let's pull no punches, the front cover of the album has become one of the most iconic and copied images in music too. The black and white photograph was originally used in *Punk* magazine and was taken by Roberta Bayley. The location of the shot of the brick wall is in Albert's Garden, situated in the Bowery in New

York with the lads cladded in black leather jackets, torn jeans and sneakers and with deadpan facial expressions. Johnny claims that on the photo, he purposely extended his middle finger though he "was really disappointed that no one ever commented on it through all those years" and he felt like he "got one over on everybody." [99] The back cover art, which depicts a belt buckle with a bald eagle and the band's logo, was designed by Arturo Vega.

The eponymous album "Ramones" was released on April 23rd, 1976. Despite the critical acclaim, it flopped commercially with only 6,000 sold in its first year in the States. The album did eventually go 'gold' in America, selling 500,000 units in 2014 and in recent years, accolades has reigned upon it in various forms. These include citations those from *Spin Magazine, Mojo, Time, Q Magazine, Rolling Stone* and in the books *101 Albums That Changed Popular Music* and *1001 Albums You Must Hear Before You die*. Back in 1976, this was the definite punk L.P and whether you like it or not The Ramones were punks and spearheading this new genre of music.

One group of punks who wanted to start their own tribute band to celebrate "the greatest punk band ever", fittingly also originate from New York – indeed just a 30-minute drive away from Queens in a hamlet located on Long Island known as Bethpage. The original line-up saw Lawrence on vocals, Sean 'Crusher' on lead guitar, Tomy playing bass and Don Don on the drums. Indeed, it was the stick man who came up with the appropriate designation of the band – *The Rawmones* – signifying the band's intention to be play stripped down music and as Lawrence proclaims be "*fast, loud and proud.*" By 2018, the lads had practised sufficiently and were ready to start gigging and just as The Ramones had done all those years before, took on stage-names in a sign of unison with the guitarist, for example, taking the moniker of Sean Rawmone. There has been one enforced line-up change due to the sad passing of much-loved drummer Don Don in March 2023 with Danny Rawmone now in charge of percussion. Danny is an ardent Ramones fan and had many first-hand experiences of the band. He recalls that his initial viewing of the group was in 1984 at *the Nassau Community College* which is based in New York. He and a school friend "left an internal suspensionto go to the show" and managed to also sneak in free of charge. Although they did not meet the band, on the way home, the two friends saw The Ramones eating pizza – "all very inspiring" the drummer recalls. Interestingly, the New Yorker also hung out with Arturo Vega a few times and actually spent some time in the designer's *awesome* loft and once met Danny Fields who was also there.

A look at the band's set list shows a near 30 strong catalogue which covers various stages of The Ramones' illustrious career. Those younger fans, whose formative years were in the 1980s and '90s, will relish such tracks as "I Wanna Live", "We Want The Airways", "Bonzo Goes To Bitburg", "The KKK Took My Baby Away", "Mama's Boy", "R.A.M.O.N.E.S" and the often overlooked "Time Has Come Today". Although not technically a Ramones song, the band can be forgiven for also throwing in "What A Wonderful World" from Joe's solo album "Don't Worry About Me" which was released posthumously in 2002. Devotees who maybe are getting a little more long in the tooth will undoutedly appreciate the picks of "We're A Happy Family", "I Don't Care", "Rockaway Beach" and "I Just Want To Have Something To Do". Of course, a Ramones cover set would not be complete without some choices from that seminal debut album and listeners will not be displeased with no less than six songs selected - "Beat On The Brat", "Judy Is A Punk", "Havana Affair", "Loudmouth", "53rd and 3rd" and inevitably the punk anthem of "Blitzkrieg Bop". The Rawmones have played many gigs over the course of their five-year existence but when pushed singer Lawrence cited his favourite venue as possibly their shows at *Mr Beery's*, a venue that has just celebrated 30 years in business and described as "Long Island's version of *CBGBs*." [100] It is also a club where patrons and fans are extremely supportive and kitted out in their shirts to back the band whilst bassist Tomy recalls the fantastic reception they received there for Don Don's memorial gig. Although I couldn't find any footage of these shows, a hunt on the online videoing sharing platform *Youtube* gives viewers extensive coverage on a gig at *The GOAT* in Staten Island. First impressions are always telling they say, and you immediately get the feeling that these rogues must have somehow escaped over the wall from *Rikers Island,* the notorious state penitentiary of New York City. Adorn in torn jeans, T-Shirts, black leathers, one thing was sure, you would not want to meet this motley crew on a dark night. Coming out to the instrumental "Durango 95" as a trio, Lawrence Rawmone walks on to the stage in the nick of time as the knockout "Cretin Hop" is blasted out. Other tunes on offer include "53rd and 3rd", "Blitzkrieg Bop" and "Go Lil Camaro Go" although the package unfortunately does not include blonde bombshell, Debbie Harry to co-sing! There are some interesting quirks to the group - mics are used for both guitarists for instance, whilst there is more chat between songs than is the norm with the other band members even being introduced individually just before "I Wanna Be Sedated". My personal favourite is undoubtedly "Pinhead" but be prepared as it comes complete with a hideous, masked, hunched monster, creeping around on both floor and stage.

Photograph courtesy of Marianne Ruscillo

The Rawmones will continue to keep playing, not only to keep the memory of Don Don alive but also for Joey, Tommy, Johnny and Dee Dee who were instrumental in shaping punk music back in the 1970s and one of the most influential American bands of all time.

Warthog
United States Of America

1974 and 1975 saw The Ramones play just one venue outside of their home city of New York at the *Palace Theatre* in Waterbury in the state of Connecticut. However, by February, 1976 these adventures had expanded with gigs in Nashua in New Hampshire, and amongst others in Cambridge situated directly across the Charles River, just three miles away from the centre of Boston. Boston, is the capital and largest city of Massachusetts, as well as being the cultural and financial capital of New England, a region of the North eastern United States. Famed historically for its "Tea Party" in 1773 where locals opposed the tax levy imposed by its colonial British rulers, it is more recently popularised by *Cheers,* the long-running US sitcom which starred Ted Danson and Shelley Long.

Not much has been documented about *The Club* where The Ramones first played Boston on February 26th although we do know that it was situated at 823 Main Street and was later known as the *Nightstage* which was closed in about 1993. The building itself was described by one punter as "nothing too good looking, brick and cinderblock" which has since been replaced by "some slightly odd-looking condos built in 2007-2008." [101] Fortunately, there is vintage video footage of the band playing "Chainsaw" at the *The Club* from that first Boston concert and well worth seeking out. Additionally, a further early gig can be found on *Youtube* at the same venue on the 20th May which has an audio link covering every song of the concert. Commencing their set with "Blitzkrieg Bop" the pace is relentless and after less than nine minutes the audience have been treated to the early favourites of "I Remember You", "Gimme, Gimme, Shock Treatment" and "I Wanna Be Your Boyfriend".

Monte Melnick describes the early strategy employed whilst as tour manager stating that "pretty soon we realised that The Ramones weren't an opening band. We were already headlining in New York, so we decided to headline our own club tours rather than try to be a support act on these bigger shows. At first we would do short tours around the East Coast - Boston, Washington and so on - but once the album came out we started touring around the country. Everywhere they went, they picked up hardcore fans." [102]

Overall The Ramones would play in Boston more than 40 times and although they performed in other centres in Massachusetts such as Brockton, Salisbury, Amherst, Lynn, Salem, Waltham, Wellesley and Northampton, the state capital was always the preferred location. The holistic importance of these tours was not lost on founding member and drummer Tommy Ramone who deliberated about how the '*fast four*' helped jump-start the punk movement all over the world. "It was every town we hit, he cited. "We'd hit Cleveland and next week there'd be *Pere Ubu*. We'd go to Boston and then there'd be *DMZ* and *The Real Kids*". [103] Indeed, years later, this phenomenon was still taking place and in 2005 four Boston-based musicians decided to take the plunge and form their own tribute - *Warthog*. The name of the band comes from a track from the eight studio album *"Too Tough To Die"*. Sung by Dee Dee, it should come with a government health warning. It's as fast as a whippet and as hard as a steel girder. Blasting out the words incomprehensively, the bassist's jaws snaps like a hyena tears at his prey. "Wart Hog" is not your average Ramones song but then again The Ramones were not your average band.

The act is made up of Mike "The Dude" Bellofatto as vocalist, Paul on lead guitar, Eric "Pudgy" on the drummer's seat whilst Chris is now on bass after replacing the original Shiv on the four string. Like many of his contemporaries, Mike points out why he was enthused enough to start his own tribute stating that "The Ramones were (are) one of my biggest musical influences. The affect they had on my 15-year-old self was the equivalent of a brick hitting me in the face." Paul cites that "getting to play with two of his oldest friends" was a major contributory factor regarding joining the group whilst Eric enthusiastically admits that once he found out there was a drummer needed for a Ramones tribute "that was all I needed to hear." All of the band members naturally refer to their love of The Ramones music which is clearly a constant throughout this book. Maybe, not surprisingly for a band who had a lifespan of over two score years, each member of *Warthog* cites different favourite Ramones albums and tracks. These included *Ramones Mania, Brain Drain, Pleasant Dreams* and *the compilations All The Stuff And More Volumes 1 and 2* although it is hard to argue with Eric with his claim that "the first four albums are perfection." As with most of our tributes, the *Warthog* members fine-tuned their skills in previous bands. Eric, for instance drummed in *Sterns76, Hellbore and Chanticlear* whilst Paul and Chris have served in multiple bands on guitar on bass respectively. A

The band's live set contains all of The Ramones' well-known favourites with a few "oddities" thrown in to keep the band bright. Chris points out that the band always start with "Durango 95" but somewhat ironically never play "Wart Hog" with gigs between 45 minutes to an hour because it is "so physically demanding." There have been a number of memorable performances but all the band members pointed to one in particular when they opened for *Too Much Joy* at the rammed *Sonia Club* in Cambridge to quite possibly the biggest audience they have played in front of. Chris paints the picture "Everyone was jumping the whole night which is easy to do when the music is spot on, but not easy to do when everyone is over 45. Sandy (from *Too Much Joy*) jumped on stage for one of our songs, and we all jumped on stage for one of theirs." On a more personal level, Mike demonstrates the power of the tribute and how it can touch individual lives. "We have a 'special' friend", he proudly articulates "who loves The Ramones and he loves what we do. He can't say Ramones - he says Mamones. Playing his 40th birthday was beyond fun. To be able to do something like that made being in this band the best."

The band watched The Ramones perform on a number of occasions. Mike, who caught sight of them half a dozen times, agrees with bass man Chris that the most notable gig was the 1992 at *The Orpheum* with *Social Distortion* and *Overwhelming Colorfast* opening the show. The venue in Boston is at one of the oldest theatres in the United States and was built as far back as 1852 and one can only imagine the atmosphere with a sold-out capacity of around 2,700 feverish fans. Things got even better at this show for the singer as he also had the pleasure of meeting the band with the joy of getting his "Mondo Bizzarro" record personally signed. Eric recites his fondest memory of the band being at Hampton Beach, New Hampshire with *The Queers* as support. Indeed, this concert inspired the superb *Riverdales* to write a song "Hampton Beach" about that show and the boys from New York.

Warthog are reflective about The Ramones influence. Paul, for instance points to the fact that so many bands have formed in the past because of them and hopes that "there are kids still out there today that hear their music for the first time and start a band." Chris also declares that "there isn't much to say that hasn't already been said. So much music and culture can be traced directly back to them."

If you like your tributes to look like and sound like The Ramones, then I am afraid the band will not be for you. However, if you have an open mind, then this may well be your cup of tea. Looking like they are just about to speed off on a Harley-Davidson, singer Mike is philosophical when describing his band. "We are not The Ramones", he states, "we pay tribute to what they were with our own spice blended in." Although not as prolific, in terms of social media footage, there are some glimpses of the group out there live. One shows *Warthog* in action back in 2015 when they are seen performing "Blitzkrieg Bop" and "Do You Remember Rock 'n' Roll Radio?". The lads certainly have their own feel and mannerisms, slightly adapting the tunes and modifying what is sung and played but one thing is for certain is they have energy to burn as they blast out the old Ramones' humdingers. They can also be seen at the *Midway Café*, Jamaica Plain in 2022 with renditions of "Merry Christmas (I Don't Wanna Fight Tonight)" and Lemmy's ode to the band, "R.A.M.O.N.E.S" which is the pick of the bunch. As impressive is their excursion onto Boston Rock 'n' Roll TV with the programme *Sonic Lobotomy*. In the programme they start with over 30 minutes of our favourite tunes including the impressive "Glad To See You Go" and "53rd and 3rd" before being interviewed at the end of the show. Check out some of their arrangements, after the initial discomfort to your senses, you may well like it.

53rd and 3rd
England

It terms of seminal punk occasions, the date of Sunday 4th July, 1976 stands at the very summit. This heralded not only The Ramones' first visit across the English coastline but also signalled their debut gig outside of their native United States of America. Besides stirring every London fan who was lucky enough to witness the concert, it also helped stimulate those expectant punk musicians who were waiting in the wings, ready to explode and energise the new up and coming movement.

The groundwork for The Ramones visit to England can be traced back to when Hilly Kristal, owner of *CBGBs* decided to advertise the place by having the *Summer of Rock Festival* in 1975. The event received considerable publicity with *Rolling Stone* 'bigging up' the band. After that, the band started getting regular write-ups in New York's *SoHo Weekly News* and even across the Atlantic in the British *Melody Maker* and *New Musical Express*. Monte Melnick recalls that one of the things Johnny Ramone wanted was to make sure that "The Ramones went to England to take advantage of the press they were receiving" [104] and it was thereafter left to people such as co-managers Danny Fields and Linda Stein to finalise dates in England. Indeed, Danny states that Seymour Stein's wife (Seymour was president of Sire Records) was "very internationally minded" and that "from the very beginning, she properly sensed that we were likely to find an easier niche in the UK." [105]

It was a whistle-stop visit to London with two barnstorming performances on consecutive days. The first was played at the *Roundhouse Theatre* whilst the follow-up was at *Dingwalls*. *The Roundhouse* is a grade II listed building which was built in 1846-47 in Chalk Farm, London. The structure was designed initially as a circular railway turntable although it was only used for that purpose for around a decade. After this, it was converted into an alcohol warehouse for a number of years before falling into disuse before the start of the Second World War. [106] By 1964, it reopened as a performing arts centre with a theatre, cinema and art gallery amongst the many fields of entertainment on offer. A number of famed artists have performed at the venue including *The Who, The Rolling Stones, Fleetwood Mac, The Doors*, Jimi Hendrix and David Bowie.

The first show was on the Bicentennial anniversary of America's independence and the irony was not lost on Danny Fields. It was "metaphorically appropriate", he said, because "we were bringing Great Britain this gift that was going to forever disrupt their sensibilities." [107] Guitarist Johnny describes the build-up to the concerts stating that "it was a co-bill with us and *Flamin' Groovies* agreeing to alternate the closing slot, and then we get there and they refused. They insist on closing the shows. We couldn't care less. Nobody could follow us. Any band is better off going on in front of us, but if you want to close, go ahead. We were right. Everyone was there to see us. People cleared out after us." [108] In fact, there were three bands that evening with none other than those mature, menacing *Stranglers* who at the time were working the pub-rock circuit and would eventually go on to be the most successful UK band to have originated from the punk scene, taking stage first. Dee Dee

Ramone, in his book *Poison Heart,* remembers that the weather in London was particularly warm that year [109] and maybe the sauna like temperature was fitting for this red hot performance. In front of a 2,000 packed audience, there is thankfully an auditory recording of the show which begins with difficulties with the PA before the crowd start ringing out the customaries "hey, ho, let's goes" and also devotees unusually heard singing "beat on the bat with a baseball bat." There is an edginess and level of expectancy from the fan base which you can cut with a chainsaw as they eventually commence with the contentious "Loudmouth" thumping through a further 15 beauties before they finish with the equally prickly "Today Your Love Tomorrow The World". Although there is no audio record of an encore, it has been suggested that they also came back to treat the crowd with "Now I Wanna Be A Good Boy" and "Let's Dance" but this cannot be confirmed. Whether they played those extra two songs or not is largely irrelevant but what was vital was that they had unwittingly launched an entire musical, cultural movement.

The following evening on the 5th July, the band again opened for San Francisco's *Flamin' Groovies* but this time at the smaller *Dingwalls*, an iconic landmark located within a market in Camden Town. Over the course of the two shows, future punk luminaries, were there to watch and undeniably learn from the New Yorkers. On the first evening, members of *The Damned, The Pretenders'* Chissie Hynde and *The Adverts'* Gaye Advert were present whilst *The Sex Pistols* and *The Clash* attended *Dingwalls* - both groups were incidentally performing at the *Black Swan* in Sheffield the night before. This new do-it-yourself crusade was now gaining momentum. *The Damned's* drummer, Rat Scabies points out that "it was the fact that the same thing was happening in different parts of the world. It was the next generation getting angry. It made us realise we weren't alone" whilst his bandmate Captain Sensible refers to the importance of The Ramones' first album. "You could plonk their record on", he recalls "grab hold of a bass or a guitar or whatever, and jam along. That's how I used to practice… and Sid Vicious as well." [110] Members of *The Clash* were backstage with the Americans the night of the *Dingwalls* show and bassist Paul Simonon, was amazed at the buzz The Ramones had generated, and the thousands of fans who came to see them. "What is it about you guys?" Paul asked Johnny Ramone. "We've played about two shows, and we can't seem to pull in a full house even in small clubs, but you're here for the first time with two sold out shows. You must be some incredible musicians. I guess we haven't rehearsed enough, or something." "You've never seen us, right?" Johnny said. "You're coming to the show tonight? You'll see. We can't play, we're terrible musicians. But the kids don't care about that; they want a show. So we give them a show, loud and fast. They love that. You guys going to keep rehearsing forever? Nobody's gonna know. They just want to be blown away. So go blow them away, nobody gives a shit about anything else." Joe Strummer, guitarist and lead singer of *The Clash* witnessed the Dingwall's performance too and was even more forthcoming reminiscing that the show "was like white heat, because of the constant barrage of tunes. One ended, the next began. You couldn't put a cigarette paper between them." [111] One last anecdote about those early London gigs, is cited in the book *Please Kill Me, The Uncensored Oral History Of Punk*. Graphic designer, Arturo Vega, who was famed for creating The Ramones logo, recalls that Johnny Rotten asked if he could come through the back door to meet the band. Innocent enough it may seem but evidently The Ramones, according to Dee Dee, "always put a few drops of piss in anything they gave their guests as a little joke" with *The Sex Pistols'* vocalist unwittingly accepting a beer from Johnny Ramone, the callous guitarist. [112] Whether this story was a fact or just poetic license will never be known for sure but it has now gone down as one of the legendary punk yarns.

All in all, The Ramones would play in the capital over 30 times with their last show in England on February 3rd, 1996 at the *Brixton Academy* in South London. Two fans, who witnessed that final British gig were Richie Goring and Peter Revesz and although the performance was tinged with sadness as it was the end of an era, it marked the start of a new dawning in their own lives. "As we were walking out" Richie recalls, "Peter said he wanted to form a Ramones tribute band. I said I'd fill in on vocals until he found his Joey Ramone. I was still on vocals 23 years later when we played our final gig in Dijon, France." Over the years, the band had many line-up changes with vocalist Richie and bassist Pete, the only constants. The guitar responsibilities were shared by a variety of musicians with Jake in the initial listing followed by Rob Brook, Robak Zlovelock and Robin Licker. In terms of the drumming duties, the main protagonists were Eric Boitier, Martin Parrott and Marek Wasiak with Eric featuring on the stool during two different spells. All of the boys were based in the London area but the group had a multinational feel with members originating from Hungary, France, Croatia, and Poland. The band members have had much experience in other groups and too many to list in this short narrative but some of the more noteworthy actions were by Richie, Martin and Rob who all played in *Los Coños,* Eric who is currently gracing the quirky rhythm 'n' blues *King Salami & The Cumberland Three* whilst Pete, Marek *and* Robin all performed in *Short Bus Window Lickers*. Robin has also been prominent on the guitar for the East London hardcore punk band *The Restarts* whilst Rob is on the same instrument in the current incarnation of old favourites *Johnny Moped*. The name of the band, *53rd and 3rd*, derives from the chilling song about male prostitution written by Dee Dee from The Ramones' first album. It is a brutal, alarming and disturbing tale but is somehow fitting for this gritty, steely and hardy tribute.

The group played something from every Ramones album over the 23 years they performed including the whole of "It's Alive" on two occasions. In the last five years or so of the band, *53rd and 3rd* executed songs mainly from the first two Ramones albums because they were the most popular songs with the audience whilst still slipping in three or four tracks from the later albums. Richie cites a number of stand-out moments during their time including supporting *The UK Subs* several times but "probably the most memorable gig was an open-air festival in Tiverton in Devon" the singer suggests. "We'd played a gig the night before and stayed overnight at a friend's house in Bristol. We left Bristol later than planned and missed our slot at the festival, we told them we'd driven all the way from London and could we at least get free entry to the festival, the security at the band entrance told us to speak to the promoter at the main entrance. We drove to the main entrance and spoke with the promoter, he said that a lot of people had asked if we'd already played so he decided to give us another slot. We ended up playing after *Stiff Little Fingers* and before *The Stranglers*. We had a great crowd, much better than we would've if we'd played our original afternoon slot."

53rd and 3rd also met two Ramones over the course of their existence. Impressively, in 1998, the lads linked up with Dee Dee Ramone at his book signing in Croydon. The group played three songs, "Rockaway Beach", "Sheena Is A Punk Rocker" and unsurprisingly "53rd and 3rd" with their hero.

Dee Dee sings along with Richie whilst Pete plays the bass

The band also met Marky Ramone at *The Underworld* in Camden in around 2005. At the time, *53rd* were drummerless so they went to Marky's solo concert with flyers in hand thinking it would be a great place to potentially pick up a new stickman. Richie recalls "that after handing them outside we went into the gig. Pete had the ingenious idea of putting a flyer on each of Marky Ramone's drums. When the band came out to play and Marky saw the flyers on his drums and he laughed. After the gig we managed to wangle ourselves into the dressing room and had a good chat with Marky."

The singer summarises the band succinctly when he adds that "we were together for 23 years and didn't really expect to last that long. Once we'd made a bit of a name for ourselves in London we decided to start playing elsewhere. We were doing quite well organising gigs around England and then we were approached by a promoter who organised a short tour of Scotland. This promoter also promoted *The UK Subs* and *The Vibrators* at the time and got us gigs supporting one or the other and a couple of gigs with both bands on the same night. We eventually decided to stop working with this promoter because he wasn't getting us the sort of gigs we expected. We carried on playing, mostly in London, but also went to Belgium, Sweden and finally France in 2019 which ended up being our final gig."

Looking up *53rd and 3rd* is a necessity and my recommendation initially would be "Rockaway Beach" along with the improvised "Marga (Sheena) Was A Punk Rocker" at *Ryan's Bar* in London in 2014. Immediately you will get a *feel* for the band. Wearing wigs, ripped jeans and sneakers is one thing but what is immediately apparent is that this group has a dark sided, unsettled, street-fighting punk streak which has got the audiences eating out of palms of their hands. If you have a little more time, then footage from *The Unicorn* in 2016 could be for you where you are treated to a five song party. Pete, in particular, is a bundle of energy throughout, legs astride, bass low, shoulders twitching and emphatically mirroring Dee Dee's early characteristics. Unquestionably, *53rd and 3rd* are the real deal whether you are at home, in a bar or as the song reflects *standing on a street.*

Hey! Ho! Let's Go!
United States Of America

There cannot be many more recognisable chants adopted by any punk rock band than the one penned by Tommy Ramone. "Hey Ho, Let's Go", was the opening line of the opening track of "Blitzkrieg Bop" from their debut album and not only became synonymous with the group itself but a battle cry for all fans of *Da Brudders* at any Ramones gig. The inspiration of the tune maybe surprisingly stemmed from *The Bay City Rollers* with Tommy explaining that he wanted to emulate a chant-type song such as "Saturday Night" which was a hit by the Scottish pop sensations. Similarly, it also was a play on words from the *Rolling Stones'* version of "Walking The Dog" with the drummer making fun of the singing of Mick Jagger's *'high low, tippy toe'*. In one interview, Tommy also recalls that the song "was basically about a few kids going to a concert, getting away from it all and having a great time. I happened to pick up Joey Ramone's guitar, a two-string guitar with A and E strings tuned to a fifth. And I started bashing away on it and came up with the chords." It may also shock a few when Tommy reveals that the original name of the song was *'Animal Hop' rather than the now-famed designation*. "Dee Dee came up with *'Blitzkrieg Bop'* because he wanted to Ramones-ize it", Tommy recalls. "And he changed one line. It used to be 'they're shouting in the back now' and he rewrote it to 'let's go shoot 'em in the back now'. Dee Dee came up with the title and that line, but the rest of it is mine." [113]

It is of no surprise therefore that one of our tributes used this rallying call as their label for their band. *Hey! Ho! Let's Go!* were formed in 2008 and originate from San Diego, the second largest city of California. Located on the Pacific Ocean in the southern part of the state, San Diego is known for its extensive beaches as well as its close proximity to the Laguna Mountains. With nearly 39 million residents, California is the most populous state in the USA and is also the third-largest U.S state by area with only Alaska and Texas occupying a greater expanse of square miles of land. It lies in the western region of the country and is bordered by Oregon to the north, Nevada and Arizona to the east and Mexico to the south. California's economy is the largest within the United States, with a $3.6 trillion gross state product which shockingly would rank as the world's fifth largest economy if it were a sovereign nation, just ahead of India and the United Kingdom. Historically, there were more than 100 Indigenous people of California including the Chumash, Pomo and Salinan chiefdoms. Early contacts with Europeans were made in 1534 and 1542 when Spanish expeditions led by Fortun Jimenez and Juan Rodriquez Cabrillo entered the Baja California Peninsula and San Diego Bay areas respectively. In 1769, Spanish colonisation of "Alto California" began when the Presidio at San Diego, the first permanent settlement on the Pacific coast was established whilst in turn, the area became part of Mexico in 1821 after their war of Independence with Spain. In 1846, a group of American settlers rebelled against Mexican rule and after a short-lived California Republic, it would officially be a U.S state in 1850. Maybe, this period is even better known for the so-called *Gold Rush* which was triggered when James W. Marshall found pieces of the precious metal at Sutter's Mill in Coloma in January,

1848. His discovery would be the impetus of approximately 300,000 people migrating to the region to seek their fortune. [114] Although the capital of the state is Sacramento, which is home to the Government of California, there are larger cities in terms of population. Los Angeles, for instance, is the most populated city whilst San Diego, San Jose, San Francisco and Fresno have all more inhabitants living within the municipalities.

The Ramones were no strangers to the hospitality of Californian venues. Their first gig in the state was on August 11th, 1976 when they played at *the Roxy* in Los Angeles which was likewise the venue for the shooting of the live section of the movie in *"Rock 'n' Roll High School"* in December 1978. Possibly even more famously, the band's last ever show was also in L.A - this time at *The Palace* in the summer of 1996. As well as the *City of Angels*, the band, would play in a host of other California centres and clocked up altogether over 160 concerts in *The Golden State*. These included shows in San Francisco, Huntington Beach, Stockton, Berkeley, Sacramento and naturally San Diego. The Ramones would play in the latter on 19 dates with their first performance on March 12th, 1977. Interestingly, on offer at *the Backdoor* that day were two shows – a matinée as well as the more customary evening performance. *The Backdoor* was a small music venue with a capacity of just 300 which operated between 1968 and 2011. Described as being "nestled in a downstairs corner of San Diego State University's Aztec Centre next to the campus bowling alley, *The Backdoor* had almost zero ambulance but considerable appeal nonetheless." It showcased a number of notable artists including *Mettalica,* Patti Smith, Linda Ronstadt, Roy Harper, *R.E.M* and *Talking Heads* whilst the first English band *Eddie and The Hot Rods,* "performed at such a high-decibel level that the group completely blew out *The Backdoor's* sound system during the opening song." [115] The band's afternoon set list totalled 21 songs and was unsurprisingly made up of cuts from the first two albums. There is an audio recording of this show on *Youtube* and it illustrates the band at its very best commencing with the hostile "Loudmouth" and finishing with the equally contentious "Now I Wanna Sniff Some Glue".

Hey! Ho! Let's Go! has experienced various line-up changes throughout its history although has pleasingly had an unchanged formation for the last five years, which has coincided with a period of notable success. The current line-up sees Alan Alpert on vocals, guitarist Preston Orellana, Daniel Johnston on the drummer's chair and Al Venditti on the bass. Amusingly, the fellas adopt the pseudonyms of "Ho", fitting in with the designation of the band with the monikers of Alan, Presty, Danny and my personal favourite Tally Ho taken up. Along with the current band members, the dedication and contribution of former guitarist Glen Wiseman, aka Glenny Ho, should also be noted who played a significant role over the years. Front man Alan explains in detail why he personally wanted to start the tribute. "First and foremost", he points out "I am a big fan of the band and I really like their music. Secondly, this was something that I could do vocally and I can resemble my character in the band because I can look the part, which for me is very important. Thirdly, it has been nearly 50 years since The Ramones started and people still talk about them today. That does not happen with other bands. I really feel people will still be talking about them many years from now just like they do with a band like *The Beatles*. Fourthly, their influence in music history is undeniable so there was a *before* and *after*. Fifthly, I believe they are bigger now than they have ever been."

Just like many of our other tributes, the band used an adapted Ramones logo with their own names around the edge. In the early years, the group experimented with variations, including one that represented *SoCal* (southern California) with elements such as a seagull, surfboards, palm trees, and the California poppy, the official state flower of the state. Additionally, they incorporated a custom character inspired by a pinhead. Over time, due to changes in band members, *Hey! Ho! Let's Go!* simplified the logo to just the band name.

Each performance is meticulously curated, considering the venue, event type, and audience demographics. Their versatility is evident as the group have played shows ranging from fairs, festivals, casinos, car shows, rock 'n' roll marathons and triathlons. The nature of the event and whether they share the stage with other bands, influences their song choices and this is all taken into account. Indeed, Alan makes clear that "prior to each show, we thoroughly research the crowd profile to tailor our set accordingly. An all-ages show requires a different approach than a 21+ event, and the musical preferences of accompanying bands also impact our selection. If sharing the stage with heavier acts, we may emphasize our faster material; for more melodic bands, we incorporate slower songs. Despite these considerations, there are timeless staples that we include in every set, such as "Blitzkrieg Bop", "I Wanna Be Sedated", "Sheena Is a Punk Rocker", "Rock 'n' Roll High School", "Beat on the Brat" and "Rockaway Beach" ensuring a mix of iconic tracks that resonate with our audience." When asked about his favourite show, Alan points to a *CBGB* tribute night at the *Gaslamp* in Long Beach on February 3rd, 2024. "The venue was packed with a sold-out crowd of 500 enthusiastic music lovers", he recalls. "Serving as headliners, we shared the stage with tribute acts for *Blondie, Talking Heads*, and *The Police*. This particular show stands out as one of the most memorable performances in recent times, leaving a lasting impact on both the band and our fervent audience." Alan also makes clear that the band "strive to make every performance unforgettable, and it's a common occurrence for fans to approach us post-show, expressing that they'll forever cherish the experience."

When asked about The Ramones' legacy the songster feels that they had a profound and lasting influence on the punk rock genre and the broader landscape of rock music in several key aspects. Alan points to their musical style and how The Ramones "simplified rock music to its core elements, featuring short, fast-paced songs with basic three-chord structures with this minimalist approach departing from the complex and virtuosic styles dominating rock at the time." He also refers to how the New Yorkers embraced a "do-it-yourself" ethos "which became a central tenet of punk rock. Their attitude encouraged aspiring musicians to form their own bands, book their own shows, and release their own music independently, outside of the traditional music industry." Furthermore, Alan points to the speed and energy of the lads from Queens. "The band's high-energy performances and fast-paced music influenced the development of hardcore punk in the late 1970s and 1980s. The Ramones laid the groundwork for a faster and more aggressive punk sound." The vocalist feels that it was not merely in terms of music where the '*fast four*' made an impact citing their influence within fashion and imagery. "The Ramones' distinctive look, characterised by leather jackets, ripped jeans, and shaggy hair", he articulates. The front man goes on to add that "this fashion sense influenced not only the punk scene but had a broader impact on popular culture." It is also difficult to argue with his assessment when he talks about their *brashness* and how The Ramones' "rebellious and energetic attitude helped define the punk ethos. Their rejection of mainstream norms and embrace of a counter-cultural stance inspired a generation of musicians and fans to question established norms." Lastly, Alan feels that it was not just within the United States that the boys from Forest Hills made their mark - the band had an international influence "impacting the UK punk scene and reaching other parts of the world. Many punk bands cite The Ramones as a major influence, contributing to the global spread of punk rock."

A look on to their *Facebook* page shows numerous photographs and information about the band but sadly just one fantastic short clip which includes the songs "Carbona Not Glue" and "Blitzkrieg Bop" at the *Santa Fe Springs Swap Meet*. Here you will find the lads at full throttle, looking every bit like The Ramones in entire combat gear, complete with leathers and wigs. Although the footage is just a morsel, it does give viewers an idea of the electrifying pace and energy of *Hey! Ho! Let's Go!* Indeed, the pace is frightening, like a lightning bolt or in this case maybe more aptly described as a *blitzkrieg!*

The Black Jackets
Canada

1976 was a big year for The Ramones. After taking London by storm, the New Yorkers flew back across the Atlantic with their reputation significantly enhanced and with the prospect of spreading their status furthermore with gigs arranged in other parts of the North American continent. As well as heading towards the west coast of the States, part of this tour would also be to visit bordering Canada. The chosen city was to be Toronto - the capital of the province of Ontario as well as being the largest city in Canada with a population of around 2.8 million. Toronto is located on the north western shore of Lake Ontario and a short drive away from the breath-taking and majestic Niagara Falls. The band would play three seismic shows in just two days on September 24th and 25th including two appearances on the Friday. The location of the gig was the aptly named *New Yorker Theatre* in Yonge Street – originally opened as the *Victoria or Victory Theatre* in 1919, it was renamed the *Astor Theatre* in 1949 before being remodelled again as the *New Yorker* in the 1960s. As with many of the venues that The Ramones played at, the building was closed and all but a portion of its façade demolished until it was rebuilt as the *CAA theatre* in 2018. [116] Unfortunately, there is no full record of their inaugural Canadian set list but we do know that the group played "Loudmouth", "Beat On The Brat", "Blitzkrieg Bop", "Havana Affair", "Judy Is A Punk", "Chainsaw" and "Today Your Love, Tomorrow The World".

As the group became more established, they would return to Canada continuously with over four score concerts in total being screened. Although Toronto would be played more frequently than any other location, it is pleasing to see so many other centres taken in with 20 different towns and cities visited. These were: Vancouver, London, Burlington, Guelph, Ottawa, Winnipeg, Calgary, Edmonton, Victoria, Kitchener, Bala, Hamilton, Oshawa, Bridgenorth, St Catharines, Barrie, Montreal, Verdun and Quebec City. The last ever Ramones Canadian performance took place in Quebec City which sits on the Saint Lawrence River in Canada's mostly French-speaking Quebec province. The show occurred on July 7th, 1996 as part of the *Lollopalooza* tour and was held at the *Hippodrome. The Hippodrome de Québec*, to give its full name, on the face of it, was an imaginative choice for a music venue with its primary function as a horse race track. The concert is noteworthy as the fortunate audience received a double delight – not only being treated to The Ramones as a support band but also a colossuses set from headlining *Metallica*. Of course, the heavy metal gurus play their own homage to The Ramones with their own six-song tribute. If you have not witnessed it, then get on to *Youtube* in a hurry and check it out with my personal favourite the thrashing and distorted "Today Your Love, Tomorrow The World". Our boys from Queens played 22 songs that evening in Quebec including their one and only instrumental ditty "Durango 95" to kick off proceedings with other goodies such as "Psycho Therapy", "I Believe In Miracles" and "Do You Remember Rock 'n' Roll Radio?" thrown in.

It wasn't all plain sailing on their Canadian excursions. Marky Ramone recalls how in July 1979, they were booed by 50,000 people at the *Canadian World Music Festival* in Toronto's

Exhibition stadium a venue which had been reconfigured to serve the local baseball team, the *Blue Jays*. Once they had been pelted with missiles in Atlanta whilst opening for English rock band *Black Sabbath* and now history was repeating itself when they opened for Ted Nugent and thereafter followed by *Aerosmith*. "There were pockets of kids getting into it", Marky noted, but then came the booing and, by the sixth or seventh song, the artillery. It was coins, cans and whatever debris was solid enough to chuck from the crappy baseball seats." [117] Monte Melnick tells of another story of a Canadian/American border crossing which is reminiscent of a similar journey that the boys had between Belgium and France. "Dee Dee", the tour manager recalls, "was a big pot smoker. So was the crew. When we'd go to Canada they'd always search the van with dogs. Dee Dee always had pot on him and wouldn't throw it away. So what did we do? We'd pull off at the last rest stop before we crossed the border and Dee Dee would bury his pot near a tree toward the back. We went to Canada, played, and would go back and dig it up and go on our merry way. Of course, while he was in Canada he'd get more pot. Dee Dee was always a maniac. He would disappear after shows and run off and get hammered on all sorts of drugs." [118]

Virtually all the designations of our tributes are the names of songs, names of albums or plays on the word Ramones. It is quite refreshing, therefore, to have an original moniker with the connection to the icons all to do with fashion and lasting taste. Sounding like a 1930s paramilitary Italian militia group, The *Black Jackets* base their name around what the group sported and indeed what they were synonymous for – their leathers. Formed in 2018 in the French speaking Quebec City, the location of the last Canadian Ramones show, the band all take Black as their assumed names with Brett on drums/vocals, Ricky on guitar, Marty on bass/vocals and Cail Black, who replaced the original singer Benny.

All the band earned their stripes in other local bands but Marty described why the lads wanted to start their own tribute citing that The Ramones were "the father" of almost every other punk band. He goes on to add that "I wanted to have fun and play to a different crowd. The Ramones was a great pick for a tribute since the band does not exist anymore and it's the original punk band with the purest look. I love the on stage symmetry, how they blasted each song back-to-back and the down picking on bass and guitar."

The bassist also points out that after playing in a small composition band, "it was special to perform in front of a crowd which all of a sudden know each song you play." He cites a memorable show at a small venue in Quebec on Halloween called

La Source Martinière where the crowd were dressed appropriately for the occasion and The Ramones' *modus operandi* just being a natural fit. Indeed, this show has been posted on social media and I recommend a visit searching *"Black Jackets – show Party d'Halloween – 29 Octobre"*. Introduced by the obligatory recording of "The Good, The Bad And The Ugly" and thereafter "Durango 95", vocalist Benny Black emerges slightly later than his amigos as if the *animal boy* has removed a manhole cover and escaped from his darkened pit. The band wearing their wigs, jackets, and sneakers move onwards into "Teenage Lobotomy" and beyond. I love Benny's "hair flicks" and diminutive jumps both reminiscent of Joey's mannerisms, whilst Marty's shorter haircut basin is not dissimilar to the legendary bassist Jean-Jacques Burnel from the *Stranglers*. Interestingly, by the end of their performance Dee Dee miraculously morphs into C.J complete with a bandana on his head singing the classic "Strength to Endure". Their set list contains all of the usual crowd pleasers with the band attempting to play at least one song from every album whilst keeping it as similar to The Ramones live performances as possible. Some of the interesting picks from their repertoire include "R.A.M.O.N.E.S" maybe surprisingly sung by drummer Brett, "She's The One", "Too Tough To Die", "Have You Ever Seen The Rain?" and the often overlooked and underrated "Swallow My Pride" from the "Leave Home" L.P. The performance is continuous with each song merging into the next with just the audible linking by the "1, 2, 3, 4" or in this case should I say…. "un, deux, trois, quatre"?...

Loudmouth USA
United States Of America

The State of Washington is located in the north west region of the United States of America and borders the Pacific Ocean to the west, Oregon to the south, Idaho to the east and the Canadian province of British Columbia to the north. Although both named after the first U.S President, George Washington, it, of course, should not be confused with the capital city, Washington D.C which is situated just 85 miles from the Atlantic coast. Washington was admitted to the Union as the 42nd state in 1889 and whilst the capital is Olympia, the most populous city is Seattle. The Ramones played 14 times in the State of Washington and 11 of those shows were in fact performed in Seattle. The city is a sea port on the west coast and is the fourth-largest in North America, in terms of container handling. Seattle lies just 100 miles from the Canadian border and has a population of approximately 750,000 making it the 18th most populous city in the country.

The first time The Ramones played in Seattle was on March 6th, 1977 after two other Washington shows in Bremerton and Aberdeen on the two previous evenings. The venue that night was *The Olympic Hotel* which is located in downtown Seattle. The hotel was opened in 1924 and was built on the original site of the University of Washington's first campus. Bearing in mind that the hotel was noted for its Belgian marble flooring, beautiful buff-faced brick and terra cotta trim which lined the walls, along with being renowned for its famous historic guests such as Martin Luther King, Jr, John Wayne, Bing Crosby, Elvis Presley, Bob Hope, Woodrow Wilson and John F Kennedy, [119] the fact that The Ramones played at the site is quite extraordinary. Indeed, this concert has been described as "one of Seattle's most remarkable rock shows" with the build-up for the event brought to light by journalist Eric Lacitis in 2017 to mark the fortieth anniversary of the gig. It is so enlightening; I have published a lengthy part of the text.

"The seminal punk group The Ramones played in the staid Olympic Hotel, in the Georgian room, a 3,600-square-foot hall with a beautiful 31-foot ceiling. Their music literally shook the guests in the lobby as a crowd of 400 to 500, mostly kids, overflowed from the 150-person-capacity venue March 6, 1977. It likely was the loudest musical group ever to grace this grand old landmark that in its heyday was the centre of Seattle high society. And it all took place because a couple of recent Roosevelt High grads, Neil Hubbard, then 19, and Robert Bennett, then 20, made it happen" in just one week. "It was incongruous to have this venerable, old Seattle hotel with stodgy guests, on a quiet Sunday, have the lobby all of a sudden full of kids in leather jackets and torn jeans," remembers Hubbard, now 59. "Guests were complaining to the front desk." But a contract is a contract; in this case, $500 to rent the Georgian (about $2,000 in today's dollars). Bennett did kind of warn the *Olympic's* manager. "I tried to explain, they're kind of loud. He said, 'Fine. We have proms here all the time.' I said, 'All right,'" says Bennett, now 60. These two young men scrambled to book a hall for The Ramones when they heard where the band originally had been booked. It was at the now-demolished *Aquarius Tavern* at 170th & Aurora, formerly known as *Parker's Ballroom*. But being under

21, Bennett and Hubbard knew that they and their friends who made up a large part of the local Ramones' fandom couldn't get into the show. Hubbard began making phone calls and eventually got a hold of The Ramones' tour manager. "He said, 'If you can find a place to do the show, you can produce the show,'" says Hubbard. Cost to book the band for one night: $1,000. At that time, Hubbard was going to North Seattle Community College and, he remembers, "living with a bunch of punk rockers. The only one in that group with some cash was Bennett, who was working at a burglar-alarm company. They had six days to find a hall. They remember calling about 20 places, which either were booked or, having a notion of what The Ramones were about, passed. Then, whoa, the *Olympic* agreed. The two printed up a poster (all red, with "Ramones" repeating) and rudimentary tickets. Record stores on "The Ave" in the University District such as Cellophane Square and Campus Music sold the tickets."

The hoteliers, that evening, must have wondered what had hit them with The Ramones thundering through 18 tracks from the first two albums. Never a band to follow etiquette, some of the songs must have grated on the hotel guests too with "Loudmouth", "Carbona Not Glue", "Beat On The Brat" and "You're Going To Kill That Girl" all on offer. Many were surely relieved that by 10:30 that evening the gig was over although Hubbard and Bennett must have been ecstatic that they had pulled it off with the latter reflecting that "the show turned a small profit." [120] For those aficionados out there, the last time The Ramones played in the State of Washington was on July 30th, 1996 in Gorge which was just a week before their final show in Los Angeles – apart from the gigs in Aberdeen and Bremerton, it was the only time the band played outside of Seattle, in that State.

Our next tribute originates from Spokane, a city in Washington that lies approximately 280 miles away from Seattle. Formed in 2021, the band is a three-piece which consists of Ed Shaw aka Eddie Ramone on guitar and lead vocals, Tyler Arnold or Tyler Ramone on the bass and backing vocals along with Steve Durrant alias Stevie Ramone on the drums. The name of the band, *Loudmouth USA,* not only originates from their geographic location but also that untouchable eighth track off their debut album which coincidentally was also The Ramones' opening tune of the night at the *Olympic Hotel* back in 1977. [121] Undeniably, the track is one of their most aggressive and antagonistic songs which oozes punk with lyrics that just speaks for themselves. Guitarist and singer, Ed goes into more detail about their choice of name stating that "they added *"USA"* not only because there was another band with that name from another country and we wanted to differentiate ourselves but also to remind folks that the world's first punk band was from the States." Ed cites the first three albums as his personal favourite Ramones records and when asked why the lads started their tribute simply points out that "we are super fans that happen to be able to play and sing." Interestingly, bassist Tyler owns a one of a kind arcade and museum called *Jedi Alliance* that features original Ramones memorabilia. He once owned a Johnny Ramone guitar and begrudgindgly sold it for an amazing $75,000 – further details can be seen on *Loudmouth USA's Facebook* page.

Their first gig was at a biker's bar in North Idaho with Ed jokingly recalling that "we thought we might get stuffed into garbage cans or something. It was the exact opposite. We realised within about 30 seconds we were doing something right. Everyone stayed at front of stage the whole set." *Loudmouth USA's* set list is very much centred around The Ramones' debut album, "Leave Home" and "Rocket To Russia". Some of the featured songs include "Judy Is A Punk", "Commando", "You're Gonna Kill That Girl", "Teenage Lobotomy" and naturally the eponymous "Loudmouth". The boys also branch out with a couple of tunes taken from "Road To Ruin" with the crowd pleasing "I Wanna Be Sedated" and the evocative and undoubtedly often over-looked little triumph "It's A Long Way Back To Germany".

Photograph courtesy of Jake Walker

A look on to their *Facebook* page or on *Youtube* shows one glimpse of the band in action with the classic "Rockaway Beach" on show live at *Pigout In The Park* at Riverfront Park, Spokane. As always, those martinets who like their Ramones cover bands as a four-piece rather than a trio will quite possibly find the footage not to their taste but once you get past the fact that there is no front man as such, then you will find much to love. The track is sung majestically and driven home with expertise with emphasis on technical accuracy. Ed points out that *Loudmouth USA* ensure that they play "all downstrokes and eighth notes on the hi hat, both of which are the foundation of The Ramones' sound." Neither do the band try to be copycats. Yes, the group have the trademark leather jackets, sneakers, T-Shirts and jeans but as Ed rather amusingly declares "we wear no wigs, we would die of heat exhaustion! It is hard enough to keep the leathers on and very physically demanding...like running sprints." The future looks bright for the band with further gigs planned. They are scheduled, for instance, to make a guest performance and a play a set for the 45th anniversary for the movie "Rock 'n' Roll High School" at the historic *Garland Theatre* in Spokane.

When asked about what The Ramones brought to the table, it is difficult to disagree with Ed's assessment with his summary that the New Yorkers were "rock 'n' roll in its purest form." Indeed, just as that audacious song reflects, any spoilt brat who tries to contradict this statement is without doubt *"a loudmouth baby!"*

The Ramoms
United States Of America

One of the most unique and amusing bands covered in this book is without doubt *The Ramoms.* The group are not your typical cover. *The Ramoms* are a proud all-female, all mom, parody/ tribute band paying their own homage to the boys from New York in their peculiar, individual manner. Performing notable shows throughout the East Coast of the States, the band have their sights set nationwide not only featuring the favourites tunes you know and love, but also "catchy new kiddo-friendly twists that rival the originals." [122] Love them, or hate them, you certainly will smile along with them.

The Ramoms originate from Philadelphia, a city which is located on the east coast of the United States, in the north east region of the state of Pennsylvania. With over one and a half million people living there, it is the sixth most populated city in the USA and the largest in the state of Pennsylvania. Philadelphia is rich in history and was founded in 1682 by William Penn, an English Quaker and advocate of religious freedom It served as the capital of the country between 1790-1800 after the Constitution was ratified and was the seat of the federal government for a short but crucial period in the country's history. Philadelphia has many tourist attractions including the Liberty Bell, Independence Hall and Christ Church but for those of us, who enjoy more modern culture, then you may well be familiar with the 72 stone steps leading up to the entrance of the Philadelphia Museum of Art which were immortalised when Sylvester Stallone ran up them during a training session in the 1976 movie *Rocky*.

The Ramones first performance in the city came on April 9th, 1977. This was part of a full American tour, sandwiched between gigs in Westport, Connecticut and West Islip in Long Island and only a couple of weeks before the unwavering band would head off to Europe. The selected venue was at the rather grand looking *Houston Hall, University of Pennsylvania* – the first student union constructed on an American college campus. Built in 1896, it was listed as a National Register of Historic Places in 1978 and was in contrast to many of the more run-down sites such as *CBGBs* which the band were more accustomed to. Other famed performers also played at *Houston Hall,* including the new wave party-goers, *The B52s* in 1979 and ex-*New York Doll,* David Johansen, a year later. There is a partial set list documented of that evening with songs such as "Gimme Gimme Shock Treatment", "Carbona Not Glue" and "You're Going To Kill That Girl" all performed. In all probability, there would have been around 20 tunes played which was the norm for that period in the band's history.

By 1996, The Ramones had played 30 times in Philadelphia and had additionally branched out to other centres in Pennsylvania including Pittsburgh, Yatesboro, Carlisle, Wilkes-Barre, Allentown, Mansfield, Millersville, Lewistown, Harrisburg, Lancaster, Reading and Milton. One of the most infamous incidents during The Ramones' illustrious career occurred just two weeks after they had opened for *The B52s* at *Philadelphia Zoo* in the summer of 1983 promoting their album "Subterranean Jungle". Early in the hours of August 14th, now back in New York,

Johnny Ramone got into a post-concert brawl, evidently over his ex-girlfriend Cynthia "Roxy" Whitney who was drunk outside in the street. The assailant, who was Seth Macklin of the hardcore punk band *Sub Zero Construction,* claimed that he believed he was in a monogamous relationship with Whitney, something Cynthia denied. [123] According to Johnny, he never saw the blindsided attack but regardless of the precise circumstances, the fight left the Ramone battling for his life. He suffered a **fractured skull** and was rushed *to St Vincent's* hospital, where the guitarist underwent emergency surgery to stop the bleeding in his brain. In the aftermath, there was a court hearing and Macklin was charged with first-degree assault and sentenced to a few months in prison [124] whilst the incident was said to have inspired the band's next album title "Too Tough To Die". In terms of performing live, there was a short hiatus after his operation, but Johnny would be fit enough to be performing again in December albeit with the unusual sight of shortened hair.

Describing their concert "as probably one of the best shows I have seen", one fan who saw The Ramones back in 1987 was a singer named Jodi Jeffers. In 2017, Jodi decided that she needed an outlet to be creative besides being a mother and asked all of her friends that played instruments that were also parents if they wanted to be in an all-female Ramones cover/parody band – a group that Jodi feels "influenced everything. There would be no Punk Rock if there were no Ramones" she reflects. It took a while to arrange between juggling being parents and their children's busy schedules but it all came together with a lot of planning and help from their significant others. As well as Jodi on vocals, the original line-up saw Sharon playing guitar, Ginger as drummer and Cori on the bass. The group has witnessed a couple of subsequent changes with initially Molly taking over from Cori until Erica accepted the duties on the four-string in 2020. Due to their motherhood responsibilities, the name of the band was logically *The Ramoms* with the band naturally taking up the usual moniker and all becoming a Ramom. The ladies have had experience in other bands. Jodi, for instance, sung in *Dean Dean and The Sex Machines,* Sharon performed in *Lyons and The Revelatours,* Ginger drummed for *The Droogettes and The Riverside Odds* whilst Erica played bass in *Speed Crazy.*

The Ramoms' set varies depending on their mood and the disposition of their crowd. Some shows, would not involve any parody songs at all and the group would just perform the tunes as The Ramones had written them. In fact, Jodi points out that primarily "we all picked our favourite songs that we loved individually although we can collectively say we love playing 'Havana Affair'." The band then reworded some of the classic tunes in a weird satyrical type of style to play for the children. One example, for instance is Dee Dee's heroin fuelled track "Chinese Rock" which with just a little bit of tinkering, evolved into the harmless kiddies play bricks "Lego Blocks". The singer also articulates how the band "enjoy playing Halloween-themed songs like "Texas Chainsaw Massacre" and "Howling at the Moon" which of course fits snugly into any Ramones set up.

Jodi explains that they have "played a lot of shows over the years but two really stand out. We played *Pouzza Fest* in Montreal, which was a large festival with many talented bands. We very happy to be part of it! We also played '*Rock and Roll Playhouse*' performing Ramones songs tailored for kids. I don't think anything was more fun than that!" The group have already had some noteworthy achievements. Impressively, in 2017, they were named one of the top 10 cover bands to watch by the *New York Times Magazine* whilst the band have also appeared on the TV kiddies programme *The Jasper T Dragon Show*. Additionally, *The Ramoms* released three records on *Pirates Press Records*, including a split with LA-based *Dad Brains* in 2018. Other productions include "Problem Child" as well as wrapping up "Teacher's Pet", at *Noisy Little Critter Recording Studio*, which came out in the winter of 2019.

Although rather disappointingly, there is no footage of them performing live, there is plenty of audio recordings out there. If you like to hear some straight up and down Ramones covers then explore "Merry Christmas (I Don't Wanna Fight Tonight", "Rockaway Beach" or my personal favourite, a slightly speedier version of "Beat On The Brat" where the band conjures up the feelings of many a harassed parent. If you wish to explore some clever parodic verse, however, then the aforementioned "Lego

Blocks", "Gritty Is A Punk", The PTA Took My Mommy Away" or the ingenious "Going Into 3rd" will be for you. The band even has a version of "Blitzkrieg Bop" entitled "Boogie Not Snot" with adapted lyrics of "Hey Ho, Let's Blow!" In all their songs they have that essential buzzsaw guitar, thumping drums and amplified, raw vocals which will keep us punks entertained. I look forward to future Ramoms' offerings as their offspring age which will surely take into account "Teenage Lobotomy", "Rock 'n' Roll High School" and unquestionably "We're A Happy Family!"

Animal Boys
Switzerland

The first country The Ramones visited on the mainland of Europe was Switzerland, a fact that might astound many fans. Switzerland is located in central Europe and is famed for its numerous lakes, beautiful villages and mountainous peaks of the Alps. The country has the oldest policy of military neutrality in the world and has not participated in a foreign war since 1815 and was also the birthplace of the Red Cross which was founded in Bern in 1866. The country has four official languages: German, French, Italian and Romansh with each of them spoken in different regions. Although Bern is Switzerland's administrative capital and Lausanne serves as its judicial centre, the most populous cities are Zurich and Geneva and it was in these two places that The Ramones first played in the country in the April of 1977.

Their first concert was at the *Volkshaus,* a 1,200 seated concert hall located in downtown Zurich at the Helvetiaplatz. Opened in November 1910, it has been described as a "cultural institution" within the city and besides a music venue offers a wide variety of rooms which can cater for parties, seminars, conventions, banquets, meetings and exhibitions. [125] A number of famed artists had performed at the old site prior to 1977 including *Deep Purple*, Alice Cooper, *Kiss, Aerosmith, Rainbow* and *AC/DC* so the choice of venue was a natural one when The Ramones hit town on April 24th. During this tour, the band co-headlined with *Talking Heads* and tour manager Monte Melnick describes the less than perfect conditions the two groups found themselves in. "While the shows were all pretty incredible on that tour, the traveling arrangements weren't ideal. First of all, both bands were traveling together in one bus. Not a tour bus, but a tourist bus. Like a school bus, with flat rows and no bunk beds to sleep in. *Talking Heads* were all friends and we got along for the most part, but The Ramones aren't exactly the friendliest guys in the world, especially Johnny." Tommy Ramone adds further detail about the relationship between the guitarist and Tina Weymouth, the bass player of *Talking Heads,* stating that "when we get to the first city on the tour, Zurich, Switzerland, Johnny got into an argument with Tina. Johnny was telling Mitch to bring an amp up or something and Tina says, 'Well, why don't you do it yourself?' I had to get between them and go backstage and apologize." From Johnny's point of view, the bassist was "a major pain in the ass to me the whole time" whilst *Talking Heads'* drummer Chris Frantz claims that Johnny refused to talk to her after that. [126]

Starting with "Loudmouth" and finishing with "Today Your Love Tomorrow The World", The Ramones played 21 songs that night with the vast majority of the tunes from the first two albums unveiled. Their compressed roster meant that their next scheduled gig was not in Switzerland but in neighbouring France with both bands making the long journey by road to Marseilles, a port city in the south of the country. One can only imagination the anger and disbelief when it was revealed that the show had to be cancelled due to a lack of power and the only option would be to retrace their steps without playing, heading back to Switzerland. Their next show was in the picturesque city of Geneva which is on the edge of Mont Blanc and the *gateway to the Alps.* The chosen venue was at the Salle du *Faubourg* on April 27th and this would be the band's last gig in Switzerland before re-crossing the border for a five-centre tour back in France. In total, The Ramones would play just five more times in Switzerland returning in 1980, 1987, 1990, 1991 and 1994. As well as gigs back in Zurich and Geneva, the boys would perform at the *Leysin Rock Festival,* an alpine resort village at the eastern end of Lake Geneva.

One die-hard Ramones fan who saw the band more than 10 times not only in Switzerland but all over the world goes under the pseudonym of *RatMatt.* Indeed, when asked about his memories of the '*fast four*' he can boast about meeting Joey, C.J and Monte at the *Stadthalle* in Freiburg in Germany as well as watching them at other foreign gigs in The United States of America, France and Italy. He has certainly been fundamental in keeping The Ramones' memory alive in his home country of Switzerland and he recalls how a tribute came about back in 1992. "I was manager of a great Ska Band known as *"The Ventilators"* and their drummer Gugi asked me if I would sing in a Ramones tribute band" he points out. "We did that gig on Christmas Eve at the *Gaskessel/Coupole* (the oldest youth centre in the country) in Biel-Bienne and have since played almost every Christmas since!" The chosen name for the band was *The Animal Boys* with the designation heralding from The Ramones' ninth studio album. Released through Sire Records in May 1986, the band started recording "Animal Boy" in early December of the previous year at a studio in New York called *Intergalactic.* Strangely, however, some of the vocal mixes was recorded at the *Polar Studios* in Sweden with Joey flying to Europe in the middle of the winter. [127] The producer was Jean Beauvoir, who had played bass in *the Plasmatics* alongside wild singer Wendy Williams. According to Richie Ramone, the production "had a little too many synthesisers on some of the songs, which a lot of the old fans didn't like" whilst it also appears that the choice of Beauvoir was largely down to Sire rather than the band themselves. (128)

As was the norm within the group, there was much tension between the members with the end result leading to less input from an unhappy Joey and more contribution from Dee Dee in terms of writing and indeed singing. Johnny "liked the songs; they were all brand-new" but felt "this would have worked if the production had been better, but the guitar doesn't even sound like me." There was also some dispute about the title of one of their singles, "Bonzo Goes To Bitburg" which referred to President Reagan's visit to a S.S graveyard in Germany. Indeed, the track's title was converted on the album to "My Brain Is Hanging Upside Down" in order to placate the staunch Republican, Johnny. (129) One of the upturns of Joey's song writing hiatus was that it gave some opportunity for Richie to put forward his own tunes and within "Animal Boy" was a track which would go on to become a Ramones stalwart at live performances. "Somebody Put Something In My Drink" was about one of the drummer's past experiences a few years earlier at a bar called *The Ritz*. The drummer stole a drink which must have been laced with L.S.D. which resulted in hallucinations and spending the next few hours "puking like crazy." (130) Along with "Bonzo", the tune was much heralded although personally some of the harder core tracks need some beating. Most notably, the monstrous "Freak of Nature" which is bellowed out expertly by Joey along with Dee Dee's brutal "Eat That Rat". The bassist is additionally on lead vocals as he blasts out his punk ballad for Sid Vicious and Nancy Spungen "Love Kills" which he would eventually sign off to at The Ramones' farewell gig in Los Angeles in 1996. More traditional songs would come in the form of "Crummy Stuff" and "Hair Of The Dog" whilst "Mental Hell" was all about Joey's state of and according to his brother, Mickey Leigh during this period "he had really had it with the band." [131]

The album cover was shot by George DuBose with the original idea to take a photograph at the monkey house in the Bronx Zoo. Once this proved unfeasible, a fake cage was built in the photographer's loft, they got Legs McNeil to dress up in a gorilla suit and hired Zippy the chimpanzee from the *Late Night with David Letterman Show*. Originally Joey was supposed to hold the ape but it kept hopping off of him so Richie ended up looking after Zippy and becoming the *animal boy*. [132] Overall, the album was steady but failed to live up to their previous L.P "Too Tough To Die" and just like other releases it did not receive any real commercial success.

The Animal Boys was unquestionably a worthy option for the designation of a group, as Ramones enthusiasts would instantly link the Swiss lads to the New Yorkers. The original line-up saw RatMatt as the front man, Gugi on drums, Chris as guitarist and Rindli on the bass. Since then RatMatt has been the only constant member to have played every gig but what he has done is build a team around him which could be called upon on different dates and in different towns and cities. There have been, for instance, since Gugi retired, three drummers – Päscu, Stony and Urs who are still all available when needed. On guitar, PJ performed one gig whilst three musicians rotate with Aebi, Himbo Flimbo, and the still active Chris all serving. On the bass, it has been even more of a *revolving door*. Rindli has stopped performing but Resus, Balony and Stebu have all stepped up to the plate and are all still *revved up and ready to go*. Special mention should be made to Bruno who has played both bass and guitar for the *Animal Boys* along with their background crew of Nathalie Girard, Doc D. Schneider and Ernst Aschi Rieben.

Since that debut Christmas gig in 1992, the fellas have combined to perform in excess of 300 live shows. Over the years they have built up an impressive roll of honour which have included playing as the opening act for *Marky Ramone and the Intruders,* an American punk rock band set up by the drummer after the retirement of The Ramones. Similarly, the *Animal Boys* supported Dee Dee Ramone's *I.C.L.C* post Ramones project who released a 14-track album named "I Hate Freaks Like You". Other memorable events were as a support act to *Les Sheriff, Toy Tolls, Peter and the Test Tube Babies, The Lurkers* and *Electric Eel Shock.* RatMatt also cited a number of his much-loved venues including the festival at *the Openair am Bielersee,* the alternative music festival at *Barbarie,* a show across the border in Rosenheim in Germany and the famous *Solex Race* at the foot of Mount

Chasseral. The band continue to evolve and in 2024, the group have been invited to play a private show in Paris in France. *Animal Boys* have also released a live CD recorded at the Kreuz in Nidau in December 2004 for promotional purposes with the cover designed by artist Joe Merenda. The style of the artwork is similar to The Ramones' album "Road to Ruin" but significantly shows Biel-Bienne, their home town in the background. Maybe his favourite occasion, however, was the release of their own self-penned single called "This Is Gonna Be Paradise" and the subsequent celebratory party at the *Kofmehl Solothurn*. The special guest was none other than George DuBose, the same photographer who snapped the famous "Animal Boy" album shot in 1986. At a presentation, he gave the band a photo of Zippy the chimpanzee taken from that shoot.

The *Animal Boy's* repertoire has seen near on half a century of tracks in their live set with a range of songs throughout the Ramone's history and albums. If you wish to hear those *must-*

play songs– "Blitzkrieg Bop", "Rockaway Beach", "Rock 'n' Roll High School" and the like, then it will meet with your approval. If you like to hear some of the more unusual picks though, then you will certainly come away pleased too with the lads' set list including the likes of "Death Of Me", "I Want You Around", "Spiderman", "Born To Die In Berlin", "Life's A Gas" and "Go Mental". Indeed, a search onto *Youtube* or their own *Facebook* page, pleasingly finds an abundance of live material of the band. What is particularly refreshing, is that you will observe many of these less documented songs on offer rather than just the 'classics'. For instance, try out the outside concert at *Carpe Dien* in the capital, Bern from 2011. On show is an energetic rendition of the demo "Slug" which many Ramones social media followers regularly cite as an unheeded gemstone. Alternatively, a search for "Mama's Boy" at the Kufa Lyss in 2013 will not only display an appreciate audience slam dancing but fantastic heavy drumming to this mid-tempo sing-along. If you appreciate another *rocky number,* then you will certainly enjoy "I Don't Want You" live at *The UFO* in Biel-Bienne in 2012 whilst the often disregarded track "Swallow My Pride" gets an airing at the *Kofmehl* in Solothurn back in 2012. For those more punk minded fans, check out the 2007 *Moonrock Festival* at Niederried where the abrasive "Loudmouth" is performed with RatMatt alternating from English to German making it even more stimulating. There are loads more on offer but I will leave you with my personal favourite of "Now I Wanna Be A good Boy" at *The Loco* which is as fast as a lightning bolt and as hard as nails. In all the performances, you will not discover a band which are trying to look or even sound like The Ramones but what you will see is a tight group, clearly having fun with an intense energy and passion.

Les Ramons
France

The spring of '77 witnessed the group take in nine countries kicking off in the heart of the continent with their first show in Switzerland. One noteworthy fact was that they co-headlined with *Talking Heads* who of course would go on to gain notable success with hits such as "Psycho Killer", "Once In A Lifetime" and "Road To Nowhere". After playing Zurich, the lads crossed the border and headed towards the beautiful Provence Region in southern France only to find that the show was cancelled. In his autobiography, *Commando,* Johnny Ramone explains. "We made this long drive to Marseilles, and they didn't even have the proper electricity to power us up. So there was no gig." [133] Returning back north, they played their second Swiss gig in Geneva, before eventually making their French debut at *La Cigale* in Lyon on April 28th. The city is the third largest in France which is located at the confluence of the rivers Rhône and Saône to the north west of the French Alps. The venue which was built in 1925, has experienced a variety of music genres over the years including opera as well as early cinema screenings and is still in operation as a café-concert hall nearly a century after its opening. The French part of the tour was concluded with four further performances at Le Havre, Paris, Orleans and Lille before they moved on to Belgium and a gig in the capital city Brussels.

Ramones' sets at that time consisted of around 20 tunes with the shows naturally featuring tracks off the first two albums.

Indeed, the title of the second album, "Leave Home", recorded in October 1976 and released in January of the following year, referred to the fact The Ramones had left New York to tour Europe and the rest of the United States. Songs that would later give way for other masterpieces at that time included "Loudmouth, "You're Going To Kill That Girl", "Carbona Not Glue" and the more mellow "Swallow My Pride". The Ramones would periodically play in France and despite a six-year break between November 1981 to October 1987 would perform in total well over 30 gigs in the country in 19 different centres. Interestingly, this hiatus is referred to by the legendary tour manager's Monte Melnick in his Book *On The Road With The Ramones.* In it, he cites Johnny and his grievance - "We were totally roughing it. For a long time, I didn't want to go back and I refused to go back to France. We stayed in these tiny hotels with one bathroom down the hall. It was horrible." [134] Amongst other cities, the band went on to perform in places such as Bordeaux, Toulouse, Reims and Rennes.

The importance of The Ramones should not be underestimated. Even to this day, aficionados are creating groups directly because of the influence of *Da Brudders.* One such devotee is bass player Frédérik Willens who comes from the city of Douai in the Nord department in northern France. In 1995, he made the hour or so car journey across to Belgium to see The Ramones at the Dour Festival along with three mates. Such was the impact of their performance, years later these same friends were inspired enough to create their own tribute band. Fréd describes the concert having a "superb atmosphere" which also featured groups such as *Burma Shave, Clawfinger, Crumb, Daisy Chainsaw, Downset, Orange 9mm, Paradise Lost* and *Supergrass.*

Fréd had already been in a punk rock band named *Disgrâce* since the 1980s who are distinguished enough to support *The UK Subs* in France and Belgium. Two band mates, the singer, Eddy, along with the multi-talented drummer, Fabrice who converted to guitar for *Les Ramons* were

also keen to create a Ramones tribute. The fourth member of the quartet, who also went to that Dour Festival all those years before was drummer Dany with the experience of his other band, *Noise Emission Control*. The drum man had also seen The Ramones back in 1991 in Deinze, a smallish city with a population of around 45,000 in the Belgian province of East Flanders. This was the period of *Loco Live*, The Ramones' second live album release and the first release to feature C.J Ramone. He too was enthused by the idea of creating a cover band. Of course, it would not be a Ramones tribute without taking on pennames and the French slant is just *magnifique* – Fréd takes over the mantle of Didier rather than Dee Dee, Fabrice converts to Jean as an alternative to Johnny, Eddy swaps roles to Joel as a substitute for Joey whilst Dany transforms himself to Domy instead of Tommy! All four of the group, grew up to the sound of The Ramones during their formative, teenage years. Part of the reason for forming *Les Ramons*, Fréd points out is to continue to share "the happiness" that they received from the band as well as to spread the influence of the men from New York. In addition, Fréd tells us that an older friend, named Laurent, who introduced him to the group many years ago, sadly passed away and it was "in his memory that he wanted to start the band."

The group has a set list based mainly around the first three albums – the self-titled "Ramones", "Leave Home" and "Rocket To Russia" with their favourites including "Pinhead", "Commando" and "Rockaway Beach". A unique aspect of their repertoire is that they always practice and perform in chorological and album order. Hence, Blitzkrieg Bop is performed first and Pet Sematary, taken from the 1989 L.P "Brain Drain", last. Their first ever gig was played in December, 2023 at the *Orge et Houblon* in the town of Lens with approximately 60 people in attendance. The lads belted out 25 songs in around 55 minutes with great energy to an appreciative audience. A look on their *Facebook* page is certainly worthwhile where they can be observed in full Ramones regalia admirably keeping the spirit of New York's finest alive. Indeed, in their leathers and wigs and playing those great songs *Les Ramons* is like a wave of nostalgia – or maybe as the French would say, a case of déjà vu!

Rawönes
Belgium

Following on from their five concerts in France in the spring of 1977, The Ramones then crossed the border into Belgium. The journey from Lille to Brussels is a relatively short one of just over 70 miles with the boys from New York scheduled to play just one concert in the country on May 5th. Belgium is located in north western Europe and is part of a region known as the *Low Countries* and has a population of around 11.5 million. The nation is the home of two main linguistic communities: the Flemish and the French groups which constitutes about 60%/40% of the population proportinately. The capital city is Brussels which also serves as the administrative centre of the European Union. As well as its ties with the EU and its historical landmarks such as the *Royal Palace, Manneken Pis, Atomium* and *City Hall,* Brussels is also renown for its cuisine - it is famed for the waffle, chocolate, French fries and numerous local beers.

The venue for their debut Belgium gig was at the *Paul Emile-Janson Auditorium,* a university building located on Avenue Franklin Roosevelt in Brussels and rather ironically situated close to a library. A number of top artists have performed at the site which has included *Eddie and the Hot Rods, The Damned, Blondie, Television, The Cure* and *Ultravox* along with *Talking Heads* who co-headlined with The Ramones that night. [135] Like so many of the concerts at that time, there is sadly no record of the set list that evening. Three days earlier, however, at *Le*

Bataclan in Paris, the band played exactly 20 songs kicking off with "Loudmouth" and finishing with their speedy cover of "Let's Dance". Sandwiched between these two beauties were an array of goodies from the first two albums which included the soon to be vetoed "Carbona Not Glue". [136] One can only presume, that the Belgium crowd would have experienced a very similar set in Brussels with other gems such as "Listen To My Heart", "Beat On The Brat" and "Now I Wanna Sniff Some Glue" all being played.

The Ramones would return to Belgium regularly with nearly 20 performances all told in the country. As well as additional Brussels' gigs, the band would also expand and pleasingly played in various centres made up of Avelgem, Torhout, Werchter, Veurne, Hechtel-Eksel, Deinze, Ghent, Hasselt, Dessel, Arendonk, Lummen, Dour and Bissegem. Part of this inventory, included festivals such as the *Achiel Eeckloo Rockweide* and the *Festivalpark* in Torhout and Werchter which took place on July 6th and 7th, 1985 respectively. The latter concert was played in front of thousands of fans attracting such luminaries as *U2, REM, Depeche Mode* and Joe Cocker. The build up to *Festivalpark,* however, did not go according to plan. At the end of the first show, Richie Ramone along with his buddy, guitar technician, 'Little' Matt Loya, turned to *"Carlsberg Elephant beer,* which has a really high alcohol content." After downing a few, the drummer talked a local into letting him take a ride on his moped in a field. Unfortunately, as Richie states in his autobiography "all of a sudden – pow! I was off the bike and up in the air. I hit a gopher hole or something and flipped the thing. Trying to stop my fall, I stuck out both my arms in front of me and came down with all my weight on my right hand. Crack."

Richie had fractured his hand but luckily, the promoter found him a doctor, gave him pain killers and taped him up. Despite the excruciating pain of playing with a broken metacarpal, *the show must go* on and the band performed with Richie as scheduled. [137] Another interesting incident which occurred in Belgium was re-told by another drummer, this time Marky. In 1994, after playing a gig in Brussels, the promoters had completed their job by dropping them off at the Eurostar station but as they went through customs, Joey Ramone, who was seeing a chiropractor at the time for his various ailments, was detained. When Belgium security had searched the singer, they "found a massive stash of salves, concoctions and prescription medications, at least one bottle of which they were convinced was ecstasy." Eventually, with the help of Monte's "hostage-negotiating skills", Joey was allowed to get on the train and the reunited band could continue their journey. [138]

One group of friends who saw The Ramones a number of times in Belgium decided that they wanted to form their own tribute band due to their love for the music. The first line-up saw Marc as vocalist, Luc on guitar, Wim "Puus" playing bass and Koen "Spider" behind the drum kit. The band has had one change of formation when in December 2013, "Ramown" Mario took over as the singer. All of the lads knew each other from previous bands or saw each other at various gigs and were all *'Ramoniacs'* says Koen. Indeed, the group have been blessed with a wealth of experience. For instance, Luc performed in *Typhonic 5* and *The 77'ers* and was accompanied in the latter band by singer Marc. Wim played bass in *Eastbird Luis, Willy and the Wimps, Ray Lincoln and The Blueband Blisserboys* whilst Koen played in *Cocktomail Novtales, The Mess* and is currently also playing drums in a new band called *Lonnie Kahlula's Bad Samaritans*. Vocalist Ramown established the band *Funeral Dress* in the early '80s and also performed in *Void Section* along with *The Fellows*.

The group are based in the province of Antwerpen from the towns of Gierle, Vorselaar, Sint-Katelijne-Waver. The choice of the name of the band is an interesting one – *The Rawönes* which is not only a play on the word Ramones but is also a local dialect word, aptly meaning 'rowdy'. In 2004, when they started rehearsing, Koen recalls that "at the time there was no one doing this in the Benelux and we wanted to do it as authentically as possible, both musically and the looks - same hairstyles/wigs, ripped jeans, sleeveless shirts, chucks, leather jackets, poses, moves." He goes on to add that the group "wanted the same set up on stage with the position of the band members, drum kit in the middle of the stage, backdrop behind the drum kit, drum on a riser. Even the complete vintage backline has been copied: Oversized white Rogers drum kit, SVT Ampeg Bass amps and speaker cabinets, three stacked Marshall heads with all the old Marshall cabinets, same Mosrite and Fender precision guitars, guitar straps."

Over the years, *The Rawönes* have completed many memorable gigs right across Belgium, the Netherlands, Luxembourg and Germany. Some of the highlights have include performing at the iconic *Veledrome* in Ostend and playing at the *Sjock festival* in 2007 and sharing the stage with grunge band *Mudhoney*. The group have also played a lot of unusual places over the years such as performing a fashion show, a squat, a boat, a music store and some private parties. Maybe their most unique venue was at a Belgium prison with all convicts having to remain sitting throughout the performance. Drummer Koen recalls that the jail had terrible acoustics and half of the inmates "were shouting for more whilst the other half were booing." Certainly, a case of the *punishment fits the crime* for those non punks!

The band celebrated their 10th anniversary in 2014 with three gigs in their hometowns with Belgium punk rock band *The Kids* playing on every night. Amongst other guests, *The Kids'* guitarist Luc Van de Poel joined *The Rawönes* on stage to join the fun. Koen also recites that "in our first years we got quite some attention from the Belgian media: we were interviewed by *Humo*, a very famous magazine. We all had a little footage on local television after a memorable gig in Jette in Brussels and we were in the newspapers a couple of times. The band even once got asked by a Hollywood production if they could use our version of the song "Somebody Put Something In My Drink". At first we thought that was a joke but we ended up in the soundtrack of the horror movie *Cabin Fever 2*."

Photograph courtesy of Staf Van Den Daf

During all the years of many performances and rehearsals, approximately 60 songs have been attempted. Although the band vary the songs to keep it fresh, there are always a few which they play in each set. These include "Teenage Lobotomy", "Blitzkrieg bop", "Rock 'n' Roll High School", "Pinhead", "Today Your Love Tomorrow The World" and "R.A.M.O.N.E.S." One of the things is that is vital is that all the songs are carried out as The Ramones performed them live.

A view of the band's performances will please all enthusiasts who like their tributes to look and move like the originals. Dressing like *Da Brudders* and adorn in appropriate wigs, the guitarists have their mannerisms spot on with the pair, for instance, suitably spread-eagled in a fashion that was particularly reminiscent of The Ramones in the late '80s and '90s. Indeed, the band acknowledge the need to attempt to make the contribution as close as possible with Koen stating that "we indeed wear wigs and dress like lookalikes. It is nice to deliver the audience a *bouquet parfait*, meaning that we combine the audible with the visible."

A suitable introduction to the band is at the *Sjock festival* where a packed audience are treated to great renditions of the mid-temp songs of "Somebody Put Something In My Drink" and "The KKK Took My Baby Away". The "KKK" camera footage also delivered angles from the stage which gives a real feel of the atmosphere of the outside concert. The same tune can be heard at the *Rock Stenen* from 2013 which also presents viewers with first-rate shots of the crowd and continues to give a flavor of the band. Alternatively, refer to the *Fashion Show* from Antwerp in 2014 where you have the surreal sight of the boys blasting out the vintage "Blitzkrieg Bop" whilst a troupe of beautiful models prance along the catwalk. Unsurprisingly, most of the crowd's eyes are not concentrating on the band and it is certainly one of the more bizarre unions I have witnessed. More to my taste are the two short extracts from the 2006 gig at Brecht. Here you find the fellas in fine form driving home the numbers "53rd and 3rd" and "Commando". Without doubt, *The Rawönes* are as tight as a camel's ass in a sandstorm and still bright-eyed and bushy-tailed as they deliver the New Yorkers' finest hits.

Photograph courtesy of Geert Kennis

Just like many of the other bands highlighted throughout this book, it is clear that the American punk icons touched people in a variety of ways and our lads from Belgium have some fond recollections. Ramown "Mario" watched them in 1991 at *Brielpoort* in Deinze describing the gig as "memorable." Wim went to two concerts at Werchter and Arendonk whilst Luc managed to see them four times. Indeed, the guitarist articulates that in 1988 at Hechtel, "it was funny to see them in the afternoon before the performance. From the stairs of their dressing room container they were having a competition to see who could throw oranges the furthest!" Luc also recalls the 1993 gig at Dessel. "I was standing next to the steps of the stage with the band members of The Ramones and *The Cramps* when The Ramones were ready to take the stage as headliner", Luc recollects. "I heard Johnny say to *The Cramps*. "If you want to see the show from the stage you have to go on together with us because they close the curtain as soon we hit the stage, no one is allowed on stage immediately after us. So I rushed to the other side, where C.J played, stood next to their monitor mixer and was able to see the entire unforgettable show from there." Koen declares that "I was supposed to see them at *Zwemdokrock* in Lummen in 1995 but I was sick and couldn't go, so I never watched them afterwards. I did see a lot of bands with Marky, C.J and Richie and went on a pilgrimage in 2010 to the *Hollywood Forever cemetery* to pray for Johnny and Dee Dee."

When asked about The Ramones legacy, Ramown "Mario" is not shy in coming forward when describing their influence. "The Ramones were definitely the pioneers of punk rock around '74 in New York", the front man states. "Later on, *The Sex Pistols* followed their example. Even though Johnny Rotten thinks he started punk rock and tries to explain it by talking about the totally different sound between his band and The Ramones. The New Yorkers changed music and lifestyle. They let us know that anyone can make pretty fine songs without putting endlessly boring solo guitar playing in a song. What's so great about them is they made it totally on their own, without having support, for example: no airplay. So it is amazing they turned themselves into punk rock heroes just on their own. At a certain point music world could not put this band aside anymore. And that is so fucking great about them. One could not ignore these guys anymore! If I may compare to *The Pistols* again: The Americans did not need the Malcolm McLaren circus to put them on the map. The Ramones put on their leather jackets, jeans and just played. Straight forward! Don't get me wrong: I got heaps of *Pistols'* records and they made great music. But sure as hell they took The Ramones as an example."

There are positive vibes for the group and as Koen asserts "we made a lot of friends in other bands during the past 20 years and we're not thinking about slowing down soon! It's just something magical to go on stage and when "The Good, The Bad And The Ugly" is playing, knowing you'll jump on that train of buzzsaw guitar noise for the next hour sweating your ass off under those wigs. It's our duty to show the kids how awesome The Ramones were and to make the veterans in the audience believe they see the lads again after all those years. It just feels damn good to do this!" Possibly the most heart-warming anecdote about the *The Rawönes,* however I have saved until last. Back in 2015, the tribute played a gig in Erfurt in Germany where singer Ramown met his future wife. Subsequently the couple had a beautiful daughter and when it came to naming her, there could only be one fitting choice - take a bow sweet, sweet, little *Ramona.*

The Hormones
The Netherlands

In total The Ramones played 28 times in the Netherlands. Their first gig in the country took place in the *Paradiso Grote Zaal*, arguably the most famous rock concert hall in Holland. The venue is a three-story brick building in Amsterdam which was built in 1879 and originally used as a church by the "Vrije Gemeente", which translates to "free congregation". It is located on de Weteringschans, standing on the edge of the Leidseplein, a square packed with nightlife. In 1967, it was squatted by a bunch of hippies looking for a place to party and although the police eventually kicked them out, the city officially opened the building as a youth entertainment centre one year later. Over time, the music scene took hold and it now regularly offers raves, themed dance nights, smaller gigs by indie bands as well as the renowned concerts by international stars. Some of the artists who have performed there include David Bowie, Madonna, *Pink Floyd, AC/DC, The Rolling Stones* and *Nirvana* whilst it was also noted as the venue that witnessed Glen Matlock's last gig for *The Sex Pistols* in 1977. For a high-profile concert, the *Paradiso* would be well-suited. The main hall has a capacity of 1,500 whilst its original function as a church serves perfectly in terms of its excellent acoustics. There is also a secondary concert venue for smaller acts and emerging talents which holds 250 people. It was at this venue on May 6th, 1977 that The Ramones first performed on Dutch soil and took place just a day after performing in Brussels. During their stay in the Netherlands they would play four more occasions in just five days in Eindhoven, Groningen, Rotterdam and Utrecht before moving on to the next stage of their European tour in Denmark. One thing is for sure, no-one could ever accuse these workhorses of lethargy or laziness. Although, there are no records of the set list at the *Paradiso,* there is one from their performance at *De Lantaren* in Rotterdam on the 10th of May. Starting with the confrontational "Loudmouth" and finishing with the cover of the 1962 hit by Chris Montez, *"Let's Dance",* all told the band blasted out 22 gems which included two encores.

The Ramones re-visited Holland 13 more times – some for one-off gigs whilst other times for minor tours. During their visit to the country in the early autumn of 1978, Marky, in his book, Punk Rock Blitzkrieg, describes events in Holland focussing on some of the antics of Dee Dee Ramone. Two years earlier, there was an official policy of tolerance for drug use and the Dutch parliament had decriminalised possession of cannabis of less than five grams. The legendary bassist, famed for penning "Chinese Rock, "Carbona Not Glue" and "Now I Wanna Sniff Some Glue" must have been in seventh heaven as he had a continuous and ready-made supply of dope on tap. On the upper balcony of the Paradiso, where the band were playing that evening, there was indeed a legalised pot seller. Marky, points out how Dee Dee's wife, Vera, amazed and at the same time infuriated the local kids. In all probability sent up by her husband, rather than buying a small bag of pot or hash, Vera and a friend purchased everything on his stall amounting to two thousand guilders or approximately $800 leaving the natives absolutely nothing to get high on. After the next Dutch gig in Arnhem, the band headed to

Paris by bus through Belgium. This was a considerable problem for Dee Dee because drugs were illegal in both in France and Belgium and he was carrying a stash. At the border, there was an establishment to exchange guilders for francs and the bassist seized his opportunity. "Dee Dee walked around to the back of the one-story brick customs building, and I followed him. He looked around a bit at the concrete planter with some shrubs and poked at the dirt with his hand…Dee Dee picked a spot between the second and third shrub from the left and started digging with both paws like a beagle burying a bone. Once he got about a foot deep, he pulled two large clear plastic bags out of his jacket and placed them in the hole. Then he filled in the hole and patted it down. This wasn't a first time for Dee Dee. He had buried pot, dope and pills all over New York." (139) Dee Dee himself acclaimed the joys of Amsterdam in his book Poison Heart. "The hash store in the club would open after the sound check" he commended. "I would try and buy the largest amount of hash they sell me and would explain myself with hand signs and

Photograph courtesy of Daisy Nieuwmans

signals." (140) It has often been cited that The Ramones helped vitalise the punk movement. Monte Melnick, Ramones' tour manager felt that "despite the culture shock and a couple hairy moments, those first few European tours were very important for The Ramones. They established the band as headliners and kick-started the UK punk scene, which spread like wildfire around the world. We became very aware that we had started something, that this punk thing was gonna be big and we were at the forefront. Back home in the States, where punk was still a cult phenomenon, the band was still struggling. Yet everywhere we went, new bands, imitators, were springing up. We knew we were onto something." (141) Years later one such group from Holland who took inspiration from the New York icons were the *Hormones*. Like many bands, the outfit has undertaken a number of changes with the only constant, guitarist Antoine Gribnau. Indeed, at one stage, the band used five musicians although this has now been cut to the more customary four. Previous members were Jordy Kevin Bunschoten on vocals, Martin on bass, Lenny Gribnau on guitar and both Erik Vissers and Frans Koopsen on drums. Nowadays, Antoine has been joined by Ed Nieuwmans as drummer, Sander Verheijen on bass whilst Sabrina Radix has the mic. Indeed, the group is refreshingly unusual for a Ramones cover band as they are mixed in terms of gender – the singer being female whilst the other members are male. The present line-up cut their teeth with a number of different punk rock bands including *StinksisterS, Deaf Minds, The Stiff, Durango, HumanBeanz, Chihuahua Pearl* and *Alvarez.*

Part of the fun of any Ramones tribute is undoubtedly taking up the various aliases. Ed naturally takes up the moniker of Eddie Hormone, Antoine has the pseudonym of Tonie Hormone,

Sander's designation has become Sandie Hormone whilst Sabrina has morphed into Sabbie Hormone. Antoine explains why he started the group in 2017 stating that "I love the simple but brilliant and energetic style of the pioneers of punk." He also talks about The Ramones' legacy stating that "they started a new way to experience music which is copied and modified until this day." Singer Sabbie, clearly a "diehard" fan, saw the band six times, the first one being in Rotterdam in 1980 and shares some of her experiences. "I was very young but felt the sound, power and energy" she says. In August, 1986, the vocalist watched them at *the Melkweg* in Amsterdam which had been moved away from the *Paradiso* because of building renovations. "After the concert they had a drink in the *Mazzo* restaurant where it was so busy around them that there was no way I could get close" Sabbie reflects whilst she still owns the ticket from the the *Nighttown* in Rotterdam where she was on the guest list.

Their set involves all the classics with his personal favourites of "Glad To See You Go", "Havana Affair" and "Bonzo Goes To Bitburg". Interestingly, the group diversifies a little playing "What A Wonderful World" from the solo album by Joey Ramone "Don't Worry About Me" and even the speeded up jingle of "Happy Birthday To You" which featured on the popular television show *"The Simpsons"*. There have been a number of memorable gigs which included a Ramones Tribute Festival at *De Duiker Hoofddorp* in 2019 and more recent ones in 2023 at *Sound Dungeons* in Rotterdam along with the *Koningsdag, The Trucker Pijnacker* where they get lots of positive feedback. It is always worth checking out groups and the promotional video on *Youtube* featuring "Blitzkrieg Bop", "Poison Heart" and "Beat On The Brat" gives a real flavour of the band although at this point they were a five-piece band rather than a quartet. Interestingly, their version of "Commando" has rather a 'metal' feel for it. Sandie and Tonie, shrut their stuff, legs apart down-stroking methodically either side of Sabbie who with her deep, throaty voice keeps the listener engaged whilst further back, drummer Eddie keeps time immaculately ensuring a solid foundation.

Our Dutch *Hormones'* performances would not be complete without stage accessories - cue the baseball bat, an air alarm to introduce "Commando", plus cardboard "Hey Ho, Let's Go" and "Gabba Gabba Hey" signs" – the latter particularly for all you pinheads out there. Other information on the band can be found on their *Facebook* page or better still at their website on *www. thehormones.nl.*

The Brats
The Netherlands

After their inaugural gig in Holland at *Paradiso Grote Zaal* in Amsterdam, the next leg of their tour was around 80 miles away in Eindhoven on May 7th, 1977. Eindhoven is the fifth largest city of the Netherlands with a population of around 368,000, lying on the Dommel River and situated in the south of the nation. The venue of choice was *The Effenaar* which is located in the centre of the city and is now one of the largest music halls in the country. Built in the late 19th century and originally housing an old textile factory [(142)], it was once used as a squat in the early '70s before being set up as a music venue in 1971. A number of top artists have performed at the site including *The Fall, Joy Division, Orchestral Manoeuvres In The Dark, Red Hot Chilli Peppers, The Sex Pistols* along with *Talking Heads* who co-headlined that night with The Ramones.

Just like the *Paradiso* gig there is unfortunately no inventory of the set list at *The Effenaar* but we do know that concerts at that time were predictably aimed to promote the "Leave Home" album. This was the most recent production with the name heralding from the fact that The Ramones were now gigging away from their home city of New York. Released on January 10th, 1977 through Sire Records and produced at Sundragon in New York by Tony Bongiovi and Tommy Ramone, "Leave Home" was the second studio L.P fashioned by the *'fast four'*. Whilst the production of the album had a slightly 'tinnier' feel and expansive mixing than their debut, nonetheless, it was jam-packed with delicious goodies and much lauded by critics – "Glad To See You Go", "Gimme Gimme Shock Treatment", "Commando", "Pinhead" and the only cover "Californian Sun" would all became pivotal live favourites throughout the band's calling. Although first designed in 1976, "Leave Home" was also the first album to feature the now famous Ramones logo on the back of the L.P cover. Using the seal of the US Presidency as inspiration, Mexican-American graphic designer, Arturo Vega, a friend of Dee Dee Ramone, made subtle changes to create one of the most-savviest recognisable marketing creations. The first adaption was to replace the olive branch by an apple branch signifying that The Ramones were as "American as apple pie". Vega added that "since "Johnny was such a baseball fanatic, we had the eagle hold a baseball bat instead of the arrows" whilst the bat also relates suitably to one of their most infamous songs. Vega completed some other tweaks to the design which saw jagged red and blue arrow stripes running up and down and inserted them into the badge in front of the eagle whilst the name of the band members replaced the words "Seal of the President of the

United States" around the outside of the logo. In early versions of the emblem, including the one on "Leave Home" he replaced the Latin words "E pluribus Unum" (which translates to out of many, one) on the ribbon by "Look out below". Later this would be altered to "Hey Ho, Let's Go" to link in with the celebrated chorus in "Blitzkrieg Bop". The Ramones insignia would not only be used on backdrops at gigs but would be seen on T-Shirts all around the world with ex-manager Danny Fields claiming that "they sold more T-Shirts than records and probably they sold more T-Shirts than tickets." [143]

Many of our tribute bands throughout this book have adapted this logo to form their own recognisable crest and one such emerging group are *The Brats.* Heralding from Eindhoven, a stone's throw from *The Effenaar,* the boys got together in February 2022 in order to share their

love of The Ramones with the crowd. The name of the band stems from the belligerent second song from their first album written by Joey Ramone. According to the singer he was inspired to write "Beat On The Brat" after watching a spoilt child screaming in a playground and was "the kind of kid you just wanted to kill." [144] The initial line up of the tribute included Hans van Bommel on drums, Dennie Janssen as the singer, Stein van den Akker on bass and backing vocals and Geert de Jonge on guitar. Geert soon departed, however and has been replaced by Jesper Meessen. As expected the musicians have gained much experience in a host of previous bands. Drummer Hans, for instance has played in *Hemaroids, Grey Days and Cutting Ties*, vocalist Dennie has sung in *Error 51, True Insanity, Liquid Courage* and *Bad By Nature* whilst Stein on the bass has had spells with *The Knockaround Slackers, Digital Orchestra, The Jeffrey* and *OneTwoThreeFour*.

The Brats cite the first three Ramones albums as their favourite records with a typical set being one similar to the "It's Alive" album which was recorded on New Year's Eve, 1977 at the *Rainbow Theatre* in London. The group also pick a handful of the later tracks from the '80s to use for their encores.

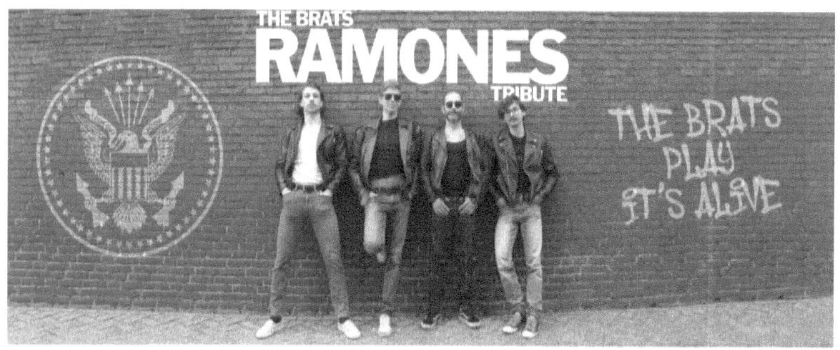

Photograph courtesy of Lisanne Reuser

Some of the more notable concerts include supporting the band *Linkshangendj* at *The Curve* in Echt, the *Kingsnight Festival* at the *Popei De Pub, OJC Comeet Someren in* Zuid-Oost Brabant and the *Café De Fantast* in Valkenswaard. Fortuitously, a number of their songs can be seen on their own *Facebook* page along with a host of photographs and I urge all of you to take a look. A good induction would be the *Turf Festival* in Asten-Heusden where there is a five-minute compilation of their performance. The lads are shown smashing through parts of nine edited songs at breakneck pace with "Gimme Gimme Shock Treatment" in particular going into hyper-speed. Other snippets include the old favourites of "Surfin Bird", "Judy Is A Punk", and "Now I Wanna Sniff Some Glue". Frontman Dennie is somewhat reminiscent of *Queen's* Freddy Mercury whilst his crooning vocals are not unlike Eddie Vedder's emotive tones during "Any Way You Want It" at The Ramones farewell performance in L.A. Stein is found with bass slung low, strutting his stuff whilst Jesper has knees bent and is seen rapidly downstroking to give *The Brats* that distinctive *Ramoneseque* type sound. Behind this trio, on the drum stool, Hans completes the quartet with his aggressive, hard skin trouncing keeping it all in check. If you do have a little longer, then refer to *Youtube* where you can see the full show lasting nearly an hour.

More treats are also on offer on *Youtube*, with footage from *Café 't Spektakel* in Asten good value and definitely beneficial to look over. On show is "Blitzkrieg Bop", "Rockaway Beach" and my personal favourite, "Teenage Lobotomy" which ticks all the right boxes.

Drummer Hans points out that "we do not wear wigs." For them "the vibe is more important than looking like them so we only use leather jackets, a baseball bat to back up "Beat On The Brat" and the "Gabba Gabba Hey" sign to support "Pinhead" as those are symbols for the band." Hans also recognises the significance of The Ramones claiming that they had a "big influence on the entire punk/hardcore genre" – and unless you are a spoilt *brat* – who could disagree?

Rumbones
The Netherlands

After performing at the *The Effenaar* in Eindhoven, *Da Brudders* travelled just over 160 miles northwards to the city of Groningen for the third leg of their inaugural Dutch tour. Described as the *capital of the north,* Groningen is the sixth largest city in The Netherlands and the main municipality of the Groningen province. It is noted in the fields of education, business and music and it was here that The Ramones and co-headliners *Talking Heads* chose as one of their early European venues. The club that night on May 8th, 1977 was the *Huize Maas,* a venue in the centre of the city. Founded in 1926 by dance teacher Herman Mass, the building was transformed and expanded into a dance hall by local architect Evert van Linge. Three years after Mass' death in 1960, the building was renovated and the venue enjoyed orchestra events, parties and organised dance evenings throughout the '60s. By the 1970s, it had become a smallish music venue and enjoyed the likes of *The Police, The Boys, The Jam, The Damned, Dire Straits* and *The Sex Pistols.* [145] Nowadays, it doubles up as a restaurant but still hosts the annual *Eurosonic* festival each January and is the permanent location in Groningen for the *Popronde,* a traveling Dutch music festival which takes in over 40 centres. As with the first two stages of the Dutch circuit, there is sadly no record of their set list that evening in the *Huize Maas* [146] so we can only surmise that they followed the normal protocols of that tour. This would have probably seen a score of songs with all tunes from the first two albums, the eponymous "Ramones" along with "Leave Home".

The Ramones would re-visit the city on two further occasions and both times the location would be at *De Oosterpoort*, a music venue described as "the most important music building in Groningen and the surrounding area." [147] On each juncture, however, the boys from Queens would come back to the municipality with a different line-up compared with the original formation of Joey, Johnny, Dee Dee and Tommy which graced the *Huize Maas* stage in 1977. On June 10th, 1988, for instance, Marky had taken over on the drummer's stool for their second concert in the city whilst C.J was in place on bass for their third and final Groningen gig on December 10th, 1992. For those Ramones buffs out there who love to know the minutiae details - the last time The Ramones played in the Netherlands was at the *Paradiso* in Amsterdam on January 31st, 1996.

Our next highlighted band from The Netherlands originate from a town named Stadskanaal which lies in the north east of Holland and just a 40-minute drive from the city of Groningen. The group were formed in 2014 and consist of lead singer Hugo Koch, Niels Withaar on bass, guitarist Richard Veen and Erik Kluin on the drums. Vocalist Hugo explains how the band came about stating that "we were all long-term friends and we started just for fun and wanted to play rock and roll!" The source of the band's name is quite unique with the lads initially unable to decide upon a suitable moniker. Instead they ran a competition on *Facebook* with fans able to put up suggestions with *The Rumbones* coming up trumps and being chosen as the best designation. In the same manner of a many of our tributes covered in this book, the group's title, along with the four musicians' names, would soon find itself as part of an adapted logo akin to the famous design by Arturo Vega – not only a sign of recognition for the *'fast four'* but also a mark of union amongst the newly formed band members. All of the musicians have had experienced in other groups with Hugo also the singer of the Dutch heavy metal band *Burning* whilst Niels, Richard and Erik played in *Rascal Rudy* between 1989 and 1995.

The group have played over 70 concerts with their debut show in the village of Onstwedde. When pressed about their favourite gigs, Hugo declares, that "we loved to play the *Zwarte Croos Festival* in Lichtenvoorde because it's such a huge event in The Netherlands." In addition, the lads have performed at the *Heroes of Rock and Blues Festival* in the city of Tiiel which had 1,500 in the audience along with the *Rock Tribute Festival* in Raalte. "We played three times at the *Gonzo Bar* in Tegelen which coincidently was the same club that Dee Dee used to regularly frequent when he lived in the town in the '90s. We also performed at the *Little Devil* in Tilburg on three occasions which is a great local bar with a crazy audience, the singer recites." Impressively, the band have crossed the border and played in Germany, for example in the city of Uelsen whilst back in Holland, in February, 2024 *The Rumbones* played at the *Spontrock Festival* in front of 200 visitors.

The Rumbones' set list remains pretty constant with the majority stemming from those seminal albums of the 1970s. Examples include "Teenage Lobotomy", "Blitzkrieg Bop", "Rockaway Beach", "Beat On The Brat", "Today Your love, Tomorrow The World", "Judy Is A Punk", "I Don't Wanna Go Down To The Basement", "I Just Wanna Have Something To Do" "Suzy Is A Headbanger" and "53rd & 3rd". In order to give a broader spectrum of the New Yorkers' career, however, there are some splendid picks taken from more contemporary L.Ps with the likes of, "Chinese Rock", "Rock 'n' Roll High School", "Spiderman", "Pet Sementary", "She Talks To Rainbows", "Outsider" and "Somebody To love" all on offer.

I always enjoy viewing all of our tributes and fortunately there are a number of opportunities to review *The Rumbones* on the internet network. Check out, for instance, "Cretin Hop" on *Youtube* taken live from Tiel in April, 2022 or "Commando" from a concert one year earlier at *the Zeeltje Festival*. You will not find the group in wigs but you will discover the band clad in the customary leather jackets, jeans, sun glasses, appropriate T-shirt and sneakers. More importantly, with their pounding drums, fizzing guitars and clear love of the songs, the band just oozes energy and their uplifting style would no doubt get the fan coming back for more. If you have additional time, then a visit on their own *Facebook* page is well worth checking out. On the social media platform there is a host of material about past events, information on groups they have performed along-side, links to forthcoming shows and also many photographs and videos of the band. Possibly my favourite is the explosive footage of "You're Going To Kill That Girl", "She's The One" and another version of "Cretin Hop". In front of a hugely appreciate audience, the three-pronged attack on your senses hits you with the force of an incendiary device. Alternatively, go find the classic "Sheena Is A Punk Rocker" or a snippet of "I Wanna Be Sedated" from an outdoor gig in 2022. I guarantee, Ramones fans will enjoy.

It is fantastic to see *The Rumbones* still going from strength to strength and still planning future gigs to honour the New York icons. Hugo points out that "they were the most unique band in the world" and it is therefore splendid to see the Dutch quartet recognising the Americans in June at the *Pagefestival.* Billed as an event to not only mark The Ramones' 50th anniversary but also to celebrate *The Rumbones* ten-year landmark, I have a sneaky feeling that the lads might just play the ditty "Happy Birthday" that night. Of course, not at regulation speed but in the style of *Da Brudders* from the 1993 TV show "*The Simpsons*"! Wouldn't that be just apt!?

Ramones Tribute - Denmark
Denmark

The Ramones performed five times in the Netherlands in the spring of 1977 with the final gig in the country taking place in Utrecht. The next stage of their European tour would see them perform in Scandinavia for the first time as they travelled to Copenhagen. The city is the capital of Denmark and with an estimated population of 650,000 it is the most populous municipality in the country. Copenhagen lies on the islands of Zealand and Amager and is separated from Malmö **in Sweden by the Öresund straight. Interestingly the two cities and therefore the two countries are connected by a combined roadway and railway bridge** which is the longest in Europe spanning for nearly five miles from the Swedish coast to the artificial island of Peberholm. The crossing is completed by the Drogden Tunnel which runs from the Peberholm to Amager. Copenhagen boasts some world famous landmarks including the Tivoli Gardens, The Amalienborg and Christiansborg Palaces along with The Little Mermaid that The Ramones, just like thousands of other people, visited to sightsee. [148]

The band would play just one night in Denmark before moving on to Stockholm in Sweden. The venue in Copenhagen on the evening of May 12th, was *Daddy's Dance Hall* or sometimes just shortened to *Daddy's*. The site had been a favoured disco establishment at the end of the *Palads* cinema on Axeltorv in the '70s and '80s and went on in recent years to become a popular night club. A multitude of notable artists have performed at the establishment including Patti Smith, Little Richard, Chuck Berry, Iggy Pop, *Television* and *Blondie* but it was possibly best known for hosting *The Sex Pistols* in the summer of 1977 at the height of the punk explosion. For any *Pistols'* enthusiasts out there, the audio of this gig is readily accessible on the web with the Pistols' first number that evening, their debut single, "Anarchy In The UK".

The Ramones would play in the country a further six times in 1980, 1981, 1985, 1987, 1990 and 1994. As well as Copenhagen, they also performed in Roskilde whilst their last performance in the country was at the *Midtfyns* festival in Ringe. In the book *On The Road With The Ramones*, according to the roadie Mitch "Bubbles" Keller, a Danish gig was an important landmark in terms of the evolution of the "Pinhead" song. It was traditional for the drum roadie, initially David Moon, to put on a *Pinhead* mask and wave the "Gabba Gabba Hey" sign. Bubbles claims that "he decided to take it one step further" and came on to the stage wearing the *Pinhead* dress for the first time in Copenhagen. Furthermore, Bubbles also points out that he *invented* the "*jerk dance*" which would be part and parcel of later shows. [149] Although Bubbles does not state the year of the *Pinhead* development, there is no doubt that at the time of their second and third tours of Denmark between 1980 and 1981, tensions between band members would have been strained. Indeed, the connection between singer Joey and guitarist Johnny had such animosity that the two would not talk to each other for years. Not only did they differ politically with Joey a liberal and Johnny a staunch Republican but "thanks to a twisted love triangle, the pair's relationship would be broken without repair."

[150] Joey Ramone had started dating Linda Danielle as far back as the autumn of 1978 and soon enough she had taken up residence with Joey in Arturo Vega's loft. Johnny claims that by the end of 1980, he and Linda would meet frequently for lunch and she had become his best friend and by 1981 they were "pretty openly hanging out." [151] Mickey Leigh, brother of Joey, concurs with the timings and although he had heard rumours about a possible association between Johnny and Linda previously, by the spring of 1981 he was convinced that an affair was occurring and confronted his brother about the possibility. After a heartbroken Joey challenged Linda soon after, she moved out of the apartment and according to Mickey, Joey told him that "Johnny crossed the line with me concerning Linda, he destroyed the relationship and the band right there." After that the two group members "couldn't agree on anything" [152] and eventually even had others such as Dee Dee acting as middlemen to facilitate communication. [153] It would have been within this volatile environment that the group performed during those tours to Denmark.

Despite this, performances at gigs did not suffer and enthusiasts would not have necessarily known about these riffs. Two fans who grew up listening to The Ramones were stickman Jesper Hartvig Brun and bassist Joakim Frank Ernst. In March 2020, the pair went to see Richie Ramone at a sold out show in Copenhagen and even had the chance to meet the drummer before the gig. The lads were so "blown away" by his performance that they decided to form their own Ramones tribute band soon after. Another musician, guitarist Jeppe Dick Olsen also attended Richie's show and when Joakim wrote to him a few days later to join the project, he was keen to take part. The band just now needed a singer and added Christian Willer to their line-up, with the group ready to start performing in 2021. The chosen designation of the new band was simple – what you see is what you get – and taking into account their geographical origins, The *Ramones Tribute - Denmark* was born. Jesper originates from a Køge which is near Copenhagen whilst the other lads herald from Næstved, a town located in the southern part of Zealand in Denmark. Three of the fellas have had experience in other groups. Jeppe still plays in the Danish punk bands *Ræzårmave* and *Social Nedtur,* Christian had gained experience in *Stöjvold* and *Make It Sweet* whilst Joakim previously performed in *Loud 'N' Proud* and is still active *with Ten Beers After* and *Steamy Blues Band.*

The band play a mixture of the early definitive material along with songs the '80s/ '90s era. Bass man Joakim points out "we just play the songs that we like to play and of course what we think the audiences wants to hear. We're very much 'forced' to play the classics like "Blitzkrieg Bop", "Rockaway Beach", "Sheena Is A Punk Rocker", "I Wanna Be Sedated", "Pet Sematary" etc, but we also like to bring in some rarer songs in the set list. Songs like "Outsider", "In The Park" and "I Don't Wanna Grow Up" are fine examples. Great and funny songs to play live!" *Ramones Tribute - Denmark* also change their repertoire once in a while in order to give the shows some variety and to keep the band themselves motivated.

In their short existence, the boys have already had some memorable experiences such as supporting the legendary pub rock group *Dr. Feelgood* in Denmark in September 2022. It was the British band's first show in Denmark in 20 years and ironically The Ramones also played with *Dr. Feelgood* at *The Bottom Line* in New York back in May 1976. The lads have also shared the stage with popular Danish bands such as *Kings Of Rock* and *The Courettes* as well as performing their very first headlining show in January 2023 when they played at the legendary *High Voltage Club* in Copenhagen.

Searching the web for live performances, is a prerequisite for each tribute and pleasurably there are a number of *Ramones Tribute - Denmark* videos out there. A great way to kick off would be the gig at the *High Voltage* where you can find "Blitzkrieg Bop", "Now I Wanna Sniff Some Glue", "I Wanna Be Sedated" and "The KKK Took My Baby Away". Alternatively check out the earlier "Beat On The Brat" from December 2021 at *The Beach* in Næstved where guitarist Jeppe has still got his music stand and notes as an aid! For a more intimate viewing look up the studio practice sessions of "Oh Oh I Love Her So" which is my personal favourite and the equally superb "Pinhead". In all the footage, you will see a high energy band which does justice to all the tunes on offer. As Joakim states "we don't wear any wigs. We just like to be Jeppe, Joakim, Jesper and Christian on stage. We do our very best to keep the spirit alive in our own personal way. We just love their music." The bass man goes on to add that "The Ramones might be the most influential band of all time. 'Blitzkrieg Bop' is a true classic and the '1...2...3...4' part is a trademark in rock 'n' roll. Just to see kids today wearing their merchandise makes us very happy! It is very important for us to keep the flame burning. At least in Denmark." Undoubtedly, they are succeeding.

Ramånes
Sweden

May 1977 saw The Ramones travel to Sweden as part of their first full European circuit. It was the second stage of the Scandinavian section of the tour crammed between gigs in Denmark and thereafter further two concerts in Finland. Sweden is a Nordic country which borders Norway to the west and north, Finland to the east and is connected to Denmark by a bridge-tunnel in the south west. It is the largest Scandinavian country by area and the fifth largest country in Europe. The nation has a population of 10.5 million people and a low density of population with 25.5 inhabitants per square kilometre. Sweden is a land dominated by forests, lakes and rivers and the country has an extensive coastline. The country is a highly developed, ranked seventh in the Human Development Index. Politically, Sweden works under a framework as a constitutional monarchy with executive power exercised by the government within a parliamentary democracy. The capital of the country is Stockholm which has just under a million people living within the municipality. The city stretches across 14 islands and has more than 50 bridges on an extensive Baltic Sea archipelago. As well as being the most populous city in the country, it is also the cultural, media, political, and economic centre of Sweden as well. It was therefore logical that when The Ramones first came to the nation, Stockholm was the chosen hub.

For Swedish fans, this was sadly going to be a fleeting visit with just one gig organised at the *Jarlateatern* theatre on May 15th. The building for the selected venue was erected in 1931 as the Civic School's auditorium and was also used at that time for theatre productions. Initially called the *Borgarskolan,* it had been re-named in 1973 after the original building had closed. In the 1970s, the record shop *Skivfabriken* arranged rock concerts there and indeed, the location had attracted some top artists of the day with *Thin Lizzy, Television* and fellow New Yorkers and eclectic pioneers *Blondie* all gracing the stage at some point. Between 1979-2000 it was also used by the Stockholm Operetta Ensemble whilst eventually in 2005 the building was rebuilt and now houses other businesses under the name *Sollévihuset.*

Thankfully, there is a record of the set list that evening with the group as expected as quick as a flash, blasting out a breath-taking 23 songs. As was the norm during that period, the band opened with the combative "Loudmouth" and immediately moved on to the equally antagonistic "Beat On The Brat". Other confrontational picks from the show comprised of "Carbona Not Glue", "You're Going To Kill That Girl" and "Chainsaw". Without exception, of course, the band would always include one or two more mellow tunes *for all you lonely hearts out there* and two ballads were thrown in at this performance. The tracks "I Remember You" and "I Wanna Be Your Boyfriend" at least gave the audience some recovery time before it was back on the roller coaster ride with the inclusion of the more customary *speedsters* "Glad To See You Go" and "Havana Affair".

One fan who was in that audience in 1977 was Pelle Almgren who would eventually be part of a Swedish tribute called *The Ramånes.* He was "blown away" by The Ramones performance that evening and had never seen or heard anything like it from any rock act at that time. "The crowd were so psyched the first five rows were trashed into pieces" he recalls adding that "the whole punk movement started from there in Sweden." He also remembers that despite using an outdoor PA "the music was so incredibly loud." Pelle had the pleasure to have seen original drummer Tommy Ramone, aka Tamás Erdélyi, who not only later served as a producer but is also given credit for the band's creative steer.

By the time the Americans returned to Sweden for a second time in the early autumn of 1978, there was a different Ramone sitting on the drummer's stool with Marky firmly now in place. All told, The Ramones would play 19 times in Sweden. As well as Stockholm they also played in other centres as well including Malmö, Ronneby, Lund, Gothenburg, Karlskoga, Hultsfred and Skellefteå. Some of their more interesting dates include the 1991 concert with Iggy Pop at the *Isstadion* in the capital and the 1993 Hultsfred festival at *Folkets Park.* Their last performance on Swedish territory was on June 24th, 1995 at the *Festivalområdet* in Skellefteå, a fixture on the northern Swedish festival circuit.

Another local, who saw The Ramones during that second tour of Sweden on September 7th was Janne Lagerström who went on to see them on a further five occasions. As a teenager, he and a bunch of school pals were so enthused by the release of The Ramones' debut album in 1976 that it drove them to pick up instruments themselves. After meeting up at Janne's bithday bash in the year 2000 they decided to take it one stage further and create their own tribute band. This would initially see Pete as singer, Pepe' on guitar, Christer Österlund on drums and Janne picking up the bass. Like many other groups, the band has undertaken some changes in personal with Janne Nilsson replacing Pepe' as guitarist in 2008 and Pelle Almgren, who had seen the New Yorkers all those years ago in '77, coming in as vocalist in 2015. As with so many of our tributes, the tradition of taking pennames was adhered to. Janne Nilsson would become Nils, stick man Christer took up the moniker of Chris, Pelle has the alias of Paella whilst bassist Janne Lagerström would naturally become Jee Jee Ramåne. The group had not only had experience in other bands but have also produced various records over the years. For example, Pelle was involved with the *Warheads* EP in 1979, a collaboration with Sam Yaffa in 1986 and various solo releases. Impressively in conjunction with Wow Liksom he also had a national hit with the song "Omåomigen" **with 15 million streams on** *Spotify* and on the Top List in Sweden in 1991. Janne Lagerström's discography included work with *Badboll* in 1979 and 1981 whilst *The Ramånes* released CDs purely of Ramones songs in 2004 and 2011.

Their first gig was on February 10th in 2001 and since then the boys have clocked up over a century of concerts. There have been a host of highlights both home and abroad. In Sweden, for instance, memorable gigs have included those in Malmö and in Åre, the famous ski resort. Nearer to home, two Stockholm performances stand out at Nalen and possibly their favourite performance of all in Terminalen. *The Ramånes* have also toured overseas and visited places such as Malta, Cadiz and Bologna. The Bologna festival which took place in 2006 was particularly noteworthy with over 2,000 in the audience. This figure, however, will undoubtedly be shattered in the summer of 2024 as the band have been chosen to headline at the *Kings Square Festival* in Stockholm with organisers expecting around 20,000 people to attend.

As with so many people, bass player Janne cites the first four albums along with "It's Alive" as his most precious L.Ps. The Ramånes live set certainly features many of the classics from these early cuts but there are also some renditions from their later albums too with "The KKK Took My Baby Away", "Rock 'n' Roll High School" and the short but noteworthy instrumental "Durango 95" in their armoury. A delve onto social media shows a plethora of material from the band to review with a great starting point a studio version of "Pinhead". Complete with wigs and American twanged accents, the boys look like they have been dragged out of the black lagoon and make no mistake these creatures are here to mean business. If you prefer a live performance, then check out the renditions of "Sheena Is A Punk Rocker" and "Let's Dance". This time, the quartet remove the wigs but more importantly the speed and energy is maintained. Even better than these glimpses then pore over "The Ramånes – The True Documentary Extended Edition" which not only provides many of our much-loved knees-ups but also gives you nearly 45 minutes of continuous tongue in cheek amusement. Founder member, Janne Lagerström, describes The Ramones influence as "huge" and points out that that the first tour in 1977 was a game changer, with many bands forming to replicate their punk sound. In order to honour the band, the bass player has also initiated and co-written a book – "Ramones i Sverige". Within it, many relevant Swedish rock stars participated along with Mickey Leigh, Monte Melnick and guitar tech, Matt Lolya. Additionally, Janne took part in a pod on National radio in 2023 to keep the memory of the band alive and celebrate their work - What more can you say apart from?... "Hey Hå, Let's Gå!"

Photograph courtesy of Angelika Cavonius

Gabbagabbahey -
The Helsinki Ramones Tribute Finland

After their one-off performance in Sweden in 1977, it was straight to neighbouring Finland for a double header on May 16th and 17th in Helsinki and Tampere. Helsinki is the capital, largest and most populous city in the country with over 1.2 million inhabitants. It is located on the shore of the Gulf of Finland and is situated just 50 miles north of Tallinn in Estonia, 250 miles east of Sweden's Stockholm and 190 miles west of Saint Petersburg in Russia. Their first show in the capital was at the *Kulttuuritalo,* which is described as *The House Of Culture* and one of the most iconic music and event venues in Helsinki. Designed by Alvar Aalto, the construction work commenced in 1955 and was carried out mainly by volunteers until its completion in 1958. The building was owned by the Finnish Communist party until 1990, when financial difficulty forced its sale to the government and is now owned by the Senate Properties. From the outside at least, it is a rather bleak building which is more akin to a planetarium than a music hall although it seats more than 1,400 and evidently offers excellent acoustics. [154] There have been a number of celebrated performers at the venue including Jimi Hendrix, *Cream, Led Zeppelin, Queen,* Tina Turner and *Metallica.* The next day, The Ramones moved on to *Teknillinen Opisto,* the Polytechnic in Tampere, a city in southern Finland. On both occasions, they played 24 songs including "Suzy Is A Headbanger" and "Now I Wanna Be A Good Boy" from the "Leave Home" album and "I Don't Wanna Walk Around With You" and "Listen To My Heart" from their debut.

The band would return to Finland in 1978, 1988, 1990, 1991, 1992 and 1994 with 11 performances all told in the country. They would also branch out to three other centres - Seinäjoki, Turku and Hummijkrvi as well as returning to Helsinki and Tampere. One of the most prominent Ramones gigs often shown on social media from the '80s is the *Provinssirock*. Organised since 1979, it is a large rock festival which is still held each year in the city of Seinäjoki in western Finland. Taking place on the 4th June, 1988, in front of a flag waving, animated and energetic audience, this should have vintage Ramones written all over it but somehow it does not hit the heights that you expect from *Da Brudders*. Dee Dee, for instance, is seemingly less enthused, less on edge, more stationary. Yes, he still has his moments of individuality but watch this video and it paints a picture of someone who is *going through the motions* – Indeed, in around a year's time, he would quit the group for pastures new.

There was conflicting views amongst the band regarding their time in areas sometimes coined as The Land of The Midnight Sun. Johnny Ramone, on the one hand, hated it. "Scandinavia would be misery to me" the guitarist said. Going on to add that "the low sky, just clouds and overcast, and if you get too far north, it doesn't get dark at night, or it's dark all day. It was so depressing." (155) Marky, on the other, loved the latitude, little darkness and "the cool and very crisp air." In his autobiography, he also reflected on his time touring in Finland in 1978. One anecdote, refers to Joey's much publicised Obsessive-Compulsive

Disorder (OCD) and the drummer recites that the singer "had as much trouble leaving a stage as he did leaving the room." Indeed, when he tried to poke his head back through the curtain which separated onstage from offstage in Helsinki, two of the roadies, had to literally grab the vocalist to get him away from the eager crowd. Another poignant recollection referred to the fanatical Finnish fans on that "Road To Ruin tour" who greeted the band with incredible energy and "were glad we were still doing what we were doing and not watering it down." (156) One local enthusiast who particularly loved The Ramones, was Damian Cullen who fronted his own group, The Damian Cullen Band. He had the idea that by creating a tribute, he could not only play the songs he loved but also do something worthwhile by raising money for valuable causes in charity concerts whilst still keeping the memory of The Ramones flourishing. In 2010, therefore, he started to get together a group of Ramones fans who had already had experience playing the odd Ramones cover in their own bands such as Daggerplay and The Riot Soul and by 2011 these were ready to perform their own complete set. The name of the band not only derived from the geographical location but from the masterpiece "Pinhead" taken from a scene from the 1932 movie Freaks. Long-winded maybe but nobody will forget *"GabbaGabbahey – The Helsinki Ramones Tribute"*.

The last line-up involved Johnny Suanto on bass, Sirpa Immonen on the drummer's seat, Anssi Örkkilä playing guitar, Pekko Mantzin also on guitar and backing vocals as well as singer Damian. Previous members who also served were vocalist Miika Kokko and guitarists Julian McGourty and Misty Fingez. With the concept of the group to help raise money, there were other guitarists and bass players around who occasionally joined in along with a number of guest vocalists from different punk rock and rock band vocalists who shared the stage. These included Joey Luumäki (from *Ne Luumäet*), Tumppi Varonen (*Problems* and *Pelle Miljoona*) Otto Grundström

Photograph courtesy of Ansku Mkinen

(*Tehosekoitin* and *God Given Ass*), Miika Söderholm (Pojat!), Vesa Häkli (*Vandaalit*), Sammy Aaltonen (*Private Line*) and Miqu December (*Plastic Tears*). Indeed, guitarist Pekko paints the picture eloquently when he states that "there was always some kind of controlled chaos on the stage all the time."

Pekko feels that all of their events were memorable as they were for good causes which meant that they were pleasingly always packed with concert goers. However, he does cite the gigs at such places as *On The Rocks*, *Tavastia* and *Backstage* which were particularly inspiring with the clubs and fans donating much needed money to charitable foundations such as *Vva ry*, a non-profit making organisation whose purpose is to reduce homelessness and to improve the services of homeless people.

Of course, with rammed venues comes responsibility and as Pekko describes "a hell of a lot of work was made in order to get the sound extremely tight." The set list changed all of the time depending on the circumstances with *GabbaGabbaHey* playing something like 15-20 songs at the first gig at *On The Rocks* in the centre of Helsinki whilst their longest set was at the *Tavastia*, the legendary rock club in the capital, when the band played an incredible 42 tunes. During the last song at this concert, the rousing "Pinhead" was met with true punk mayhem with every performing artist and devotees from the audience on the jam packed stage and you can just imagine the booming cries of "Gabba Gabba Hey" as the ditty neared its end. The last concert the band performed was at the *Vastavirta* music club in Tampere in 2014. The group never officially folded but the musicians were busy back then and are still busy working now. Pekko admits it "would be great to do it again but it would take a lot of effort to make it sound as good as it once was."

Pekko points out that Ramones are still a very important inspiration for his present band *Daggerplay* with some of their tunes heavily influenced by their style with even one tune named "Now I Wanna Listen To The Ramones". He goes on to add that "there is a song contest, also organised here in Helsinki, dedicated to *'Ramopunk'* which is simply a "genre" to come up with the best and most original songs in Ramones' style."

There are two easily accessible videos of the group, *GabbaGabbaHey* on *Youtube* and both are well worth examining. Take a look at "I believe In Miracles" from way back in 2012 with Sammy Aaltonen guesting on vocals. Those sticklers who like their Ramones cover bands as a four-piece rather than a quintet will probably find it somewhat uncomfortable but as soon as you get past the extra guitarist you will find a well-crafted outfit who are as tight as duck's arse. Even better, is their version of "Poison Heart" from 2014 with stunning vocals from Damian Cullen and superb percussion work from the female drummer Sirpa Immonen. Both samples on offer are, of course, mid-tempo beauts and disappointingly I cannot find any faster Ramones' crackerjacks to get my teeth into. Nonetheless, check out what is on offer, you will not be disappointed. Indeed, once you start watching you might just not want to finish…or should I say Finnish!?....

Ramoaners
Scotland

The Ramones' first gig in Scotland was at *The University of Strathclyde* in Glasgow on May 21st 1977. This came near the end of their first extensive European tour and like most subsequent excursions north of the border it was sandwiched between concerts in England. Their first song on Scottish land was fittingly the seminal anthem "Blitzkrieg Bop". It's not hard to picture, a frenzied crowd, fist pumping synchronised with the hearty cries of "hey ho, let's go". Other landmark sing-alongs would of course follow including "Havana Affair", "Commando" and "Chainsaw". However, it was not all machine gun etiquette, with the slower more melodic tunes of "I Remember You", "Babysitter" and the gorgeous "I Wanna Be Your Boyfriend" inserted between the more customary driving punk numbers.

Another cut off their first album which The Ramones sang that night was "Now I Wanna Sniff Some Glue" - Dee Dee's self-confessed adolescent craze to help pass the time. Not only a cheap and easy way to get high when you were a bored teenager but unfortunately a hasty way to blow some brain cells too. The problem, as James Havlin articulates in *Ripped and Torn*, one of the first punk fanzines, was that "alarming statistics and stories emerged; including, after a spate of a dozen or so deaths, the growing menace of solvent abuse. According to the Glasgow Health Board there were a couple of thousand kids in the city sniffing glue. Stories circulated about terrified communities, particularly of old people afraid to go out at night due to the behaviour of feral gangs of kids, high on glue." With the Scottish press featuring glue sniffing teenagers almost on a daily basis, this came to a head when a 16-year-old died after inhaling gas canister vapour. With The Ramones ground-breaking first album celebrating the art of glue sniffing and brat beating along with the mesmerising iconic street fighting gang lookalike L.P cover, some blamed the band for the boy's death particularly after it was found that he had purchased a copy of that album. There were calls for the record to be banned which fell on deaf ears although some DJs refused to give their tunes any airplay. [157]

The Ramones shrugged off the controversy and all in all, played 16 times in Scotland concentrating on the two major populated cities. This amounted to five in the capital, Edinburgh and 11 in the second city, Glasgow. Their last ever performance in *Caledonia* was at the *Barrowland Ballroom* in Glasgow on September 23rd, 1994 and featured Scottish rock band *Goodbye Mr Mackenzie* as support. The *Barrowland* is a dance hall and music venue located in the Calton District with an original building built in 1934. [158] Regrettably, this building was completely gutted by fire in 1958 and a completely new build took place which opened on Christmas Eve, 1960. With a capacity of 1,900 standing, many well-known artists have played there. The venerated Northern Irish punk band, *Stiff Little Fingers,* for instance, performed sold-out gigs every St Patrick's Day since 1992.

One fan who remembers The Ramones at *Barrowland* in 1985 was Glasgow based, Bryan Robertson who would eventually play bass for the *Ramoaners*. Like so many other individuals who observed the band The Ramones left an instant impression. "My ears hissed for a week and the songs were so fast and loud that they were almost finished before you could identify them" Bryan reminisces. Little did he know that he would be standing on the very spot Dee Dee once starred, playing those same songs some 30 years down the line performing in his own Ramones tribute.

The band's origins can be traced right back to 1984. Vocalist Tony Gaughan, who promotes Scottish artists as well owns the aptly named Glasgow music store *Blitzkreig,* answered Bryan's advertisement for a singer. Tony was instrumental in reforming *Goodbye Mr Mackenzie* and also managed singer Martin Metcalfe. Tony and Bryan went on to form *"Wages of Sin"* and although the band broke up, in 2014, met up by chance in the queue for an *Echo and the Bunnymen* show in Glasgow. Now back in touch, Bryan describes how the *Ramoaners* came about. "It was by accident really. Tony was looking for a Ramones act for a Roller Derby fundraiser and I stupidly suggested that we could do it better than what was on offer at the time. After one show we all wanted to do more."

The original 2014 *Ramoaners* line-up featured Jimmy on guitar and initially Rico on drums, followed subsequently by Jay Jay. Bassist Bryan would take the moniker of CC whilst singer Tony naturally took the title of Tony Ramonaner. By 2016, Gordon Adams or GG came in and provided real authority on guitar whilst a third drummer, ex *Esperanza* band member, Jason Good was introduced on the drummer's stool in 2019 amusingly becoming the second Jay Jay Ramoaner. Impressively, Jason, was at the legendary gig at the *Rainbow Theatre* in North London on New Year's Eve, 1977 which has been often cited as the best ever live punk album. *The Ramoaners* live performance is indeed based on this finely tuned *"It's Alive"* core with other tunes rotated in and out.

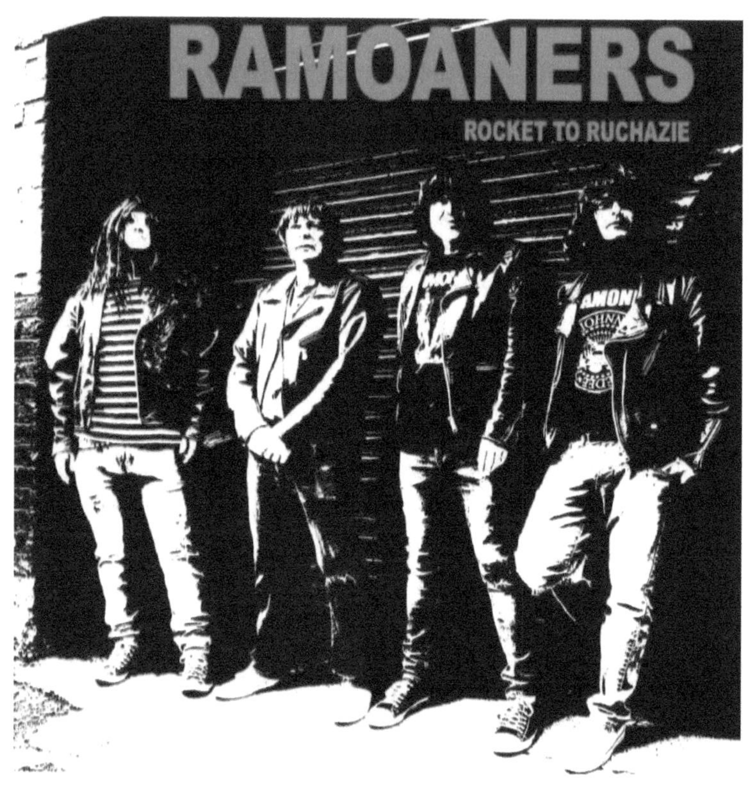

Although always difficult to judge, Bryan felt that the standout shows would be two outings at the *Barrowland Ballroom* in 2014 and 2019. The have also worked with *The Dead Boys* and *Vice Squad* and have travelled extensively from Stornoway to Southampton. In addition, the group played three shows in quick succession at London's *Dublin Castle*, a venue where two-tone heroes *Madness* began their career and where celebrated vocalist Amy Winehouse frequented.

An examination of the band is essential and a visit on *Youtube* shows the band in action. *The Ramoaners*, live at *King Tut's Wah-Wah Hut* in Glasgow in aid of cystic fibrosis on Joey

Ramone's tribute night, for instance, is a decent unveiling of the Scots. As with virtually all Ramones gigs post "Too Tough To Die", they commence with the instrumental "Durango 95" and just before the start of the next track, "Rockaway Beach" singer Tony strolls on with pint in hand – a must watch. Other worthy performances include "Teenage Lobotomy" live at *McChuills* and "Oh Oh I Love Her So" at the *Ivory Blacks* in 2022. There are many videos of the band on the social media platform and well worth taking a look.

When asked about the cover act, Bryan was quite reflective in his response. "We are all about authenticity in sound and image but recognise the absurdity of middle aged men in wigs and leather jackets (which are murder to play in). There is a lot of criticism levelled at tribute acts for cashing in on others creativity but I am pretty certain we have never made a cent from playing as *Ramoaners*. What we have done I hope is to deliver blistering sets in the manner they were originally meant to be played and allowed many who never saw the band to imagine what it was like. There is always someone after the show who really gets it and that is sufficient reward for all the effort. I don't think UK punk would have taken off without The Ramones' guitar sound and imagery.

When I was introduced to their music by a school friend my small record collection was immediately redundant. I really enjoyed seeing that same friend at a couple of our shows 40 years later. We are 10 years in and a good bit older than The Ramones made it to. It gets ever more physically demanding but we aren't finished yet." Indeed, long may this continue. The band is still playing - still keeping the New Yorker's legacy alive ensuring that there is no *moaning* going on - just pleasingly plenty of *Ramoaning*!

The Marones
England

Maybe another one of those rather surprising statistics brought up in this research is that The Ramones played six times in Bristol. Enveloped in the hills of south west of England and located between Gloucestershire and Somerset it is possibly not a centre where you would expect the boys from Queens to perform no less than half a dozen times. Yet play there they did, with the first time occasion as early as May 30th 1977 along with periodic returns to the city in 1978, 1980, 1986, 1989 and 1992. The history of the city is interesting and in the 19th Century, it was associated with the Victorian engineer Isambard Kingdom Brunel. It was Brunel who engineered the Great Western Railway between Bristol and London, built the renown Clifton Suspension Bridge which spans the nearby Avon Gorge and River Avon and designed the world-famous Bristol stream ships - *The SS Great Britain* and *The SS Great Western.* [(159)] Nowadays, the population of the city is estimated to be around 479,000 people at the end of June 2022 and it is the 11th largest in the United Kingdom.

Their first gig in Bristol was at *Colston Hall* which is now a grade II listed building. The establishment opened as a concert venue way back in 1867, and became a popular place for classical music and theatre and in the 1950s even hosted wrestling bouts. Rebuilds and refurbishments took place in 1901 and 1951 and by the late 1960s it had become one of the most important rock venues in Britain. The list of famed artists who performed there is certainly impressive and includes the likes of *The Beatles, The Rolling Stones,* Tina Turner, *Jim Hendrix, Elton John, David Bowie, Queen, Thin Lizzy, The Who* and Bob Marley. The venue has seen further repair and development and in 2020 has been rebranded under the name of *Bristol Beacon.* [160] The Ramones co-headlined with *Talking Heads* in Bristol but sadly there is no record of their set list that night and the precise details of the gig have been lost in the mists of time. One week earlier at *Barbarella's* in Birmingham, however, we do know that they performed 26 songs with three encores [161] so there is a fair likelihood that the west country crowd would have experienced a similar feast. Songs would certainly have been taken from the first two albums with "Suzy Is A Headbanger", "You Should Have Never Have Opened That Door", "Oh Oh I Love Her So" and "Now I Wanna Be A Good Boy" particularly aimed to plug "Leave Home", the latest cut. The New Yorkers would play at *Colston Hall* for a second time in February 1980 and would also perform in the city at *The Locarno,* twice at *The Studio* and finally at the *Bristol Rainbow* on the "Mondo Bizarro" tour in December 1992.

One tribute that originated from Bristol was *The Marones* which formed in 1996 at the tail end of The Ramones' career. Right from the offset, the group decided to take up monikers akin to *Da Brudders* and originally consisted of Wiggy Marone on guitar, Jerry Marone on bass, Gary Marone as singer and Jonny Marone on drums. The band generally had a consistent formation although did experience one line-up alteration in 1998, when Steve Croom aka Spider, as he liked to be coined, came in as front-man to replace Gary. It was Wiggy who thought up the name of the band with the guitarist wanting it to be a play on the word *moron* which naturally fitted in with the nature of so many Ramones' tunes. Wiggy also describes why the lads decided to start their tribute stating that "just for the hell of it – and we were of course all die-hard fans." The band members were all in various local groups with Spider particularly gaining recognition with *The Seers,* a rock group which were active between 1984 and 1991 and who were signed to Cherry Red Records releasing two albums. Indeed, *The Seers* supported The Ramones a number of times in West Germany, France, The Netherlands and in England in the summer of 1988 whilst they also became the first unsigned band to play at the *Reading Festival*.

The Seers pictured with The Ramones backstage at The Paradiso, Amsterdam in June 1988. Spider can be seen to Joey's left.

The Marones concentrated on playing a similar set as "Loco Live" but at the "It's Alive" tempo ensuring that it was not, as Wiggy suggests, "stupidly fast." The group entered the stage to

"The Good, The Bad and The Ugly" and would immediately blast into the instrumental "Durango 95" before Jonny would pound into the drum introduction of "Teenage Lobotomy". "Loco" included many tracks from the '80s and the likes of "Rock 'n' Roll High School", "The KKK Took My Baby Away", "Somebody Put Something In My Drink" and "Do You Remember Rock 'n' Roll Radio?" all performed by the Bristol based group. Naturally, the band also discharged the older favourites with Wiggy reminiscing that "I used to love playing "Commando" and "Pinhead" - 'D.U.M.B everyone's accusing me'! I also enjoyed playing "Bonzo" because of those backing vocals, he states."

As well as using the Loco Live" set list as a starting point for their own repertoire, the group adopted some of the other familiarities associated with The Ramones. Firstly, *The Marones* adapted the unmistakeable eagle crest which was designed by Arturo Vega but with one noticeable difference - their personal names would be placed around the edge of that trademark logo. Secondly, their friend and roadie, "Mouse" would dress up in a clown's costume and would run about with a "Gabba Gabba Hey" sign, executing the so-called "*jerk dance*". This would of course feature so prominently in the New Yorkers' concerts of the 1980s and 1990s.

Wiggy points out that "we played several shows around Bristol and found it was easy to get a decent gig because so many people loved The Ramones." When asked about his favourite concerts, the guitarist fondly recalls those at the *Fleece & Firkin* in Bristol where they performed many times, with the venue often hosting a number of other tribute bands. Other establishments included *The Full Moon, The Underground* and *The Hobgoblin*.

Wiggy recollects that "we played a club supporting a band called *Hi On Maiden* and we got a great reaction because it was The Ramones. We even once took part in a *Battle of the Bands* and won! We would wear the full outfit, leathers, T-Shirts and jeans. Gary/Spider wore a wig and pink sunglasses. I already had long hair although not a bowl cut," the guitarist pronounces. It was not always easy and Wiggy ruefully remembers that "my hands would hurt playing barre chords for over an hour! Nonetheless, we played it hard and fast. Honestly it was just a bit of fun between four good friends in two different bands. A release from playing our own material that was mostly metal."

As with so many of our tributes and cover bands featured in this book, it is apparent how much The Ramones were appreciated and deeply loved. Wiggy, for instance, saw the *'fast four'*, a number of times including the Bristol *Studio* and *Rainbow* gigs and twice at the Brixton Academy in London including that final tour with the guitarist simply affirming that "they were memorable." Not only that, but Wiggy additionally saw Joey Ramone play Coney Island High at a small club in New York City whilst on a trip to the States. "I got to say hi to him and we shook hands", he recalls. The musician goes on to add that it was "purely because I was English. He ignored everyone else. Dee Dee and Daniel Rey were in his band. Wayne Kramer played a set, as did Scott Asheton and Ronni Spector. It was quite the night, and we just luckily stumbled across it." When asked about the impact that The Ramones had, Wiggy believes they were "hugely influential, unwavering and dedicated. They were also underrated, he articulates."

At the end of 1998, after just two years, *The Marones* decided to call it a day in order to concentrate on their own bands. Nevertheless, they were an important cog in keeping The Ramones' legacy alive – the group was one of our earliest recorded tributes with their formation coinciding with the American's retirement ensuring that at least some fans would still hear those blistering tunes – a decision which was certainly saner than *moronic*!

Gabba Gabba Hey
United States Of America

With around 2.7 million inhabitants, Chicago is the most populous city of Illinois and the third largest in the United States of America after New York City and Los Angeles. Located on the shore of Lake Michigan, its geographical location is described as in the Midwest. The *Windy City* as its been coined, is possibly best known for a period of organised crime in the 1920s where after Prohibition, rival gangs fought for control of the illegal sale of alcohol along with protection rackets and gambling dens. During this period, Chicago was the location of the infamous St Valentine's Day Massacre in 1929 when Al Capone sent four of his men down to shoot members of a rival mob leading to the murder of seven members of the *North Side Gang*. Nowadays, the city is famed for its bold architecture with huge skyscrapers piercing the skyline, coupled with its professional sports teams such as the *Chicago Bulls* of the NBA.

Although The Ramones had performed in Illinois a handful of times previously in 1977, it was not until July 6th that they played in Chicago itself. This was part of a full American tour, with the lads having just performed in Milwaukee in Wisconsin two days earlier and with the knowledge that their next concert would be in Lebanon in Illinois two days later. The chosen Chicago venue that evening was the *Ivanhoe Theatre* which played a chunk of early national punk shows in the 1970s. There is a saying that "good thing comes in pairs" and this was certainly the case that night with fellow New Yorkers, *The Dictators* also on the bill for those lucky fans who were in the audience.

There is no official record of their complete set list but in all probability they would have played around 20 tunes from the first two albums that night as was customary at that time in their career. Thankfully, there is footage of the concert and readily available on *Youtube* with five songs on offer. Here you will find absolute vintage Ramones - "Now I Wanna Sniff Some Glue", I Don't Wanna Walk Around With You", "Pinhead", "Suzy Is A Headbanger", and "California Sun" all blasted out in *Gatling* gun fashion. Both guitarists are at their very best – Johnny mean and menacing, jestering his guitar like the thunder god Thor yields his hammer whilst Dee Dee is a jittery bubble, a live wire of electric energy. At the back, cymbal thumping Tommy is seen keeping it all together whilst Joey, precariously hangs over the stage like a dark menacing delinquent as he chews and spits out those famed lyrics.

The Ramones would return to Chicago regularly throughout the rest of their calling and performed in the city over 20 times with *The Aragon Ballroom, Metro Chicago* and *The Riviera Theatre* regular haunts throughout the years. One fan who originates from Chicago is bassist and singer Mike Pecci who saw them on numerous occasions and would be instrumental in the formation of our next tribute. Mike recalls that he "first learned of The Ramones on a cable TV show called *"Up All Night"* on *USA* channel. They played "Rock 'n' Roll High School" and I fell in love with them, immediately going out and to buy their first three albums. The fourth was released but they had sold out of it so I had to wait two weeks before

I could get the "Road To Ruin" L.P." The first time Mike saw them was on the 1983 "Subterranean Jungle" tour at a small venue called *Haymakers* in a suburb of Chicago called Wheeling and he remembers that "the place was a dump" and that The Ramones were "incredibly loud."

In 2005, Mike and guitarist Bill Pratt III had the idea of creating a tribute group because of their love of The Ramones and because they did not think "they got the proper thanks or recognition that they deserved." As well as Mike on the four string, doubling up as vocalist along with Bill on guitar, the initial line-up was a three-piece which saw Kevin Elwardt on drums. It was Bill who came up with the title of the band, *Gabba Gabba Hey,* heralding from the catchphrase in the tune "Pinhead". The origins of the infamous song stem from the 1932 film, *"Freaks"*, which was a movie thought to be too horrific at the time of release and nowadays too politically incorrect to air due to the fact that it "included characters from travelling shows such as real conjoined twins, the 'living torso', the bearded lady, dwarves and a microcephalic or *pinhead* called Schlitzie." Evidently, after an outdoor concert was cancelled due to bad weather, The Ramones watched the film and adapted the freaks' chant from 'Gooble, Gobble, we accept her, one of us' to 'Gabba, Gabba, we accept you, one of us' which is, of course, is the mantra we all now readily associate with the band. [162]

Their first ever gig was at a bar on the south side of the city called *O'Malleys* on the 11th March, 2005. The group had no lead vocalist at this time so singing duties were carried out by Mike who recalls that "I loved it, lots of people were there and dancing around" with the set list focussing on songs from the first five albums. Soon after, the band found a lead vocalist, Don Batryn Jr. and the quartet continued to play the local clubs and bars of Illinois such as the *Abbey Pub, The Penny Road Pub* or *Bada Brew*, gradually expanding their set list to incorporate more contemporary tunes from other L.Ps as well. *Gabba Gabba Hey* eventually had a number of different sets depending on the needs of the venue ranging from 30 minutes, 40 minutes, one hour or even 90 minutes. "I would normally sing 'Spiderman' and 'Love kills', for the extended sets." Mike reminiscences. "I really liked singing and playing." When asked about his favourite shows, Mike points to a couple of stand-out memories. The first was a sold out gig at *Reggies Rock Club* in Chicago. "All I could see from the stage was a sea of people. The best compliments we got were on that night. one girl said, 'I'm too young to have seen them, and now I feel like I have.' Another middle age man told me, 'I saw The Ramones several times and you guys are the most accurate copy I've seen. I especially like the fact that your guitarist plays all downstrokes like Johnny would and I understand that is very hard to do'." Another remarkable event was when the band featured on Channel 9, *WGNTV* morning news and played three songs live – "Blitzkrieg Bop". "Teenage Lobotomy" and "I Wanna Be Sedated". Mike articulates that it all was over in a flash and that "I barely remember playing the songs although what does stick out was being told not to move around too much because they didn't want us to bump into their new expensive roving camera!"

The four musicians had all previous experience in other bands. Mike and Bill, for instance, had played together in *Fresh Flesh, Uncle Crusty,* and *Crook County,* Kevin had performed in *Brothers In Arms* whilst Don Jr. was in *Zoso*. The group experienced a couple of line-up changes – one temporary and one permanent. In the short-term, Don Batryn III played guitar and subbed for Bill for six shows whilst Andrew Cielo took over on the skins after Kevin left in 2010. The new drummer is currently performing in the band *Sex Dream*.

A look on to the band's *Facebook* page will see a host of activities related to The Ramones as well as *Gabba Gabba Hey* including an array of fantastic photographs. It is immediately noticeable how closely the lads look like the originals. Garnished in leathers, T-shirts, knee-holed jeans and sneakers there is no mistaking that these boys are honouring Forest Hills' finest. Indeed, Mike elaborates and declares that "two of us (Bill and I) wore wigs at first, but I grew my hair out" with undoubtedly the end result a resemblance of Dee Dee. The second distinctive feature are the variations of the trademark Ramones eagle logos which are dotted around their site and adapted to feature the band's name around the periphery.

When asked about The Ramones' impact, Mike brought up how the band affected him personally stating that the New Yorkers "have greatly influenced my playing and song writing." As with all bands, at some time or another, musicians "move on" and after a cancelled gig in 2011, the band decided to call it a day. With six years of playing Ramones' songs and keeping their name alive, they had certainly made their mark and Ramones fans in the Chicago area will undoubtedly thank them for that. Or maybe more pertinently rather than gratitude, in this instance recognition is key with the apt sentiments of *"we accept you, one of us"*, the perfect, fitting send off.

the abbey
@murpho

Sedated - The Ultimate Ramones Experience United States Of America

By 1976, The Ramones had ventured away from their New York base to take in other venues. Gigs started with performances in New England in New Hampshire and Massachusetts but soon expanded across the Atlantic to London along with concerts in California on the west coast of the States in the summer of that year. Maybe surprisingly, the boys from Queens did not perform in Texas until July 1977 which was after their first full European tour. Texas is the second largest U.S state by both area (after Alaska) and population (after California) and is situated in the south central region of the country. Native American tribes who lived inside the boundaries of modern day Texas include the Apache and the Comanche whilst the region was once controlled by the Spanish until the Texas Revolution - probably best remembered for the famous Battle of the Alamo where William Travis, James Bowie and Davy Crockett met their heroic deaths. Their first gig in Texas took place on July 14th at the *Armadillo World Headquarters* in Austin, the state capital. The venue was an influential music hall and beer garden which was built just after the Second World War. The bizarre sounding name of the establishment was inspired because the building was an old armoury and local artist Jim Franklin used the armadillo as a symbol for the new venture. The *Armadillo* opened its doors in

August 1970 and quickly became the centre of much of the city's musical culture with an eventual capacity of 1,500. Enjoying an eclectic concert calendar, the music hall was able to host a variety of top acts including Bruce Springsteen, Ray Charles, Frank Zappa, the Pointer sisters, *ZZ Top* and *The Clash*. The site lived on a shoestring budget and eventually closed its doors because of financial difficulties on New Year's Eve, 1980.

The full set list for the Austin show has been lost over time although we do know that the masterpieces "Now I Wanna Be A Good Boy", "53rd and 3rd" and "Today Your Love, Tomorrow The World" were all part of the show. In all probability it would have naturally centred around both of the first two albums and numbered around 20 songs which was the norm for this period of their career. After Austin the band played five further gigs in the state in four different centres: Houston on two consecutive nights followed by San Antonio, Killen and Dallas before moving on to the next stage of their tour in California. Monte Melnick describes life on the road with The Ramones which not only gives a feel for the continuous workload of the group and the tedium which accompanied the long bus rides between locations but also the humour and practical jokes which was integral with the touring band. When reciting a narrative regarding places to stop for refreshments the tour manager laughs "we'd ask the promoter where one was on the way out of town or near the hotel, and grab some snacks or magazines. It started off casually, but then they became obsessed. After the first decade or so I knew to do this. They knew I knew and yet would still come and bug me every night. 'Monte, find a 7–11, we gotta stop.' Then half the time they'd wander around in a daze and not buy anything. One time in the early days we were wandering through a Texas gas station mini-market. We had been driving for hours and the guys were stiff from sitting all day. You can imagine what they looked like, piling out of the van, all stinky and stiff. They were wandering around the gas station in a zombie-like daze, like something out of 'The Living Dead', when the attendant turns to me and says, 'It's so nice of you to take care of these retarded boys.' I cracked up. The band was oblivious." [163] Monte and his *cretin family* performed nearly 60 times in Texas all told with the last one taking place on the July 25th, 1996 in Ferris at the *Old Fort Dallas*. By this time, their song repertoire had of course altered featuring tracks such as "I believe in Miracles", "The KKK Took My Baby Away", "Wart Hog", "R.A.M.O.N.E.S" and "Spiderman" which the band originally recorded for a tribute album named "Saturday Morning: Cartoons' Greatest Hits".

A common theme with the conceptions of Ramones tribute bands has been a love of their songs and wanting to keep the memories of the band going and relevant. One such band who had these sentiments is *"Sedated – The Ultimate Ramones Experience"*. Rather uniquely, the band have three different line ups. The "core" group is based in Dallas, but there are also regional line ups in Houston and St Louis. Formed in 2015, the band members adopted pseudonyms ending with "Sedated" with the singer, for instance known as Joey Sedated.

The band's live set is rotated but typically likes to base itself around the *"It's Alive"* album with other later songs such as "Durango 95", "Psycho Therapy" and "Pet Sematary" also embraced. It is imperative to check out their performance for yourself and a great starting point is the punk psalm "Blitzkrieg Pop" *"Live at the Amp Room"* in 2022. Dressed in basin wigs, black leathers, dirty white plimsolls and the obligatory blue knee-hole jeans, *Ultimate Sedated* radiates energy. At the front, Johnny has that steely look, threatening to launch his flailing guitar on any unsuspecting audience member whilst he also gives us that mandatory circular spin in the middle of the number made famous during his Ramones performances. Dee Dee is the jack-in-the-box; twitchy, edgy and hyper-active with bass slung low and knees bent. Joey is hunched over the mic, nodding head appropriately and punching the air in time with the "hey, hoes" as Tommy, hidden by Joey's giraffe shaped figure is the splice that brings it together, keeping time flawlessly. Another notable video on *Youtube* which worth investigating is "I Wanna Be Sedated" live at the *Black Circle Brewing* in Indianapolis. Playing with a different line-up, the number probably doesn't quite hit the heights of "Blitzkrieg Bop" but is still performed at lightning pace and frantic vigour.

The singer cites a number of memorable gigs with the most notable including the *House of Blues* in Dallas in 2016 and most recently at the *Handlebar* in Pensacola, Florida as part of a 50th anniversary for *CBGGs*. Impressively, the band also took part in the reunion for the *"Rock 'n' Roll High School"* party in 2019 at the *Texas Theatre* in Dallas. At this event PJ Soles, who played Riff Randall in The Ramones cult movie, was in attendance and witnessed the group perform at the end of the event.

Joey, the vocalist of *Sedated*, feels that without The Ramones' influence, music "would not have thrived." He also goes on to add that "he is very proud of what we have been able to accomplish; playing in 11 U.S states. More importantly has been the relationships I have fostered as a result with the *extended Ramone family*: Mickey Leigh, Vera Ramone, Roxy Ramone have been in contact online whilst David Erdély, John Holmstrom, George Seminara and Matt Loyla were met face-to-face when we played in New York City at the *Pyramid Club*".

Lobotomen
United States Of America

Oregon, is situated in north-western United States and is one of just three states in the contiguous US with a coastline on the Pacific Ocean. The Colombia River largely defines Oregon's border with Washington state in the north whilst the evocatively named Snake River forms a section of its state line with Idaho in the east whereas the celebrated 42nd parallel north defines the borders with California and Nevada in the south. Oregon has a population of 4.2 million people and although the capital is Salem, the largest city is the major river port, Portland, with a population of just over 641,000. Sitting on the Columbia and Willamette rivers and in the shadow of the snow-capped Mount Hood, Portland also has one of the most vibrant music scenes in the US and it was in this city that The Ramones first played in Oregon on August 5th, 1977. The designated venue was the *Paramount Theatre,* an ornate and lavish building costing $1.5 million which still stands as an architectural treasure in Downtown Portland. Movie fans lined for hours to get a glimpse inside the 3,000 seated auditorium on the opening night in March 1928 and it has since been the home for the *Oregon Symphony* and as a venue for concerts and other enterprises such as the *Portland Youth Philharmonic.* [164] When the performing arts centre was opened in 1984, it was renamed *The Arlene Schnitzer Concert Hall,* an American arts patron and philanthropist. Those who have performed at the venue reads like a *who's who* of the very best musicians including Louis Armstrong in 1954 and 1959, Frank Sinatra in 1957, Liberace in 1962, Bob Marley in 1978, *Abba* in 1979, Madonna in 1985 and *Oasis* in 2000.

The Ramones' supporting act that night was the rock band *Tom Petty and the Heartbreakers* who had already performed together on the previous night coincidentally at another *Paramount Theatre,* but this time in Seattle. There is no record of their set list in Portland but in all probability it would have incorporated around score of songs and undoubtedly focused on the first two released albums. The gig was just four days before the filming of the *Don Kirshner's Rock Concert* in Los Angeles and is now readily available on *Youtube.* During that show the band played 12 tunes to a minimal audience but it still remains one of their best performances – go take a look.

In total, the band would play in Oregon just a dozen times. Along with Portland, Eugene would be the only other city The Ramones visited in the state, playing there on three occasions in February 1978, May 1983 and December 1984. During that visit in the spring of '83 would see a new recruit to the band early on in his fledgling Ramones career. Richie Reinhardt, better known by his stage name Richie Ramone would play in the band from February 1983 until August 1987 and would be the third drummer to sit on the prestigious stool. In his autobiography *I Know Better Now,* the stick man describes how he got the gig in one of punk's premier outfits. Richie was tipped off by Larry Chekofsky, a drum tech from a band that Richie had played in named *The Shirts,* that Marky was about to be fired by the band due to his alcoholism and was asked if he fancied joining The Ramones. [165] A couple of months earlier, Marky had evidently persuaded road manager, Monte, that he was capable to getting to the next gig in a friend's car rather than travel together along with the rest of the band as was the norm. When his lift fell through – a 600 mile trip from Cleveland to Virginia Beach – the alarm bells started to ring, the alcohol started to flow and the drummer never got to the show despite last ditch efforts to hire a private plane. Things went from bad to worse when he got busted stashing vodka during the recording of the seventh studio album "Subterranean Jungle" which eventually led to the inevitable phone call from front man Joey. "Marc." He said. "I gotta tell you something. You can't be in the band anymore." [166] Marky's last gig during his first stint with the group was on November 27th, 1982 in West Islip, a hamlet on Long Island in New York. With Larry Chek, as he was known, acting as a middleman between Richie and Monte, a rehearsal was set up at The Ramones' space at the *Daily Planet* in Manhattan. The would-be new drummer was not familiar with their songs so just perfected what he considered the three most famous tunes - "Blitzkrieg Bop, "Sheena Is A Punk Rocker" and "I Wanna Be Sedated". His strategy paid dividends though and he must have made an impression playing along-side Dee Dee and Johnny as he was asked back for a second audition two days later. With Joey also present at this additional try-out and with the same three songs performed, things went swimmingly again and the following morning, Richie got the call he was waiting for from Monte telling him he had got the job. [167] Interestingly, the tour manager immediately talked about finances with Richie asking for $400 per week which was negotiated downwards to an agreed figure of $375 with the additional prospect of making money from record sales too. [168] Richie's first concert with the band was on February 13th, 1983 in Utica in the state of New York.

Half way through the show, his drumming was 'off' and much to Richie's bemusement, perfectionist Johnny stopped playing to correct him. [169] By the time he reached Eugene at the Erb Memorial Union at the University of Oregon, he would have been still *wet between the ears* having performed for less than three months.

Photograph courtesy of Joe Saffer

In 2019, the Portland based drummer Brendan "Mack" Hagin put out an advert for "a Ramones cover band looking for our Joey." The potential band already had Paul Burke or as he was soon to be coined Pauly Damone on bass and Frank Goulart aka Frankie Sparks as guitarist. When another drummer, Ken Weiner saw the ad, he immediately thought "I'm doing this" as he always wanted to try his hand as lead vocalist. The first practice was seamless and with Mack putting it all together, they blasted through a bunch of songs. The line-up was now settled with Ken taking up the pseudonym of Monty Vega inspired by the often unheralded duo of Monte Melnick and Arturo Vega, once termed as "the fifth Ramone." [170] Mack, Paul and Frank had only seen *Da Brudders* a handful of occasions in total, due to the fact that they performed more

sporadically on the west coast but interestingly, the singer, who had grown up in the New Jersey/New York area in the 1980s, had witnessed The Ramones over 60 times. As a 20-year-old, also had the pleasure of meeting Joey Ramone at a record store signing in Brooklyn. Ken also had the chance to meet PJ "Riff Randle" Soles, who starred in the 1979 film "Rock 'n' Roll High School" along-side The Ramones and managed to get her autograph on the soundtrack.

The name of the band derives from the eighth tune on the "Rocket To Russia" L.P and one of their most popular - "Teenage Lobotomy". Typical of the New Yorkers sick sense of humour and completely *don't give a damn,* non-politically correct stance, the *Lobotomen* is a perfect moniker for the cover. The group members are Ramones maniacs or as Monte phrased it "Ramoniacs" and believe that their influence and style is found in most rock that succeeded them.

All the lads had previous experience with other bands. Monte, for instance had played drums for *The Screamin' Furys* in the past whilst is currently drumming for *48 Thrills* as well as being front-man for *Monty Vega & The Sittin' Shivas,* an act heavily influenced by The Ramones. Paul plays guitar and sings backing vocals in *The Sittin' Shivas* whilst he is also involved with *Dirty Graves and Scourge of Ians* and intriguingly had a previous project called *The Ramodes* which played Depeche Mode songs in the style of The Ramones! Guitarist Frankie cut his teeth with the groups *Watchlist, Captain Crunch/Flesh Packs* and *The Flue* whilst Mack in the past hit the skins for *The Breach, Edgies* and *New Idol Son.*

Lobotomen typically run through around 20 songs on average for a set and have currently an impressive catalogue of roughly half a century of picks to choose from. "Our motivation", Monte states, "is to try and recreate more of their album orientated sound, rather than the lightning fast live pace." The singer goes on to add that they heavily "focus on vocal harmonies, especially like those on the first three albums." Similarly, the band do not wear wigs. "It's strictly about the music, specifically paying tribute to what the boys did in the studio." When asked about his favourite gig so far, the songster had no doubt and pointed to a 2023 concert in Portland at the *Swan Dive* to celebrate Joey Ramones' Birthday Bash where a big crowd raised $500 for lymphoma research. As well as The *Lobotomen* performing the whole of "Rocket to Russia", other artists gave up their time such as the all-female band *The Fauxs* who ran through The Ramones first album and *The Beat on Brats* completed "Leave Home". *Monty Vega & The Sittin' Shivas* closed the evening with a short set of originals and some covers which included "Don't Come Close", "Danny Says" and "What A Wonderful World".

Searching social media finds the band in fine form with four tracks observed. Take a look at "The KKK Took My Baby Away" at Portland's *Alberta Pub* in 2019 or "Howling At The Moon" and Pet Semetary" from the annual Halloween celebration at the *Chinese Restaurant* in the autumn of the same year. These rocky, more melodic numbers undoubtedly suit their tuneful emphasis it seems somewhat more compared to the head-splitting punkier "Commando" which was also on offer. Monte, stands perched with left foot forward, sideways on, Joey style whilst Frankie, legs astride and downstroking is not dissimilar to our driving force, Johnny. Paulie not only cries out the "1, 2, 3, 4s" and the "heys and hoes" with gusto but also harmonises expertly particularly on "The KKK". Mack keeps everything ticking along, rivalling the meticulousness drum head spanking renowned by Tommy, Marky and of course that *newbie* Richie. Take a look at these boys because if you don't, you certainly need that lobotomy.

Photograph courtesy of Alex Wrekk.

Rockaway Beach Boys
United States Of America

The state of Maryland is located in the Mid-Atlantic region of the United States and is bordered by four other states – Pennsylvania to its north, Virginia in the south, Delaware to the east and West Virginia towards the west. Maryland's name honours Queen Henrietta Maria, wife of Charles 1st the monarch of Great Britain who signed the 1632 charter to establish the colony and famed as the only English King to be tried and beheaded for treason. Although the capital of the state is Annapolis, the most populous city in Maryland is Baltimore with just over 576,000 inhabitants and is situated only 40 miles away from the capital of the country, Washington D.C. It was in Baltimore that The Ramones first performed in the state in the autumn of 1977 after a gruelling schedule which must have taken its toll both physically and mentally. Indeed, after the breakthrough year in 1976 where they had not only helped stimulate the punk scene in London but also cement their reputation in other parts of the North American continent, 1977 saw them expand even further. Their hectic programme had embraced further American gigs such as in California in February and March, along with a European tour between the months of April and June. After the return journey back across the Atlantic, The Ramones would again set off traversing the States, this time taking the Midwest and even further south in Texas in July. After recording, "Rocket To Russia" in August, more gigs and new centres would follow and by October, they had been billed as the support act for Iggy Pop and the pairing would hit Baltimore on the 15th of that month. In his book *Commando*, Johnny Ramones claims that there was some chicanery between the two acts. "We did some shows that fall with Iggy Pop in the east and Midwest," the guitarist recalls. "It was with the best band Iggy had assembled post-*Stooges*, with the Sayles brothers. But the shows were ruined by rock star bullshit. Iggy kept taking lights from us each night, and finally we got to Chicago and we were down to one red light. We told him we weren't going to play. They gave us another light." [171]

The selected venue in Baltimore was the *Baltimore Civic Centre*. It was built on a location rich in history with the old site of the Henry Fite House, which became known as "Congress Hall", briefly serving as the new United States seat of government from 1776-77. A new building, established in 1962, has been used for several sports teams such as the *Baltimore Bullets* of the National Basketball Association, the *Baltimore Blast* of the indoor soccer league and the *Baltimore Clippers* of the American Hockey League. The site has had a number of other designations – *the Baltimore Arena, 1st Mariner Arena, Royal Farms Arena* and currently the *CFG Bank Arena.* According to one web site, the building "is no longer the outdated dump of arena that is in so many people's memories" [172] and now has the seating capacity to hold 14,000 after a $250 million revamp. [173] Past performers at the venue read like a music aristocracy which include *The Beatles, The Rolling Stones, Led Zeppelin, The Jackson 5, Gladys Knight and the Pips*, Jimi Hendrix and Bruce Springsteen whilst the venue is also famed for holding a Martin Luther King Jr. speech there back in 1966.

Although there is no record of the set at the *Baltimore Civic Centre,* there is a partial one chronicled from their concert just three days previously at the *Tower Theatre* in Upper Darby in the neighbouring state of Pennsylvania and a full listing registered from a Montreal gig in Canada a week before that. There is little doubt that fans at the Baltimore performance would have largely caught the same 20 or so tunes which was customary practice by the *'fast four'* during that period. Indeed, the majority of the songs came from the first two albums but four were chosen from the forthcoming "Rocket To Russia" L.P which would be released in less than a month. Those promoted were "Rockaway Beach", "Cretin Hop", "Sheena Is A Punk Rocker" and the slower paced, melodious "Here Today Gone Tomorrow"

The Ramones would return to Baltimore the following spring with the all-girl rock band *The Runaways* in support and altogether, the band would perform in Maryland on 34 occasions with 23 of these in Baltimore. Five other towns and cities within the state would be visited which were College Park, Ocean City, Saint Mary's City, Columbia and Salisbury. Their last ever gig in the state was at the *Hammerjacks,* a music venue in downtown Baltimore on February 24th, 1996.

One musician who saw The Ramones over a dozen times who is based in Baltimore is drummer Pat Kim. He first met guitar player and singer Chris Hubbard through a mutual friend who was starting a Ramones tribute act but when the mutual friend left, Chris and Pat decided to create their own cover band. After a series of bass players, the pair recruited Mikey Methven on the four string with the trio sharing the vocal duties. It was Kim who came up with the name of *Rockaway Beach Boys* which perfectly describes what they do. The drummer expands stating "we play

Ramones songs as they are recorded but we add *Beach Boys* style, barbershop vocal harmonies to all the songs." Interestingly, all three of the lads perform in another band, *The Beatnik Termites*, except they play different instruments. In *The Termites*, Kim is on guitar, Chris plays bass whilst Mikey plays is on drums and this group remains their focus with The Ramones cover, more of a side-project.

"Rockaway Beach" was of course one of the classic Ramones tracks. Written by Dee Dee, the only beach goer in the band [174], it was the second track on their definitive third album, "Rocket To Russia". The catchy song, on the face of it, conjures up a bright, breezy and optimistic imagery with carefree and joyful recollections of summer fun. However, journalist and founder member of *Punk* magazine, Legs McNeil, reflects that the song is a typical case of The Ramones irony and humour and were "accurately writing and singing about our living conditions." Legs points out that "they were putting it in a kind of *Beach Boys* rock 'n' roll context which is what made it so hilarious." The author tells us that *Rockaway Beach*, which is located in Queens in New York City, in reality "is a sewer." He goes on to add that "the one time I went there with Joey Ramone, there were crowds of vicious girls in bikinis and – I swear – high heels, drinking tallboys of beer out of little brown paper bags, waiting to get into the next fight. Everyone was stoned on Quaaludes and Tuinals, and I witnessed six different fights in half an hour – girls fighting girls, engaged in brutal hair-pulling contests, or running through the sand in their high heels, looking for empty quarts of Budweiser to crack against their opponents' skulls…The real place was never so 'bouncy' and innocent as The Ramones' song and to romanticize such a toilet was akin to writing a ballad about finding true love at Spahn Ranch."[175] But that's what was so cool about it – and revolutionary…Lets take everything crappy and miserable about our lives and celebrate it!" [176]

Founded in 2011, *The Rockaway Beach Boys* usually play small Ramones tribute type shows at 'dive bars'. The band did perform at the *Beer Bacon Music Festival* in Frederick in Maryland but with *the Termites* as their main focus and with the emphasis on having fun with *"Rockaway"*, the fellas are not really trying to expand to play bigger venues. In terms of their set, the lads can pretty much play anything from the first self-titled record through to "Subterranean Jungle". They also chose some select songs off of "Too Tough to Die" and "Animal Boy" but do not play any tunes from the latter material. The band avoid looking like The Ramones so there are no wigs, for instance and as Pat explains "we don't really do the costume thing. However, we pretty much dress like The Ramones in everyday life…well-worn Levis, T-shirt, Perfecto leather jackets and sneakers."

A look on the band's *Facebook page,* immediately de-mystifies the genre of the group. *"We play Ramones songs in the vein of the Beach Boys"* it clarifies and like the famous no nonsense British TV advertisement this statement *does exactly what it says on the tin.* A viewing of their videos gives greater insight, instantly portraying a uniqueness and not merely because there is no traditional front man and only three in the band. Check out, for instance, their acoustic version of "The KKK Took My Baby Away" which is probably the best example of how *The Rockaway Beach Boys* stamp their own individuality on a Ramones classic. Here you will find a barbershop vocal harmony carried out by all three lads reminiscent very much of days gone by. Another song which is perfect for their melodic style is Bobby Freeman's "Do You Wanna Dance?" which unsurprisingly has a 1950s feel and was indeed also covered by arguably a better version by the *Beach Boys* themselves in 1965. One of the most interesting tunes the band take on is "Glad To See You Go". Somehow the band adapt the punk anthem, by slightly slowing it down and harmonising skilfully to create a tune which could be danced to at a high school prom. One just gets a snippet of "Blitzkrieg Bop" which in all honestly doesn't sound too dissimilar to the original whilst "I Wanna Be Sedated", "Judy Is A Punk" and even the solvent abuser's ode of "Carbona Not Glue" has arrangements which emphasises the tight vocal harmony and one which will surely get even grandma bopping along to.

One of the songs which I couldn't find, however, was remarkably "Rockaway Beach". All was not lost though, as a visit on to the social media platform *Youtube,* directs viewers to Mike Love's *Beach Boys* with a special guest – none other than Marky Ramone who temporarily took the drummer's chair.

The show was at the *Paramount* in New York City in 2019 with the performance aimed to help promote their forthcoming album which covered The Ramones ditty. Although Joey's love of *The Beach Boys* as a youngster was well publicised, [177] there does seem something ironic about the Californian outfit, noted for their clean-cut, sleek songs about girls and surfing, paying homage to New York's finest punk rockers.

The *Rockaway Beachboy,* Pat Kim, speaks frankly when discussing the iconic band's legacy. "If The Ramones hadn't existed, the vast majority of bands wouldn't exist today whether they are aware of it or not" the drummer states. "Not only in music but a lot of fashion styles wouldn't prevail either, due to their influence at the start of the punk movement." In this short narrative, it is apparent that their influence has moved away from solely punk based. Old Guard Ramones fans who like to see their tributes as a quartet, in wigs and as close to the original as possible will no doubt shudder at the mere thought of this creativity. With no distorted barre chords, some will feel that you take away the very essence of what made The Ramones special. However, what is abundantly clear, is that their simple melodies, catchy hooks and uncomplicated patterns lends itself to all sorts of styles. Go have a listen, *it's not hard to reach!*

Rockit To Russia
United States Of America

The third album released by The Ramones was "Rocket To Russia". Recorded at the *Mediasound* studio in New York City, in the August and September of 1977, it was released on November 4th of the same year. The band had a considerably larger budget than previously with Sire Records allocating between $25,000 and $30,000 on the production. Though the album cites Tony Bongiovi and Tommy Ramone as the head producers, much of the album's production was done by Ed Stasium. Indeed, according to one music website review, Johnny Ramone went so far as to insist that Bongiovi was "not even there" during the band's recording sessions. [178] Johnny also remembers that it took seven days to record the music and then two days for the vocals. [179]

The album's cover work was directed by John Gillespie, John Holmstrom and Johnny Ramone. In fact, the guitarist states that he sought after a "military theme and playing into my strong anti-communist stance in a cartoonish manner." Johnny goes on to add that he "wanted drawings to represent all the songs on the inside sleeve" and that he "had the concept for the back cover too." Johnny recalls that "I asked for a pinhead riding a rocket over a cartoon map of the world. There were specific details I wanted on the map too, like the Empire State Building for New York, and the Capitol Building for Washington D.C." [180] As a teenager, I personally remember laughing at the various characters dotted around the globe particularly the depiction of the grim-looking monarch located in the United Kingdom and the freakish Count Dracula hovering over Eastern Europe. The celebrated front cover album photograph of the four Ramones, lined up against a wall was fittingly taken outside the back door of the sleazy but popular *CBGB's*. The shot itself was taken by their manager, Danny Fields and has probably become synonymous with the band, at least matching the iconic snap from their debut L.P.

According to John Holmstrom and publisher Ged Dunn, when enthusing about "Rocket To Russia", The Ramones "were a fusion of bubblegum" mixed with "The Stooges/MC5 wall of sound" and that the group "had a special class and intelligence, a simplicity that took sophistication to appreciate…especially when it came to appreciating their sense of humour." [181] This ironic wit is crystallised superbly throughout the album with a number of classic tracks. Dee Dee's wonderful "Rockaway Beach", for instance, has a title and lyrics which draws up romantic images of sun-kissed vacations whereas in reality, although seemingly improving in recent years, still has a tarnished reputation with some. Another authoritative song is "Teenage Lobotomy". For Ramones fans, it has everything – a pounding drum beat followed by bass and guitar intro, crazy lyrics culminating in the screaming chorus which seemingly relishes some frontal lobe surgery. It is full head-on Ramones which would become a necessity at all concerts. Dee Dee's warped sense of humour is shown in full glory as the band's next victim is lying in a bottle of formaldehyde in one of the band's forgotten treasures – How "Why Is It Always This Way?" isn't lauded at the highest level of punk echelons is a mystery to me. Nor was it a song that was even favoured as a live pick. It's superb – if you have not heard it before – it's essential listening. If you are looking for caustic cynicism, then look no further than "We're A Happy Family". Legs McNeil felt it "always seemed to be one of the great rock 'n' roll theme songs establishing why the band happened" likening it to the *Monkees'* signature tune. [(182)] As the relationships within the band deteriorated, particularly between Joey and Johnny, and as other members of the group departed, the irony of this live favourite becomes even more accentuated. The list of prodigious songs goes on – "Cretin Hop", for instance, an ode to those early fans from *CBGBs*, at face value seems hardly an accolade but that's the beauty of this twisted, ludicrous jocularity. Ramones fans would take all this in their stride as a back-handed compliment. If "Blitzkrieg Bop" was the flagship song from their debut album, then Joey's, commercial "Sheena Is A Punk Rocker" would lead the way on "Rocket". Although, it did appear on some issues of the "Leave Home" L.P, due to the removal of "Carbona Not Glue", this is no doubt the definitive version of the song. It was also released as a single and reached number 22 and 81 in the UK singles chart and the USA's Billboard Hot 100 respectively. The "B" side of the 45 also featured on the album – "I Don't Care" was one of the first song's Joey ever penned and one which he had already written before The Ramones had formed. [(183)] Mid-tempo it maybe, but it has a driving bassline and I challenge any fan not to join in with Dee Dee's catchy, ungrammatically correct but just so perfect backing vocals of *"he don't care"*. Another medium paced ditty written by the vocalist was "I Wanna Be Well". According to one critic this "appears to explore a desire for well-being and escape from the challenges and disappointments of life" with the repeated chorus expressing a "strong longing for a state of being that is free from the troubles and burdens experienced by the singer." [184] There were two covers chosen for the album "Do You Wanna Dance?" and "Surfin Bird". Both would be live mainstays with particularly the latter, originally performed by *the Trashmen*, a firm crowd pleaser. Just like "Why Is It Always This Way?", perhaps another overlooked song from the album is "I Can't Give You Anything". Rarely picked as a live choice, I urge fans to have a listen to the tune from Stoke on 29th December, 1977 just a couple of days before their more famous concert at the Rainbow in London with the ditty emphasising their electrifying pace and power. Johnny Ramone felt that "this was the best Ramones album, with the classics on it." He also stated that "the band had reached its peak both in the studio and live." [185] Whilst it is hard to disagree with the guitarist's verdict regarding the live performances, I certainly would not concur about the album itself. Undoubtedly a superb recording but still not quite as good as their debut. Maybe some of the *album fillers* such as "Locket Love", "Ramona" and "Here Today Gone Tomorrow", for instance, are a notch below the level of the less famed tracks on their first.

Despite universal critical acclaim, "Rocket To Russia" failed to make that breakthrough commercially. Legs McNeil felt that this was inadvertently due to *The Sex Pistols* becoming "the quintessential punk rock band in the world" at this time and this "killed any chance "Rocket To Russia" had of getting any airplay." Seymour Stein, President of Sire Records thought that when the album "didn't live up to expectations, The Ramones became somewhat indelibly stamped in everybody's mind... as a cult band that wasn't for everybody. [186] The L.P also signalled the last album which would feature Tommy as drummer although he would continue as co-producer for the next album, "Road To Ruin" and later for their eight album, "Too Tough To Die".

One band who used the album as a title for their own name originate from South Florida in the States. Changing just one letter in their designation, an "e" to an "i", *Rockit To Russia* cleverly plastered their own individual identity whilst still being clearly linked to The Ramones. Formed in 2001, the original line-up consisted of Nicky 'Rockit' as front man with Tommy on drums, Saul playing guitar and Cat as bassist. Over the years, the only constant has been Nicky with many changes on the other positions. For instance, there have been a further two musicians taking up responsibility as stickman – Johnny and Marky whilst five other bass men have performed on the four string – Bobby Reinhardt, Mikey, George, Brett and Bobby BadFollow. On guitar, *Rockit To Russia* has also seen a further four artists take part with Blackkie, Mikey Reinhardt, Vicktor Cuba and Zacky at one point or another. The band was the idea of original Columbian bass player Cathy and singer Nicky sets the scene. "We wanted to play *Black Sabbath* music since I had the voice," he recalls. "It never went anywhere but we built a friendship. One day whilst glancing over an ad for a Ramones tribute band from Tommy, we both called each other at the same time… Next thing we know, we are in a rehearsal studio now called *Musica Turista* on 149th Street in North Miami with the coolest guy on guitar, Saul and the most organized drill sergeant Tommy on Drums. It was a train wreck and it was awesome. We rehearsed for six months every weekend at Saul's home in Coral Gable until we got with *Nasty and Nasty* productions on a tribute Show. We were so in tune and perfect, people on the other side of the bar wall thought it was a live recording of The Ramones."

When asked about unforgettable gigs, Nicky's immediate response was there were "too many. All are memorable." However, when pushed the singer picked out a few which really stood out including one at the *Chili Peppers* club in Fort Lauderdale and two to celebrate Independence day on the Fourth of July. One of these was played on a roof in Fort Lauderdale whilst the other was performed in Miami Beach. Additionally, *Rockit To Russia* opened at the legendary *Churchill's Pub* in Miami for *Independence*, a band managed by Joey Ramone as well as supporting, American punk rocker, Joe Queer. The group also performed in a memorial show for the late Bobby Reinhardt, a cousin of Richie Ramone. During this, there was a live Karaoke with everyone taking it in turns to perform. The evening included *The Stingrays* with *Rockit* sharing the stage with members of the band *Death Becomes You*.

The act's set list would feature all of the usual favourites with some interesting anecdotes thrown in including the fact that rather uniquely they often had a local 14-year old opera singer come on stage to sing before they would go on to perform! Amusingly, Nicky reminisces that guitarist Zak would play Michael Jacksons "Beat it" as we then popped into "Beat on the Brat", baseball bat and all. In addition, "the 'KKK' was sung half Spanish, half English, so we called it *Quen Quen*" whilst the front man ruefully also remembers that they used to give some songs fun names. "We did 'Havana Affair' and 'Commando' transitioned together so we called it 'Have Man Do' he laughs." The group would always start with Ennio Morricone's "The Good, the Bad the Ugly" from the movie directed by Sergio Leone and enter as the trumpets peak with the Iconic "1, 2, 3, 4" before driving into "Durango 95". *Rockit To Russia* would likewise end with the track "R.A.M.O.N.E.S" with Nicky stating that this was "a play on the fact we are a tribute band playing a tribute song to the band we are attributing." The group would invariably play "Wart Hog" and who can argue with Nick's comment "that it is the definitive song for punk rock. It has everything." The band learned the whole of The Ramones' shows from "Live In Italy" in 1990 and the definitive "It's Alive" gig at the *Rainbow Theatre* in London on New Year's Eve, 1977. The group took inspiration not only from The Ramones but also other projects associated the New Yorkers. This might be Joey's solo work, Marky's *Blitzkrieg,* Richie's post Ramones band or even groups such as *U2* who cover classics such as "Beat On The Brat". Similarly, *Rockit* would listen intently to Joey's phrasing in order to mirror them as much as possible - how he drops his jaw and relaxes his words, Dee Dee was Doo Doo. His transitions on "u do know dis¬Beneath your feet Liiiise, the pet cemetery…"

There are some fascinating clips on *Youtube* of the band. Dating back from 2008, you will find *Rockit* live at *Churchill's* blasting out a that *punked up* finale of "R.A.M.O.N.E.S". If you have a little more time, then the 2012 gig at the same venue could be to your liking. Here, the band start off as a trio with the lightning "Durango 95" before the singer climbs the stage and begins the rant of "53rd and 3rd". Bassist Bobby looks like a young C.J, complete with cropped hair, whilst the other three musicians are wigged appropriately in typical Ramone fashion. "Rockaway Beach" is then delivered with "oohs and arghhs" akin to *The Beach Boys* whilst "Blitzkrieg Bob" has a unique introduction with the band stamping their own style over the classic. Even more singular, however, is at the *South Florida Fair* in West Palm Beach where the band perform another definitive tune aided by *Zippy,* their own personal "Pinhead". All in all, *Rockit To Russia* are an extremely interesting band and well worth exploring – conveying the songs we know and love but in a manner which is not entirely in a copycat fashion.

In 2018, the band decided to break up with a hectic work and family life schedule meaning the time needed for the group was difficult. Nonetheless, Nicky is quite forthcoming with his views on the punk icons stating that "The Ramones are the top five most influential bands in history - *U2, Metallica*, etc have a debt to them." The front man also talks about how they influenced him admitting that they "saved my life, music saved my soul. To be able to play music is scary", he feels. "You would hear *Led Zeppelin* and say, "No way!!" and stop. But, when you heard The Ramones take what *the Kinks* started and make it obtainable. We saw bands emerge, influenced by the simplicity of Johnny's chords, like a Chuck Berry in overdrive. Joey singing like *the Ronettes.* Dee Dee's writings. You could tell which song was Dee Dee's and which was Joey's, one was about lobotomy and one was love. I'm happy I did this. The Ramones… well, they are in the hands of every child picking up a guitar with their dad." Indeed, just like Nicky Rockit, hopefully, there will be a few more boys or girls inspired enough to blast off!

Carbona Not Glue
Scotland

In terms of longevity, one of the oldest serving groups originates from Scotland - *Carbona Not Glue* - who have been blasting out Ramones classics from as early as 1995. Indeed, this band of brothers actually formed a year or so before the boys from Forest Hill High School officially hung up their leather jackets and headed off into the sunset for that much earned retirement. Originating from Leith within the city of Edinburgh, the group started life covering a mixture of Ramones and *Undertones* songs but soon narrowed their set down and removed the material from the Northern Irish band. The name of the group stems from the infamous fifth track from the "Leave Home" L.P released early in 1977. At that time, there was somewhat of a mystique about this song as many fans would not have necessarily had a chance to have heard the melody. This was because the company that manufactured *Carbona* did not want their stain-remover product to be associated with the glue sniffing fad which was prevalent at the time. With potential legal action threatened, Sire Records made the decision to withdraw the tune from the original album. Consequently, therefore, there would be three versions of the L.P. As well as the first cut, the tune was replaced with "Sheena Is A Punk Rocker" on the American re-pressings whilst this side of the Atlantic got treated to the sweeter-sounding "Babysitter". *Carbona Not Glue* was undoubtedly a great choice of name for the band, however, as aficionados would immediately associate the group with The Ramones.

Although The Ramones performed in Scotland 16 times, most of these had been centred in Glasgow rather than in the capital, Edinburgh where they played on just five occasions. Edinburgh is steeped in history, the seat of the Scottish Government and Parliament and was recognised as the capital since at least the 15th century. The city is the second largest in Scotland and the seventh in the United Kingdom with a population of just over 526,000. The band's first gig in the city was on December 18th, 1977 after they had just performed the evening before in Carlisle, a city in Cumbria just south of the border in England. The chosen location was at that time known as *The Clouds* in Tollcross which is a major road junction in the south west of Edinburgh. The club hosted hugely famous acts in the 1970s and '80s including *Pink Floyd, The Jam* and punk legends *The Clash* so it was the common-sense selection when The Ramones hit town. The venue has had a number of different monikers being also known as *Coasters* or *The Cavendish Ballroom*. Previously it had been a popular dancehall since the forties and in its time was also known as *Outer Limits, Bermuda Triangle*, and *The Network*. Supported by the offbeat locals *The Rezillos,* the gig has been cited in *The Scotsman* as one of the all-time Edinburgh's legendary concerts with one patron reminiscing that it was "the best gig I went to… £2 to get in… *The Rezillos* were great and went down a storm and then The Ramones were superb. They got three encores and played 13 songs." [(187)] Although there is no documentation of the set that night, this was part of the "Rocket To Russia" tour so tracks would be solely focussed from the first three albums. It is also worth noting that in just under two weeks they would perhaps perform their most famous concert of their career at the *Rainbow Theatre* in London under the flag now known as "It's Alive".

The Ramones would return to the capital of Scotland four more times between 1978 and 1986 gracing the stage at the *University of Edinburgh, The Odeon Theatre* and twice at the *Edinburgh Playhouse*. One fan who witnessed the band at the *Playhouse* in both 1980 and 1986 was guitarist, Robin Woods. It was Robin who helped form *Carbona Not Glue* back in 1995 along with three other enthusiasts which saw David Hall take the mic, Simon Kettles on bass and Calvin Burt behind the drum kit. Three of the lads, have gained experience in other bands with Robin, for instance in *Vatican Shotgun Scare*, a late 1980s punk band and *Salt*, a post punk band which is still performing today. Bass man Simon played in '80s pop band *The Ruby Suit* whilst Calvin has drummed with the *Thanes, The Off hooks, The No Things* and *The Hook 'n' Pull Gang*.

Over the 28 years or so *Carbona* have tried nearly 60 songs including Joey's solo release "What A Wonderful World". A look at their set list is a collection of Ramones masterpieces and it is great to see some of the more overlooked diamonds given an airing. Examples include "I Don't Wanna Go Down To The Basement", "Why Is It Always This Way?" "Zero Zero UFO", "Life's A Gas" and even the demos "Slug" and "Yea Yea" which eventually showed up on the "Rocket To Russia" and "Road To Ruin" remastered releases respectively.

There have been many memorable gigs over the years but one Robin particularly remembers was at the *Tap O' Lauriston*, a famous punk venue in the heart of Edinburgh. Opening for a festival, the audience was split between a bunch of old punks and 'office types' who liked The Ramones. "A pint was knocked over and an ensuing fight broke out. We played through it, ironically the song was 'Beat on the Brat'", Robin drolly recalls.

The guitarist also points out that "we recently played a mini tour with *Teenage Werewolves*, a *Cramps* tribute band, playing bigger venues with the band continuing to go down well. The group has a backdrop, made over 25 years ago and painted by John Burgess, an artist from Seaton Sluice in Northumberland in England. With its subtle joke and aptly publicised "Leith Home" proudly centralised, it is still being used despite many a theft attempt at their gigs.

Carbona have had the pleasure to meet C.J Ramone at his solo concert at the *Opium* in Edinburgh in 2017. The band presented the bassist with their own T-shirt gift and just like any good humoured Scot, Robin isn't shy about being careful with the cash claiming that the merchandise provides the band with "a good, wee bit of revenue." The guitarist also has the delight in owning a signed Mosrite by Johnny Ramone, number 3/30 which he acquired from a company in California for £1,200. Robin states that the guitar is surprisingly light in weight and tells the story how once after a gig in the Scottish countryside, he "placed it safely in a tree whilst loading the van!"

A swift probe onto social media, shows numerous *Carbona Not Glue* performances. If you wish to have an instant introduction to the band then check out Lemmy Kilmister's parting gift to *Da Brudders* and *Carbona's* great encore song "R.A.M.O.N.E.S", live at *Leith Depot*. Alternatively, explore the even better "Chinese Rock" starring Calvin, the impressive silhouetted drummer, whose shadowy figure would be equally at home in a Hitchcock movie as he is with the sticks. If you have more time, then a stroll down memory lane back to 1998 at the Edinburgh *Ross Bandstand* on Princess Street is a must. Not only will you discover five Ramones prize pieces of work including a superb version of "Let's Dance" but you will also find Robin, in shades, looking not dissimilar to Dee Dee circa 1984 off "Too Tough To Die." If you wish to see a more up to date performance, then their recent summer performance of 2023 could be for you. Although traditionalists be warned – our guitarist, Robin shouts the "1, 2, 3, 4s" rather than the bassist Simon whilst our two guitar players are each found on the uncustomary side of our wigged vocalist David. To counter that, it must be said that early footage at *CBGBs* in 1974 of The Ramones depicts Johnny, for instance to Joey's left rather than his accustomed stance to the singer's right. The one overriding element to *Carbona's* performances is that there is no doubt that they *feel* the songs. They *get* it. They *live* it. Playing Ramones is their therapy as long as their brains are, of course, not stuck from shooting glue.

Gabba
England

Guaranteed to put a smile on your face, our next band had the art of the 'mash up' down to a tee with their unique blend of power punk music. Performing the Swedish pop super group *Abba*'s famous hits but in the stripped down, razor sharp style of The Ramones, *Gabba* certainly left their mark creating their own self-coined *discopunk* brand of chaos. Claiming to be sweeter than the Swedes and faster than the Americans, one thing is for certain, whether you are a fan of Benny or an admirer of Dee Dee, this bunch of jesters will brighten up your day.

The origins of the band were the brainchild of Cliff Homow. In 1988, Cliff had the idea of fusing *Abba* with The Ramones and asked ex school-friend Jon Lebar to consider being the singer. Indeed, Cliff explains how he came about with the idea of the hybrid-band. "I was fascinated by the similarities and differences between *Abba* and Ramones songs and styles and realised that they were actually incredibly similar, one highly embellished, the other stripped right back. Plus, I loved The Ramones! I think their influence is massive and speaks for itself, both musically and stylistically." Interestingly, Cliff only saw the New Yorkers once but what an occasion he picked as it was the famous New Year's Eve gig at the Rainbow on December 31, 1977, which was recorded and became the 'It's Alive' album. "It was amazing", he recalls. "My ears were ringing for hours and I never wanted to see them again, fearing that it would ruin my memory of that night!"

Just before the turn of the century, Jon agreed to sing and whilst Cliff never played in the band himself, except as guitarist on some early demos, Stig Honda as he was coined, would be instrumental in terms of writing 'original' lyrics, and managing the group. Incidentally, Cliff's stage name was taken as a spoof from Stig Anderson, best known as a lyricist, music publisher and as manager for *Abba*. Cliff also brought in Alan Way as part of the project. The two had met at Brighton Polytechnic, in Sussex and had been in an art school cabaret band called *Little Green Hondas* between 1984 and 1988. Cliff persuaded Alan to join as producer taking the name Phil Smegma, a play on the famous "End Of The Century" producer, Phil Spector. The original line-up started taking shape in 1999 with the band mostly rehearsing at *the Survival Studios* in Acton, West London. Advertising in NME for musicians, Cliff met bassist Jimmy Lacey who coincidentally had been at the same school as Cliff and Jon albeit much later. Vocalist, Camilla Engdahl, was introduced to Cliff by a mutual friend with whom she worked whilst guitarist Edmund (Ed) Dudley met through Cliff's ex-girlfriend with whom he worked, and they had recorded a few musical pieces together. The last piece of the jig-saw saw drummer, Jerome Bisgambiglia join the band who was friends with singer, Jon. It was Cliff, or should I say Stig, who chose the name for the band with *Gabba* the perfect designation. "I chose the name *Gabba*, the manager points out, "because it's integral to the concept of the band, *Abba* in the style of The Ramones." Of course, the band would have to take on pen-names and indeed take on the personalities of the fusion of band members. This would be done acrostically with each first name the initials of the word G.A.B.B.A. Hence:

- Geeky - guitar
- Anneky – lead vocals
- Bjöey - lead vocals
- Bee Bee - bass, vocals
- Abby - drums, vocals

Bjöey and Bee Bee were the only constants over the years and the band experienced a number of personnel changes but rather than change their monikers, new musicians would simply step into their ready-made names. *Gabba*, for instance, would see Charlotte Owens soon take over as Anneky in 2000 and Tiffeny Walsh become the third female vocalist in 2006. Two further guitarists would take the role of Geeky with Mik Stanger, active between 2002-2004 and he in turn replaced by Mattias Hedenborg in the last couple of years of the band's existence. On the drums, three other stick men assumed the moniker of Abby with Alan (Pilly) Pilsworth, Reiner Cole and Tommy Shotton all performing on the drummer's stool for various lengths of service. As with many of our tributes, *Gabba* adopted the famous Ramones logo with their pseudonyms around the circular edge along with a couple of other noticeable differences – firstly, the Swedish flag, the yellow cross on a blue background was centralised replacing the red, white and blue of the United States and secondly, rather than the having the words "Hey, Ho, Let's Go" above the eagle's head, this was switched amusingly to *Gabba's* own catchphrase – none other than "Hey, Ho, Disco!"

In order to get a taste for the band, a great starting point would be their much celebrated album, "Leave Stockholm". Released in 1999 on Stigma Records, just a look at the C.D cover is enough to get any *cretin* chuckling with Bjöey towering over his geeky bandmates which of course includes blonde glam-dressed and booted, Anneky. The parody is there for all to see but make no mistake the record is not just a gimmick and the tracks are top drawer – Driving

guitars, crashing cymbals, catchy hooks and after a couple of plays, I guarantee you will be singing along to those well-loved ditties. Much of the fun is that *Gabba* cleverly merge the two bands - taking "Mama Mia", as an example, the tune is based on the *Abba* classic but not only is the pace and power fully akin to the New Yorkers, it also somehow manages to incorporate aspects of The Ramones songs "Cretin Hop", Commando", "53rd and 3rd" and "We're A Happy Family" to boot. Stig undoubtedly deserves much credit here with the amalgamation of some of the favourites into their own original arrangements in tracks such as "The Pinhead Takes It All", "Gabba Gabba", "Hej Ho, Disco" and "Super Shock Trooper". My personal preference, however, has to be "Gimme Gimme Gimme (Shock Treatment At Midnite)" which has an opening riff, every bit as catchy as some of *Da Brudders'*. For those of you who enjoy tunes covered in their entirety then you will not be disappointed – *Abba's* "Waterloo" and "So Long" as well as The Ramones' "Rockaway Beach" are on offer with the latter, the final track of the album. It is also refreshing how the band alternate the vocal duties between the male and female singers and all in all, "Leave Stockholm" is a must for all Ramones fans.

The band played around 25 gigs all told and at their second at the *Grosvenor* in Brixton, the group was *spotted* by DJ Steve Lamacq who subsequently asked them to do their next show, broadcasted live on BBC Radio from *Maida Vale Studios* for his evening session. A search on their *Facebook* page or on *Youtube* will see a host of their material. Try out their Brighton concert, for instance and "Knowing Me Knowing You" (later adapted to "Knowing Me Sniffing Glue") where you will see the peculiar sight of two blondes up front - Not only does Anneky strut her stuff centre stage but Geeky appears more like Björn than Johnny with his mop of golden hair as he blasts out his buzztone guitar. As if to maintain the status quo, at the back, however, dark haired, Abby, keeps time immaculately, all so reminiscent of Tommy, whilst Bee Bee is a live-wire of tricks, head nodding and restless in his stars and stripes T-Shirt looking like he had just been dragged from the corner of 53rd and 3rd. Next to Anneky, hangs the hovering creature which is Bjöey, perched like that famed Ramones eagle, he not only looks like Jeffrey Hyman but also scoffs out the words in that same duteous fashion. If you wish to examine a different gig, then check out the Brixton show and the tracks "Ring Ring", "SOS" and "Fernando". More to my liking is the *discopunk* anthem "Hej Ho, Disco" where the guys really ham it up, naturally in the best possible taste and of course, with the emphasis on fun.

Stig won the *Portobello Film Festival 2002 Special Independent Film Award* for the *Gabba* film, "Gimme Gimme Gimme Shock Treatment at Midnite". In the video, which is posted on *Youtube,* it depicts the hideous hybrid of the band emerging from the laboratory from the remains of the bones of *Abba* and The Ramones. Again, it is great entertainment and well worth searching up. By 2007, *Gabba* decided to call a halt to proceedings with Stig being quite frank about why they packed up stating that it "became too much work trying to find the right people for a non-commercial concept band. It is still my belief that *Gabba* could have become a franchise and that there could have been a *Gabba* in every continent. I did notice that a band in Sweden started using our name and our concept a few years ago", he reflects. Nonetheless, there is no doubt that those *'mashed up'* crossbreed musicians gave us some great memories and it only seems right to give them a proper thank you and farewell. Or maybe more appropriately as *Abba* and indeed *Gabba* would say, *so long*!

Ramoanz
England

"Hey, we're The Ramones, this one's called Rockaway Beach". This emphatic declaration, barked out by Joey Ramone at the *Rainbow Theatre* on New Year's Eve 1977 captured the anticipation of all those who were lucky enough to witness any concert by *Da Brudders*. Yet, we all knew there was better to come. Enter the bundle of energy hovering to Joey's left. In an instant, the "1, 2, 3, 4" was bellowed out from the greatest punk bassist of them all. Dee Dee's famous count drew Tommy's crashing symbol and Johnny's grinding guitar right on cue and so the assault on your senses began.

"It's Alive" was the first live album released by The Ramones taking its title from the 1974 horror film of the same name. It was recorded in Finsbury Park, London on the last day of December in 1977 although not released, until April 1979. Produced by Tommy Erdélyi, aka Tommy Ramone and Ed Stasium, the album consists of tunes solely from the first three L.Ps. The build-up to what many describe as the ultimate punk live album, can be traced back to more than a year earlier. In 1976, the New Yorkers had performed at London's *Roundhouse* and *Dingwalls* on July 4th and 5th to enthusiastic crowds and often cited as the springboard of punk in the country. From April 24-June 6, 1977, they undertook a gruelling six-week tour which included most of Europe and the U.K. so by the time they returned to Britain in the December of 1977, this was their third visit to the country and were performing to extremely receptive audiences. During the tour, Ed recalls that "we recorded a shitload of shows in England. We recorded Manchester, Stoke-on-Trent, Aylesbury and others… We used the Island Records mobile truck, which had been used by the Stones and Zeppelin and had a Helios console." [188] The producer also recites that "I travelled with the band and road manager Monte A. Melnick on the 'tour' bus, which was not anything like the luxury liners that one sees today. This bus was more of a coach with large windows and rows of seats. It wasn't mentioned, but I immediately noticed that the practice of having "assigned seats" was mandatory on this trip. Dee Dee's allocated area was right across from mine, and he kept himself well entertained with a stack of Scandinavian pornography (the likes of which I had never seen) and his knife collection. Apart from Dee Dee enjoying his switchblade stockpile, Johnny, Joey, and Tommy did not seem to have an interest in any hobbies; they would sleep, read magazines, and gaze out of the huge windows at the English countryside, probably dreaming of being back in the States. It was apparent that they were seeing the light at the end of the tunnel, and the tension of a lonely Christmas away from home would add a peculiar energy to the shows that would transpire over the next few days. The first three dates we recorded were in clubs. Nothing special. The Ramones, the Basing Street Mobile crew, and myself looked at these shows as a run-through for the recording of the New Year's Eve gig. The band was performing virtually the same set every night, honing the tunes and playing tighter and tighter, with military precision." [189]

The chosen venue for their last concert of the tour was in London with the band supported by *The Rezillos* and *Generation X*. Previously known as the *Finsbury Park Astoria, Finsbury*

Park Paramount Astoria and then the *Finsbury Park Odeon, The Rainbow Theatre* as it is now known, was built in 1930 and is a grade II listed building. Before its use as a music venue, it had been a cinema and maybe surprisingly is now used as an Evangelical church. There is no doubt that the establishment impressed the travelling Americans with Ed Stasium reminiscing that "in the '60s, rock concerts began taking place at the venue, when it was named *The Finsbury Astoria*. On March 31, 1967, Jimi Hendrix poured lighter fluid onto his Fender Stratocaster and lighted it on fire for the first time, changing the dynamics of live 'Rock & Roll' forever. In the '70s, the venue was renamed *The Rainbow Theatre*, and on November 4, 1971, The Who was the first artist to perform a concert under the new moniker. Tonight it was The Ramones' turn. When Joey, Johnny, Dee Dee, and Tommy arrived for sound check, they looked around in amazement, a big wow written all over their faces. According to Monte, they had never played in such a large hall before. This was a beautiful theatre with a capacity of approximately 3,000 and a foyer with a dang fountain in it! At this juncture, the group had played only small clubs and theatres; this evening, *the Rainbow* would be filled with several thousand Ramones fans." [190]

From the opener of "Rockaway Beach" to the finale of "We're A Happy Family" there is not a duff song amongst the 28 on offer which was blasted out in just under 54 minutes. Drummer, Tommy remembered that to add to the atmosphere, because "it was New Year's Eve, our management brought in some balloons and gave everybody these 'Gabba Gabba Hey' signs to wave around. It was very celebratory. Johnny Thunders was there, and Sid Vicious with his new girlfriend, Nancy Spungen. Elton John was there, dressed up like Marlon Brando in The Wild

One. We'd honed our craft really sharp by then. The Ramones' sound was basically the essence of rock 'n' roll. That's what we were going for." [191] As well as the audio L.P, there still exists video footage of half of the concert and for any fan who has not seen it, then it is essential viewing. Take a look, for instance, at "Pinhead" to get a feel for the evening. The Ramones are quite simply at their live peak with both Dee Dee and Johnny tearing up the stage with their energy and constant movements. Talking of tearing up, then the wild and hysterical audience can be seen smashing and throwing seats, presumably to enable pogoing, as early as the song "Listen To My Heart". According to one website, the first 10 rows were damaged. [192] Producer Ed, remembers the atmosphere of the night. "The din in the hall was overwhelming, not so much for us out in the truck, because I had the audience microphones muted in my monitor mix, so that I could carefully listen to the sound of the close microphones. In the cold London night outside of the truck, you could practically feel the electricity in the air as The Ramones were about to claim their throne." [193]

It has been said that the live recording was not as 'pure' as some might believe with a lot of studio work thrown in. Indeed, although Marky Ramone had not joined the band at this time, the future drummer pointed out that he heard that "It's Alive" was redone in the studio. "You keep the drum track, the stick man points out "and then Joey and Dee Dee and Johnny did it over in the studio". [194]

In 2019, a 40th anniversary re-release was produced which included four shows of that UK tour in December 1977. In addition to the London show, the concerts at *Top Rank*, Birmingham on December 28th, *Victoria Hall* in Stoke-on-Trent on December 29th and at *Friars* in Aylesbury are part of the package. There were just a few differences in the track listings with "I Can't Give You Anything", for example played twice and "Judy Is A Punk" only played at *The Rainbow* and "Havana Affair" discarded in Birmingham and Stoke.

The album has been universally acclaimed by critics and fans alike. Joe Marchese, for instance, when reviewing the 40th Anniversary Edition describe the four concerts as a "jolt of pure adrenaline and gleeful punk furore" going on to add that it "is a definitive document of one of rock's great live albums." [195] In a joint collaborative review during the Covid-19 outbreak and subsequent lockdowns, Amorosi, Aswad, Barker, Tangcay, Trakin and Willman pick "It's Alive" as one of 50 live albums "so good, you may find yourself wanting to quarantine with them even after concerts resume again." [196] Critic Mark Deming is even more praising stating that "it's not only the best Ramones live album, it's one of the best and most effective albums in the rock canon. [197] In 2005, the L.P was ranked 279th in *Rock Hard* magazine's book of "The 500 Greatest Rock and Metal Albums of All Time." [198]

For many Ramones and punk fans alike, "It's Alive" was almost like a *mantra,* a rallying cry signalling how a live set should be played. One such band, which formed in 2023 are the *Ramoanz,* who if in any doubt about the tempo of their songs, refer back to that seminal live album aiming to replicate the "It's Alive" pace rather than the studio cuts or later albums such as "Loco Live". "I first heard about the group roughly at the time they performed "It's Alive" and my first concert was in 1980, co-incidentally also at *The Rainbow",* front man Mark Leadon points out. "I went on to see them in London on every tour subsequently, right up to their last show in Britain in Brixton in 1996. Make no mistake, they were quite easily the best band I have ever seen live particularly in their younger days with Dee Dee's energy breath-taking. I always felt that The Ramones lost something at the end of their career when they went into that warp speed mode. There is no doubt in my mind that Joey's vocals suffered in terms of it being difficult for him to phrase appropriately as did Johnny's ability to nail every note with his downstroking technique. Don't get me wrong, they were still awesome but probably peaked at that 'It's Alive' period."

Based around the Greater London area, the band's formation was a lengthy process. Initially it was linked to an idea of bassist Peter Revesz, who wanted to create another cover group after his established tribute *53rd and 3rd* decided to call it a day. Pete asked Mark to join his new act and with two other friends were about to gig under the title of *Gabba Gabba Oi* when tragedy struck – Pete died and effectively the idea of this band ended too. Six months or so later, however, Mark decided to try again, simply because of his love of The Ramones. After a number of potential musicians initially responded to on-line requests, four *old school punks* hit it off and started rehearsing regularly at *Sanctuary Studios* in Watford in Hertfordshire. On the bass is Ken Spearpoint who had previously performed in punk bands *Holocaust F, Sulphate, Graffiti Nightmare*, the '60s garage band *St John's Wood Affair* and is currently still playing in the *Dicemen*, an indie-folk band which he has served for 13 years. Sitting on the drumming stool, is Beana Burns who has had a vast amount of experience in an array of bands including *The Act, Image, Mr Breeze, The Tantrums, Bad Habits, Fury Of The Hand, Snide* and *Blind Panic.* The quartet is made up of Greg Simpson who answered Beana's Ramones advertisement on a music website and as he wryly points out joined the project because he wanted to "thrash chords to my heart's content". Greg has played guitar for the Midlands based punk group *Anti-Climax* and the Essex cover band *Bad Cadillacs*. Interestingly, Greg was born in Ferryhill in County Durham and went to the same school as Pauline Murray, Gary Chaplin and Robert Blamire, the founding members of the punk group, *Penetration*, probably most famed for their 1977 debut single, "Don't Dictate". Indeed, the guitarist was family friends with both the Murrays and Chaplins with Greg referring to *Penetration* as a huge influence which "really changed my music preferences towards punk as a 14-year-old."

The name of the group was the idea of drummer Beana with the lads wanting to get a designation as similar as possible to the original so as there was an immediate link between themselves and The Ramones. Shortly after, and as with many of our tributes, the group adopted the famous Ramones' eagle logo with their own names around the perimeter to cement another link with the New Yorkers and used this emblem as a backdrop at their gigs. The stick man was also heavily involved in posting links on social media and put out a variety of the songs on various platforms even before the group played gigs. The band established their own style and incredibly, the *Ramoanz* swiftly became somewhat of an internet sensation with literally thousands of hits amassed on *Youtube* and *Tic Toc* – take a look for instance at "I Don't Wanna Go Down To The Basement" or "Rockaway Beach" to not only get a feel for their style but also to get an awareness of their on-line following. The quartet did not want to go down the copy-cat, wig wearing, clone route with Mark explaining that "this has already been done by so many bands with various degrees of success whilst we wanted to stamp our own authority on those wonderful Ramones songs. My music roots are certainly punk-based so we try to add a little of that 1976/1977 British punk sound. At every opportunity we try to *punk it up.*"

Their debut concert was on December 10th, 2023 at the *Fiddlers' Elbow* in Camden, North London. Their set list comprised much of "It's Alive" and naturally focussed on the early favourites. However, as well as the *must play* gems including "Blitzkrieg

Bop", "Pinhead" and "Cretin Hop", the band wanted to ensure that there were always some of the often discarded jewels in the repertoire so tracks such as "Loudmouth" and "Why Is It Always This Way?" were given an airing. The group also used "It's Alive" as a basis of the order of their set-list having similar runs of songs – "I Don't Care, "Sheena", "Havana Affair" and "Commando", a prime example. The band's performance at the gig earned rave reviews with music critic Amelia Vandergast rich in her praise for the boys stating that "London's premier Ramones cover band, *Ramoanz,* is bringing a brand-new energy to the punk legacy, as evidenced by their recent performance." The on-line author goes on to add that the "Ramones may have spoken to the disfranchised youth, but the four old-school punks who grew up listening to the three-chord structures of the NY-hailing antagonistic visionaries are extending the conversation to every generation while proving that the music is as timeless as the taste for rebellion. By keeping pace with the frenetic rhythms with razor-sharp precision and putting visceral oi punk-esque volition behind the vocals, *Ramoanz* aren't just paying homage to their idols, they're starting their own revolution in the UK." [199]

Soon after, due to the success on social media, the band was invited to play a 30-minute session on *Tic Toc* live from the studio with 15 songs blasted out in the allotted time. Gigs followed at *The Ship* in Aveley and subsequently they supported the cover band *Six Little Fingers* at *Duffy's Bar* in Leicester which Beana particularly enjoyed because of the "audience interaction." The concert at *Duffy's* was also the first where the band adapted The Ramones' classic "Sheena Is A Punk Rocker" fittingly modified to "Beana" in the last verse. "It might be corny", bass man Ken points out, "but it gets a laugh!"

The Ramoanz made a conscious decision to expand the setlist and take in some of the songs from the fourth album onwards although would keep to that "It's Alive" tempo guideline. The new tracks included "I'm Against It" and "I Wanna Be Sedated" from "Road To Ruin", "All The Way" and "Chinese Rock" from "End Of The Century", plus "Danger Zone" from "Too Tough To Die". The lads also decided, maybe against convention, to play a non-Ramones classic – "White Riot" by *The Clash*, just simply because they love the song. The group will always be a Ramones tribute, first and foremost but they have not ruled out maybe adding one or two of the more well-known punk definite tracks. Stay tuned for a couple from the English punk elite from *The Damned, Stranglers, Pistols* or *UK Subs.*

The fellas all cite their favourite shows as the ones at *The Dublin Castle* in Camden in north London. After playing there in February 2024, the boys went down so well that they were invited back for another concert shortly after. That additional gig was billed as a celebration of the 50th anniversary of The Ramones' first show at *Performance Studios* and it was fitting that there were some stalwarts from the British Ramones' tribute scene also able to join in the festivities. Andy Johnson (Shamones), Richie Goring (53rd and 3rd) and Lee Drury (Erazerhead) all guested for one song to make it a particularly memorable occasion.

The future looks promising for the band. Not only has their fan base grown but they also have a number of prestigious gigs lined up including the Dorking festival, an event to herald the 75th anniversary of the Harley Davidson Riders Club of Great Britain at the *Ace Café* and a show in Blackpool during *Rebellion* week. What is abundantly clear is that fresh groups such as *The Ramoanz* are continuing to emerge, ensuring that the

New Yorkers legacy is maintained and their music remembered. Indeed, although that *Rainbow* gig may have taken place nearly 50 years ago, our tribute certainly ensures *it's still alive.*

Morones
United States Of America

By the time The Ramones journeyed down to Florida they had already released three ground-breaking albums, moulded a unique minimalistic music style and taken Europe by storm helping to galvanise punk rock as we know it. So the visit to the Sunshine State was for many long overdue when they toured the area in the spring of 1978. Florida is located in the south eastern region of the United States and bordered by Georgia and Alabama. It is the only state that has coasts on both the Gulf of Mexico and the Atlantic Ocean and is just 450 miles away from Communist Cuba. With a population of over 21 million, Florida's major cities include Jacksonville, Tampa Bay, Cape Coral, Tallahassee, Miami and Orlando. Indeed, it was in Orlando at *The Great Southern Music Hall* on March 2nd that The Ramones would play their first show in the state. The building was built in 1921 and at that time was known as the *Beacham Theatre* named after a Mayor of Orlando who commissioned the build. The Theatre played an important role as an entertainment centre and served as a gathering spot for movie-goers, music lovers and performers alike. In the 1970s, the theatre suffered both from disrepair and declining audiences, symptomatic of the urban decay which plagued the Orlando area at that time and the venue was sold. The new owners re-named the site *The Great Southern Music Hall* in 1976 which could seat 700 fans, ushering in a new era of live performances ranging from laser light shows, dinner theatres and live musical acts. Ray Charles,

Devo, Judas Priest and Robert Palmer are just a few examples of performers who have made appearances at the setting. After a number of name changes, since 2011 the theatre is now known simply as *The Beacham* and features disc jockey acts as well as playing the "top 40", Hip hop, Latin music and Reggaeton. [200]

The Ramones played one night in Orlando before moving southwards with a 235 mile hike down to Miami. The next venue was at the *Gusman Cultural Centre* and concert goers were in for a double helping of goodies as the support act was *The Runaways*, the all-female rock band, probably best known for the provocative single "Cherry Bomb". Gratefully, The Ramones set list was recorded for posterity that evening. As expected the selection of songs derived in the main from the first three albums of the self-titled "Ramones", "Leave Home" and "Rocket To Russia". We are treated to such trinkets as "Listen To My Heart" "We're A Happy Family" and the slower paced "Here Today, Gone Tomorrow". Interestingly, there was one track, "I Just Wanna Have Something To Do", thrown in off the forthcoming "Road To Ruin" L.P which was released in September of that year. The album would be the first to credit new drummer Marky and in essence, after the two Florida concerts, Tommy would have just a couple of months left in the band. Remarkably, Tommy actually worked on that fourth album as he explains "everything was working fine and then the last day they cut me out. We worked on 'Road To Ruin' for a long time: several months. I put a lot of work into those songs and was supposed to get a quarter-share of the song writing. On the very last day, John came to me and said, 'You're not going to get the publishing.' Their excuse was that I was going to get production royalties. I got some, but not much." [201] In fact, the original cover for the album which was drawn by Gus MacDonald featured Tommy in the picture.

After the line-up change, John Holmstrom was brought in to alter the image and include the new stick man. [202]

By the time The Ramones retired they had played over 40 concerts in Florida expanding their influence and increasing the chances of new fans witnessing them. Other locations were included such as Gainesville, Tampa, Hallendale, St Petersburg, West Palm Beach, Destin, Tallabassee, Coco Beach, Miami Beach, Jacksonville, Melbourne, Fort Lauderdale and Panama City Beach. Their last concert in the Sunshine State took place on July 18th, 1996 at the *Coral Sky Amphitheatre, South Florida Fairgrounds* in West Palm Beach.

Although they were not fortunate enough to see The Ramones live, four musicians were suitably enthused by the band to form their own tribute. Originating from Orlando, the same city as the New Yorkers made their debut gig in Florida, the *Morones* were formed in 2022. Indeed, the fact that tribute bands are still forming over a quarter of a century after The Ramones last ever performance puts into context just how significant the boys from Queens still are today. The band started as members of other punk cover bands and all professional musicians with years of gigging, touring and recording experience across many rock genres. Whilst on tour, the singer and bassist came up with the idea and the band name and started building a set list on *Spotify* which kept growing and growing. The boys took stage names, as is customary, with Joey, Johnny, Dee Dee and Tommy Morone taking up the mantle. When the drummer left on good terms for another project, up stepped a new man with the drum sticks and Richie joined the party. Singer Joey describes the choice of name for the band. At the time "we had a couple of ideas", he recalls. "One was the *Class of '74* and one was the *Marones* but at the time we were playing with a *Green Day* tribute called *American Idiots,* so we thought idiots and morons was funny" and it evolved. The vocalist expands into further detail why the band was created. "First and foremost", he states, "we love The Ramones" but also points out some of the logistical useful pointers. "We play in other tributes so we know the venues, the bookers, the other bands in the scene. Ramones is one of those bands that, while never a huge commercial success in the US, there is a broad fan base. There are only a couple others doing this in the US and none are in Florida, so it made sense for us to start one up. We try really hard to do it justice because we're huge fans." The singer also points to The Ramones' influence feeling that it is "undeniable." Joey utters "you hear it in everything from their peers they influenced in the '70s and '80s, to *Nirvana, Green Day,* and even the Pop Punk bands of the '00s. One of the things we love about Ramones is their passion for straight up rock n roll - stripping away the glitz and corporate look, getting back to the simple but effective musical approach of '50s and '60s rock with gritty production and in-your-face live performance."

In order to prepare for the *Morones* gigs, the group vigorously consumed the live footage from the New Yorkers over the years. Joey again stating that "the ones that stand out are *the Rainbow Theatre* '77 (aka It's Alive), Don Kirshner's Rock Concert '77, and *Winterland* in San Francisco in '78. The pure energy in these shows is just amazing. Not to mention, this period is arguably the best they ever sounded live. Later live performances were cool too – the *US Fest,* all the way up to *Lollapalooza* with a different vibe, but I love to watch Johnny and Dee Dee or C.J moving in unison downstage." The band play up to 90 minutes if headlining, 60 minutes if co-headlining, possibly less if it is a festival or multi-band gig. The group rotate the tunes in the set to keep it pristine but will always perform the crowd pleasers such as "Blitzkrieg Bop", "I Wanna Be Sedated", "Sheena" and "Lobotomy". "As a relatively new project", Joey clarifies that "we haven't played any massive shows at this time, but no question our favourite to date is *Tuffy's Music Box* in Sanford in Florida because it's a great stage and sound system."

For a perusal of the band, a good induction is on their *Facebook* page which posts videos of their shows. The boys, attired in wigs, black leathers, jeans and plimsolls, appear as if they have recently ascended from a damp, slimy sewer from the darkest depths of downtown Orlando. Musically they are tight and melodic with their style particularly akin to the rockier Ramones numbers of "Poison Heart", "I Believe In Miracles", "I Don't Wanna Grow Up" and the "KKK Took My Baby Away". It is also amusing that there is a use of props so watch out for the accessories such as the "Pinhead" mask, "Gabba Gabba Hey" signs and an inflatable baseball bat. Whether you think these guys from Florida are idiots, cretins or just plain morons, you judge for yourselves but there is little doubt they are keeping The Ramones music alive.

Take It Dee Dee
United States Of America

Possibly the first major crisis the band had to face was indeed that period in the late spring of 1978 when Tommy Ramone decided to quit the band. According to John Holmstrom "he was more than just a drummer. He was the manager, the general, he produced the first four records and he created The Ramones sound." Indeed, the editor and illustrator of *Punk* magazine felt that "they fell apart when Tommy left the band. He was the glue of The Ramones." [203] The reasons for his departure has been well documented. In Mickey Leigh's autobiography he cites the drummer who declared that "after a while they wore me down. I was startin' to go nuts, which they all thought was amusing. They were on thin ice themselves. Looking back, I think I was suffering from clinical depression, which I didn't know at the time." Tommy also went on to add that "I was really into the recording process and writing the songs and making the albums, but not the logistics of touring with a bunch of very eccentric, high-strung, crazy people, from one shit-hole to another. It was pretty depressing. I was making practically nothing." [204] Indeed, in an interview the founding member expands stating that that "in a studio, I was in control and creating" going on to add that "on the road, I was a passenger, basically being bossed around and not treated very well, actually. I felt like I was losing my mind, and I would explain to people, 'I think I'm losing my mind,' and they would find this amusing. So the choice was me

"

staying on the road and becoming a vegetable, or helping them write the songs and producing the records—which I felt would be a little more productive—and bringing in another drummer." [205] There may have been other reasons for his departure too. In the book *On The Road With The Ramones,* Tommy talks about a power struggle which was occurring at that time. "They were always paranoid I would take over, which I had no intention of doing. They were in denial about what my role in the band was and they still are. They were trying to create a fantasy of what The Ramones were, and part of their fantasy was that my contribution didn't count or something like that. They needed it for their own psyche. Joey and Dee Dee sort of sensed that I was leaving and said, 'Don't leave.' I explained to them that I was going to have to. They tried to talk me out of it, not very strongly, but they did try. Johnny was shocked and surprised, but he didn't make a scene out of it. I said, 'I don't want to tour anymore. I don't need to play drums. I can show someone how to play these parts and you can go on the road with him and I'll just work with you guys in the studio." [206]

There seems to be mixed reaction from those in or close to the band. Dee Dee, who evidently along with Joey, was the first to be told by Tommy did not seem that surprised. "I had been watching him deteriorate on the road. Tommy didn't hold up too well – he wasn't really made of the real stuff that rock stars are made of. Then one day he was gone. We could never recapture that classic punk sound after Tommy left, but with Marc in the band we got a very hard player, the bassist stated." [207] Lighting and art director, Arturo Vega was more stunned. "When Tommy left I couldn't believe it", he recalled. "Why would anybody leave this band at this time? I thought it was completely irrational.

We were all going out of our minds." [(208)] Even Johnny seemed genuinely sad by his departure. "Tommy was starting to fall apart and have a breakdown. He was becoming catatonic and having trouble dealing with everything. He couldn't take the road," the guitarist pointed out. "I never thought he'd leave. I mean, for Tommy to leave, this was terrible. Tommy was fun to have in the band, and I wish he had stayed in The Ramones forever. He was a good friend. I was really worried when Tommy left, because he had been a buffer between me and the rest of the band. He was the mediator, so problems were going to start; I knew it right then. Tommy leaving was not good." [(209)]

Tommy's final gig as a Ramones drummer was fittingly at *CBGBs* in New York on May 4th, 1978 and his final tune performed was rather ironically "We're A Happy Family". This was a benefit show to help pay medical bills for *Dead Boy's*, Johnny Blitz. The Cleveland based drummer had been hospitalised after an altercation in Manhattan which had seen him stabbed five times. Tommy's replacement would be Marc Bell, an experienced drummer who had played with the hard rock three-piece band *Dust*. The skin basher sets the scene about how he joined the band. "Wayne County was the first person to ever play me The Ramones' first album. I was upstairs at *Max's*, where he was moonlighting as a DJ and had The Ramones' first album. I'd seen them live, but wasn't a fan yet. But when I heard the album I thought, 'What the fuck Is this?' I'd never heard anything like it. I was doing all this technical stuff, triplets, double strokes, different time signatures, and I hear this and I knew at that moment that this was going to change things. It didn't matter how simple it was. It was like a tidal wave, a train, intense power and electricity, a wall coming right at you. Richard

Hell had something, but The Ramones had something special." (210) In his book *Punk Rock Blitzkrieg*, he expands in more detail. "Every time I ran into Dee Dee at *CBGB*... he told me I ought to join The Ramones... He said the band was having trouble with Tommy, their drummer, and I was a little upset to hear that. I didn't want the original line-up of The Ramones to break up. I was a fan. But I didn't put much stock in what Dee Dee said. He was a nut and known to exaggerate... But when Johnny Ramone asked to meet with me about joining the band, the whole proposition turned real." After laying down some ground rules such as wearing leather jackets, Marc thought it was a done deal but he was asked to go to an audition and he had heard through the grapevine that The Ramones had already auditioned several drummers." (211)

The 'try-out' was at Performance Studios in Manhattan and although Holstrom recalls that they "auditioned drummer after drummer and everyone showed off" (212) according to Johnny "there was never anybody else we seriously considered. There were names tossed around, like Johnny Blitz of The Dead Boys and Paul Cook of The Sex Pistols... we had some choices – and we wanted to make sure we had the right one" the guitarist recollects. (213) Such was his love for The Ramones, Tommy clearly still wanted the band to thrive and helped Marc in those initial steps. Marc recalls his audition remembering that "I go down and there are 20 drummers there on this long couch. I sat behind the drums and did 'I Don't Care,' 'Sheena Is A Punk Rocker' and 'Rockaway Beach'. The next thing I knew I got the call. Once I joined, we rehearsed at Daily Planet and I met Monte. Tommy was sitting behind me at the drum set and we were going through "Road To Ruin" and their live set. I had to change my drum style.

This was simplicity at its most simplistic." Johnny realised that "once we started playing with Marky, I felt we'd be fine, as far as the sound of the band." He also added that "Tommy showed him his certain style and Marky caught on pretty quick. He played Tommy's parts and would interpret

Photograph by Tom Hearn

his own playing into Tommy's style. It was obvious that Marky was the better drummer, but we lost someone with Tommy's intelligence." Indeed, something which highlights this seamless transition is a photograph of Tommy playing his penultimate gig at the Shaboo Inn in Willamantic, Connecticut on April 29th, 1978. Here one can see Marc Bell or should I say the 'wannabe' Marky Ramone, watching on intently, observing the original drummer's style.

Marky Ramone as he was now coined, played his first show for The Ramones in Poughkeepsie, New York on June 29th. "I was a little nervous, but I pulled through" the new recruit said. "After the show Dee Dee was very happy. He knew I was in the group, so now he had someone to drink and party with. After that I took John into a room and said, 'This is what I want for the album. I want half of what you get to start. I don't expect a whole or even three-quarters. I know you formed the band so it wouldn't be fair for me to get a full amount. Just give me half.' 'No.' I go, 'John, you're going to have to. At this point, if I leave the group and you have to get another drummer it's going to look ridiculous. People already know I'm in the group.' So I got my 50 percent to their 100 percent on that album and later it went up." (214)

Marky's first show outside of the state of New York and second performance was in New Brunswick in New Jersey on Independence Day, 1ˢᵗ July. The band had already played a number of times in the *Garden State* and all told would perform over 100 times there over the course of their career. One tribute band that heralds from Union County in New Jersey is the fantastically named *Take It Dee Dee.* Formed in 2020, it originally comprised of singer Bill the Butcher, Kevin Battery on drums, Alex Rosen on the bass and Brian Grecco as guitarist. The quartet had plenty of experience in other bands with Bill performing in *The Blisters* and *Fetal Rage* and Brian in *Pom* and *KQHYT.* Alex and Kevin both played in *Battery Electric* with the former also gracing *Hot Blood*. Singer Bill was instrumental in starting up the tribute stating that "it was for the sheer love of the band that spans a lifetime." He goes on to add that "I saw them around 30 times. Still one of my favourites was the first in July 1983 at the *Convention Hall* in Asbury Park, New Jersey. To put into context this would have been during the "Subterranean Jungle" tour and just a few weeks before Johnny got beaten up and hospitalised in a street brawl which resulted in a five-month hiatus for the band. Bill had the fortune to meet Joey and the relatively unknown Richie before that show describing the surreal events "I was at 17-year-old kid and I just remember seeing this larger than life man hunched over a girl in tight leopard skin skirt walking down the boardwalk in 90° weather and 'saying Holy shit that's Joey'. I immediately asked for an autograph and then he headed towards the arcade where I hung out with him while he played pole position and other video games. I even finished his game because he had to walk off for a minute." In terms of the concert itself he recalls "as soon as they came out, I shot to the front to witness this life changing event." At the time, Dee Dee was "still jumping around" and it was Bill who chose the unique designation of his tribute, *Take It Dee Dee*. He goes on to clarify that he just "loved the phrase" and wanted it to be more original than have a spoof or a play on the word The Ramones which most tributes opt for. Like so many other tribute band members followed in this book, the front man is clearly a Ramones *geek* and confesses to once putting in a bid for Joey's tinted glasses. "I'm not done yet", he states, "one day I will buy them." Interestingly, Bill also took drum lessons from Marky Ramone in early 1987 which would have been just prior to the stick man re-joining the band for his second spell with the group. Bill still has the handwritten notes from Marky with advice on the key elements in order to improve his technique.

Take It Dee's set is mainly taken from the first three albums of the late '70s with examples including "Suzy Is A Headbanger", "Swallow My Pride", "I Don't Wanna Walk Around With You", "Gimme Gimme Shock Treatment" and "Cretin Hop". The group also adds some tunes from other L.Ps such as "Go Mental", "I Just Wanna Have Something To Do" and "I Wanna Be Sedated" and as Bill points out they "never play the same set twice" which keeps the group fresh and fans engaged. One of their favourite gigs was from a "Rock 'n' Roll High School" movie event in Pennsylvania where the crowd was dressed as characters from the film whilst the band have also performed at various local venues in New Jersey including *Stone Pony, Dunellen Theatre, Pino's, Salty's Beach Bar* and *The Vogel.*

After three years, the band experienced some line-up changes and in October 2023 a new re-vamped *Take It Dee Dee* took to the stage. This saw current *Cynz* drummer, Mike Wretched on the skins, Ronny taking over on the four string and Anthony Bones performing on guitar. Both guitarists play for the famed *Accelerators,* a band noted for covering one of the great accolades to the iconic bassist - "I Wanna Be Like Dee Dee Ramone" – if you have never heard this then it is well worth a visit on to *Youtube,* it is first class. Rather amusingly, Bill states that as front man he wears a *Joey* wig and "as we speak is working on the rest of the band to follow suit!"

Photograph courtesy of Deb von Olden

As always, I recommend looking into all our tributes and *Take It Dee Dee* are no exception. I love their version of "Beat On The Brat" at *the Low Dive* in Asbury Park, New Jersey which shows Bill hovering over the front of the stage with his bat in hand poised to yield his deadly instrument – not to attempt to complete a home run of course but to pound any young spoilt upstart who happens to get in his way. Other great snippets come from the *Dunellen Theatre* which shows a fantastic interpretation of the old masterpiece "Pinhead". Indeed, the tune comes complete with the most hideous looking masked freak clutching his "Gabba Gabba Hey" sign as if his life depended upon it. Clad in his jeans, T-Shirt and leather jacket, he completes the customary "*jerk dance*" at the front of the stage before the watching audience. Possibly my favourite, however, is a great rendition of Dee Dee's "Chinese Rock" which really does cut the mustard and again emphasises how much better the live account is than the lame, tame version that Spector served up on "End Of The Century".

When asked about The Ramones' legacy, Bill is not shy in his praise to the boys from Queens. "Their influence is everywhere in all good music", he claims adding that "every band I have ever played is to some extent derived from The Ramones." Likewise, Marky Ramone's impact should also not be forgotten and Bill

Bill and Marky: Photograph courtesy of Cathy Kleemeyer

still occasionally bumps into the legendary stick man in New Jersey – the same drummer who once gave him those lessons all those years ago and of course the same man who helped fend off The Ramones' first real crisis when Tommy left back in '78.

The Shamones
Wales

Wales is one of the four constituent countries which makes up the sovereign state of the United Kingdom and is bordered by England to the east. The Principality has a contrasting geography - in the south, flat coastal plains give way to valleys, whilst in the central and northern parts, there is a range of hills and mountains with the highest peak at Snowdonia. Indeed, the country is renowned for its awe inspiring landscape which includes three national parks and five areas of national beauty. Wales has its own identity and language and according to the 2021 census 17.8% of the population can speak Welsh. [215] The modern Welsh name for themselves is Cymry and the Welsh name for Wales is Cymru with many public and private signs written in both English and Welsh languages. The *Land of My Fathers,* as coined in their national anthem, has a population of just over 3.1 million with the largest city being Cardiff with around 362,000 inhabitants.

It was totally rational, therefore, that The Ramones took to the stage in the capital when they crossed the Severn bridge from neighbouring England for the first time on October 3rd, 1978. The chosen venue was *Cardiff University* and the location within this Institution where the gig took place is known as *The Great Hall.* With a capacity of 1,600, the site has attracted many popular acts since the '70s – examples include *New Order, The Stranglers, Van Morrison* and *Motörhead* to name but a few. [216] Seven songs from their most recent album "Road To Ruin" was on the set list, which numbered an impressive 28 in total. [217] "I Don't Want You", "Go Mental", "Don't Come Close", "I Just Wanted To Have Something To Do", "Bad Brain", "She's The One" and "Needles And Pins" were all chosen to help promote the latest cut. The support group that night was *The Snips* and one of their band members Jackie Badger, recites an interesting memory about the New Yorkers stating that "before they go on stage The Ramones play through their entire set, acoustically, in the dressing room, and then went straight out to do it all again. I guess they want to hit the ground running; it was a strange sight." [218]

The Ramones would come back to Wales on just two more occasions and each time *Da Brudders* would perform at *Cardiff University*. The next was in January 1980 on the "End Of The Century" tour whilst their last visit was in the October of 1987 to promote the album, "Halfway To Sanity".

One fan who saw the boys from Queens on those last two Welsh visits was Andy Johnson who would eventually form his own tribute band. The musician originates from Barry, a town situated in the Vale of Glamorgan on the south coast of Wales and is located just 10 miles south west from Cardiff. The place is famed as a seaside resort with its beautiful beaches and the *Barry Island Pleasure Park*. For those who enjoy television, it is also renowned for the setting of the wonderful TV sitcom *Gavin and Stacey* written by James Corden and Ruth Jones.

The band was a three-piece and consisted of Andy on guitar and lead vocals, Dave Johnson on drums and Bryn Merrick on the bass with both Dave and Bryn joining in on backing vocals. In one interview in the *Repeat Fanzine*, Andy describes how he put the tribute together. "We started rehearsing in September 2010 after me and Bryn met up and I persuaded Bryn to come out of an 18-year musical exile and start playing again. We decided on The Ramones because it was the simplest form of music to play being mostly three chords, two verse/one chorus pop songs. We had grown up with The Ramones' music after being sent the first album, back in 1976, by a mutual friend." When asked why honour the Americans rather than say *The Clash* or *The Sex Pistols*, Andy's response was straight forward. "For me and Bryn, The Ramones were the first 'real' punk band to influence us and make us want to play in a band. The simplicity of the songs and the image is just so appealing", he pointed out. [219] The last piece of the jigsaw was when Andy recruited his younger brother Dave to join the band and *the Shamones* were born. Fascinatingly, the designation of the group was not the idea of one of the members but was inspired by Andy's wife, Rachel, who came up with the name. Not only did the moniker immediately link the band to The Ramones but also gave it a *tongue in cheek*, humorous feel - undoubtedly a stroke of genius. As with so many of our tributes, part of the fun of a Ramones tribute is taken up various aliases and the lads from Barry played their part, all having the collective stage sir name of Shamone. Andy took up the penname of Johnny, Bryn transformed into Bee Bee and Dave morphed into D. Jay Shamone. The boys also adapted the famous Ramones logo with the trio of names sitting around the outside of the celebrated eagle, baseball bat and apple branch which they prominently had on display as a backdrop at their gigs.

Before performing in *The Shamones*, the group members had previous impressive links at the top end within the punk echelons. Andy, for instance was a member of *Victimize*, one of South Wales' foremost punk bands of the late 1970s who supported the likes of *The Damned, Stiff Little Fingers, The UK Subs, The Lurkers* and *The Skids* and even had a song "Hi-Rising Failure" played on the illustrious John Peel's radio show. In the '80s he was also part of the group, *The Missing,* who opened for *Hawkwind* at Stonehenge in 1984 and supported *The Damned's* 'Anything' tour in 1986. Bassist Bryn had an even

more illustrious upbringing having played with punk icons *The Damned* between 1983 and 1989. The bassist once explained how he managed to secure the role as the bassist of one of punk rock's most notable outfits. "I was on the dole, living in a flat in Barry, not really doing much musically", he recalled. "I got a call from Roman [220] saying Paul Gray had been sacked by *The Damned* and he had suggested me as a replacement. The band agreed to audition me. I had seven days to learn 30 songs for the upcoming British Tour, followed by a tour of the States. I passed the audition and rest is history, as they say." Bryn also went on to add what it was like playing for the group stating that it was "nerve-racking but exciting. It sounds corny but I was 'living the dream'. It was a life's ambition. The whole experience shattered my illusion of 'pop stars'. Most of them were down to earth. Ozzie Osbourne was great, a big hero of mine from my *Sabbath* loving days" he recalled. [221] Stick man Dave gained experience in *The Generals,* before teaming up with his older brother in *Andy & the Johnsons* as well as spending an 18-month spell in the band *Fallen Through* which cut a three track demo back in 2010.

The Shamones first gig was on the 3rd December, 2010 at a local pub in Barry and they soon started to play all over the country with gigs in Carmarthen, Chepstow, Cardiff, Houghton Regis, Wolverhampton, Ipswich, Melton Mowbray, Birmingham, Cannock and Romford to name but a few. The Welshmen also performed at *Tribfest* which was Europe's largest tribute festival taking place in Hull. When asked about his favourite concert, guitarist and singer Andy responded by stating that "every gig was memorable. We travelled the length and breadth of the UK playing as often as we could. Sometimes we played to a handful of people and on other occasions we'd play to packed venues. We often played on the same bill as other punk tributes including *Radio Clash, The Pistols, Sex Pistols Tribute, Blond-E, Transmission (Joy division)* and countless other bands at tribute festivals."

Andy recalls that the band "played a repertoire of 54 songs covering tracks from every studio album." Indeed, *The Shamones*, when playing as a single band, would regularly perform two 45 minute slots with a short break between sets maximising the number of tracks they could play. Along with the expected classics such as "Blitzkrieg Bop" "Sheena Is A Punk Rocker", "Pinhead" and "Teenage Lobotomy", the band also continued to cover some of the much loved early songs that The Ramones stopped performing live including "Loudmouth", "I Don't Wanna Go Down To The Basement" and a superb, more aggressive version of "Swallow My Pride".

As always I urge people to check out all of our tributes on social media and a visit on to *Youtube,* will give you lots of opportunities to see *The Shamones* in action. For instance, a first port of call could be the audio link of "Cretin Hop" which is one of my personal favourites. The sound is not only close to the original but you also get an insight what the band was about - buzzsaw guitars, sung with passion and a pounding drum beat. Another little gem is "Rockaway Beach" which again, not only has an audio of the definitive song, but some wonderful photographs of the group on show too. In both extracts, Andy somehow manages a slight New York drawl which adds to the fun of the tunes and compliments the concept of the tribute. If you wish to see some video footage then I suggest a noteworthy starting point is "California Sun", live at *Central Park* in Barry which shows the band in fine form and also reflects both the melodic nature of the band but also their ability to *drive home* the song in typical Ramones fashion. If you have a little more time, then take a look at "Shamones live" at the *Park Hotel* in Barry. Amongst others you will find "Beat On The Brat", "53rd and 3rd", "Now I Wanna Sniff Some Glue", "Gimme Gimme Shock Treatment", "Today Your Love, Tomorrow The World", "Judy Is A Punk", "I Don't Wanna Walk Around With You" and "Glad To See You Go". It is nearly 20 minutes of continuous Ramones pleasure which blasts out those memorable tracks in a barrage of relentless noise and energy. I know there will be sticklers out there who will nit-pick about the fact that the band was a trio rather than a classical quartet or that the "1, 2, 3, 4s" were cried out by Johnny rather than Bee Bee, but I will *go to war* with anyone who argues that these are not the real deal. There is no doubt that these guys are *no sham.*

The band folded when bassist Bryn Merrick developed throat cancer and sadly passed away in September, 2015. James Hewitson, or JJ Shamone as he was coined, took over for the final few scheduled gigs of that year but it was never going to be the same. Bryn certainly left those who knew him or witnessed the band with some great memories and it is fitting that his buddy, Andy, should have the last words. "It was an honour to play so many of The Ramones' great songs to audiences across the UK. We enjoyed keeping the music and spirit of the band alive and introducing the music to new, younger audiences as well as old punks. We prided ourselves on being as accurate as possible when playing the songs. There were only three of us but we were still a band of brothers with the same attitude and hard, fast delivery as the original band. The Ramones were the most influential band in the history of rock music. They inspired ordinary people to form bands and also inspired many musicians to pick up instruments and learn to play. Their fan base across the world is largely made up of misfits, freaks, loners and outcasts but everyone can relate to the band in the same way." Indeed, if ever there was a summary of *'we're a happy family'*, that will do nicely!

Hamburg Ramönes
Germany/Republic Of Ireland

1978 was an action packed year for the band. The first part of it had witnessed the group tour the United States with the much-loved Tommy in the drum seat but by the end of the year, Marky had seamlessly slipped into the position as the precision skin thumping Ramone. As well as this, the boys embarked on another European tour in September to publicise their fourth Album "Road To Ruin" which had also been released in the same month. After completing three gigs in Sweden, the *'fast four'* moved on to Germany with their first concert on German ground in Hamburg on September 11th. Hamburg is one of Germany's three city-states and is the nation's second largest city after Berlin with a population of over 1.9 million. It is a major port in the north of the country and is connected to the North Sea by the river Elbe. The city is an important domestic and international tourist attraction and is famed for its many bridges which cross the extensive network of rivers and canals. Musically it is also well-known for the development of *The Beatles* who in the early '60s honed their skills and widened their reputation at different clubs within the city. Their first performance was at a venue known as *Markthalle Hamburg* which is a convention centre located at Klosterwall, Hammerbrook. Built just prior to the start of the World War One in 1913, the site can hold up to 1,000 people and has seen such notable artists as *Guns N' Roses, Nirvana, The Police* and *AC/DC* perform there. The group played 24 songs that evening but maybe surprisingly only four being chosen from the forthcoming L.P, "Road To Ruin". Nonetheless, "I Don't Want You", "Go Mental", "She's The One" and the enticing "Don't Come Close" were all given airings to whet the appetite of their German hosts.

One of our most interesting bands in this book in terms of logistics and location originate from the city where The Ramones made that German debut - Hamburg. Formed in 2001, the original line-up consisted of Tommy Ramöne as vocalist, Ecki Ramöne on guitar, drummer Hansi Ramöne and Jenzzzi Ramöne playing bass. Whilst the singer and guitar positions have remained stable there have been some changes on the other two instruments – the aptly named Marky Ramöne took over as stick man in 2006 whilst the bass has seen both Janny and Axel serve until present Olli Ramöne took over on the four string in 2019. Remarkably, Olli is now based in Galway in the Republic of Ireland and has to travel across to mainland Europe for gigs and studio recordings. More on the Irish connection later – first of all I want to concentrate on the inital conception of the band in Germany.

Photograph courtesy of Lothar Felkel

The founding members had been pretty active and successful musicians in their younger days but then took time off to raise their families. Ecki and Jenzzzi, for instance, were both members of the 1980s German outfit, *Der Moderne Mann* whilst the bass player was also in *Gigantor*. When the quartet got together at a friend's wedding they decided to take the instruments off the wedding band and play a few Ramones songs. They loved it so much, the lads stuck with it, formed the group and played Ramones music ever since. The chosen name for the tribute speaks for itself and is based on their geographical locality – *Hamburg Ramönes*. "It's simple and did not require too much thinking about", quips spokesman Olli.

The group quickly evolved – initially they played purely Ramones songs and wore wigs to impersonate the Americans but soon shed this idea and started to write their own catchy original numbers but in true Ramones fashion. Since then, they have released seven albums including the humorous titled "Free Phil Spector" which has sold in 22 different countries and a follow up "Long Black Hair". [222] For full details of their various Ramones inspired releases, a visit to their website is well worth investigating.

The *Hamburg Ramönes* amusingly adapted The Ramones emblem not only to include their own names around the perimeter of the logo but also to take into account their origins. A white castle on a red background is displayed which heralds from the Hamburg coat of arms whilst a more contemporary bottle of larger is seen in the eagle's right claw signifying one of the city's more famous industries. Above the eagle's head lies the words "black leather" which of course relates to the lad's attire.

Their set list tends to kick it off with the instrumental "Durango 95" before playing a mixture of definitive Ramones songs along with their own original numbers. Olli points out that "The Ramones classics we play vary but you can't leave the stage without playing 'Blitzkrieg Bop', 'Sheena', 'Commando', 'Pinhead' and 'Cretin Hop'. "We try to change the songs around", the bass player adds. "For example, when we play with a surf band, "California Sun" will be in the set."

Hamburg Ramönes have played many great gigs over the years establishing themselves initially on the local scene in Hamburg. Some of the more memorable achievements include playing at the "ball-room" at their beloved FC St. Pauli football stadium, a professional team in Hamburg, along with a *Brexit* Tour of the UK and Ireland in 2017. With a quarter of the band living in Ireland then links with the *Emerald Isle* are inevitable. The group played at the *Fibber Magees* in Dublin just before the pandemic and also returned to Ireland in the August of 2023.

The Ramones also performed in the Republic of Ireland playing four shows in Dublin in total. The first, on Sunday, September 24th, 1978, was just a couple of weeks after their German debut and was played at the *State Cinema*. Fortunately, we have two eye-witness accounts of that show which paint a glorious picture of events that evening. "That night changed my life", said Irish promoter Eugene Connelly. "The speed, power and other worldly visuals has resulted in me thinking about Joey, Johnny, Dee Dee and Tommy/Marky every day since. The way Joey didn't bother pronouncing Blitzkrieg Bop properly…Bbbeee Bop! I couldn't believe it! His huge lips seemingly dripping with an unending saliva supply and that occasional one-legged body shift at the mic…On the bus home, we all knew things would never be the same again." [223] John O Sullivan was another local fan who managed to get a ticket for the show, reminiscing that the *State Cinema* in Phisborough in Dublin was "a new venue, putting on its first ever gig, promoted by *Big D*, pirate radio station." He recalls that once inside "the first thing I noticed was the seats were still in place. Do they not realise this was a Ramones gig?" John goes on to add that the Dublin crowd had a reputation for gobbing but "on the night there were only a small number of gobshites spitting" and that "the place was heaving; I had never experienced a gig like this before. As the crowd cleared afterwards, the full extent of the damage was clear, 75% of the seats were in bits on the floor." [(224)]

The Ramones would return to the Republic of Ireland in October 1980 and for two back-to-back gigs in June 1985. Indeed, there is an excellent audio recording of the full show from one of their performances in '85 at the *TV club* in Dublin. Members of the *Hamburg Ramönes* would naturally not see the New Yorkers at these gigs but did see them play on other occasions. Ecki and Tommy witnessed The Ramones on numerous times in Germany and had the privilege to meet Joey in the '90s at one of his birthday bashes. Olli Ramöne, the youngest member of the tribute, saw them play in 1994 and has also since met C.J and Richie after gigs in Ireland as part of their solo projects.

Pleasingly, there are many links to get a feel for the band on social media. A look on

Photograph courtesy of Lothar Felkel

Youtube, for instance, will find a mixture of their own material and Ramones favourites. If you wish to hear some new original music, then take a look at the tune "Ramones Forever". "the track merely lists various old songs and isn't a *stand-out* to be honest. More impressive, however, is their number, "Flying Saucers Over Hollywood", which has a driving fuzz tone guitar and a striking catchy tune which will get your feet tapping steadily and your head bobbing to the beat. If your taste is more associated with live footage, then "Blitzkrieg Bop" at the *Hafenklang* in Hamburg back in 2014 should be right up your alley. It is particularly fitting to hear the "1,2,3,4" screamed out in the mother tongue at the start of the ultimate Ramones ditty. At the same venue, but fast forward five years, there is extensive coverage of the band from Ecki's birthday party with my personal favourite, the third section of the video covering "Sheena Is A Punk Rocker", "Havana Affair" and "Commando". If you dig a little deeper, you will also find more original material played very much in the style of The Ramones.

When asked about the legacy of the American band, Olli reaped them with praise. "I think the influences of The Ramones are everywhere", the bass player suggests. "Sometimes it's really obvious when you hear the pop-punk bands. Occasionally it's just a low hanging guitar where I think 'oh look, that sounds like The Ramones too'. I hear drum beats that remind me of them. Sometimes an 'oh-oh-oh' in a song reminds me of Joey. Famous musicians such as Henry Rollins mentions them a lot still. Plus, the many Ramones T-shirts you still see around. They are everywhere."

Hamburg Ramönes should be congratulated – there's no doubt that performing for over 20 years is an outstanding feat.

The band continue to press on, performing in Germany and with plans to play in England and Ireland in 2024 as well. Indeed, the hope is to carry out a small west coast tour of Eire visiting Galway, Cork, Kerry and Limerick with Irish fans able to hear Olli cry out those immortal words of *"eins, zwei, drei, vier"* in his adopted homeland.

Commando Berlin
Germany

After performing in Hamburg on September 11th, 1978, the following day The Ramones travelled south-east to the divided city of Berlin. Berlin is the largest city of Germany both in terms of area and population with over 3.8 million inhabitants. It is located in the heart of the North-German plain lying on an east-west commercial axis which helped establish it as the capital of Prussia and then, after unification in 1871, the capital of the country. After the fall of the Nazi regime at the end of World War Two and its subsequent occupation by the victorious nations, the devastated city was divided. West Berlin became a political enclave, a piece of territory completed surrounded by East Berlin and East Germany between the years of 1948 to 1990. During this period, known as the Cold War, Bonn became the *de facto* capital of West Germany and officially designated as the "temporary seat of the Federal institutions." Back in Berlin, in 1961, the construction of a concrete barrier, including armed guard towers placed along the walls, was set up with the primary intention to stop East German citizens from fleeing to the west. After the fall of the Berlin Wall in 1990, the city was reinstated as the capital of the country and Germany was once again united as a nation.

One of the band members was well accustomed to life in the country already. Douglas Colvin, better known by his stage name Dee Dee Ramone, was born in Virginia just six years after the end of the Second World War. His mother was a German whilst his father was a Master Sergeant in the US army. Due to military requirements, the family was relocated initially to West Berlin and subsequently to a number of other towns in Germany. The young Dee Dee would spend hours in old-bombed-out buildings searching for war relics and Nazi memorabilia to sell in antique shops [225] and there's no doubt that these formative years shaped the man that for many would become the most iconic punk bassist the world has even seen. Germany was *in his blood* and this was often reflected in his song writing, heard for example, in the much loved but controversial "Today Your Love Tomorrow The World" or the hugely underrated, medium paced and rocky "It's A Long Way Back To Germany".

The Ramones' first performance in West Berlin, was at the *Neue Welt,* a concert hall where, in 1930, Adolf Hitler once gave a speech and set out his vision for a *New World*. There were two buildings at the venue with the smaller site holding 1,500 people and the larger one accommodating twice the capacity. During the 1960s and '70s, it was a popular location for rock and pop concerts with the likes of Jimi Hendrix, *Deep Purple, Blondie, ZZ Top, The Clash* and *The Police* all gracing the stage. The old establishment closed in 1982, but nowadays, it has been revamped with a change of designation. It is now known as the *Huxley's Neue Welt* and enjoys artists still regularly performing at the arena. There is no record of the set list that day so one can only assume that it would have been very similar to the previous evening's work in Hamburg which saw over 20 songs performed in total with four tracks taken from the most recent album "Road To Ruin".

After the Berlin gig, the lads headed west again recording a live television show named *Musikladen* at the *Beat Club* in Bremen on September 13th. For all Ramones buffs, this is quite simply a requisite viewing with the band at its very best blasting out a score of songs. It is rather fitting to witness Dee Dee screaming "*eins, zwei, drei, vier*" as the starter to the German associated named anthem "Blitzkrieg Bop" but also somewhat off-putting to witness the Saxon punks calmly sitting at tables whilst *Da Brudders* perform ferociously in front of them. Collectors might also wish to note that a shortened version of this show was released in 2001 as a live EP under the title "You Don't Come Close."

The Ramones played in total just over 60 times in Germany over the course of their career. As the group's reputation increased, the band naturally ventured to more centres across the Fatherland, not only to cities in the old West Germany such as Munich, Hanover, Bonn, Cologne and Düsseldorf, but also to places in the Old Communist controlled East Germany including Leipzig and Halle as well as a return to the now unified, capital Berlin. In the book *On The Road With The Ramones*, author Melnick cites both the 'cold-war' shenanigans witnessed and the new-found liberty of post-wall knock down as perceived by some of the road-crew. For instance, front of house soundman, John Markovich and drum tech, Mitch 'Bubbles' Keller describe the situation at the Brandenburg Gate and notorious *Checkpoint Charlie* crossing-point with the East German security brandishing automatic machine guns towards their western antagonists. The band was also in the city just after the infamous Wall had been brought down in November 1989 with Bubbles recalling that "we all grabbed picks, chisels and hammers and started chipping away and taking pieces of the Berlin Wall" whilst C.J, who by now had replaced Dee Dee in the band, "reached through a hole in the wall with some money and bought a cap and belt buckle off the guy." (226)

One fan who saw The Ramones twice was a musician named Alexx whose most memorable show was indeed in 1989 at the Berlin *Eissporthalle* during that period after the wall had been brought down. Alexx describes the situation at this historic time stating "I had come from the eastern part of Berlin, so this was my first ever concert in the free world." Although a drummer by trade, Alexx additionally always wanted a chance to be a lead singer and loved The Ramones so much that in 2002 he asked some of his musical friends to start a cover band. Indeed, the vocalist feels that "The Ramones were one of the greatest bands of all time and had a huge impact to all types of music." The founding line-up also saw Ron on guitar, Traudl picking up drumming responsibilities and Fröhlich on bass and backing vocals. After many re-shuffles within the line-up which included the guitarists Mecker and Nilo, bass man Ulli and drummers Steffi and Oli, the band folded in 2010. Fortunately, in 2019 the band reformed and has now seen a stable format comprising of vocalist Alexx, Tobi on bass, Steffi in the drummer's seat and Ron back on lead guitar. The name of the band, *Commando Berlin,* not only originates from their geographic location but also the untouchable twelfth track off the second album "Leave Home" and the title of the autobiography of none other than Johnny Ramone. It is a fantastic and natural choice for a German tribute with the verse ostensibly focusing on American soldiers fighting the Cold War whilst the chorus has those thumping emphatic lyrics including *"The Laws of Germany".*

Although the band have gigged extensively, Alexx cites his personal favourite experience as maybe the *TouRussia* in 2007, where they played a few gigs in and around St. Petersburg. For those of you who would like to explore life on the road in Russia including footage of other bands then a quick search on *Youtube* and *the Rockumentary* will do the trick.

In terms of the set list, the band have played around 35 different songs which has varied depending on the line-up. It has centred around The Ramones early material such as the favourites "Havana Affair", "Now I Wanna Sniff Some Glue" and "You're Gonna Kill That Girl" but also throws in later material too including "Bonzo Goes To Bitburg". Unusually, *Commando* also serve up an original number, "Overdose", wrote in dedication of Dee Dee Ramone.

The band have also had many distinguished achievements along the way. In 2004, after a show to celebrate the 30 year's anniversary of the creation of The Ramones, the idea for founding the first "Ramones Museum" came to super fan Flo Hayler. The site which was situated in the Kreuzberg borough of Berlin would open a year later and has more than a thousand objects of memorabilia associated with the New Yorkers. More information on the now world famous museum can be found on their web site at www.ramonesmuseum.com although the establishment is unfortunately closed at the moment whilst a new site is sought.

Another milestone was when the band recorded a handful of Ramones songs in the studio although these were never formally released until a few years later and only on vinyl as a limited edition of 100 sets. For further details, refer to the band's own website. Pleasingly, a search on social media finds a couple of extensive clips of *Commando*. As always, I urge you to look at these features yourself as they provide an interest one way or another. The first port of call, I suggest, is live at the *Magnet Club* in Berlin back in 2004 and the fore mentioned 30th birthday bash. Introduced with the *Spaghetti Western* theme from "*For A Few Dollars More*" rather than the habitual "The Good, The Bad And The Ugly", the lads kick off with a first-rate rendition of "Blitzkrieg Bop". Led from the front by the dangling, Alexx whose shadowy form is reminiscent of the alien from the 1979 science-fi movie, you will discover nearly 30 minutes of Ramones dearest tracks. Alternatively, a second performance worth surveying is the more recent performance in 2019 at *Blackland Berlin Club*. In both shows *Commando* do not try to emulate or copy The Ramones but attempt to create their own distinctive, fun style whilst still reverberating those piercing guitars and pummelling drums. This is highlighted not only in their movements but also the way they play with the backing vocals and as Alexx states lots of "uuhhhs and ooohs." The singer is also evocative of Joey's more theatrical and flamboyant approach prancing around *the CBGBs* stage in their earliest video back in 1974 with his early Glam Rock *Sniper* influences still apparent. Interestingly, the group invite another vocalist to sing in a duo for the "KKK Took My Baby Away" whilst after a few songs Alexx removes the Joey wig to again seemingly herald that the band want to play in their own rather offbeat and entertaining fashion. Undeniably, there's no doubt about *Commando's* German law, the first rule is *we must entertain you.*

Melones
Germany

Another tribute originating from Germany are the *Melones*. Remarkably, the band do not herald from just one city within the country but are scattered across the Fatherland with members originating from Hanover, Hamburg and Berlin. The group were formed way back in 1987, which to put into context, was at the same time as The Ramones released their tenth studio album, "Halfway To Sanity". This certainly means that the band have played with each other for even longer than The Ramones performed together and undoubtedly puts the *Melones* up there as being one of the longest surviving Ramones covers.

The idea of creating a tribute was initiated by a guitarist named Svenni along with a former singer called Karo. Svenni started listening to Ramones around 1984 and wanted to recreate the raw and fast music of *Da Brudders* live on stage. As with many of our groups, the boys have had some line-up changes over the years. Karo left and was replaced by Christian Meissner, aka Dicki as the frontman, whilst the current set-up also sees Lütti on drums and Tommi playing the bass and supporting with backing vocals. The origin of the band's name is fascinating and Dicki tells the story about the practicalities of using technology all those years ago. "Svenni and Karo used the name *Melones* by simply trying to create something out of the existing Ramones typo/font of the 'Road To Ruin' record" he remembers. "They went to a local shop and did several photocopies. The original

"ONES" could be used and also the "M" and the "E". And the "L" was simply a portion of the letter "E" - imagine it was in 1987 with no computers. *Melones* was the easiest way to form a band's name out of what was available within The Ramones name and it had to have the same amount of letters." Dicki also remembers that it was former bass player, Maxi, who cleverly adapted The Ramones logo and eagle with a hand drawing encorporating a knife and a slice of watermelon to signify their own unique designation. Dicki adds that "actually *Melones* had nothing to do with the fruit at first but we made it that way and now play along with the joke. Because of the name, folks often think *Melones* are from Spain or from Latin America" which is an experience which the tribute shared with the New Yorkers. Before Danny Fields had seen them play, for example, he initially thought The Ramones "were a cha-cha band. The name sounded Spanish." [227] Like so many other Ramones covers, all of the group take up the same stage name with the guitarist for instance, morphing into Svenni Melone. The present quartet have gained a host of experience from performing in previous bands which have included *Sanity's Dawn, Tank Shot, Nice Guys, Ostzonensuppenwürfelmachenkrebs, Mastino, Der Moderne Mann and C.E.O.*

From their debut gig in Hamburg in September 1978 to their swansong in Hanover in January 1996, The Ramones would consistently return to German pastures. There are many interesting narratives from their stints in Germany and I will share just a few. Marky Ramone, in his autobiography *Punk Rock Blitzkrieg,* gives the reader information about the broader picture of the punk world of 1978 at a gig in Berlin. "The spitting was getting out of control" with the German punks so accurate that he could "no longer hide behind a *Paiste* cymbal" he states.

Joey evidently attempted to get the fans to stop the *gobbing* and had some success but it wasn't until Dee Dee said something in German that the crowd stopped drenching the band with saliva. The drummer also witnessed first-hand Dee Dee's love of war memorabilia when the pair had some time to sight-see at the Brandenburg Gate before the wall was brought down. "There were street vendors selling a variety of Nazi daggers, and Dee Dee had a field day", Marky recalls. "The Nazi Party logo was there on the brown handle. But the big thrill was the etching on the ten-inch-long carbon steel blade: *Alle für Deutschland. Everything for Germany.* The dagger, however, was only one hundred deutschmarks. A few steps to the left, Dee Dee spotted a Hitler Youth dagger with the etching: *Blut und Ehre! Blood and Honour...* 'Yeah, why not, he said. One for the road'." [228]

Fast forward to the summer of 1990 for the fan's perspective of the band at the *Bizarre Festival* at the *Freilichtbühne Loreley*, an open air amphitheatre on top of the Lorelei rock in Sankt Goarshausen. At a gig described as "memorable" by Dicki and also attended by Svenni Melone, the frontman managed to catch a plectrum thrown into the audience from Johnny. It was double delight for the fan because he was also able to snatch one of the drumsticks thrown into the crowd by Marky as they departed the platform. "At the other end of the stick", he recalls "was a big guy pulling it too and Dicki's friends had to help him to ensure he wouldn't let go!" In the end his potential adversary made him an offer to break the stick into two which they did with Dicki fortunately getting the part with Marky's signature on it. There is superb coverage of this concert on *Youtube* with a choice of either an audio of the full show lasting just under 60 minutes or a half-hour video. All the band managed to see the '*fast four*' at some stage or another with other glorious Ramones nights at the *Große Freiheit* in Hamburg in 1987 or at the *Live Music Hall* in Hanover in 1992.

Another interesting show was the *Freizeitpark Festival* at Alsdorf in June 1992. By this time of course, C.J had replaced Dee Dee in the band but was involved in a motorcycle accident on his Harley with the bassist suffering a broken wrist shortly before the gig. Under pressure to continue to perform, primarily from Johnny because of the decent pay-day that the German event secured, he went into the show bandaged up, with a splint and on heavy painkillers. C.J describes that once they started to play "pretty soon it's clear I'm useless, so Johnny has them turn the bass off in the house and I faked it. I didn't play a note." Fortunately for C.J,

Photograph courtesy of Jörg Volker

he did not have to endure the full set as a crash barrier gave way and the band had to stop the show for health and safety reasons in any case. Only six songs were played that day – "Durango 95", "Teenage Lobotomy", "Psycho Therapy", "Blitzkrieg Bop", "Do You Remember Rock 'n' Roll Radio?" And "I Believe In Miracles" before the band left the stage. Incidentally, The Ramones had a short hiatus of nearly three months after this Festival in order to allow C.J recovery time. [229]

The Melones cite a number of their own unforgetable gigs over the years. Some of their favourites include the *UJZ Kornstraße* concert in Hanover in 1990, a performance at Bielefeld at *AJZ* in 2002 and one in Munich at the *ISPO trade fair* for East Pak in 2005. They have also been involved in large events such as Berlin's *Uncle Sally's* festival in Columbiahalle in Berlin in 2004 which included *Anti Flag* headlining and the *Punk & Disorderly Festival* at the *Astra Kulturhaus* with *Peter and the Test Tube Babies, Perkele, Discharge, Red London* and *The Cockney Rejects* also performing. What is noticeable is that the band have managed to perform all over the country despite the logistical difficulties of living in different cities. Dicki reflects that "this means a little more of coordination than others might have, but we got used to it. We know each other for more than 30 years now and it means a lot to us playing in this band." The group even hope to reach out further in the future and tour Poland in the east and Holland towards the west.

The *Melones* love to play Ramones songs from their early years and particularly tunes from the "It's Alive" recording. In general, Dicki highlights that it is the "Dee Dee Ramone era of the late '70s until mid/late '80s that we pick." The live sets have variations from gig to gig, but of course all sets include classics such as "Blitzkrieg Bop", "Teenage Lobotomy", "Commando", and "Pinhead". It is Important that the band never changes anything from the original song arrangements, the vocalist stresses with "no interpretation, nothing added and nothing re-arranged." Indeed, he goes on to say that they "imitate both the music and look as well as we can. For example, we play with the original Rogers drums and Mosrite guitar, we wear wigs, Schott leather jackets and some of the shirt designs that were worn by Joey and Johnny."

All you cretins out there will know by now that my favourite part of compiling this book is watching each and every tribute band. A search on to *Youtube* immediately finds a compilation of *Melones* snippets with "53rd and 3rd" the first port of call and specifically the Dee Dee break, or should I say the Tommi, part of the song. As if to keep the listener dangling, however, this offer is just a mere morsel as it morphs quickly into "Pinhead" complete with our escaped hospitalised *dumb* victim, suitably clothed in his pyjamas, masterfullly waving his "Gabba Gabba Hey" sign and proudly performing a full *'jerk dance'*. There are more goodies to sample and for you headbangers out there, there is a brief piece of the guitar break on "Now I Wanna Sniff Some Glue" before more cranium rattling in the shape of "Go Mental", "We're A Happy Family" and "I Wanna Be Sedated". Now *my brain was completely upside down,* up stepped my personal favourite and a full version of "Commando" live in Hanover to a packed, appreciative audience. I had to blink twice, however, as Svenni aka Johnny is found on the uncustomary left side of our singer Dicki with bassist Tommi to his right. Talking of Svenni, he is the perfect natural Johnny Ramone look-a-like – infact a double. He also has his mannerisms clocked to perfection with a sneering, scowling face, legs astride with guitar at that pefect inclination. Dicki too is frightingly similar to Joey – Tall, lean, left leg forward, at a precarious 45% angle and of course kitted out with those tinted glasses. Tommi Melone screams out the *1,2,3,4s* and barks out those backing vocals, alternating his movements back and forth. Perched stern side and sporting his sun glasses, sits Lütti who keeps time impeccably, canvass bashing in perfect Ramones style. The band are seen continuing to perform extracts of our favourites such as "Rockaway Beach" and "Cretin Hop" and all I can say is if you like your tributes as authentic and as similar to the originals as possible get on to social media - you will not be let down.

Dicki is passionately about the American's pioneering legacy and talks from the heart. "The Ramones are immeasurably important for almost any punk and rock band around the globe. They shaped the music world because so many bands started to play music because of them. They just went out and played even they were fairly bad musicians in the beginning, but never gave a fuck. They introduced a new way of making music. Their approach challenged the conventional wisdom that songs had to be long and complex to be successful. They totally redefined the idea of what a song could be and left an indelible mark on the music world. It is a enduring testament in the history of popular music - we simply love The Ramones."

No Matter
Northern Ireland

Northern Ireland is the smallest of the four constituent countries which makes up the United Kingdom with a population of just over 1.9 million inhabitants. The capital and largest city is Belfast with just over 293,000 people living within the city boundaries and 671,000 living within the metropolitan area. The country was created in 1921 when Ireland was partitioned, creating a dissolved government for the six north eastern counties which still wished to remain part of the United Kingdom. Nowadays, the Northern Ireland assembly has responsibility for a range of dissolved policy matters, whilst other areas are reserved for the UK government in Westminster. The governments of Northern Ireland co-operate with the government of Ireland in several areas under the terms of the Belfast agreement and it now shares an open border to the south and west with the bordering Republic of Ireland. Much has been written about the historical and political landscape of Northern Ireland which was for many years the location of a brutal and resentful ethno-political conflict. The *"Troubles"*, which started in the '60s and continued for over three decades, consisted of persistent acts of sectarian violence between elements of Northern Ireland's nationalist community, predominantly Roman Catholics who wanted to be politically united with The Republic of Ireland and the unionist majority, principally Protestants who wished to remain part of the United Kingdom. The violence was spearheaded by the armed campaigns of paramilitary groups such as the provisional Irish Republican Army and Ulster Volunteer Force and the activities of these organisations meant armed British soldiers took to the streets of Ulster in order to attempt to maintain law and order. By the late 1970s, *war fatigue* was visible in both communities and included the formation of a group known as the "Peace People", which won the Nobel Peace Prize in 1976 for its efforts. It was therefore within this social and historical context that The Ramones first took to the stage in Belfast in the autumn of 1978.

Their first concert in Northern Ireland took place on September 23rd and was the opening show of their fourth visit to the United Kingdom in two years. The selected venue was the *Ulster Hall* which is in the heart of Belfast's city centre. Opened in 1862, the hall's purpose was to provide the city with a multi-purpose sufficient sized venue and as well as music concerts, it has hosted classical recitals, craft fairs and political conferences. Despite *Ulster Hall* staging a number of notable artists over the years, it is perhaps most famed for two gigs not completed. The first saw a *Rolling Stones* concert abandoned in 1964 after only three songs due to hysterical fans breaking up the show [(230)] whilst a second involved punk giants, *The Clash*. The group, who had embarked on their *Out Of Control* tour in the autumn of 1977, heard the show had been cancelled after their sound check due to the promoters not gaining a letter of liability from an insurance company – no doubt holding their breath at the thought of London's punk finest treading the boards in Belfast during "*The Troubles*". Although maybe a "storm in a tea-cup", it did result in a mini-riot from disgruntled fans and five arrests being made. [(231)] Other noteworthy musicians who did manage to perform at the venue include *Led Zeppelin, AC/DC, Simple Minds, Metallica, The Undertones* and *Stiff Little Fingers.*

There is an excellent primary source of that first concert in Belfast on the web. Written by Adrian Thrills of the *NME*, the critic informs us the "the boys from the Bowery" performed 26 songs that evening "honed, polished and delivered in just under one hour." He also points to the fact that this was their first visit to the province as a date from their last tour had to be called off again citing the difficulties with venues and insurance. Thrills goes into detail about the concert stating that "they've got a new drummer, but, basically, it's the same Ramones. The visuals, for a start, are just as expected; the Regal Eagle backdrop, the ripped jeans, the jackets - as old hat as the odour of stale Airfix. Joey even still brings the "Gabba Gabba Hey" banner on stage during 'Pinhead'. But don't for a moment doubt that it's anything but peerless stuff. Sure, everyone wants change, but, in a nutshell, if The Ramones were to drastically alter their music…well, they just wouldn't be The Ramones, simple as that, and that would be sad indeed. They're the exception that proves the rule. However, any allegations that they don't care about the quality of their gigs are patently untrue. The *Ulster Hall* audience gob as if caught in a mid - 1977-time warp, making it difficult for Johnny and Dee Dee to work the stage properly. But even on the slippery, slivered boards, they put in a whole lot of effort." Who can disagree with the journalist as overall he describes the New Yorkers as "still a great live group." Interestingly Thrills points to a mistake by Johnny in the introduction of "Surfin' Bird" and dislikes the latest single of the day "Don't Come Close" along with the addition of half a dozen songs from the "Road To Ruin" album. He summed up by stating that the best moments were the highlights from their two bona fide classics, "Rocket" and the unsurpassed "Leave Home", although worth a mention is the bulldozing fanfare of the charging "California Sun", an extra 'specially impressive moment and a blitzing Clash *tour0style* medley of old stuff towards the end - "Today Your Love", "Judy" and "Glue" making a magnificent three-pronged encore." [232]

The Ramones visited Northern Ireland on two more occasions. The next gig in the country was part of the "End Of The Century" tour in October, 1980 and was also performed at the *Ulster Hall*. Their third and final visit to the province was in the summer of 1985. By this time, their third stick man, Richie was sitting on the drummer's stool and he and the rest of the lads would perform at a different venue - *The Queen's Student Union*. The building, now known as *Mandela Hall*, has a 1,000 capacity and is a concert, club and comedy venue in the heart of Belfast's bustling University Quarter. In its various incarnations, it has played host to some of the finest local, national and international music and comedic talent including Ed Sheerin, *Blur, Radiohead* and *The Clash*. [233] Sadly, no record of the set list exists from this gig but based on other shows from "The Too Tough To Die" tour, punters would have been treated to around 30 songs with probably five picks from that latest album. As well as the title track, fans would have seen "Durango 95", Mama's Boy, "Danger Zone" and "Wart Hog" with its inflammable guitars and Dee Dee's undecipherable, devilish vocals.

Four musicians who were heavily influenced by The Ramones are the band *No Matter*. Originating from different parts of Northern Ireland but using Belfast as their practice centre, the group was formed in 2010. The quartet is comprised of Jarlath Cowan and Dan Kennedy both on guitar, Caitlin Palmer playing bass and Jamie Wilson on drums with Jarlath, Dan and Caitlin taking it in turns as lead vocalist. The group is another variation in terms of the way they have 'honoured' The Ramones and have covered songs rather than being classed as a tribute act. Indeed, the band usually play original material and have been described as a "fast-paced energetic melodic skate/pop punk" outfit and as "one of the greatest things to come out of Northern Ireland." The group have gained a reputation for being extremely hard-working, having toured extensively across the UK, Ireland and Europe." *No Matter* have also made appearances at several punk festivals and have also crossed the Atlantic playing shows in Canada. [234]

Jarlath points out that "the band always have fun putting together a cover set when they get the chance" and in 2014 and 2016 performed two gigs solely of Ramones tunes at the *Black Box* in Belfast. Indeed, their repertoire was impressive with songs taken from a number of albums stretching the full length of The Ramones' illustrious career. At one end of the continuum, for instance, we have tunes such as "Beat On The Brat" and "Now I Wanna Sniff Some Glue" taken from the eponymous debut album whilst at the other end of the timeline, *No Matter* performed "I Don't Wanna Grow Up" captured off the 1995 swansong "¡Adios Amigos!" L.P. There were some interesting picks on the list which included the often forgotten treasures of "Outsider", "You're Going To Kill That Girl", "She's The One" and the melodic "She's A Sensation". In addition, the group covered some of the traditional choices such as "Sheena Is A Punk Rocker", "Cretin Hop" and "Glad To See You Go" to give a real balanced range of the *tried and trusted* to the more personal preferences.

"Sadly", Jarlath states, "none of us ever saw them live." Indeed, the guitarist wasn't even born when The Ramones first came to Northern Ireland. He goes on to add that "when The Ramones were in their prime, Northern Ireland was experiencing the height of *'The Troubles'* which would have deterred many touring bands from coming over here to play - it never seemed to stop Ramones from playing though." Pleasingly, *No Matter* have had first-hand experience of one of The Ramones when, in 2016, the band played three shows in Ireland supporting Richie and his group. Jarlath adds the detail remembering that "one of the shows was in a small venue called *Lulu's* in Dungannon, a town close to my hometown of Cookstown, where some of my first bands (before *No Matter*) played regularly when we were teenagers. Back then, around 2005, *Lulu's* was known as *The Common Room* and I spent many nights performing numerous Ramones cover on that stage, so to have Richie come and play there was quite a wholesome, full-circle kind of moment for me, personally."

When asked about the influence of The Ramones, Jarlath talks about his personal experience. "I always recall the scene in the 'End of the Century' documentary when Johnny says something along the lines of "You could spend years practicing to be the next Jimi Hendrix, or you can just get out there and play." At the age of 14, when I was starting to learn guitar, hearing someone as iconic as Johnny saying that was very inspiring and is a rule I still live by to this day. In terms of their legacy, you just have to look at almost any sub-genre of alternative music today and you can guarantee that if the bands within their respective genres aren't directly influenced by Ramones, whoever did inspire them almost certainly was."

In May 2023, *No Matter* played in New York City and Jamie, Cat, Dan and Jarlath could not resist the opportunity to take a snap in the exact same spot where The Ramones once stood outside *CBGB* – a real flash back to the past. However, what is apparent is that the band are also looking to the present and to the future to continue to keep The Ramones' memories alive. "We played another Ramones cover set in March 2024 in a new Belfast venue called *The Sanctuary Theatre* alongside *Goon Squad* and Brian Young (frontman of legendary Belfast punk band Rudi)" Jarlath says. "These Ramones tribute nights are a semi-annual occurrence that are organised by the guys at the Belfast-based independent record label *Time To Be Proud* who, much like ourselves, are big Ramones fans." Indeed, *no matter* what you know of the band, that's gotta be good news!

Photograph courtesy of Emma Cunningham

The Ramonas
England/Scotland

To the unacquainted, Brighton might seem a rather odd place to stage a concert for punk rock legends like The Ramones. The town, is a charming seaside resort, located in the county of Sussex in England just under 50 miles south of the capital, London. It is famed for the rather grand Royal Pavilion which was constructed under the guidance and patronage of the Prince Regent who would later be King George IV. This majestic establishment was designed in an Indo-Saracenic style prevalent in India in the 19th century and was built between 1787 and 1822. Other allures had been built in the town including the Palace Pier and the West Pier during the Victorian period and indeed, Brighton's setting appears to make it more akin to a tourist attraction as opposed to somewhere which would provide a venue for these top punk rockers. However, these simplistic truths hide some of the more social nuances about the town. It is also now renowned for its diverse communities such as a large LGBT population, shopping areas, large and vivacious culture along with a vibrant music and arts scene. In fact, Brighton had always hosted a number of top artists at their premier venue, *The Top Rank Suit.* This building was opened in 1965 with a ten-pin bowling alley and an ice rink added a year later as part of the new West Street/Churchill Square re-development after the war. In 1972, the building was re-named the *Kingswest* and it was split into several bars and a cinema. As one resident pointed out "local people had a love/hate relationship with the building, many saying it was ugly and not in keeping with the buildings on the seafront. Others, mainly the younger generation, loved it for its entertainment." (235) By the 1970s the building was used for a music venue with some celebrated acts performing including Suzi Quatro, *Wizzard, Thin Lizzy,* Iggy Pop, *Squeeze, 999, The Damned* and the pretty boy punk peacocks *Generation X* so maybe when the New Yorkers hit the *Top Rank Suit* it should not be regarded as such a surprise.

The Ramones played Brighton twice with their first performance on January 16th, 1980 as part of the tour to promote the "End Of The Century" L.P. For many old-school Ramones fans, this album was maybe not quite a catastrophe but at the very least did push our punk boundaries to the limit. Yes, fans did understand the need to achieve that much sort after chart breakthrough, but at what cost? This 33 rpm was just too damned *poppy.* Indeed, producer, Phil Spector, the creator of the "Wall Of Sound", might well have been the springboard to stardom for the *Ronettes,* but did he have the right credentials to galvanise The Ramones whilst still amplifying Johnny and his buzzsaw guitar? For those of us who witnessed that tour, we need not have worried with absolutely zero *watering down* of their legendary live show. Although there is no written record of their set list that night, we do have accounts of the chosen tracks around that time and we do know that they were supported by the tuneful power-punk band *The Boys.* One song which they would have almost certainly have played was already established as a favourite with another New York band, the *Heartbreakers.* Dropping the "s" The Ramones took the junkie ditty of "Chinese Rocks" and performed their own version of "Chinese Rock" paving the for it to be one of their mainstay live tunes throughout the rest of their career. Interestingly, Dee Dee maintained that although credit was given to Richard Hell as a co-writer of this song, it was almost entirely written by the Ramone himself. As well as tunes from "End Of The Century" there would undoubtedly have been a number taken from the fourth studio album "Road To Ruin" too with "I Don't Want You, "Go Mental", "I'm Against It" and "I Wanted Everything" all featuring heavily on this tour. The second and last time the band would visit the *Top Rank Suit* would be over six years later in May 1986. By this time hard hitting, Richie had replaced Marky on the drummer's stool with the band promoting their ninth studio album "Animal Boy".

As well as the title track, three other gems are included off that album with "Crummy Stuff" chosen along with the harder core tracks of "Freak Of Nature" and "Love Kills". That night, the Brighton audience would be treated to 27 songs altogether. [236]

Although too young to have witnessed The Ramones play live, four females - three based in Brighton - have since seen and indeed supported the individual acts of Marky, Richie and C.J. Indeed, the *Ramonas* have now become one of the busiest and easily recognisable Ramones tributes in the UK and beyond. The band's concept was actually

Photograph: Yuki Kuroyanagi

conceived by someone well known to Ramones buffs around the globe. Clare Misstake, aka Clare Pproduct or Noizee now keeps the memory of the New Yorkers alive by playing bass for Richie Ramone's superlative solo project. She is a bundle of energy, fearsome to watch and with a punk aggression and attitude which slaps you in your face. Although Clare has long since left the *Ramonas*, she initially started the group due to her love of the boys from Queens. The bassist, at that stage was playing for *AntiProduct* who back in 2004 performed alongside Marky Ramone at the *Underworld* in London. "That show inspired me to start the *Ramonas*", Clare says, going on to add that "I was recording the guitar tracks for the first *Ramonas* demo on the same day that Johnny Ramone died (September 15th 2004). I didn't know till after, but I thought it was really cool that I was playing Johnny's chords on the other side of the world the day he died. Though it totally freaked me out the next day when I found out... I wore my Ramones shirt for an entire week in a sort of smelly vigil." [(237)]

There have been a number of changes to the line-up over the years. The longest serving members are vocalist Lisa Lathwell (who incidentally is the one member who does not come from Brighton but from Scotland) and bass player Victoria Smith who both joined in 2008. Guitarist Maxine Cahill took up the role in 2017 whilst Sadie Brown is the newest recruit starting in 2022. Some of the amusement of a Ramones tribute is surely taking up the various pseudonyms and the *Ramonas* are no exception. Lisa has the penname of Cloey Ramone, Maxine cleverly converts into Rohnny, Sadie's title becomes Skitchy, whilst my favourite nickname is undoubtedly Vicky's who miraculously transforms into Pee Pee. All the girls have performed or still take part in other music projects with Vicky, for example, an ex-member of the all-girl rock band *McQueen* and still involved with blues artist Dani Wilde.

The band base their sets around previous song lists used by The Ramones usually playing about 30 songs in total per gig. As with most cover groups, the *Ramonas* always play "the classics" but change the set frequently to keep it as fresh as possible adding in a few more obscure tunes along the way. Refreshingly, the band also take requests from the audience at the end of the show for their encore keeping the punters as happy as possible. The girls cite a range of favourite albums as their inspiration ranging "Brain Drain", "Animal Boy", "Rocket To Russia", "Leave Home" and of course the self-titled debut. In terms of individual tracks, "it changes all of time" Maxine reflects but I always come back to "Bonzo" referring to the outstanding "My Brain Is Hanging Upside Down" a rare political song about president Ronald Reagan's visit to a Nazi war cemetery in Bitburg.

The band pick out a number of concert highlights with Vicky reminiscing "in November 2011 we played a show at Camden *Underworld* with Richie Ramone. It was a dream come true, he joined us on drums and then vocals. I almost didn't make the gig as there was a crash and I was in standstill traffic for hours, luckily I did make it but I was so embarrassed in front of Richie!" Guitarist Maxine talks about her stand-out gig stating that it "was my second time playing *Rebellion* - 2018 on the *Casbah* stage. I was nervous because it was the biggest crowd I had played to at the time, but I'll never forget the rush I felt after that show. It was amazing and inspiring."

With over 10 years playing the pubs and clubs as an all-girl tribute to The Ramones, 2016 saw The *Ramonas* launch their self-penned material with their debut EP "You Asked For it". This was followed a year later with the album "First World Problems" which also encompasses many of the girls' wider musical influences with hints of early *B-52s, The Cramps, Siouxsie and the Banshees, The Runaways, Descendents* and *Motörhead.* The band has followed this up with further releases including "Acoustic Problems", "I Want To Live In Outer Space" and "Haphazard". A hike on to their official website at *www.ramonas.co.uk* is well worth a visit where you can hear many of their top picks.

As an all-female group of course it would not be fitting to wear Ramones type basin wigs. Lisa reflects that "we are pretty much ourselves but with some Ramones moves thrown in. For us it's about the power and energy of the music and keeping it alive and true". Vicky agrees affirming that "the live energy is really important at our gigs, plus the moves and capturing the speed and things that are unique about The Ramones. There's definitely some bass faces thrown in too!" There are a host of video clips and links to the band out there and I recommend that patrons always go and view for oneself. If you have time, a great starting point would be the 2022 *Rebellion* full concert superbly filmed by Demon Knight. Indeed, drummer Sadie points to this as her personal favourite gig. "The room was packed and the energy was high" she says. "The Empress Ballroom" is a beautiful room to play." Opening with the introductory instrumental "Durango 95", the band then blasts out all our favourite sing-alongs such as "Teenage Lobotomy", "Rockaway Beach" and "Blitzkrieg Bop". Indeed, by the time the "hey ho, lets goes" are ringing out on that signature tune, the crowd have become fully absorbed and joining in enthusiastically. The band transgress occasionally and play some of their original work but more often than not it is jammed packed with the likes of "Commando", "Pet Sematary", "Let's Dance" et al. If you have not time to see a full-set then check out "Gimme, Gimme, Shock Treatment" at the *Scarborough Punk Festival* which will whet your appetite. Although it does take some time getting used to the female vocals and therefore the consequential different pitch range, you cannot fault the energy and power of any of the girls in the band. Their all action style is contagious and endless whilst you have never heard the "*1,2,3,4s*" screamed so ferociously or quickly.

As with our other tributes, the band acknowledge The Ramones legacy with singer Lisa claiming that "it kicked off the punk movement" and bassist Vicky recognising that "The Ramones influence goes beyond music, it's the whole punk movement." These four girls may not be *sweet, sweet little Ramonas* but without a shadow of doubt *you kids in the crowd, will like it when the music's loud!*

UK Ramones
England

Even by Ramones standards, 1980 must have been a gruelling, yet exhilarating period. To give an insight into their heavy schedule, one can take their touring programme of the United Kingdom as an exemplar. In that calendar year alone, they visited Britain on three different occasions, performing in 30 different shows. Their first leg of the country took place in January and February and during the tour they played in some towns and cities which many might regard as unusual choices – maybe not *backwaters* as such but the selection of places such as Brighton, Norwich, Exeter, Aylesbury, Lancaster, Bournemouth and Colchester may raise a few eyebrows nowadays. Yet these centres were all designated and on January 24th, 1980, The Ramones ended up on the south coast in Hampshire to perform in Portsmouth, another option which may surprise the unenlightened.

Portsmouth, affectionately known as Pompey, is a port city and naval base on the south coast of England. It is probably best known for its maritime heritage and the historic dockyard which is the home of the interactive National Museum of the Royal Navy. Here thousands of tourists each year, visit sights such as the Henry VIII Tudor flag ship, *The Mary Rose* or view the largest, fastest and most powerful vessel of Queen Victoria's fleet, the first iron-hulled and armoured battleship, *HMS Warrior*. Even more famous, is *HMS Victory* which lies in dry dock and is the oldest naval vessel still in commission. One can still see the exact spot where Admiral Lord Nelson died at the Battle of Trafalgar in 1805 just prior to hearing that his British fleet had gained a crushing victory against the combined forces of the French and Spanish. Portsmouth is the most densely populated city of the United Kingdom with just over 208,000 inhabitants recorded with most of the conurbation located on Portsea Island.

The chosen venue for The Ramones that evening was the *Portsmouth Guildhall*. The original building was built in 1890 which was heavily damaged by Luftwaffe bombing in World War Two, resulting in the establishment being entirely rebuilt in the 1950s. The *Guildhall* now operates as a concert, wedding and conference site and according to *Visit Portsmouth's* own website the *Guildhall's* "reputation as an illustrious live music venue is guaranteed; it having hosted not only *The Beatles*, but also the world's first live airing of seminal *Pink Floyd* album, 'Dark Side of the Moon'." It also lists other eminent bands and artists "to have walked the Guildhall stage" citing amongst others *Led Zeppelin, The Jimi Hendrix Experience, U2, Blondie, The Rolling Stones, Iron Maiden*, Bob Dylan, Elton John, *The Beach Boys, The Jam, Status Quo, The Kinks* and The Ramones. [238] The support band throughout their first section of their 1980 British tour were London based power-punk band *The Boys* who are possibly best remembered for their 1978 single "Brickfield Nights". There is a partial Ramones set list documented that evening with "Rockaway Beach", "Judy Is A Punk", "Chinese Rock", "Rock 'n' Roll High School" and "Do You Remember Rock 'n' Roll Radio?" all performed with the last three songs all aimed to promote the latest album "End Of The Century".

Those locals who witnessed The Ramones that evening would be fortunate as it would be the one and only time the band performed in the city. One fan who did see the group was bassist Alan Weeks who along with three other musicians went on to form their own Hampshire based tribute in 2011. As well as Alan, the group comprised of George Hart on vocals, Nick Smith as guitarist and Harry, ex member of *Some Kinda Wonderful (SKAW)* on drums. The band initially never really got off the ground until 2014 when Steve Kirk replaced Harry on the drummer's chair with the stick man detailing how he got involved. "The band had been playing a little earlier but never really did many gigs and certainly none outside the local area", Steve recalls. "I was playing in quite a few bands such as *Night of Treason, Mid Age Rampage* and *The Money Shots* and I got a call from George who I knew from years earlier when he fronted local legends *Emptifish*. He asked if I was interested as they wanted to give it another go as a Ramones tribute. I met the others and we all clicked from the word go. We rehearsed intensely and started to book gigs all over the place." Just like many of our cover bands, the lads took on stage names akin to the boys from Forest Hills with Georgee, Nicky, Stevie and A. Jay the preferred monikers whilst the band's title was simplicity itself – *the UK Ramones* not only immediately linked themselves with the American punk icons but also portrayed their geographic location as well.

For those fans familiar with The Ramones' set during the late '80s and early '90s, then *Pompey's* finest were very much reminiscent of these times. Indeed, just as many of our tributes have based their repertoire around "It's Alive", it would be fair to say that *UK Ramones* was more affiliated to "Loco Live" which ran through the much loved songs in the same tried and trusted order. This would see, for instance, "Durango 95", "Teenage Lobotomy", "Psycho Therapy", "Blitzkrieg Bop" and the obligatory favourites delivered in rapid fire succession. Steve recalls that his first gig with the band was on the 1st November in 2014 and he went on to perform over 50 times with the group in total. When asked about his favourite concerts he recalls a number of stand-out shows highlighting, the gig at the *Beat Generator* in Dundee in Scotland. After pretty much an eight-hour drive and straight on stage they played a blinding gig to an exceptionally appreciative audience. As well as north of the border, the group have also travelled across the River Severn to perform in Wales. Co-headlining with a *Blondie* tribute for a show at *The Globe* in Cardiff the drummer recalls a raucous crowd "up for it right from the start." At the other end of the scale, Steve recites a last minute gig at *The Box* in Crewe where they performed to just two people, a father and son, who just happened to stumble upon the gig. They had a great time and we played as we would have done to a full house and we still got paid, put up and fed," he laughs. Other great shows include the *Fighting Cock* in Kingston and the *Holroyd Arms* in Guildford where Steve remembers that there were "loads of youngsters, going mental!"

Fortunately, there are many opportunities to observe the band in action and I would strongly recommend either a visit on to their *Facebook* page or on to *Youtube*. The most noticeable factor is how reminiscent the lads from Portsmouth are to the boys from Queens. Centre stage, is Georgee – wigged appropriately, wearing his hooped shirt, tinted glasses and clad in leather jacket and gloves, his left foot forward thrusts forwards as he hovers sideways on, as if playing a forward defensive. Flanked to his right, Nicky blasts out the classics like a machine gun disperses bullets. Ripped jeans, bowl haircut, plimsolls and capped T-shirt, make no mistake he has Johnny's mannerisms to perfection. To the front man's left is A. Jay. Hair swirling, bass low, legs astride - just for a split second I was sure we were caught in a time warp, transported back to say *hola amigo* to Christopher Joseph

Ward. Sitting behind them is Stevie, cool and composed, hunched over the drum set, sun-glasses perched, adorned in his T- shirt and very much reminiscent of Marky at his peak. There are some great clips of *UK Ramones* and a wonderful starting point would be the renditions of "Cretin Hop" and "Suzy Is A Headbanger" at *Southsea Skate Park*. If you have more time, check out the outside gig live at the Bandstand from August 2017 which gives us nearly 25 minutes of high-tempo fun. Their last concert was in October of the same year with Steve admitting that "at the time, we were talking about mixing up the set and introducing new songs but it never really got past the discussion stage. No one left and we certainly didn't split, it just kind of stopped." There is no doubt that many on the south coast and beyond will be hoping for some kind of change of mind, with the UK Ramones' version of the Pompey chimes ringing out again!

The Outsiders
Italy

The Ramones first hit Italy in February 1980 coinciding with the recent release of their fifth album *"End of the Century"*. Produced by Phil Spector in a variety of studios in Los Angeles, it used more advanced standards of engineering, such as high-quality overdubbing and echo chambers but has been much criticised by many fans as being "over-produced" or too commercial or merely the dislike for the non-jacketed and coloured T-Shirt album cover. The production period encountered much conflict between Spector and the band members, particularly Johnny and Dee Dee who were used to a far speedier recording process. In their respective autobiographies both guitarists cite their distain of the producer with the bassist claiming "he levelled his gun at my heart and then motioned to me to get back in the piano room". [239] Johnny informs us that he "had me play the opening chord to 'Rock 'n' Roll High School'…for three or four hours" going on to add that "if he would have shot any of us, it probably would have been Dee Dee. Somehow, he irritated him even more." [240]

Away from the studio and back on the road, you can only presume that the band were more at ease without Spector as they left Belgium and headed for Italy, the fourth nation of their mini-European tour. The band's first gig took place on February 14th in Reggio Emilia, a city in northern Italy with a population of just over 170,000. The gig took place at the *Palazzetto dello Sport* which is an indoor area primarily used for sporting events such as basketball or volleyball. Opened in 1968 it has a seating capacity of 4,600 and has witnessed notable artists such as *The Police, Black Sabbath* and *Anthrax.* All Italian fans that tour, would have been spoilt rotten – in addition to The Ramones there was more punk royalty in store as the support band was none other than *The UK Subs* with the famed Charlie Harper at the helm. The set list that night naturally included works from "End Of The Century" and as well as "Rock n Roll High School", "This Ain't Havana", "I'm Affected", "Do You Remember Rock 'n' Radio?", "Chinese Rock" and the understated gem "All The Way". Indeed, this wired, frenzied, raw live version of the track makes a mockery of Spector's lame, tame studio effort.

The band went on to play three other centres in the country taking in Udine, Milan and Turin before heading northwards to Paris. Fortunately, for Italian Ramones fans they would not have to wait long for another taste of the group and in the September of the same year, the boys returned. The New Yorkers played five gigs in Sanmero, Genoa, Rome, Casalmaggoire and again in Milan and it was here in the second city at the *Velodomo Vigorelli,* an oval venue originally used for cycling racing, where Marky Ramone walked off stage during a rendition of "Commando". "I didn't use my cymbal a lot in that song", he points out, "but suddenly there was a crash that didn't come from my stick. A large rock hit the symbol and fell to the ground." [241] With the band joining him backstage soon after and with the tense crowd on the verge of rioting, the drummer and his bandmates braved the potential backlash and went back out to finish the set.

Overall, The Ramones would play in Italy over 40 times with their last gig in Milan in January 1996. Interestingly, most of their gigs were confined to the northern regions of Italy with only the occasional venture to places such as Rome where they played in the capital just four times. Exploring *Youtube,* however, will find a superb sound check of the jewel "Cretin Hop" from 1980 with the formidable *St Angelo Castle* in the backdrop and well worth an inspection. Maybe surprisingly, the band did travel once to Sassari in Sardinia in 1994 but at no time did they perform down south 'in the boot' of the peninsula or the "Stivale" as the Italians call it.

Based in Conegliano, in the province of Treviso in the north east region of Italy, another bunch of fanatics who were suitably *revved up and ready to go* are *The Outsiders.* The choice of band name is an interesting one which stems from arguably the best track from The Ramones' 1983 album *Subterranean Jungle.* So good in fact that the mass market maestros and Californian punk luminaries *Green Day* covered the tune themselves on the "B side" of their single "Warning" at the turn of the new millennium.

Formed in 2016, the group have gone through a series of line-up changes which have included Fabiola "Sheena" Bellomo on guitar, Michele Daresi as bassist as well as Matteo Spinazzè and Matteo Amadio both at one stage on drums. The present quartet now features Alessandro Spagnol on vocals, Andrea "Andrix" Rossi playing guitar, Matteo Zaccardelli on bass and Steven "Grinch" Franzin taking control at the drummer's stool. Alessandro has been with the band since its formation, both Andrea and Matteo joined a year later in 2017 whilst Steven is the newest member of the band starting in 2018. After a three-year hiatus between 2020-23, the group are now back in full swing, reinvigorated and gigging again.

As with most tributes, the musicians have had much experience playing in other bands. Alessandro, for instance, has sung for *Qupram, Lacerator Swarm, Athwart, Evome* and when he is not *Joey* is now also playing as bass man for *Obscure Obsession*. Andrea was also in *Qupram* along with the *Silverbones* whilst Matteo performed for *Silver Trash, Slane* and also plays bass for the group *The Goodwin Sands* when not doubling as our Dee Dee. Lastly, multi-skilled Steven played drums for *Stadium Arcadium* - a *Red Hot Chilli Peppers* tribute along with currently switching instruments on to the bass for *Xbox,* a *Green Day* cover band.

Although *The Outsiders* are too young to have seen The Ramones, Alessandro describes why he started the band. "In 2015, I lost a very important person in my family. At that time, I was playing in two metal bands which broke up for various reasons. I was on the verge of quitting playing music because any rock/metal genre piece didn't give me the same feelings after the loss of my grandmother. One day, purely by chance, I was listening randomly on my Ipod and a track from The Ramones' Anthology collection came on. Suddenly I felt a new energy, which surprised me because I knew The Ramones well but had not listened to them for a number of years. It was there that I realised that giving up everything didn't make sense, so I decided to start again from there. In addition, besides the fact that in my country, Italy, there aren't many tributes to the '*fast four*', so I decided to reproduce as faithfully as possible, the music of the most influential group of the last 50 years in punk rock."

Like so many other artists, the singer refers to the significance and legacy of The Ramones pointing out that "they began a process of evolution. If you think about it, bands like *Blink 182, Green Day* and *The Offspring,* have in a way kept The Ramones' punk rock style alive, of course putting their own spin on it in terms of composition and themes."

One of their most memorable concerts was when the group headlined the 2018 the *Ca' Rimoto Festival* where the band were invited to inaugurate a new motorbike meeting with *the Outsiders* going down so well that they carried on performing until one in the morning. Citing the first three albums along with the 1989 *Brain Drain* as the most inspiration L.Ps, the band's set features many of our customary favourites. An interesting viewing is the *"Outsiders Official Teaser"* from 2017 on the social platform *Youtube* to get an impression for the band. Here they present "Blitzkrieg Bop", "Pet Sematary", "California Sun", "Rockaway Beach" and "Poison Heart" as well as two tracks from Joey Ramones solo adventure - "New York City" and "What A Wonderful World". If you enjoy "a rocky" and more melodic cover band then you will relish *The Outsiders* with Alessandro's pleasant sounding voice giving a rather mellow feel for the songs.

Wardogs
Italy

In terms of keeping the memory of The Ramones alive and kicking, one of the most prominent cover bands has undoubtedly been *The Wardogs*. With around 500 live shows under their belt in Europe and in the United States of America and with a catalogue of experiences as long as your arm their *curriculum vitae* is indeed impressive. The group were formed in 2009 in the city of Treviso in northern Italy which is located approximately 25 miles north of the beautiful canal city of Venice. The band consists of Sandro Mariuz on guitar, Simone Morettin as drummer, Paolo Mariott as the bass man and Simone Baldi holding the mic. Three of the lads had previous experience with other bands prior to the *Wardogs* – Simone Baldi in *Evilsonic* a *Slipknot* tribute, Sandro in *Wanted,* a speed metal band and a juicy mix of *Metallica* and *Motörhead* whilst Simone Morettin is still in *Evelking*, a folk metal group.

Guitarist Sandro enthusiastically remembers past Ramones concerts stating that all in all "we saw them around 30-40 times. Every gig was like a train in your face! And every gig was memorable." Indeed, other Italians recall the New Yorkers having similar lasting effects on them as well. One such fan, was an 18 at the time of the 1980 *"End Of The Century Tour"* and writes his personal story in a blog. He went to their fourth gig on that tour in Turin - another northern Italian city, situated around a four-hour drive from the *Wardogs* home of Treviso. Although made famous for the Christian religious relic of the *Holy Shroud,* Turin also has a nightlife which is impressively varied so it was apt that The Ramones hit here on February 18th at the *Palasport Ruffini.* This indoor arena was built in 1961, primarily for as a sports venue for basketball and volleyball but was also used for rock and pop concerts. Music genres were varied with examples of artists who had performed there including *Iron Maiden, The Cure* and *Jeffro Tull.* It has a capacity of around 4,500 and of course for the punk dream double header of *The UK Subs* and Ramones, it was sold out. The young fan cites that this gig "definitively changed my life" and also points to the political tension in the air at that time as well as the eye-opening experience of a punk gig. "Many people from the "right" wing (Fascists I can say without any doubt…) were listening to The Ramones. Fascists hated punks. They just listened to them because of the way they were dressing (leather jackets) and lyrics of a few songs (Blitzkrieg Bop or Commando). The venue was clearly divided in four big groups. The Fascists, the punks (few), communists (do not care about the music just want to kick some Fascist ass type of guys) and music fans just like me and my brother… When The Ramones started their gig the place went nuts. It was a total fight but the police did not intervene this time. I was not in the "centre of the action" (fortunately) but I had a good view of it. It went on for the whole set. That night I did not notice but, years later, I found out that The Ramones has been forced to modify, or censor, lyrics of some songs for the Italian tour. Commando, for example, the "third rule" of the song [242] was simply not sung by Joey… Ramones set was tight as usual but, since I've never seen one of their shows, I only knew their music from their record. songs where twice faster than the studio version. Even songs from "The End of

The Century" songs sounded 'punk'. I was amazed. Hit by this wall of sound seeing a real punk group playing as fast as they could. I guess I must have looked like a child at the luna-park hypnotized, with a dumb smile on my face." [243]

Wardogs guitarist Sandro recalls how his band was formed. "We love The Ramones and trash metal music. We all played in different bands but at one point we decided to start the tribute. Our idea was to keep their legacy alive after they had stopped." He goes on to add that "we didn't want to make a copy of the original band but, respect the tradition. Our sounds reflect this philosophy - we are *heavy, dirty and direct* like The Ramones."

The band have certainly kept to their promise. Their work is without doubt tireless and endless which mirrors the dogged originals. Many of their extensive exploits have been in conjunction with Marky Ramone – on New Year's Eve in 2011, for instance, they played with the drummer at the *Treviso Palasport* in front of 7,000 people. Two years later, he awarded them the honour of

Photograph courtesy of Andrea Compa

"Official Italian Ramones Tribute Band". In 2014, their splendid relationship with Marky saw them play together not only on three occasions in New York but also at the Italian *"Home Festival"*, a 40 year's anniversary of the band which attracted 16,000 people. Marky and the *Wardogs* continued on tour playing a number of Italian towns. In 2023, this collaboration was sustained with the release of "Pet Sematary"/ "I Don't Want To Grow Up" whilst they also commenced the *"High Five For The Kids Tour"*.

Besides their association with Marky Ramone, there has been many other memorable heights. In 2013 they released the cover album *"Raw & Dirty"* which featured 20 of the very best Ramones tracks including maybe a couple of the more unusual picks such as "Main Main" and "Spiderman". Indeed, the former song featured on the recording of "1, 2, 3, 4", the compilation album which was performed by a number of Italian bands a year later. The *Wardogs* have also been in associated with the "extended Ramones family." In 2014, they worked on the publication of tour manager, Monte Melnick's Italian biography, *Sulla Strada con i Ramones* whilst four years later they worked with him again on the *"On The Road Tour"*. In 2017 producer and writer Daniel Ray played guitar along-side the group in *Treviso* in a rendition of the famed "Blitzkrieg Bop". In addition, the band have been fortunate to support a number of well-known artists such as *The Cockney Rejects, Discharge, Prodigy, LA Guns, The Dictators, Meteors, Napalm Death, Morlocks, Warrior Soul and* Liam Gallagher of *Oasis*.

The band play songs from every album, from the first to the last. Normally they would define a list and play it for one year before changing the set. When asked about his personal most loved albums, Sandro felt it was "very difficult to choose" but maybe "Rocket To Russia" and "It's Alive" by a whisker with "Rockaway Beach" as his favourite individual track. A quick search on social media reveals a number of *Wardogs'* tunes with my personal preference a cover of "Go Mental" which featured on The Ramones' fourth album "Road To Ruin". The Italians released this as a single in 2016 and promoted by the original drawing created by John Holmstrom back in 1977. This was first used on the inside sleeve of "Rocket To Russia" and aligned to "I Wanna Be Well". Other easily accessible tracks include "Censorshit" in Turin, "Havana Affair" at the *Dragonfly* in Salzano, "Teenage Lobotomy" at the *Alcatraz in* Milan, "Tomorrow She Goes Away" at the *Factory* in Verona and "Psycho Therapy" at The Ramones convention in Treviso. Throughout these and other records by the band, the influence of thrash and heavy metal seeps through not only with their intense, powerful and distorted guitars along with emphatic drum beats but also with the general demeanour, black clothes and long hair styles. Sandro wraps up The Ramones' impact stating that "their influence is enormous and you can see it everywhere, when you listen to music (punk or metal), when you wear leather jacket or ripped jeans. T-shirts with their logo are everywhere and when young boys start a band, they are not perfect musicians there but they could be The Ramones."

Shock Treatment
United States Of America

Da Brudders performed in Iowa just three times overall in a career which spanned over 22 years. The state of Iowa is situated in the upper Midwestern region of the United States and forms a bridge between the forests of the east and the grasslands of the high prairies to the west. Bordered by the famous rivers of the Mississippi, Missouri and Big Sioux, it is also bounded by six American states– Wisconsin, Minnesota, Illinois, Nebraska, South Dakota and Missouri. The state's name is derived from the Iowa Native American people who once inhabited the area whilst the capital and most populous city is Des Moines with just over 212,000 inhabitants living there. [244]

Their first gig in Iowa, which took place on May 10th 1980, was not in the capital, however, it was at the *Darby Gymnasium*, a private college at Grinnell. Already that year, the group had toured Europe and parts of the USA and Canada. Their gruelling schedule should never be underestimated as in 1980 alone they would also go on to visit Japan, Australia, New Zealand and return to Europe and the United States. The show in Grinnell has unfortunately no documentation of those tracks played that night although we do know that it would be aimed to promote the "End Of The Century" album and five or six songs would no doubt have been chosen from this cut.

Far more details have been recorded regarding their second visit to the state on June 1st, 1983, in surely one of the most bizarre venues imaginable - on the jam packed top floor of a Holiday Inn in Des Moines with the site known as the *Top of the Tower*. There is a comprehensive account online of that evening under the guise of '*1983: When The Ramones Conquered Des Moines*' and set out below are two extracts from different people who were at the gig which highlights the surreal circumstances. The first is from an unnamed blogger who states that "The Ramones rocked the revolving banquet room atop the *Holiday Inn* in downtown Des Moines. As one might expect, it was a concert that would be talked about years afterward, and it was the initial footprint of punk rock's influence in Des Moines. The band was on the back end of a rigorous eight-day run. Having played Omaha, the night before, they stormed into Des Moines early and booked a room at the Holiday Inn on the corner of N.E. 14th Street and Euclid Avenue (now where Community State Bank sits). After checking into the Holiday Inn, the band made an appearance at *Music Circuit*, a local record store that moonlighted as a concert promotion company. Hundreds of people lined up to meet these punk rock legends, and asked them to sign everything from record albums to baseballs. A number of the people that would later shape the Des Moines underground scene were there…One thing is for certain, however… After this show, punk rock finally had a foothold in Des Moines, Iowa." Another person who was at the show was Mark Penner who was the guitarist in the support band that evening *"Universal Will To Become"*. He recollects that "The Ramones were really on that night. I've seen them since; this was easily the best of the shows I'd seen. I also remember them being very loud…Looking back, that show was when the scene in Des Moines changed. Before that show the 'punk' scene was very small, very diverse and very tight knit." (245)

The 1983 tour was to help endorse the latest L.P "Subterranean Jungle" which was The Ramones' seventh studio album. Recorded in October 1982 and released in the following February through Sire Records, the 33 was produced by Ritchie Cordell and Glen Kolotkin and recorded at the *Kingdom Sound Studio*, Syosset in Long Island, New York. Due to his alcoholism and imminent sacking, it was also the last album to feature Marky on drums until his return on "Brain Drain" in 1989. The photograph on the front cover was taken by George DuBose which shows the band inside a subway car at the 57th Street stop on the B train – the final stop before entering Queens. Marky's placement in the shoot says it all with the drummer isolated peering out of a window rather than standing with the rest of the band by the door. Although Johnny Ramone felt the band were "going in the right direction", [246] it is hard to argue with journalist Gil Kaufman's review "that the strain within the band shows in the album's track selection: nine original songs in 33 minutes, padded out by three covers." I think most would agree that the one truly classic tune from the album, which would go on to become a mainstay in their live set, was "Psycho Therapy". This was the only collaboration between Dee Dee and Johnny and it marked an upturn in their relationship and has all the hallmarks of a perfect Ramones song: "lyrics about a psychotic teen, random acts of violence, Tunial-popping and the obligatory trip to the psych ward. [247] Other notable songs included "Outsider" and "Time Bomb" which both feature Dee Dee on vocals – the former mid-song and the latter for its entirety. As Marky points out "the guitar was aggressive, and the lyrics, largely thanks to Dee Dee, were sufficiently warped." [248] Although other tracks fail to hit the summits from early albums there are some *steady eddies.* "In the Park", for instance, appears to harp back to the bassist's youthful experiences whilst the only decent cover, "Little Bit O' Soul", despite its non-punk title, includes some driving guitars reminiscent of a *vacuum* sucking up dirt and grime. Lastly, the catchy "Highest Trails Above" should never be forgotten. Not just because it has some decent hooks with an exquisite melody but more touchingly because some of the words that Dee Dee penned from this song were placed on his headstone. Interestingly, the soon to be ousted Marky, hated the album and in his autobiography states that the drumhead sounded "as if it had a towel over it" and told Cordell that he was "fucking with The Ramones sound." [(249)] I would have to concur and for punks like myself, there were too many slower, mediocre, pop numbers. Notwithstanding from those tracks already mentioned, the rest of the album, would merely be classed as *also-rans* and spend little or no time on the stereo turntable. Indeed, the worst of the bunch - "Everytime I Eat Vegetables It Makes Me Think Of You" is more like a *turnip* than *10 carat gold.*

There would be only one song, "Psycho Therapy, chosen from the "Subterranean Jungle" album which would make it on the *Lollapalooza* tour. During this circuit, the group visited Iowa for a third and final time, playing in Des Moines at the *Iowa State Fairgrounds* on June 28th 1996. Although they never got the chance to see The Ramones play live, four musicians emerging from Iowa decided to form their own tribute band in 2016 due to their love for Ramones' songs and style, as well as wishing to share the music with a new generation of live audiences. The band consisted of Ryan Miller as vocalist, guitarist Davis Coover, Karl Schlotterback on the drums and Lincoln Hinzman as bassist and backing vocals with Ryan coming up with the group's designation of *"Shock Treatment"*. The choice of the band's name is noteworthy, stemming from arguably the best track from The Ramones' second album "Leave Home". The link, of course, is invaluable as would-be fans would immediately associate *"Shock Treatment"* with the New Yorkers. Many of our cover bands have enjoyed taking up the various pen names and the lads from Iowa did the same with Ryan assuming the title of Jodey, Davis having the pseudonym of Jimmy, Karl having the nom de plume of Tony whilst Lincoln having the superb hybrid stage name of Dee-Jay Ramone. Ryan, Lincoln and Karl all had past experiences of playing in other local bands around Cedar Rapids which is the second-most populous city in Iowa located about 122 miles away from the capital, Des Moines.

Singer Ryan reflects that "one of our most memorable gigs was at *The Liar's Club* in Chicago, Illinois. The staff was really great and it was a fun crowd." A swift look at their set list which last around an hour will give you an idea why they went down so well with a 30 strong repertoire and so many crowd pleasers performed. Although *"Shock Treatment"* concentrate on songs from the first three seminal albums, there are some tunes which postdate "Rocket To Russia" too including "Chinese Rock", "It's A Long Way Back

To Germany", "I Wanna Be Sedated", "I Wanna Live", "Pet Semetary" and of course "Psycho Therapy". I also love the fact, that as well as the favourites such as "Teenage Lobotomy", "Beat On The Brat", "Judy Is A Punk" and "Cretin Hop", the band perform some of those live songs which were disregarded over the course of time by The Ramones. Examples include "Loudmouth", "I Don't Wanna Go Down To The Basement", "Carbona Not Glue" and "You're Gonna Kill That Girl". Some brief exploration on to *Youtube* soon unveils *"Shock Treatment"* live at *Brauerhouse* in Lombard, Illionois in June 2019. If you wish for your Ramones tribute to look like the prototype, then you will immediately be impressed. Four punk urchins clad in their torn blue jeans, black leathers, murky white sneakers and bowl haircuts appear to have crawled from a dark, dingy maintenance hovel from the dimmest of pits. Joey, or more accurately Jodey, is suspended over the stage like a hideous wigged creature from *War of the Worlds* whilst Johnny, aka Jimmy, blank expression, legs split holds his guitar as if it will convert to a bayonet at any given second. Dee Jay's movements and gesticulations have early Dee Dee written all over them – restless, disturbed, hunched, knees bent and head bobbing. In front of the impressive backdrop Ramones logo, the converted seal of the US Presidency, sits Tony who is a dead ringer for Tommy. Just like the original drummer, he drives the band forward with both precision and energy. Four songs are on offer at the club with "Sheena Is A Punk Rocker", "Rockaway Beach", "Commando" and my personal favourite "Glad To See You Go" all whizzed through in typical style. If you have more time to spare, then refer to the *Liar's Club* in Chicago in August 2019. Commencing with the punk anthem "Blitzkrieg Bop" and finishing with the appropriate "Gimme Gimme Shock Treatment", the band delivers more than half an hour of vintage Ramones tunes.

By 2019, the lads decided to call it a day, primarily because after the mandatory Covid-19 break, some of the members were getting old and less energetic. As Lincoln points out "if the tribute can't be done accurately, then it's not really a tribute at all." Nonetheless, for those three years, *"Shock Treatment"* helped to keep alive the name and legacy of The Ramones. "We think they influenced generations of people musically, and culturally" states the singer. "Spearheading a genre with minimalistic, primitive, yet aggressive song writing while creating the sound, style, and attitude of punk rock. They had more of an impact than any other band and we could go on in greater detail but would like to keep our reply just as their music…short and to the point."

Uramones
Japan

By 1980, The Ramones had truly become a global band. Previously, the boys from Queens had been limited to tours of North America and Europe but the new decade saw them embark on trips to countries across the Pacific with gigs in Asia and Australasia too. Indeed, the summer of 1980 included five locations in Japan – the first on June 27th in the capital, Tokyo. Playing at the *Seibu Gekijou*, they co-headlined with *Sheena and the Rokkets*, a popular local rock band. The theatre was a well-known high-profile landmark within the city and had already attracted other notable guests such as Elvis Costello and *The Attractions* and *The B52s* so would have been a natural venue to kick off the tour. According to Marky Ramone, the venue was impressive. The *Seibu* was an auditorium seating several thousand but situated on the top floor of a large modern commercial building which had opened as recently as May 1975. "Where we come from", Marky points out, "auditoriums either occupied the entire building or, like a swimming pool, were at the base of one. But the Japanese were innovators." There is no doubt that the Japanese fans loved The Ramones – dressing like them, knowing the lyrics of each and every song and applauding appropriately. The drummer, however goes on to describe a more unique experience shortly after the gig. "On the way back to the dressing room, we knew something strange was going on…There were cracks along the concrete walls. They weren't wide cracks you could stick your finger in – more like hairline cracks. There were more along the staircase. I knew we played loud, but this was ridiculous." It soon transpired that there had just been an earthquake, not a major one but registering just under 5.0 on the Richter scale. Marky just remembered one of the songs they had just played "Gimme, Gimme Shock Treatment" and the irony was clearly not lost on him. (250)

In the following days, the group would play in various cities taking in Nagoya, Kyoto, Osaka and Fukuoka. Overall, the workaholic band would play on seven different dates in the "Land of the Rising Sun" with some venues allocating two shows per day totalling an impressive 12 gigs in just eight days. Never short of eyeing up an opportunity for a quick buck and with Marky now well and truly established in the band, many fans purchased the "Non Stop World Tour" T-shirt which aptly summarised this international development as well as signalling the new recruit within the group. Along with the usual favourite singalongs, there were some new additions to the live set during this period taken from the latest L.P - "End Of The Century". Although "I Can't Make It On Time", "Let's Go", "I'm Affected" and "All The Way" did not become regular features on The Ramones' future set list, three tracks certainly did. "Chinese Rock", "Do You Remember Rock 'n' Radio?" and "Rock 'n' Roll High School" would all emerge as integral features and "must play" tunes at any concert throughout the rest of their career.

The Ramones went on to tour Japan half a dozen more times in 1988, 1990, 1991, 1993, 1994 and 1995. The increased frequency of the visits to the nation was no doubt a sign of the popularity of the band in the far east as well as the group members' affection for the country. Johnny Ramone enjoyed his excusions to the country for sure. In his autobiography *Commando* he pointed out "everything would be dead silence, then you'd come on to play a song, and they'd go crazy. The song would stop, and they'd all listen to what you were saying, even if they didn't understand the language. I loved it there. They'd all get the look just right, too. The whole audience would come with the black leather jackets on. They'd all have the punk look down, nice and neat, and perfect – clean. Every little detail." [251] One such person who was lucky enough to see the group once was Yoshikazu Kushima who could not forget the emotion he felt when he observed The Ramones on that final tour of Japan. In fact, so inspired by the band in 2013 he started his own tribute band taking up the moniker of Kussie Ramone.

Kussie ran a rehearsal studio and is based in the city of Sabae, a densely populated area located in the Fukui Prefecture region of Japan, just over 100 miles north of Osaka. The drummer had already played in over 10 punk and hardcore groups and knew long-term friend Tatz Ramone on guitar, who had also been through several punk bands previously. The quartet was made up of two customers of the studio with Ackey Ramone on bass and Zoe Ramone as vocalist. Ackey had already had experience in other covers whilst singer/songwriter Zoe had played in his own projects as well as singing solo.

The band's live set is usually taken from the classic "It's Alive" album or material from the greatest hits "Ramones Mania". The group particularly enjoy the early material and the first three definitive albums when Tommy was part of the band.

Kussie cites three memorable gigs which attracted audiences of between 150-200 ecstatic fans. In 2016, *Uramones* visited Taipei in Taiwan with the groups *"Take This"* and *"Bazooka"* on the bill whilst in 2018, they also played in Beijing in China. It is of course, worth pointing out that The Ramones never toured either Communist China or the unitary semi-presidential republic of Taiwan due to the political tension at that time. The fact that *Uramones* are reaching out to audiences and indeed countries who never experienced the originals is surely a major argument in favour of the concept of the tribute. Another noteworthy concert was back home in Japan where around 100 Tokyo fanatics viewed the band blast out the usual favourite tunes to a wildly enthusiastic crowd. At their concerts, grateful enthusiasts tell them about their memories of The Ramones whilst the band's goal is to raise awareness of the New Yorkers, increase the number of new Ramones fans and of course, bring back these recollections of the older fans.

A quick search on *Youtube* shows *Uramones* in fine form blasting out their versions of The Ramones classics. I would recommend *"Live at Tabby's Guitar"* which screens a dozen gems or *"Live at the Bar Basic"* to get a real feel for the band. Wearing wigs, sneakers and the customary leather jackets, the boys have their mannerisms down to a tee with Dee Dee, or should I say Ackey, absolutely nailing the bassist's movements and motions. Tatz wields his guitar like a samurai exercises his katana sword whilst Zoe stands at the front like a praying mantis hovering over his intended next victim. At the back, Kussie ensures the unit is bound together, emulating the precision skin slapping noted by Tommy Ramone. If you like your tributes, as close to the originals as possible – *Uramones* are the *real McCoy.*

When asked about The Ramones legacy, drummer Kussy noted that "many people now copy them in terms of clothes, style and fashion, even if they do not realise it." He goes on to add that "such is their importance that many people may not be fans of The Ramones but are often fans of bands who followed The Ramones." *The Uramones* are still playing to this day and to coin a phrase from the classic song "Zero Zero UFO", they *might not look like they came from Japan* but undoubtedly are helping to immortalise those boys from Queens in this part of the world.

Road To Ruin
Australia

After a successful tour of Japan, The Ramones hit Australia for the first time in July of 1980. For many Australians, the visit of *Da Brudders* was long overdue. On the music community website, *I Like Your Old Stuff,* for instance, one Australian summed it up succinctly enough:

> *"Long before their logo became a ubiquitous T-shirt design and indeed long before their sound was translated for millions of kids around the world by the likes Green Day in the '90s, The Ramones had a special relationship with Australia. Going right back to their first album and beyond, The Ramones struck a chord here; one that went beyond being just the opening salvo of punk. There was something about the guitars and the beat of The Ramones music that resonated with us, and something about their simple pure rock'n'roll that hooked us."* (252)

Australia have had a history of producing top draw loud rock 'n' roll. One example, was in the form of Sydney's hard rock super band *AC/DC,* with high pitched, gritty vocals and their dirty riffs amplified to the max. Another was the early Brisbane based punk pioneers, *The Saints.* Chris Bailey's snarling and sneering voice may have been somewhat different to Joey's more melodic, dulcet tones but the blistering fuzz tone guitars were certainly shared by both the Saints' Ed Kuepper and our Johnny Ramone. It's no real surprise therefore that when the New Yorkers finally landed "down under" there was an eagerly awaited anticipation from the locals.

Supported by the Melbourne based punk band *La Femme*, their first gig within *Terra Austalis* soil took place at the *Capitol Theatre* in Sydney on July 8th. Sydney, is the capital of New South Wales and is the largest city in terms of population with nearly 5.3 million inhabitants. It is perhaps best known for its picturesque harbour complete with the distinctive bridge and illustrious Opera House. The *Capitol Theatre,* itself began its life in 1892 as the New Belmore Markets selling fruit and vegetables but was converted to a hippodrome during the First World War specifically for a circus. Within 10 years, this venture had proven to be unviable and in 1927 it was adapted again to a picture palace or movie theatre. (253) In 1972, the theatre received a shot in the arm and was chosen for the production of *Jesus Christ Superstar.* As well as musicals, the theatre secured famous performing icons such as *Thin Lizzy, The Boomtown Rats, Black Sabbath* and punk titans *The Clash.* Fortuitously, that first Ramones show was recorded and indeed can now be listened to on social media under the humorous title *"Gabba Gabba G'Day"* or purchased as a C.D albeit as an edited version under the guise of *"Broadcast Collection – '77-'95".* Rather aptly, Joey commences the gig with the words "Well we've finally made it", no doubt referring to their Australian debut being considered long overdue by some. Without time to blink, Dee Dee discharges his war cry of "1, 2, 3, 4" like a battleship barrage and with the aesthetic built on quicker, quicker, quicker, the punk anthems of "Blitzkrieg Bop", "Teenage Lobotomy" and "Rockaway Beach" was demolished in six minutes flat. With "End Of The Century" tracks featuring more prominently than usual, it is worth listening to some of the often forgotten tunes. The rawer live version of "I Can't Make It On Time", for example, is undoubtedly a step up from the studio take. Altogether, The Ramones would play 10 shows that tour with other centres visited such as Melbourne, Adelaide, Wollongong, Canberra, Brisbane and the Gold Coast. Some superb photographs of the band performing at the Festival Hall in Brisbane have been collated at the John Oxley Library, Queensland and also available online. [254] I would strongly recommend a visit to the website to check these rare photos out.

By the time they touched down on Aussie turf for a second tour in 1989, C.J had replaced Dee Dee on bass. C.J has fond memories of his time *down under*. "That Australian tour was right after I joined the band", C.J recalls. "Actually, my first tour was in Europe – that was my 'break in' tour, where I got my cherry popped – but Australia, because I already had one tour under my belt, that was the first tour that I could really kick back and enjoy. I really had a good time there, and I've said ever since that if they ever chase me out of the States I'll be beating a path out by you guys. That was a really good time to see the band too, because I'd just gotten into the band and Joey and Johnny were more fired up than they had been in a long time with Dee Dee gone. Dee Dee had just gotten pretty difficult there near the end, so they were excited about being out again too and we probably sounded as good as we ever did right there." Although C.J might have seen it as his new job after leaving the US Marine Corps, music journalist Steve Bell felt that this period "revived the band's spirits after a period of unease, his (relatively) youthful enthusiasm rejuvenating the ranks like a breath of fresh air." [255] In the book *On The Road With The Ramones,* C.J also describes life on tour giving a glimpse about what coming into an established outfit must have been like. "There was one rule" he remembers "no drinks before a show. We were in Australia and I was so unbelievably jetlagged. I went down to the lobby and had a gin and tonic and fuckin' got busted. Johnny was, like, 'You know the fuckin' rule, this and that.' I could smoke pot. I could smoke cigarettes. The agreement was, if I missed one show, I lost a week's pay." [256] It was thankfully a short-term hiccup and C.J carried out the almost impossible task of filling Dee Dee's sneakers impeccably. The Ramones toured Australia two more times in 1991 and 1994 with nearly 30 gigs completed in total in the country and *Oz* continued their love affair with the band.

"Road To Ruin" was the fourth studio album released by The Ramones, which hit the streets on September 22nd, 1978 after being produced at *Mediasound* in New York City. It was the first album which featured Marky and heralded some marvellous tracks such as "I'm against It", "Go Mental", "I Wanted Everything", "Don't Come Close" and "She's The One". Although Tommy had left the band, he stayed on to help produce the album along with Ed Stasium which had elements of heavy-metal influenced guitar solos within it. *Road To Ruin* was also the moniker used by four Australians when they started their own tribute. Formed in 2021, the group were based in Castlemaine, a small town in Victoria around 75 northwest of Melbourne. The driving force of their formation was Mik Weir who explains how the band came about. "I was transitioning from drums to guitar, at the same time as I was really getting into The Ramones" he reflects. "Covid hit and I decided to learn as many Ramones songs on guitar and vocals as I could. From here I formed the band." Indeed, Mik recruited three other Ramones enthusiasts with Dean Turner initially on drums, Brandon Alford on bass whilst rather unusually Ben Fraser was on guitar and lead vocals along with Mik. After a year, Dean left the group and *Road To Ruin* was restructured into a three-piece. Mik reverting to his first love and moving to drumming duties and Ben taking responsibility solely on guitar and lead vocals. The musicians had already developed their skills in other bands with both Mik and Ben performing in *Luke Yeoward and The Halfway* whilst the drummer had also served in in *The One Twos* and *The Rebelles* whereas Ben had played in the *Go Set* as well. Bass man Brandon had gained experience in *Boob In A Test Tube*.

Although he never observed The Ramones perform, Mik did see Richie on one occasion and Marky and C.J Ramone twice on their solo tours, the first time at the *Reverence Hotel* in Footscray where "I met all band members and had my album signed" he recalls. *Road to Ruin's* live set naturally contained most of the "usual favourites" but also was dependent on whether they were being used as a support or headlining act. Amusingly many of the usual *'wanna'* picks are there including "Do You Wanna Dance?", "I Wanna Live", "I Wanna Be Your Boyfriend", "I Want To Be Sedated" and "I Just Wanna Have Something To Do". Interestingly they also execute Joey's solo cut, the charming rendition of "What A Wonderful World" but rather peculiarly, the *Misfits'* song "Hybrid Moments" is sneaked in their stockpile too. When discussing, his favourite Ramones tracks Mik feels "It's hard to go past the first three albums, but honestly, I'm a big fan of everything up to "Pleasant Dreams" and like most of the material after that album." He also cites a number of personal much-loved gigs whilst performing in *Road To Ruin* such as their debut at the *Taproom* in Castlemaine or concerts at the *Theatre Royal* whilst supporting *The Rebelles* and *The Ska Vendors*. "Other musicians joked", he ruefully recalls, "that it was easy to play Ramones songs – it wasn't! Whatever part of a song you were playing changed within 20 seconds! With the shorter songs, you were always moving from one section of the song to another. If the chords were similar, or the lyrics were repeating, you really had to focus on which part of the song you were up to. Ramones songs were relentless, especially when you tried to imitate the band by moving from one song to the next with minimal fuss."

When searching *Road To Ruin* online, there is unfortunately less video material than other Ramones tributes. One performance which can be seen is live at the *Sound Systems Studio Bar* in Sunbury, Victoria. The version of "Blitzkrieg Bop" is as a four piece as opposed to the later three. You cannot fault the energy and vigour although having three guitarists at the front is admittedly a shock to the system. As Mik understandably points out, however is that "the approach of our band was to let the music speak, so we didn't wear wigs or 'tribute' – we just played the songs!"

Road to Ruin have recently stopped playing with the logistical difficulties of travelling a major contributory factor. No doubt, however, that Mik and the rest of the boys have helped keep The Ramones' memory alive and there's no doubt according to the musician just how astounding their influence was in return. "I started hearing The Ramones in so many other groups. By the '90s, many popular bands were openly acknowledging the influence of either The Ramones music or simple approach, or both, on their own music."

Der Ramoans
New Zealand

At the end of their first Australian tour in 1980, The Ramones left the Gold Coast on the east shoreline and headed across the Tasman Sea to New Zealand. The island country is located in the south western region of the Pacific Ocean and consists of two main land masses and over 700 smaller islands. The South Island is the largest of the two, although the North Island is more populous and is home to about three-quarters of New Zealand's total population. Historically, the country was settled by the Māori, the indigenous Polynesian people who arrived in New Zealand in several waves of canoe voyages between approximately 1320 and 1350. The country is blessed with a variety of landscapes ranging from spectacular glaciers, scenic fjords, rugged mountains, rare hot springs and geysers, subtropical forests, volcanic plateaus, rolling plains and sandy beaches. The three biggest cities in the country are Auckland, Christchurch and the capital Wellington and all these were visited by The Ramones during that first visit.

The Ramones' first gig in New Zealand was on July 21st in Auckland at the *Logan Campbell Centre*. Named after a Scottish-born New Zealand public figure, who represented the electorates of the city in the 19th Century, the venue became a prominent music centre in 1980. Although it was claimed that its "close proximity to the city's Central Business District and the airport, its 3,000 max capacity and the 2,000 onsite parking spaces" made it Auckland's "ideal medium sized concert venue" not everyone shared New Zealand's *Event finder's* sentiments. [257] In fact, critic Chris Schulz was in celebratory mood with the news that there was a liquidation order in 2020 stating "goodbye and good riddance to Auckland's worst music venue" citing parking problems, coldness, poor sound, health and safety worries and a lack of charism. [258] Whatever the quality of provision, a number of notable performers took to the stage at the venue over the years including *The B-52s, Tom Petty and the Heartbreakers, XTC, Thin Lizzy, Coldplay, Green Day, INXS* and *Incubus.* The support band that day was a New Zealand rock outfit named *The Whizz Kids* who coincidentally had a member named Mark Bell in their line-up. This guitarist, however should not be confused with drummer Marc Bell aka Marky Ramone.

The next two days would see them play firstly in Wellington at the *Winter Show Buildings* and then on to the South Island at the *Christchurch Town Hall.* Marky recites a story about the Christchurch gig which had around 2,500 fans in attendance. After he had smoked some hash with his future wife Marion, the couple fell around eight feet backstage whilst the support act was performing. Despite his right ankle and knee being badly injured, he fortunately managed to play through the pain barrier and get through the gig. [259]

Sadly, there are no records of their set lists from any of the concerts in New Zealand but in all likelihood it would have been similar to those from the recent Australian leg of the tour. These witnessed around 30 songs performed at each show with tracks from the latest album "End Of The Century" complimenting the usual goody bag of older favourites. After their virtual day in, day out routine of playing since late June, which had taken in Asia and Australasia, the band would fly back to the States before performing again in the first week of August at Long Beach, Long Island. For those Ramones aficionados out there, there is a fantastic rare 1980 interview on *Youtube* by New Zealander Dylan Taite. The journalist speaks to both Johnny and Joey with questions regarding the start of the band, success and their role in kick-starting punk rock. Go have a look.

There would be a hiatus of nine years before the New Yorkers returned to New Zealand where they would play two shows in Auckland on October 31st and November 1st of 1989. Both gigs were held at the *Powerstation,* a smaller establishment which holds around a 1,000 located in the Eden Terrace of the city and these performances would sadly be the last time The Ramones visited the country. The tour was part of the promotion of the "Brain Drain" album which Dee Dee alluded to as being a "tough recording" to have been part of. "Everyone took their shit out on me" the bassist confided. "I dreaded being around them. It drove me away – I didn't even end up playing on that album." [260] Indeed, it would be the bass player's last attributed L.P with the group as soon after he left the band.

Although too young to have witnessed the group perform live, four musicians who wanted to play Ramones music decided to set up their own tribute in 2005. Heralding from New Plymouth, a city on the North Island with a population of just over 80,000, the first line-up saw Wazza on vocals, Stefan X as guitarist, Craig Pyscho on drums and Von Toxic on bass and backing vocals. The origins of the cover started when 15-year-old Stefan met Toxic and Psycho at a gig one of their bands were performing in. The guitarist told tales of Ramones downstrokes whilst wearing leather jacket and kneehole pants. After one jam, they still needed a singer as their original potential front man was initially not committed but fortunately another friend Wazza knew the words and was invited to join. *Der Ramoans* was born with Toxic amusingly stating that the name of the band was "trying to be dumb and smart at the same time." The band played their first short set on New Year's Eve in 2005. By the following year the group had a tight 21 song list. In 2008, Wazza stepped down on vocals and was replaced by Ryan who coincidentally was the same singer who was at that first practice in 2005. The band members had played in and continue to be in their own original groups. In fact, *Der Ramoans* would in reality be a side-project and sometimes be on the same bill as one of their other bands. "We did this for fun on special occasions" the bass player Toxic points out but also adds that "it was always a good way to end the night." Some of the other bands which the musicians played include *Horror Story, Red Hot Pussy Liquor, The Stunngrenades, Hateseeker, Nefarious* and *G.F.N.R.*

Photograph courtesy of Suspect Pics

The group played for three years and only performed in total around 10 gigs due to the heavy commitments of their other bands. The live set consisted of a score of songs and included all our favourites mainly focussed from the first three albums such as "Cretin Hop", "Sheena Is A Punk Rocker" and "Today Your Love, Tomorrow The World". There were some great picks from other L.Ps too with the cover of *Motörhead's* masterclass "R.A.M.O.N.E.S", and the more medium paced "I Just Wanted To Have Something To Do" and "The KKK Took My Baby Away" both discharged. *Der Ramoans* did not wear wigs but would always where the leather jackets, jeans and sneakers. Just like The Ramones "we would stop by the fifth song to take our jackets off and it was just too hot!" Toxic recollects. When asked about his most memorable concert, the bassist jokingly called it the *"You're Going To Kill That Girl"* infamous gig at *Kings Arms* in Auckland. He recalls the scene in vivid detail. "I asked a girl who was holding on to my mic stand to take her hand off or it will end up crashing into me if she bumped into it," he states. "Her next move was to smash me in the face with the stand/mic, shattering my front teeth. Realising she had done something stupid, the woman backed up and headed toward the female toilet with the crowd parting for her like the Red Sea. I spat out my teeth and launched my Fender precision bass through the air. The girl was about 5 metres away and almost at the toilet door. Surprisingly, the bass guitar hit her with *'Fender precision'* in the head with enough force to drop her. As she went down, the bass slid down her body to the floor. A minute later, with the bass retrieved the band kicked back into action with none other than the fitting "Glad To See You Go" as the now standing offender was removed from the bar." The bass man laments that the episode "cost him hundreds in dental work but at least the bass was ok."- *Anarchy in N.Z maybe?* A search on *Youtube* reveals just one video available, the aptly named, *Basement Bar* in New Plymouth with the drug themed "Chinese Rock", "Glad To See You Go" and "Now I Wanna Sniff Some Glue" on offer. It's well worth checking out and you will find a hard edge, punk fuelled outfit. By 2008, the band had to cease as they started to get bigger than they intended and the lads just did not have enough time to devote to *Der Ramoans* coupled with their other commitments. The last show was a fitting way to go out though, as they headlined with two other New Zealand punk tributes - *The Clash* and *Sex Pistols* in support. The boys had a short but enjoyable experience as a cover band and even if it was a brief project, they still deserve credit for preserving The Ramones' memory. The last words, I will leave with the bass man as he sums up the New Yorker's legacy and what it was to play some of those tunes. "The Ramones, like the *Misfits* are rooted in pop culture, B movies and '50s rock 'n' roll", Toxic suggests. "The great song writing combined with the velvet rich vocal, chainsaw guitar and the beat that drove it, was all good fun with a switchblade knife!"

We Need Cash
Norway

Despite performing in Finland, Sweden and Denmark in 1977, it wasn't until three years later that the band played upon Norwegian terrain. The Nordic country has a population of nearly five and a half million people and is bordered by Sweden to the east and Finland and Russia to the north east. Norway has an extensive shoreline which is formed along the North Sea, the Norwegian Sea, the Barents Sea and the Skagerrak and along those coasts feature many fjords, islands and bays resulting in a low-resolution coastline of over 16,000 miles. Part of northern Norway experiences the *midnight sun* which is a natural phenomenon that occurs in the summer months in places north of the arctic circle. Conversely, during the winter months these areas will experience *polar night* where the sun does not rise at all. Historically, the country is probably best famed for the Viking period which started in the eighth century. It is known that Viking Norwegian explorers, for example, discovered Iceland and visited Newfoundland in Canada and raided coastal regions in Great Britain. The capital and largest city is Oslo which has just over one million inhabitants and it was here that The Ramones first played on August 30th, 1980.

The Norwegian gig was sandwiched between a couple of concerts in Sweden with the boys having performed two days earlier in Stockholm and another scheduled for Lund the following day. The venue in Oslo was at the *Chateau Neuf,* a student's union building, just south of the main campus of the University of Oslo at Blindern. In the early '70s, the institution presented a number of prominent artists, including glam rock stars *T. Rex* and *The Sweet* and even hosted pop *super group Abba* in January 1975. Other notable musicians to grace the stage include *Status Quo, Hawkwind,* Leo Sayer, Suzi Quatro, Chuck Berry, *Slade, Thin Lizzy, Madness and The Kinks* whilst the venue was not averse to welcome punk bands through their doors as well - *The Buzzcocks, Blondie, The Clash, Sham 69, The Undertones* and *Stiff Little Fingers* all performed at the establishment between 1978-1980. Thankfully, when the premier American punk band outfit chose this location, there is a record of the set list that evening. Opening and closing with two classics, The Ramones commenced with "Blitzkrieg Bop" and ended with "Pinhead". In between the 'Heys', 'Hoes' and the 'Gabbas' there were over 20 songs played but it was cut short due to health and safety issues as the show was interrupted with members of the audience climbing on the stage. It did feature a salvo of six of the best from the latest L.P "End Of The Century" with "All The Way", "I Can't Make It On Time", "I'm affected", "Let's Go", "Rock 'n' Roll Radio" and "Do You Remember Rock 'n' Roll Radio?" on the agenda. There would also be a selection from previous albums including two of our beloved covers - "California Sun" and "Surfin' Bird". The Ramones would return to the country a further three times and on two occasions these were played in in the capital. In 1990 it was back to the *Chateau Neuf* whilst in 1993, the group played at the *Rockfeller Music Hall* which is located in downtown Oslo and has a capacity for 1,300 people. Their last show in Norway was on June 25th, 1995 at the *Festivalplassen* or *Kalvøyafestivalen* which was an annual Norwegian music festival arranged at Kalvøya in Bærum. Here they delivered 25 songs which included many of the latter day favourites such as "Strength To Endure", "Cretin Family", "Take It As It Comes", "I Don't Wanna Grow Up" and "7 And 7 Is".

Too young to see The Ramones play live, three teenagers, originating from the city of Tromsø in northern Norway, were so enthused by the New York punk rockers, that they decided to form their own tribute. Tromsø is a city situated in northern Norway and one of those places, due to its high latitude, where you can observe the northern lights, the beautiful displays of dynamic patters of brilliant lights that appear as curtains, rays or spirals covering the sky. There is little doubt, however that it wasn't the *aurora borealis* that was on the adolescent's minds when they formed their outfit in 1992. To put into context, at the time of the cover's conception, The Ramones were still very much in fine fettle having just released their "Loco Live" album and had just recorded their twelfth studio L.P "Mondo Bizarro". The group was the idea of drummer and backing vocalist Andreas Lorentsen and guitarist and lead vocalist Ulf Ivan Olsen. Andreas describes in detail the history of the band's formation and the influence these Americans had on his life. "I started playing different instruments from an early age. When I was 10 years old, I was introduced to The Ramones by my uncle, who was my mentor and the one who sparked my interest in music and rock history from an early age. I remember it very vividly. That day, the first time that I heard "Rocket to Russia" and later "Leave Home", something just clicked into place in my head. It was like the missing piece of the puzzle that I didn't know that I was supposed to look for. It was like nothing I'd ever heard up to that point, and it just changed my life really. My uncle gave me both of the L.Ps. I think he might have been aware that I showed some remarkable progress on my playing, perhaps on the drums in particular, and he probably noticed right away the near catatonic impact this event had on me. I've always had a keen eye for details, and by the end of the year, I'd learned most of the songs on "It's Alive". The trickiest part was of course mastering the blistering fast tempo and copying Tommy Ramone's trademark 8th note Hi-hat technique. It takes a lot of practice and stamina to do it properly. I was practicing so much that my right arm started living a life of its own. I recall that it annoyed the living crap out of the primary school teachers. However, after countless hours playing on drums, pots and pans and everything, I finally mastered it really well. In the fall of 1989, I met Ulf. He was one year older than me, and he had a guitar. He had a natural good ear and he still is an out of the ordinary talented guy and quick learner. We played together for some years, practically all the time, anywhere that was possible. That's how it all started for me. Playing music was my only interest, and Ulf came from a similar background. His reaction to hearing The Ramones for the first time was like a *deja vu* of my own experience. We were just kids, but we had shared something on a higher subconscious level. Like turning on a light switch. Click. No turning back. Ramones was the glue that we bonded to. As if we had no choice. In fact, to this day, I feel the same way every time I meet someone with similar interests. All the *cretins* and *pinheads*, forever marked and sealed by invisible ink from that special brotherhood known as The Ramones."

Andreas and Ulf were desperately looking for a bass player and like-minded Ramones fan and fortunately *stumbled upon* Jimi Keith Tangerud who had just moved into Tromsø after his parents had secured jobs at the local university. Andreas remembers that "I could tell right away he was 'one of us', and he just invited me home one day and told me everything he knew about The Ramones. He even had a white Fender Precision bass like Dee Dee and lots of live Ramones videos on VHS." After mastering the chosen songs, the three youngsters played their first gig under the designation of *WNC* which was an abbreviation of *We Need Cash*. Curiously, their moniker had no connection with The Ramones but was more to do with their financial situation as they were a bunch of 14/15 year kids strapped for money. The three-piece played their debut gig on May 4th, 1992 at a local festival at the Brygga (Ungdommens Hus) in Tromsø. Andreas looks back with pride as he describes their debut stating that "I think it's fair to say that the element of surprise was on our side as we blasted through 12 classic Ramones songs, almost non-stop. We had done all of our homework down to the smallest detail. We quickly won the crowd that night, and I later learned that we left a solid jaw dropping impression on some of the older punks that watched our performance. We became quite a cult phenomenon, at least on a local scale, and from time to time, some people still remember me as one of The *Ramones kids*." Their set that day included some of the more common picks such as "Cretin Hop", "Blitzkrieg Bop" and "Rock 'n' Roll High School" but also some of the more unusual gems such as "Palisades Park", "Mama's Boy" and "All The Way".

WNC went from strength to strength with an expanded set list which included "Surfin' Bird", "Pet Semetary", "Here Today Gone Tomorrow", "Poison Heart" and "I Don't Wanna Grow Up". The group played around a dozen gigs overall performing periodically over the course of seven years. Other highlights included playing at the Åsgårdspell festival in 1993 and being recorded live by a local television station, a subdivision of *TV Norge*. By 1994, bass man Jimi moved back to Oslo and left the group with initially Finn Stenberg taking over the responsibilities on the four-string before Jostein Tveit was thereafter recruited in 1997. Sadly, the group disbanded in 1999, with Andreas pointing out that "it's a shame really because we never sounded better but everyone just moved to different places." The drummer, however, is still very much involved in keeping the boys from Queens' name alive and created the logo for the thriving Tromsø Ramones Fans Association Club. Indeed, there is little doubt that with the drive and determination of people like Andreas, just like the sun in northern Norway, The Ramones' legacy will never set.

Ramons
Spain

For many fans, the first chance to witness the band would arrive courtesy of the "End Of The Century" tour in 1980. After just completing a successful five-centre tour of Italy and then a one-off gig in Montpellier in France, The Ramones journeyed on and into the Iberian Peninsula. For Spanish enthusiasts, the first glimpse of the group would be on September 19th in Barcelona. The city lies on the north eastern coast of the country and is the capital and largest city of the autonomous community of Catalonia, as well as the second most populous municipality of Spain. With a population of 1.6 million within city limits, it is one of the largest metropolises on the Mediterranean Sea. The Ramones would not be headlining that day but supporting Mike Oldfield, famed for his haunting theme tune, "Tubular Bells", which was used for the soundtrack to the horror film *The Exorcist*. The rather odd musical pairing would see 250,000 people witness the event at an outdoor venue. The chosen site was on a broad, shallow hill, at a place named *Montjuïc* (which translates to 'Jewish mountain') and was the location of a medieval Hebrew cemetery [(261)]. Happily, there was an audio recording made of this first Spanish concert and it can be heard on the online video and social media platform, *Youtube*. Kicking off with "Blitzkrieg Bop" the band apparently played 30 songs that day although by the time they got to "Commando", the sound system went off and the show was stopped. On the soundtrack, as well as this song, "Here Today, Gone Tomorrow" and "I'm Affected" are lost for future generations and were never taped. Fascinatingly, as the show progresses, Joey is heard to experiment with his vocals somewhat and songs like "Judy Is A Punk", "California Sun" and "I Don't Wanna Walk Around With You" lose their characteristic familiarity. For those who enjoy some variety, it makes this gig well worth dissecting.

After the Barcelona performance, the boys headed on to Portugal performing three shows in that country before travelling back into Spain for a further two appearances in Madrid and San Sebastián. The Madrid concert is noteworthy for taking place at the *Plaza de Toros de Vista Alegre,* a venue which is still used for bull fighting to this day.

The Ramones returned to Spain a further seven times in 1981, 1989, 1990, 1991, 1993 (twice) and 1994, clocking up in total over 50 concerts in the country. Indeed, the 1991 shows at the *Sala Zeleste* in Barcelona, recorded on March 11th and 12th, were chosen as the second live album released by the band and the first Ramones L.P to feature C.J. Produced by Adam Yellin, "Loco Live" was overdubbed at the *Electric Lady Studios* in New York City and interestingly has two versions. A 1991 Chrysalis version includes the tracks "Too Tough To Die", "Don't Bust My Chops", "Palisades Park" and "Love Kills" whilst the 1992 Sire format replaces these four tracks with "I Just Wanted To Have Something To Do", "Havana Affair", "I Don't Wanna Go Down To The Basement" and "Carbona Not Glue". Compared with their definitive first live album "It's Alive", there is no shirking the fact that "Loco Live" is a big disappointment. By this time, they had speeded up to such an extent that something was being lost. Indeed, according to Marky, this was a conscious decision by the band which was being pushed by Johnny to cater for a younger audience, who were listening to hardcore and thrash. Whatever the rationale both Joey's "phrasing suffered" as did Johnny's guitar sound who couldn't now play "true eight notes with a downstroke at those tempos." [262]

As well as Barcelona, San Sebastián and Madrid, over the years, the group visited extensively. Other performances took place in Valencia, A Coruña, Zaragoza, Murcia, Valladolid, Vigo, Pamplona, Mondragón, Bilbao, Melgar de Fernamental, Solsona and Gerona. The '*fast four*' also visited two off-shore islands playing Las Palmas of Gran Canaria and Palma de Mallorca, the largest city of the Balearic Islands. Their last visit on to Spanish terra firma was on September 21st, 1994 when they played the *Plaza de toros Buenavista* in Oviedo, a city in the north of the country.

Life on a continuous tour along-side the same bandmates and crew took its toll accentuated by the fact that within the outfit stood two polar opposites. Although not well publicised to fans during their playing days, it is now well documented that Joey and Johnny did not like each other. Politically they differed in their opinions and both were romantically involved at some point with Linda Daniele who first dated Joey before marrying the guitarist. Another theme which caused friction was the vocalist's health. Johnny of course wanted things regimented and got frustrated by Joey's mental difficulties and other health problems. Joey was eventually diagnosed with Obsessive-Compulsive Disorder (OCD) and in her article *"How OCD killed Joey Ramone"*, Cat Jones succinctly describes how the affliction was so severe that his mother was once told by doctors that he would never be able to take care of himself. [263] The condition is characterised by recurrent, persistent obsessions or compulsions. Throughout his life he felt compelled to repeat things, to carry out little acts that only he seemed to be aware of. If he touched something, he had to touch it again. If he entered a door, he had to leave through it again. If he moved something, he had to move it back. [264] This disorder nearly proved to be fatal in Spain as Marky Ramones describes when he was crossing the road in his book *Punk Rock Blitzkrieg*. "Joey had done an about-face to touch the opposite curb and then run out of green time" the drummer reminiscences. "In Barcelona, as in New York, drivers had no time to waste" and Marky recalls how "we had our hearts in our throats as Joey twirled through the air and hit the street still spinning sideways" after being hit by a car. [265] Thankfully the singer got up and no lasting damage was done.

Fortunately, the internal squabbles between The Ramones' members at no stage affected their recording capabilities or undoubtedly their live act and four Spanish musicians from Puzol in Valencia were suitably impressed to create their own cover band. The act was formed by chance on New Year's Eve of 2007 after performing the entire "It's Alive" set to celebrate the 30th anniversary of The Ramones classic album at the *Durango Hall* in Valencia. Under the moniker of *Cromañones,* which was the name of their own group at the time, they were witnessed by a promoter who was suitably impressed and hired the band for an upcoming festival. The quartet consists of Sergio "Ruso" Mateo on drums, Kike "Bandido" Bayarri on the bass, Javi "Ramone" Climent on guitar and unusually a second guitarist with Soti "Cromañon" Poza also doubling up as the vocalist. With a new vision as a Ramones tribute, the lads changed their name labelling themselves *The Ramons*. As well as the *Cromañones,* all of *the hombres* had experience in other bands with all four members also playing in *Soul Bandidos*. Sergio featured in *Los Asoirantes* and *Inhospito,* Javi played in *Two Skulls, Tittixx, Frankenstein Dandys and Redneck Loosers* whilst both Soti and Kike performed in *The Bastard Cousins Band.*

Guitarist, Javi is keen to recreate The Ramones sound at their own concerts. Indeed, he witnessed The Ramones a number of times - citing the first two gigs in 1989 *at The Arena* in Valencia as possibly his favourites as Dee Dee was still on bass. He also observed the New Yorkers in 1991, 1992 and three times in 1993 with one in *Anoeta,* San Sebastian described as "unforgettable" adding that he feels "they were the most influential band in the history of rock 'n' roll." In order to re-create The Ramones experience, the musicians are zealous to replicate as much as possible with the wearing of wigs, ripped jeans, comparable T-shirts, equivalent chains on the leather jacket's shoulder and the usage of two American army pins adorned like Johnny and Dee

Dee. The band always attempt to play in the same downstroke style and perform with a matching guitar as Johnny's - a Mosrite. Javi feels that Stickman Ruso has a similar panache to Marky and also states that "I have been a Ramones fan for almost 40 years and I have never heard anyone who sings in such a similar fashion as our singer Soti compared to Joey." Their set list varies depending on the length of time the band have for the concert and without support it can sometimes be as long as an hour and a half. The *Ramons* pick songs from all Ramones albums, although always keep to the traditional introduction of "Durango 95" and "Teenage Lobotomy". The line-up has played at big festivals all over the country in front of thousands of people but Javi picks out some smaller clubs such as the legendary *Mardigrass* at A Coruña, *The Gruta 77* in Madrid or *The Durango club* in Valencia as special memories. When pushed for a favourite venue he fondly choses *The Four Seasons* in Castellon stating that "it is always special to play here because the audience in this city is the foremost Ramones fans in Spain."

As a starting reference, one should explore the Ramons' own *Facebook* page where you can cultivate a taste for the act. Searching on-line for their performances yielded fewer results then hoped although the menacing singsong "Somebody Put Something In My Drink" which related to the evening when drummer Richie had his alcohol spiked with LSD, can be observed. Having two guitarists and a bass man certainly differentiates the group although in all honesty, it does take some getting used to for any Ramones purist. As Javi pointed out, vocalist Soti, unquestionably has a sweet but powerful, plangent voice reminiscent of Joey's and there is no doubting the vigour and vivacity of the foursome. Long Live The Ramones or as they say in Spanish *"Larga Vida!*

Ramonada
Portugal

The one and only occasion, The Ramones visited Portugal was in the autumn of 1980. Placed between gigs in Barcelona and Madrid, the boys from New York played just three times in the coastal nation over the course of their entire career. Portugal is located on the Iberian Peninsula in south western Europe and features the Cabo da Roca, the most westernmost point of the continent. The country is bordered to the north and east by Spain and to the south and west by the Atlantic Ocean. One of the oldest countries in Europe, the nation is immersed in history and was at the forefront of maritime discoveries and explorations in the 15th and 16th centuries establishing a far reaching Empire. The capital of Portugal is Lisbon with a population of just under 550,000 people whilst the second largest city is Porto with over 237,000 inhabitants.

According to Portuguese radio celebrity, Luís Filipe de Barros, until the end of the 1970s, Portugal was very much on the periphery in terms of the choice of preference on the international music circuit. However, by late 1979, groups such as *The Stranglers, Dr Feelgood and Elvis Costello & the Attractions* had pathed the way for other artists including Peter Gabriel, Chuck Berry, *UFO, 999, The Skids, Iron Maiden, The Police* and The Ramones to venture into the country in 1980. [266] The allocated venue for The Ramones' Portuguese debut was in Porto at the *Pavilion Infante Sagres* and this site had already seen the likes of

Mike Oldfield, *Nazareth,* Lene Lovich and Lou Reed perform at the establishment. [267] After the single show on September 22nd, the American punk icons travelled around 215 miles down the coast to play the next two nights in Cascais, a town just over a half hour's drive away from the capital city Lisbon and located in area described as the Portuguese Riviera. The venue for both the gigs was held at the *Pavilhão* **Do Grouo Dramãtico E Spotivo De Cascais** or known more simply as *Dramãtico De Cascais.* Opened in the 1970s, it has been dubbed as "one of the mythical concert halls" although was sadly demolished in 2003. [268] There is no record of the set list from any of the three Portuguese concerts that September although one can only surmise that it would have been very similar to the performance in Barcelona, a few days earlier. Here, we found a mixture of the old and new - five tracks, for instance off the "End Of The Century" album including "All The Way" and "I Can't Make It On Time" but also more familiar favourites such as "Beat On The Brat" and "Today Your Love, Tomorrow The World". A search on *Youtube* finds a couple of interesting Portuguese related clips of the band. The first one comes under the title of *"Ramones em Portugal, 1980 + UHF"* and displays a variety of photographs, tickets and posters connected to the pocket-sized tour, accompanied by a song from the group *UHF* which opened the three concerts for the '*fast four*'. The second, described simply as *"The Ramones live in Portugal, 1980"*, has a short but excellent extract of "Blitzkrieg Bop" on offer. For all Ramones fanatics, I strongly recommend tuning in to these less well known videos – they will meet with your approval.

Despite extensive exploration on social media and Ramones related literature, there is little other coverage of the time the band spent in Portugal with those trio of concerts proving to be their only excursion into the country. Three friends who were too young to get a glimpse of The Ramones back in 1980, however, still wished to form their own tribute act. Based in Peniche, a seaside municipality around 65 miles away from Lisbon, the group consists of drummer and backing vocalist Carlos Marques, guitarist Joao Guincho along with Paulo Franco as bass man and lead singer. Drummer Carlos sets the scene when he described how the three-piece got together. "We knew each other for many years, since we were teenagers and some of us played together previously in other punk rock bands or met at gigs," he recalls. Carlos goes on to add that "we all love The Ramones and during our rehearsals we used to play Ramones songs for fun because we really enjoyed it. As The Ramones had stopped performing and some of the founding members had already passed away, we decided to pay them homage by joining our skills together." As with so many of our covers, the lads decided to take suitable pennames, almost as a sign of solidarity and unity with Carlos taking up the mantle of Marqy Ramone. Joao transforming into Jonnny Ramone and Paulo naturally converting into Paul Ramone. The band started rehearsing in 2003 and soon after were ready to perform under the designation of *Ramonada*. Carlos explains the choice which was "a slang word adapting the band's name to the Portuguese language. We used to say the word every time we wanted to play a Ramones song during a jam session like: "Vamos tocar uma ramonada!" ("let's play Ramones!"). We all agreed on the name because it sounds Portuguese and everyone would immediately associate it with the band." As well as being a three-piece rather than a quartet, the outfit also have the unusual peculiarity of having Carlos or should I say Marqy, bellowing the "1, 2, 3, 4" battle cry from the drummer's throne. All the musicians had previous experience with other groups. Paulo and Joao, for instance had both performed in various rock bands such as *Pigs In Mud, Dapunksportif, Rock'n'Roll Station* and *Os Dias Da Raiva*. The guitarist had also teamed up with Carlos in the hardcore unit *Vade Retro* whilst the drummer has additionally played in the punk groups *Carpe Noctis* and *Vae Victis*.

In terms of their set list, the fellas initially played the entirety of the famous "It's Alive" album at every show. The speed of the songs would have even surpassed the boys from New York with Carlos claiming that they performed "all the songs in 35 minutes!" He also believes that "we really think they are the greatest band of all time, and we consider this live album as the greatest ever." *Ramonada* followed this routine for the first six or seven years "as the audience loved it" before digressing in 2009. The skin-basher expands stating that "we changed our set, removing some songs and adding others. We thought of including more recent tunes and not make the set so long. We also thought of playing the songs at a slower tempo, making it sound more like the studio versions." Further tracks include "I Just Want To Have Something To Do", "I Wanna Be Sedated", "Pet Sematary", "I Don't Want To Grow Up" and "R.A.M.O.N.E.S." with their repertoire per gig usually comprising of 22 songs or so.

In terms of memorable gigs Carlos points to a number of stand-out shows. The first was at their debut, back in 2003, at the *Vilar de Mouros Festival* and in spite of the fact it was their first show, they co-headlined to an extremely appreciate audience of around 3,000 people. Another unforgettable evening was in 2009 at *Mercantil Badajoz* in Spain. Here *Ramonada* topped the bill with 500 in the crowd to a very knowledgeable Ramones fan

base who demanded countless encores. In addition, the drummer loved the *Musica de Ca Festival* in 2016 which had another 1,000 concert goers in attendance and was the first time the band played their new set list in their hometown of Peniche. The stick man proudly recollects that "we were considered the best act of the festival" and also delightfully recalls that the band added "I Wanna Be Your Boyfriend" with his 13-year old daughter coming on to the stage to sing and play guitar. Carlos amusingly recites another story where the trio were invited to play in a motorcycle club festival. "When we were at the middle of the set, there was these four topless dancers roaming around the stage, waving at us, almost rubbing us while we were playing", he chuckles. "Once we finished the song, we told the show organisers that we could not play like this and we had to take a break because our mind was all over the place. When the show was over, they still came harassing us backstage!"

Ramonada never had the intention of imitating The Ramones and therefore did not wear wigs or attempt to copy the New Yorkers. Instead, as Carlos indicates "we just try to play from our very heart and soul and make the music sound as similar as possible." This was all about "the *feel* rather than the look." Indeed, the drummer is certainly fully aware of The Ramones importance stating that they should be "celebrated as influential pioneers who revitalised rock music and set the stage for the punk rock movement." Carlos, is not backward in coming forward when describing The Ramones' legacy believing that "their lasting impact is evident in the continued admiration and influence they have on subsequent generations of musicians and fans. Even today many bands refer The Ramones as their main influence. They are a big influence on us for sure." One thing is for certain is that *Ramonada* are still performing to this day and according to Carlos playing Ramones "*is in their blood.*" Now doesn't that just sound so similar? ....

The Cavrones - The Ramones Tribute Experience
Italy

Verona is situated in the north eastern part of Italy in the Veneto region and is famed for being the setting of Williams Shakespeare's *Romeo and Juliet* as well the site of an ancient Roman amphitheatre. The city is central to our third narrative from this country and is the home of another Italian band named *The Cavrones – The Ramones Tribute Experience*. The group were formed in 2009 by long standing friends who had known each other since their childhood. The band consists of frontman Cristiano Sartori, Michele Cantelli as guitarist, Pierluigi 'Gee Gee' Apollonio on drums and Alessandro Adami on the bass and backing vocals. After gaining experiences in several music ventures, singer Cristiano states that starting up the group was "an opportunity for the friends to play together" whilst also recalling that bassist Alessandro said that "we must play in a Ramones tribute because the singer was so tall!" *The Cavrones* cleverly adapted The Ramones logo to take into account their own unique geographical location with the eagle replaced by a goat's head and a ladder taken from the banner of their hometown city of Verona. The words were also changed to humorously read *"poga e tasi"* which translates to "do the pogo dance and shut up!"

The Ramones never performed in the city of Verona or even in the Veneto region. However, they regularly played in neighbouring Lombardy in the city of Milan which is located around 96 miles away from Verona. One of the quirky facts about their visit to the second city in 1981 was that they played two shows on November 6th due to the fact that they lost a show the day before because of an airplane strike. [(269)] At both the early and late performance, the group would feature six tracks off the most recent album "Pleasant Dreams" – "This Business Is Killing Me", "The KKK Took My Baby Away", "You Sound Like You're Sick", "Come On Now", "We Want The Airways" and my personal favourite from that vinyl "All Is Quiet On The Eastern Front". The L.P was the sixth studio album by the band released on July 20th, 1981 through Sire Records. Johnny Ramone cites that there were internal problems concerning issues at the time of making the album - the image and the direction of the music. This probably started with "End Of The Century" and got worse with "Pleasant Dreams" he said. [(270)] Although the band wanted British record producer Steve Lillywhite who had had commercial success with *Siouxsie and the Banshees* on their debut single "Hong Kong Garden, Sire instead chose another Englishman Graham Gouldman. The unlikely coupling of New York punk's finest and of the ex-*10cc* musician seemed doomed to failure even before they started. Some of the tracks certainly had a pop-feel about them with vocal harmonies and guitar overdubs with tracks such as "She's A Sensation", "Don't Go", "It's Not My Place (In The 9 To 5 World)" and "7-11" having no punk credence. Johnny was as frank as ever affirming that "I didn't write any songs with Dee Dee so it no real punk songs on it; it's too light." On top of this, Johnny recalls, "nobody in the band was speaking" which would have been directly related to his problems with Joey due to the Linda love triangle. [(271)]

Interestingly, it has often been debated that the live favourite of "The KKK Took My Baby Away" was written by Joey as a direct result of Linda leaving him for the guitarist. This is disputed, however, by his brother Mickey Leigh who states that the singer penned the song "well before I'd told him what was going on." [272] Another conflict during this period centred around the band's management. Hoping for improved record sales, the band made a change after the "End Of The Century" album with the view that they needed to replace Danny Fields and Linda Stein. Even this was not a smooth transition with disagreement between the original band members who should be their 'saviour'. After much convincing by Johnny, Dee Dee and Joey agreed to go with Gary Kurfirst, a music promoter and manager also brought up in Forest Hills area of Queens. Initially the bassist and singer both felt that lawyer and business-man Steve Massarsky would be the right man for the job. During the L.P, Dee and Joey also led campaign to attribute the song-writing credits to individuals rather than to the group as a whole. Although they did not expect the financial structure to change, they did want recognition for the songs they wrote. Naturally Johnny was not keen for this to occur as Dee and Joey were writing the bulk of the songs. [273] The "Pleasant Dreams" L.P was the first not to feature the band members on the cover. Instead it appears to have some kind of artistic *bogey man* creature maybe ironically suggesting nightmares rather than sweet dreams. Who knows? The design work was created by a Texan named Guy Juke and in all honesty immediately and quite possible purposely takes away a punk rock feel and geared towards a more commercial market.

The early show in 1981 in Milan was performed at the *Rolling Stone* and was fortunately recorded and now posted on *Youtube*. On that tour, the band commenced shows with "Do You Remember Rock 'n' Roll Radio?" which in hindsight might surprise some people out there. As is customary, I urge all Ramones devotees to look the concert up – you will not be disheartened particularly with some of those more unusual picks from "Pleasant Dreams" where you will find the tracks played at full throttle and not *diluted versions*. This venue would be a regular fixture for the groups with the band returning to it a further four times. Other notable performers at the venue include *Iron Maiden, Adam and The Ants,* Iggy Pop and *The Human League*. Including this double show and past visits, The Ramones would play Milan in total 11 times which was more than any other city in Italy.

Amongst their other highlights *The Cavrones* were selected to play at the *Alcatraz*, a club also in Milan by *Bertelsmann Music Group (BMG) Recordings* and *Virgin Radio*, Italy. This was to celebrate the posthumous release of Joey Ramone's solo album "Ya Know?" in 2012. Furthermore, the band released a video from the event of their version of "Oh Oh I Love Her So" which was published as part of an Italian tribute compilation and is now readily available on *Youtube.*

The Cavrones, like so many other fans, draw inspiration from the first three Ramones L.Ps and tend to play many of the songs from the "It's Alive" album, keeping at the recording's tempo rather than the hyper-speed which was heard in the latter stages of the New Yorkers' calling. Their set list also includes around 10 to 15 songs from other albums with the boys able to play for up to an hour and a half depending on the requirement of the gig. Frontman Cristiano points out "we loved wearing the wigs and clothes and also playing the instruments *Ramones like.*" The group even researched to see which T-shirts should be worn, used similar leather jackets and ensured that other details such as the shoes or sunglasses were like the originals. The vocalist adds that "we wanted to try to reproduce the magic atmosphere of the previous work of the '*fast four*'" something which "inspired so many future musicians."

A search onto social media for "Oh Oh I love Her So" will give you two choices. One is from the compilation album with an audio version of the song whilst the other is a superb promotional video in front of a packed audience. The boys give an expert interpretation of the track with the melody beautifully sung, guitars and drumming accurately played and visually impeccable interpretations of Ramones' mannerisms. Even better is the live rendition of "Pinhead" at the *Blocco Music Hall* in 2011 where you will find the hulking silhouette of Cristiano perched like a vulture reading to swoop on helpless quarry and the jerking, skull twitching Alessandro on his low hung bass. Michele is doing what Johnny does – mean and moody, legs astride whilst Pierluigi is reminiscent of Marky in his hooped T-shirt and of course black wig. The song would not be complete without the "Gabba Gabba Hey" sign and we are not to be let down as a pinhead comes on with dress, mask and performs a *mini 'jerk dance'*. If you have a little more time, check out *The Cavrones* at the *Sabotage Bar* in Vicenza in 2010 which highlights the 1977 "It's Alive" opening of "Rockaway Beach", "Teenage Lobotomy", "Blitzkrieg Bop", "I Wanna Be Well" and "Glad To See You Go". Lastly, take a look at their *"Halloween Party"* where you will find energy to burn as they scorch through "53rd and 3rd", "Cretin Hop" "Surfin Bird" and "Sheena Is A Punk Rocker". Three of the four *Cavrones* are now working on a new project, *Black Vessel For The Saint*, and the lads have not gigged as the tribute since 2020. However, Cristiano has not ruled out a return to the stage in black leather, sneakers and knee-holed pants and I for one, hope that the Verona friends might just have a change of heart.

Too Tough To Die
Multinational

"Too Tough To Die" was the eighth studio album produced by The Ramones and was released on October 1st, 1984. With a title which was inspired by the near-fatal beating received by Johnny Ramone, the album incorporated more rasping sounds than recent L.Ps. Indeed, during the early '80s there had been a greater emphasis on the pop-punk, melodic style of watered down compositions highlighted by the release of the albums "End Of The Century", "Pleasant Dreams" and "Subterranean Jungle" and for many fans, dare I say it, *Da Brudders* were drifting into mediocrity. Yes, people assumed the need to broaden the band's appeal and gain commercial success but at what price? The band was still intense live but appearing tired and losing respect with their sound dumbed down on vinyl. The record style on "Too Tough To Die", both lyrically and compositionally thankfully leaned back to punk rock. It was a return to their roots and for many supporters, myself included, it was *music to our ears*.

There were a number of factors which were instrumental in the return to earlier methods of writing, recording and production. The first and arguably the most important was the band eased away from the celebrity producers and returned to the fellas who had fashioned their finest efforts to date – Tamás Erdélyi, aka Tommy Ramone along with engineer Ed Stasium. Even Sire Records president Seymour Stein couldn't argue with that logic and allowed Dee Dee to make the call to their ex-drummer and producer. Tommy recalls that "I was kind of shocked, but pleased, too. Actually, The Ramones had wanted me to produce 'Pleasant Dreams' and 'Subterranean Jungle', but the record company kept getting these big producers like Richie Cordell and Graham Gouldman. As soon as I started working on 'Too Tough To Die', it was like I never left." [274] You can certainly feel the difference with a back to basics rawer guitar sound, less pop orientated emphasis and a 'live in the studio' feel. Johnny would certainly welcome the change as Gouldman, who had found fame with the pop group *10cc*, once asked the guitarist to turn down the volume as his amp was buzzing too much. [275]

Another important feature was the fact that this album had a new drummer on the pew. Joey reportedly stated in The *Providence Local journal* that Richie "saved the band as far as I'm concerned also adding that "he's the greatest thing to happen to The Ramones. He put the spirit back in the band." [276] One thing for certain is that Richie not only brought powerful drumming to the party but also some outstanding song writing and backing vocals too which gave the band an added dimension. Richie's "Humankind" was picked for the album whilst arguably an even better gem "Smash You", was on the "B" side of the single "Howling At The Moon". This was thanks to the Beggars Banquet Records, an independent British record label that were licensed by Sire Records. Both tracks were perfect for the minimalistic revitalised New Yorkers – lung puncturing guitars, clean but heavy drum work at white water rafting speed.

A further vital factor was the relationship at that time between Johnny and Dee Dee and the contribution the bassist had on the L.P. Johnny cites that due to ill health with foot problems "Joey wasn't at the rehearsals for the album" and that "Dee Dee had a lot input on this, which shaped it as "our best record of the eighties." Johnny additionally recollects that the two guitarist "wrote several songs together which helped make it such a good album." [277] whilst the bass man concurs to this fact stating that he sat down with the guitarist and "wrote songs and made them real *Ramones-like*." In his book *I Slept With Joey Ramone*, Mickey Leigh also sets the scene during this period stating that Dee Dee felt he needed to try and "pull the band together." [278] The record is also the only album to feature a purely instrumental track – with the driving and penetrating guitars of "Durango 95" becoming an integral part of their live performances as an opening number. It is also the first album to have two songs with Dee Dee on lead vocals – the uncompromising "Endless Vacation" and particularly the intransigent and razor-sharp "Wart Hog" which would become an immediate crowd favourite. As Mickey Leigh states these songs, "not only allowed him to blow off steam that had been building inside him for years, but would also prevent The Ramones from falling into the doldrums, as a new form of punk rock, called hardcore was emerging." [279] Shockingly, Wart Hog, according to Richie Ramone nearly didn't make it on the album with Joey wanting it cut but Johnny pushed to get it on. With the crazy lyrics about junkies and fags, Sire was also afraid the lyrics might be offensive and blanked them out on the inside sleeve [280] which just gave the song more of a mystique and aura about it. At that time, "Wart Hog" sent out a statement – an announcement that this is what a hardcore song should be like and a declaration that The Ramones were back in business. For any buffs who have not seen the video of the track refer to the *BBC's Old Grey Whistle Test* from 1985 which gives a taste of the action. Not only will you find a spikey haired Dee Dee comparable to Sid Vicious in his pomp but also Richie screeching away on backing vocals.

The group did the shoot for the album cover photograph early on a foggy morning in a tunnel in Central Park, New York near the zoo. During one snapshot, something went wrong with one of photographer's George DuBose's strobe flashes and it failed to work properly. The picture came out shadowy and the quartet were just bluish silhouettes against the misty fog underpass arch background. This *lucky accident* was a stroke of fortune as this majestic yet eerie image was a perfect depiction for the band's new dawning. As Richie describes "here's The Ramones, coming out of the fog of the last few years, back again to show the world how this punk rock stuff is done." [281]

Other highlights on the album includes the disturbing "Danger Zone", the archetypical Ramones melody "Daytime Dilemma (Dangers of Love)"and the dark and menacing "I'm Not Afraid Of Life". The third track off the album was the title track – *Too Tough To Die* and it was this moniker that four musicians chose for one of the most unusual cover bands of them all. So unusual in fact, that these four guys never met at all, never gigged and originate from different parts of the world. *Too Tough To Die* were in fact a virtual band which were formed in 2016. Comprising of Martin "Woody" Woodstra, a guitarist from Holland, bass player Ricardo Val from Brazil, drummer Ad Van Dikj from Canada and singer Troy Durrance, a converted guitarist, from the United States of America, the lads set out to recreate the most professional videos possible as if the quartet were playing simultaneously and outwardly appearing as a *normal* band. Vocalist Troy explains that "we've all played live in different, various, bands. As a Ramones cover band, everything we recorded was shared via Google Drive for us all to work on our individual parts. Once the audio was mixed, we'd 'green screen' a video so we had something to post online. Our drummer was really into editing and never wanted to do cheesy videos. He wouldn't allow us to 

have the typical video with each of us in a corner of the screen like a Zoom meeting. We did our best to make everything look as realistic and legitimate as possible with our amateur equipment." "Some songs", Troy points out, "we would whip through in a week but some would take months to do. That was mostly my fault. I loved doing the music side of it, but hated doing the videos. I'm not a frontman by any definition."

Two of the foursome were indeed well known for posting useful tips how to play in Ramones style before *Too Tough To Die* commenced with their combined project. A search on *Youtube* for instance, will see our guitarist under the guise of *woodyamsterdam* give expert renditions of such treasures as "Loudmouth", "Let's Dance" and "We're A Happy Family" from the comfort of his own living room back in 2009. Similarly, if you need help with Ramones drumming, tune in to *Adje 1960* and check out his tutorials of "California Sun", "Sheena Is A Punk Rocker" and "I Can't Get You Out Of My Mind" to name but a few. Judging by the numerous comments posted, their outstanding musicianship has aided many would-be artists who for whatever reason wish to play Ramones numbers.

Indeed, Troy explains that it was through these sites that *TTTD* initially got together. "Martin Woodstra has a fairly large following on *YouTube*, probably close to 12k", he states. "I'd seen many of his videos and always thought how fun it would be to play some Ramones with him. Since The Ramones didn't have two guitar players, it didn't make sense. I messaged him and asked if he'd be interested in playing a song and I'd sing it. I'm not a singer, but it's punk, you didn't need to be a great singer, holding a tune was optional. He agreed. Our first song, I believe was 'Life's A Gas'. Martin mentioned that he had a friend that was a drummer and that he had worked with him (via the internet) and that he may be interested in doing some stuff, too. Martin reached out to Ad and he was interested." The trio then looked into a couple of bassists but these didn't really work out until eventually they found Ricardo. Troy recalls that "he would thrash around, swinging his long hair all over the place, Martin and I would just stand in one spot and do our thing. Ricardo brought a new energy. At some point, we were in a Facebook group chat and all agreed that we would only do Ramones covers."

There are several videos on social media of the *TTTD*. Again, if you scroll on to *Youtube* you will swiftly find Troy's personal favourite of "The KKK Took My Baby Away". You have got to say that Woody and Ad have done an excellent job in terms of the mixing and videoing and although you can tell that the boys are not physically together in a studio, once you open up your mind to the concept, then you will no doubt enjoy the various songs. "It's A Long Way Back To Germany" has a comical twist where singer Troy is presented hopping around the 'studio' and the boys make no attempt to hide that this is a virtual band with the gents very much operating *in tongue in cheek mode.* This underrated, haunting melody, however, is perfectly executed and I particularly love the evocative vocals of this tune. Another amusing performance is the video to "Don't Come Close" which starts off as a quadruple split scene before moving to 'roaring' crowds and performing as if as one. Look out for the great punk picks of "Commando" and "Gimme Gimme Shock Treatment" too. On the former, bassist Ricardo comes into his own where he can be seen head rolling, hair spraying à la C.J although on the latter, purists may wince somewhat as he appears to play purely with his fingers rather than with a plectrum. For further details on *TTTD,* a good source is the band's own *Facebook* page. Here you will not only find the band sharing general information on The Ramones but also engaging interpretations of "Swallow My Pride" and "Today Your Love Tomorrow The World". Interestingly, they have also diversified and posted their own version of the *Misfits'* tune "Attitude" which is also well worth a viewing.

The last song the band posted was in 2022. Real life and logistical difficulties just got in the way and to keep the venture functional in the long-term was not viable. Communication, for instance, was almost exclusively done via messages and group chats, which made organising projects quite difficult. However, during their existence, the guys had a great deal of fun and they provided much entertainment to Ramones fans during the Covid outbreak. At a time where live gigs were not possible they put a smile on many people's faces and they deserve much credit for this achievement.

The Ramone –
A One Man Tribute
United States Of America

Without a shadow of doubt, amongst the most original acts that has been experienced during the compilation of this book, is *"The Ramone – a one-man tribute"*. The concept of the one-man band is of course not novel. There are records of street musicians back in the 13th century who simultaneously played a three-holed flute and a drum. By the early 19th century, multipurpose individuals were delivering their own form of entertaining music using fiddles, panpipes, a bass drum, and a tambourine. Music journalist, Johnny Black cites a blind London-based street musician in 1850 that due to the unreliability of the members of his first band led him to go solo whilst goes on to describe Fate Norman of Dalton, Georgia in the United States who in 1927 was pronounced as "the one-man wonder, who plays six individual instruments in an individual band…two guitars, bells, bass fiddle, fiddle and mouth harp or kazoo." As the 20th century proceeded, other innovators such as Jesse Fuller and Joe Barrick were masters of the musical contraptions such as the fotdella and piatarbajo allowing them to give rudimentary melodies with a variety of sounds. [282] In addition, by the 1960s, one occasionally witnessed performers either on *the box* or in the streets mount a big bass drum on the back whilst playing a harmonica held by a wire-frame. Indeed, as a boy I remember a man who used to busk outside *Woolworths* in the busy shopping area of Clapham Junction in South London who would also play guitar and sing. I am sure it wasn't just me who looked at these musicians as maybe talented but also rather eccentric – slight oddballs. With the rapid advancement of technology, electronics was the chosen method for these type of artists with 19-year-old Mike Oldfield's *Tubular Bells* in 1973 probably the crowning glory of a multi-instrument production. Returning to Johnny Black's superb summary of these solo performers he succinctly points out that "although, the range of sounds and number of instruments that could be used by just one player became vastly greater than was hitherto possible, but what was largely lost was the ability to reproduce the results live." By the turn of the century, however, live looping became possible which is the recording and playback of a piece of music in real-time enabling musicians to use their previously recorded music and add, for example, their new "live" vocals or instruments. Notable artists who have incorporated these techniques are Ed Sheeran, Keller Williams and KT Tunstall.

How does this relate to The Ramones? Well one musician who has taken the ability to live loop and use it to conjure up his own unique tribute to The Ramones is Rocky The Ramone. Originating from Texas, Rocky saw the New York icons six times after first hearing the band on the *Dr Demento* radio show and thereafter watching the offbeat movie *Rock 'n' Roll High School* on TV. Not long after, he went to his first concert back in November 1984 at the *Arcadia Theatre* in his own home town, Dallas. The establishment had a chequered history. Originally opened in 1927 as a movie house with 1,040 seats, the building was partly destroyed by a fire just prior to Christmas 1940 before being rebuilt again in 1941. In November 1958, $75,000 of damage was caused by a second fire whilst the theatre closed again in 1973, whilst its owner, manager and a couple of employees were involved in a legal battle over the showing of the provocative pornographic film *"Deep Throat"*. In the '70s, it became a concert venue with artists such as Peter Murphy, *Nine Inch Nails* and *The Judy's* all performing. Interestingly, in one journal by Kris Scott named *"The Rise and Fall of the Arcadia"* the columnist asked a regular "what was the favourite show at the venue" with the local naturally responding with "you just can't touch The Ramones!" Sometime in the mid-1990s the theatre closed as a live-music venue and later re-opened as a nightclub but after a third and ultimately terminal fire in 2006 the building was sadly destroyed and subsequently demolished. (283)

At that first gig Rocky points out that "you never saw punk shows on TV and it was the first time I saw people slam dancing. It was both thrilling and scary. I became obsessed with The Ramones after that." The last time Rocky witnessed the band was at *the Bomb Factory* on March 20th in 1994 with support from Frank Black along with *The Cardillac Tramps*. This was the *"Acid Eaters"* tour and

four of the songs that evening - "Journey To The Centre Of My Mind", "7 And 7 Is", "My Back Pages" and "The Shape Of Things To Come" naturally featured from the album which completely featured cover tracks.

Rocky has been playing the drums for over 40 years and whilst being a drummer feels it has given him a deep understanding of rhythm aiding the understanding of the guitar and bass. Bored with nobody appreciating his experimental music, tired with working with some of the other musicians, he realised that the minimalism of The Ramones was perfect for the one-man show and by April 2016 had put together his own unique routine. Rocky, who for a short period was in another Ramones tribute *"Sedated"* as well as in a number of other bands, ruefully reflects that he would rather play in front of just 10 people who really *get it* rather than a larger club night citing a superb recent small gig in Aledo, Illinois. When asked what made The Ramones so distinctive, his answer was philosophical. "The thing that makes The Ramones different from any other group is that they were a brand as well as a band. The only comparable band at the time was *Kiss*. They were the first T-shirt band decades before the current trend of people wearing shirts of bands they've never listened to." He now sets up live shows playing guitar and singing vocals with bass and drums arranged through live looping. For all you whizz kid geeks out there, Rocky's main piece of equipment is a Roland P-10 Visual sampler. He has a short throw projector and a screen with a PVC pipe frame. He used to use a Roland street cube but will shortly switch to just using a zoom guitar processor. He runs it all into an eight channel direct box/rack unit and then to a headphone monitor rack unit. The last bit of gear is an extension cable into ear monitors.

Although, he usually plays the celebrated famed refrains of the band, Rocky now has a 55 long song list. His personal favourites include "All Quiet On The Eastern Front", "We Want The Airways" and the thumping harder core tracks of "Eat That Rat" and Freak Of Nature". As well as these live performances, Rocky runs Ramones karaoke events. These are shown on social media and worth tuning into *Youtube* to observe. In one viewing, whilst he plays guitars and carries out backing vocals, a member of the public is fully immersed singing "Beat On The Brat" and "Rock n Roll High School". The video also shows another fan up on the stage, beer can in hand singing "Rockaway Beach" whilst my favourite is indisputably the third enthusiast who sings "Cretin Hop" with enough gusto to earn his place in his own Ramones tribute band.

I would also recommend his *Facebook* page *The Ramone – A One Man Tribute Band* which has a number of Ramones songs broadcast with public votes organised to gauge viewer's favourite tracks Once you get over seeing Rocky split into the four components of his synchronised bass, guitar, drums and vocals routine, it is quite a compelling and indeed an amusing watch just like those old one-man bands with the mouth organ and beating big bass drum back in the day.

Ramonera
Brazil

When The Ramones touched down in South America early in 1987, they had completely underestimated their popularity within the continent. Indeed, according to Richie Ramone, a couple of his associates had told him that the band will meet with the locals' approval but they didn't have any inclination what was soon to unfold. "I figured popular", the drummer assumed, "meant it would be like it was when we played the clubs in England or Europe. Man I was wrong. It was way beyond that." [284] Johnny Ramone concurs. "I don't know how. I don't know why, but I was really surprised. It was great" he recalled, going on to add that when he called his wife Linda he told her that "we're like *The Beatles* here! This is how the rest of the world should be." [285] With fans waiting for years to see the band, the group were followed by hundreds of well-wishers everywhere they went with security guards needing to protect the musicians from the kids trying to get pieces of their clothes or anything they could get their hands on. When watching old footage, one can only describe the scenes as being *mobbed*.

Their first gigs in South America was a twin bill in Sãn Paulo in Brazil on January 31st and February 1st. The city was named after Saint Paul, the Apostle and was founded by Jesuit missionaries in 1554 [286] and is the largest city in the country, the fourth largest in the world with an estimated population of around 12.3 million and the largest Portuguese speaking city on the planet. Sãn Paulo, sits in a shallow basin with low mountains to the west and about 220 miles southwest of Rio de Janiero and just 30 miles inland from the Atlantic Ocean port of Santos. The selected venue was *The Palace Theatre*. It is regarded as a landmark of the city, significant both for its architectural value as well as for its historical importance. Construction on the building began in 1903 and it was completed eight years later. During the early days, the establishment presented opera and weeks of Modern Art and has continued to showcase classic and contemporary arts, described as "one of the most celebrated cultural venues in South America." [287] Undeniably a lavish and beautiful building, this setting was light years away from their early roots at *CBGBs*. Other notable performers at the site included Bob Dylan, *Emerson, Lake & Palmer, Kid Creole and the Coconuts* and Johnny Rotten's post-punk *Public Image Ltd*. According to Richie, the venue was sold out in advance with about 5,000 people crammed into each concert and despite some fights with skinheads outside *The Palace Theatre,* "the shows themselves were great." [288] A search on *Youtube* give us an audio chunk of the show which was part of the tour to promote the "Animal Boy" album. Introduced, not by the more common theme from "The Good, The Bad and The Ugly", but instead by the drum roll from "The Spirit of 76" by the Eastman Symphonic Wind Ensemble, the boys are then straight into the customary opening songs. You know the score by now with "Durango 95", "Teenage Lobotomy", "Psycho Therapy" et al thumped out within the blink of an eye. As well as the title track "Animal Boy", there were four other tunes chosen from that latest album – "Crummy Stuff", "Somebody Put Something In My Drink" and for the more hardcore punks, the belligerent "Freak Of Nature" along with Dee Dee's lament to Sid Vicious, "Love Kills". After the two shows in

Sãn Paulo, the Americans would move on to Argentina with an equally crazed audience in Buenos Aires.

The Ramones would perform in Brazil a total of 15 times and as well as Sãn Paulo, would reach out to the municipalities and cities of Porto Alegre, Rio de Janeiro, Bello Horizonte, Porto Alegre, Florianopolis, Curitiba, Mogi das Cruzes and Santo Andre. Each time, they returned to the country *Ramones mania* had amplified. Johnny cites that this included being a "prisoner" in his own hotel room, unable to go outside or even to the lobby for fear of being besieged by appreciative fans. During the last tour, he even had their promoter, fly friend and singer, Eddie Vedder down to South America to keep him company but the plus side was they were playing to 50,000 spectators and were awarded their first gold record for the "Mondo Bizarro" album. [289] Marky also talks about the hordes of T-Shirts and banner waving devotees who were camped outside their windows all day and night and tries to explain why felt that they were 'hero-worshipped' south of the equator. "The young people spent most of their lives dealing with shitty governments, shitty jobs and shitty surroundings" the stick man said. "A rock show – any good rock show – provided a short but relief from reality and sent a booming message to authority. A good rock band was a bunch of antiheroes. Maybe, just maybe, The Ramones – with our street look, loud obnoxious songs, and no-bullshit stage presence – were the perfect antiheroes." [290]

Heralding from Itapira, a municipality in the state of São Paulo, one die-hard hard fan who witnessed The Ramones in their last Brazilian gig on 13th March, 1996 was singer Wellington Clemente who describes the event as "unforgettable." He goes on to add that "The Ramones changed the way I listen, play and write songs, ever since the day I first heard them." As well as performing in several metal and hardcore bands such as *Incubus, Mantor, Executer, Godzilla* and *Slasher*, Wellington, has organised a range of acts over the years, to incorporate Ramones songs. These have included *Lo Cover and Banda Lira Itapirense e Ramones Cover*. The latter needs to be seen to be believed - a full brass band playing the tunes we adore accompanied with flutes, trumpets, trombones and the like. Conversely, Wellington has other strings to his bow, and if you want your punk favourites sung in a more traditional punk style then the more regular project *Ramonera*, may well be to your liking. Even more remarkable and heart-warming is that Wellington performs these from a wheelchair, showcasing his amazing courage and personal determination, something to be admired.

Ramonera has seen a number of musicians serve in the band since its foundation in 1990 denoting that were performing whilst The Ramones was still active and are one of our longest surviving tributes. Previous members have included drummers Rude Bueno and Eleandro Costa, guitarists Mauro Cintra and

Lucas Aldigheri and bass player Tiberius Santa Luccia. The current line-up consists of frontman Wellington, Dutão on drums, Krys Freitas on bass and Fabio Zangelmi on guitar, who for a spell also had a stint on the four string.

When Wellington was asked about his most memorable moments he recalled the time where *Ramonera* combined with *the Banda Lira Itapirense orchestra* and performed in front of 2,000 people. This can indeed be seen on social media with "Do You Remember Rock 'n' Roll Radio?" and "Baby I Love You" on show. There's no doubting the singer has a rich, smooth voice and I guess if The Ramones can get away with violins on BBC's *Top Of The Pops*, then Wellington can blag the French horns and cornets too. More to my personal liking is straight up and down, pure *Ramonera* with a varied set list which includes several songs that The Ramones did not play live. This includes the much loved demo "Slug" or tracks from Joey's solo material such as "What A Wonderful World" and "Don't Worry About Me". Thankfully, there is an abundance of their goodies on offer on *Youtube* and unfailingly my advice is to get out and have a look at these yourself. As an introduction, check out the studio performances of the "The KKK Took My Baby Away" and the often unheralded "I'm Affected" plus the acoustic solo version of "Here Today, Gone Tomorrow". If you prefer a live gig then refer to "She's A Sensation", "Sheena Is A Punk Rocker", "Tomorrow She Goes Away" or "Life Is A Gas" at *the Pedreira* in 2017. Both performances have a different line up with the female bassist, Krys Freitas, for example, playing live. The one constant is Wellington whose serenading, crooning tones lends itself beautifully to the more melodic Ramones numbers. Most impressively, despite adversity the singer is up there, doing it. Now where have I heard that before?

Ramonos
Argentina

After performing in Brazil, The Ramones flew to neighbouring Argentina and played their first gig in the country on February 4th, 1987. The chosen city was the capital of the nation, Buenos Aires which according to tradition was established by the colonizer, Pedro de Mendoza in 1536. The Spaniard named the area *Nuestra Señora Santa María del Buen Aire* which translates to "Our Lady St. Mary of the Good Air." [291] It is located on the shore of the Río de la Plata, 150 miles from the Atlantic Ocean and is the largest city in Argentina with 2.9 million inhabitants. Buenos Aires is the national centre of commerce, industry, politics, technology and culture so was no real shock as the preferred option for that first gig. The venue that evening was the *Estadio Obras Sanitarias* which is also known as the *Arena Obras Sanitarias* or *Templo del Rock*. The establishment is mainly used as a basketball arena hosting the club Obras Sanitarias but also doubles up as a concert hall with a capacity for 4,700 people. It was opened in June 1978 and has enjoyed a host of top artists over the years including *Iron Maiden, The Red Hot Chili Peppers, Motörhead, Duran Duran, Siouxsie and the Banshees, The Police, Black Sabbath,* Iggy Pop and *The Sex Pistols.*

A search on *Youtube* gives us over 30 minutes of the show and indicates that the Argentinian audience was treated to 31 tunes that night. Five songs came from the latest album release and were the same picks as those played in Brazil - "Crummy Stuff",

"Somebody Put Something In My Drink", "Freak Of Nature", "Love Kills" and of course the title track from the L.P, "Animal Boy". Maybe more surprisingly is that we see the unusual sight of Johnny having technical difficulties with his guitar sound with "Psycho Therapy" halted twice as the engineers sort the problem. As four or five minutes are consumed, the feverish crowd wait patiently whilst conveying their love for the band with rallying cries and fist pumps. Throughout the clips, this exuberance is transmitted and you can almost *cut the atmosphere with a knife.* Other delights that night include "Wart Hog", "Mama's Boy" and a blast from the past with "Loudmouth" on the list.

The Ramones would perform a further 25 times in Argentina and would play in the country more times than any other in South America. All bar three of their concerts would take place in Buenos Aires. However, in November 1994, they did reach out to three different cities with Rosario, Mar Del Plata and Bahia Blanca the preferential choices. Their last gig in South America would take place on March 16th, 1996 at the *River Plate Football Stadium,* a venue which is the biggest in the whole of Argentina. Opening for The Ramones that day were Iggy Pop, *2 Minutos, Attaque 77* and the German punk rockers *Die Toten Hosen.*

According to Johnny Ramone "each time we went to South America we got bigger. The first time through we played maybe like a 3,000-seat place. Then the next time it was a couple nights at a 5,000-seat place. Then we went to five nights at the 5,000 seat place and then to a 30,000-seat stadium. Then we moved up to the River Plate Stadium in Buenos Aires, Argentina, where we played for 52,000 people." [292] Marky Ramone who toured Argentina every year between 1991 and 1996 enthusiastically recalls the reception giving to them by the local fanatics particularly recalling how loud the "Hey, Ho" cries were in Buenos Aires and how the Spanish accents could still be picked up – "Ra-mon-es…Ra-mon-es…" He also recalls how many aficionados "camped out all night on the open concrete slabs" on the lookout for their favourite band in the capital. [293] In his book, *I Know Better Now*, Richie Ramone describes "how the kids down there had been waiting forever to see us. And, now that we were there, they all came out and followed us everywhere we went – like, literally *hundreds* of them. And they were all totally going out of their minds. It was actually scary at times. We had guards stationed outside our hotel room doors, and we had big security guards around us when we were walking to and from the van, because the kids would surround us and start touching and grabbing us, trying to get pieces of our clothes and our hair or whatever." The drummer, who was part of their first tour of Argentina in 1987, goes on to add that the fans used to chase the van and even used to rock it up and down but he was always most afraid that someone "was going to get run over." [294] This type of scenario is shown on a short clip on *Youtube* entitled *Ramones in Argentina – Real Ramoniacs*. During the video you will see scores of fans outside their hotel as they attempt to drive their car to the gig. Naturally and rather amusingly tour manager, Monte Melnick gets the blame as the vehicle gets stuck in the mayhem. As the car eventually manages to pull away, the fitting tune of "Cretin Hop" comes into play as numerous Argentinians chase after the boys.

Sadly, one Argentinian story which never quite came to pass was a planned short-term reunification with Dee Dee Ramone. By the mid '90s, the ex-bassist had moved to Argentina and Monte recalls that "we played a huge show there and he was supposed to come and join us onstage, but it never happened. He was supposed to meet us at our hotel but there were big crowds and lots of security guards there. The security didn't know Dee Dee, so they gave him a hard time and he couldn't get into the hotel. The band was there signing autographs and didn't see him. He felt they were snubbing him. We finally got him in the van and we're driving to the venue and he suddenly flipped out. He couldn't handle it anymore. He jumped out of the van and ran away. He could've gone on and done one song and people would have loved it. He was a big star in Argentina." [295]

One *band of brothers*, originating from Buenos Aires, who undoubtedly would have loved to have seen that transitory reconsolidation with Dee Dee are the *Ramonos*. Come rain or shine, I guarantee that this group will put a smile on your face and their unique brand of covering is quite simply infectious. These cheeky little monkeys may look like *butter wouldn't melt in their mouth* but make no mistake, the *Ramonos* pack a hefty punch and are as punk as any. The quartet consists of Alejandro Rojas Gauna on bass, Javier Christina playing guitar, Federico Eichhorn as singer and Facundo Meligene on the drummer's stool. As if to drive you ape, the rascals have all taken on stage-names with Kong Kong, Bonzo, Joe and Chitto Ramono, the chosen corresponding monikers for each musician.

Photograph courtesy of Sophie V. Blasett

The origin of the tribute band, along with the decision to wear monkey masks, was the idea of Alejandro Rojas Guana or should I say Kong Kong. Historically his links with The Ramones go way back to 1995 when was part of the band *Bien Desocupados* which actually supported The Ramones at the *Estadio Obras Sanitarias*. By 2006, he formed the *Ramonos* – a tribute made *by apes* with a section of the designation *'mono'*, aptly translated from Spanish to English as *'monkey'*. His link with *Da Brudders* even post-dates this - in December 2008, for instance, Alejandro's *Bien Desocupados* worked with C.J Ramone on the song "Punishment Fits The Crime" in "The Family Tree". This was a compilation C.D featuring 28 Ramones songs and compiled by the Argentinian label, Music Brokers.

Photograph courtesy of Sophie V. Blasett

The first gig was at the *Bahuen Hotel* in Buenos Aires, for about 30 people. Interestingly, the *Ramonos* were up to their usual monkey business when they drafted up their initial set lists with those mischievous chimps at first only playing songs that The Ramones never played live. Over time, the group then started adding the hits and now usually play around 30 tunes per concerts. Indeed, the band have gone from strength to strength with packed out gigs and rave reviews playing around 200 shows over the years. Including tours abroad to Mexico, Brazil, Paraguay and Chile. The group even performed on Argentinian television on the show *Nunca es Tarde (It's Never Too Late)* in front of a suitably impressed, Marky Ramone in the studio. After bizarrely being asked about football superstar Lionel Messi, the drummer then sat back and seemed more at home listening to the wonderful "The KKK Took My Baby Away". Possibly, the most memorable concert, however, was when they supported C.J Ramone at the *Teatro de Flores* in Buenos Aires. where 2,500 people were in attendance. Here to ensure the lads didn't *make a monkey out of him*, they asked the bassist what songs he was going to perform in order to ensure that they co-ordinated and did not duplicate any of the tunes.

Photograph courtesy of Sophie V. Blasett

Pleasurably, there is a plethora of recordings of the *Ramonos* in action. A great starting point is one of those often overlooked masterpieces – "Why Is It Always This Way?" captured live at the *Kirie Music Club* in 2017. Joe stands there, left foot forward, suspended, as if hanging from his branch, with a voice so similar to the original front man that one could have been placed in a time machine and transported back to *CBGBs* or *Max's Kansas City* – or maybe this was just some weird time dilation from a parallel world of the *Planet Of The Apes,* it's now hard to decipher reality from this dream world! Bassist Kong Kong delivers a ferocious "1, 2, 3, 4" as well as impishly joining in with the "oohs" and "heys" whilst nodding appropriately reminiscent of the spread-eagled Dee Dee at his best. To Joe's right, is of course Bonzo, attired in a cropped *Yahoo* T-Shirt, he seesaws the stage, crouched over his driving buzzsaw guitar in the style of our Johnny. Behind them, there is a glimpse of the animal boy, Chitto who expertly ensures time is kept with his playful yet pummelling percussion. If you prefer to see one of The Ramones more well-known recordings, then refer to *the Ramonos* official video of "Sheena Is A Punk Rocker" also from 2017. It is not only delivered superbly but also gives you an indication of their fan base with an appreciative packed audience frenetically pogoing to the beat. Another little gem, taken from the same "Mono Live" tour, is "I Wanna Be Sedated" which is suitably rounded off with a snippet from *The Simpsons'* T.V animation. Alternatively check out "Gimme Gimme Shock Treatment" where you will discover the band on late night Argentinian television live at the *Sports Centre.* Fortunately, there is also a full concert on offer, at *La Casa de Luca* in March, 2023. Here the band come on to mandatory recording of "The Good, The Bad And The Ugly" but interspersed with monkey chants as if the boys have escaped from the zoo. During the set, you will find over an hour of monkeying around but make no mistake, once you get over the gimmick of the ape masks, this band is a bona fide band of the highest quality. Something which should not be overlooked is the heat the lads must endure whilst performing - not only in their guises but also because of the leather jackets and the non-stop movement. According to Kong Kong, however, when "playing Ramones songs, you forget everything, even the heat!" One thing is for certain though, it certainly would *not be cold enough to freeze the balls off a brass monkey*…. For further information on the band, I would strongly recommend a visit to their *Facebook* page and although you might not find King Kong, the Empire State Building, Charlton Heston or even Roddy McDowall, you will definitely catch hold of the term "Hey, Ho, Let's Go!" Or more appropriately "Hey Ho. Mono!"

Halfway To Sanity
Canada

"Halfway To Sanity" was The Ramones tenth studio album and would be the last to feature drummer Richie after he quit the band in mid-August following the refusal to accept his request for a 10% cut of the merchandise revenue. Released on September 15th, 1987 and produced at the *Intergalactic studios* in New York, it was their first album shaped by producer Daniel Rey who would go on to also fashion "Mondo Bizarro" and "¡Adios Amigos!". According to Johnny Ramone this was "a stressful time" with Joey and Richie making it difficult for Daniel Rey and "wanting to change things and remix songs." He also claims that at this time Dee Dee did not play on the album with Daniel peforming his parts. (296) In Richie's autobiography, the drummer concurs with this stating that although Dee Dee was there he was not "a technical guy" and some of the bass parts were re-done by Daniel as were some of Johnny's parts on lead. Richie additionally cites part of the difficulties for the album was that the band had to work under a very quick time-scale and small budget which was a priority of Johnny's with Daniel being picked up at a *bargain-basement* salary. He also goes into details about the taxing period of recording but suggests one fall out was because he stood up to Johnny. Specifically, the guitarist wanted to change the introduction of Richie's *I know Better Now* because he couldn't nail the difficult opening on guitar and the stickman was having none of it. Ironically, Richard said, after "all the insanity in the studio" he had gone through with John, the album was entitled "Halfway To Sanity." [297]

Daniel Rey spells out how he became the producer for the L.P. "My band *Shrapnel* started opening up for The Ramones in the late '70s and I was producing a lot of young bands in my basement", he remembers. "Johnny heard one and said, 'It's better than our last record.' He knew that he could get me cheap and I was the only person who got along with Johnny and Joey at the same time. So I was asked to produce them on Halfway To Sanity in '87." [298] In Mickey Leigh's autobiography, *I Slept with Joey Ramone*, it appears that both Joey and Richie were not happy with the production of the record. Mickey also cites Daniel Rey's opinions with the then inexperienced producer stating "it was a tough record to make", he admitted, "because it was the first album I ever produced. My goal was to make the best record with what we had at the time. Not to make the best Ramones record ever – because that just wasn't gonna happen. The Joey-and-Johnny problems were really bad then; they couldn't be in the same room together." [299]

The photography for the album was carried out by George DuBose, who had worked with the band previously. The splendid front cover was taken in an old stairwell in New York City's Chinatown with Johnny insisting that they kept it dark. "It had to be pretty good not to make us look old" he stated "and it was getting harder and harder." [300] There were a number of interesting tracks on the album with the genres varying greatly from track to track. At one end of the spectrum we see the hard core "I Lost My Mind". It is a blast of punk rock fury as vocalist Dee Dee chews up and then spits out his sleazy, unsavoury agenda. Other stereotypical punk tunes include "Weasel Face" and "I Know

Better Now" which both fit the bill for those of us who like our songs at grease lightning pace. At the other end of the continuum stands "Bye Bye Baby", the longest track on the album and in all honesty will probably bore the pants off most. Similarly, the final track, "Worm Man", gets my vote as quite possibly the worst Ramones song from any of their L.Ps and does not befit a group of their usual quality. Ranging somewhere in the middle of these extremes lie the rather unique and uncharacteristic "Garden Of Serenity" and the rocky numbers of "Bop 'Til You Drop" and "I Wanna Live". The latter song was chosen as one of the singles from the album and in his book *Poison Heart*, Dee Dee explains at this point he was getting into rap music and he turned up for the video shoot for the song in a maroon jumpsuit, gold chains and a kangol. It was no wonder when "the rest of the band hit the ceiling." [301] The vinyl also includes the pop-punk catchy tunes of "A Real Cool Time" and "Go Lil' Camaro Go" which features the wonderful Debbie Harry as guest vocalist singing alongside Joey.

One of our most unusual ongoing projects which will be one to watch in the future, acquired their designation from that Ramones album title and were the inspiration of founder member Steph Ramone. The guitarist/bassist sets the scene. "I chose the name *Halfway To Sanity* because I am a little crazy and so were they too! With *HWTS*, my goal was to be a little different than the average Ramones tribute band. Who needs more clones that mimic their every moves? The project came to life during the 2020-2021 Covid-19 pandemic and lockdown. I was bored at home and I needed something to keep my mind occupied with something. Being a lifelong Ramones fan, the time seemed right to start a tribute." Since the government of

Québec had declared no contact and no gathering of people, it meant that a flesh and bones band was impossible under these conditions, Steph got the idea of therefore making it all virtual and added Denis Ramones on drums, latter on replaced by April Ramone on drum machine programming, Nadine Ramone on bass whilst Steph would play guitar and also sing (by default). The first stage, Steph remembers was "when everyone jammed together, each at their remote locations, using the magic of the internet. I mean, four squares on a screen and then we put it all together afterwards."

Halfway To Sanity were all based in various locations in Quebec, Canada – Sherbrooke, Gaspésie and in suburb of Québec City. It is an area which The Ramones would have been familiar with. Indeed, the New Yorkers played over 80 times in Canada in total with 14 of these in the province of Québec. Québec is the largest of the 10 Canadian provinces, mainly French speaking and is situated in the north eastern region of the country. The Ramones performed in three centres within this province – Montreal, Verdun and Québec City which was, in fact, their last gig within Canada. Interestingly, Steph saw the band back in 1992 at a relatively small venue called *La Brique* in Montreal. He recollects that they were tight, loud, fast and in-your-face, describing them as "magical" as well as "deafening." The artist also states that "I am so glad to have seen them play. I had a good seat and after seeing them, I wanted to be a Ramone too. I wanted to be more than just a fan and be a Ramones core punk rock musician."

The virtual Band was going to be based loosely on *Gorillaz,* an English virtual band consisting of four fictional characters. However, due to logistical, geographical restrictions and illness hitting one of the band member's family, as well as another group member, *Halfway To Sanity's* progress stalled somewhat as there were no recordings made or shows performed. "I had the idea to do a CGI cartoon of each members, The Ramones music is cartoony enough so it fit. But the project was aborted… but the ideas weren't lost", Steff recounts.

Determined to honour the New Yorkers in some format, Steph then decided to create his own one-man tribute band. "I sing and play guitar, and the rhythm is made by a machine, bass tracks and drum tracks", he points out. The musician goes on to add that "I cover exclusively songs that were never played live or rarely by The Ramones themselves and talked of about 200 songs! No "Blitzkrieg Bop, no hits per se. I do *"thematics"*: drugs abuse, alienation, mental issues, etc. in a multimedia environment. I have a micro gig in a small venue on December 26. Here, I'll play a few punk Christmas songs (à la Ramones), including their "Merry Christmas (I Don't Wanna Fight Tonight)". I will only play small venues gigs, just for the fun of it because I won't get paid much. If *Halfway To Sanity* flunks, then the concepts will be integrated into my solo act. And might end up on streaming platforms."

What lies ahead, will be of particular interest to Ramones fans in the province of Québec. Steph has now teamed up with guitarist and singer, Laurent Ramone, with the hope of eventually finding one or two more similarly minded Ramones maniacs to form a new live tribute. This is certainly one to watch out for and it might just keep your sanity intact – well at least half of it…

The CB Ramones
Wales

The A470 is the longest trunk road in Wales measuring a lengthy 186 miles in total and connecting the capital Cardiff on the south coast to Llandudno in the north of the Principality. Much of the road travels through the beautiful Brecon Beacons and Snowdonia National Park but it was a thoroughfare that The Ramones not once journeyed upon. Indeed, although the New Yorkers performed three times in Cardiff, they never played in the north of the country at all. Despite this, the lads from Queen's influence was huge – not only did they leave a trail of new bands in their wake wherever they toured but in addition, had eager musicians set up groups in unexpected places all over the world. One such location is Colwyn Bay, a seaside resort on the north coast of Wales overlooking the Irish Sea. It lies within the historic county of Conwyn and with a population of just under 35,000 is probably not the sort of town one would associate with punk rock. Huw Roberts, however had other ideas and in March 2018 formed his own cover band which would eventually be known as the *CB Ramones*. Nothing to do with the legendary club in New York, *CBGBs,* this was everything to do with his hometown of Colwyn Bay. A Self-confessed Ramones *nut,* Huw set up the band as he "wanted to play like Dee Dee Ramone along with being gripped with the 'It's Alive' concert and album." Indeed, Huw learnt bass specifically to set the group up and recruited three equally Ramone enthused musicians. The rest of the line-up was completed by Efion Rhys-Harper on guitar, Damo Gee as singer and Sion Jones on the drummer's seat After lots of rehearsals and around 15 gigs, the band underwent some line-up changes in 2019. Sion left the band whilst sadly Damo lost his finger in an accident and quit soon after. Gary Vaughan, who was a long-term fan, first witnessed them on the *Old Grey Whistle Test* in 1978, joined on vocals and Kev Bowyer, a fast and skilful drummer was also recruited. As in time-honoured fashion, the boys all adopted stage names with Huwey, Effy, Gary and Kevvy Ramone the preferred pseudonyms, distinctly displayed on The Ramones logo which proudly included the word Cymru, the Welsh word for Wales, in their native language.

Huw was previously in the original heavy rock outfit *King Boss* along with the cover band *G-String* and additionally a duo named *Queenie & Dee Dee*. The bass man is still active and currently plays in a band named *The Botox County Sheriff's Dept.* Kev performed in numerous well-known punk bands in Scotland in the 1990s whilst Damo was in *The Black Sheep* and is presently the guitarist of *The Retros.* Probably the most interesting of past roles *was* Gary, however, who swapped his blue suede shoes as an Elvis impersonator to a pair of dirty plimsolls in keeping with Joey Ramone.

The band's live set consisted of around 20 songs with all our usual favourites delivered. Some of the more interesting picks include "You're Going To Kill That Girl", "Censorshit", "I Can't Make It On Time" and "I Just Wanted To Have Something To Do". As Huw explains, "we didn't play at the speed The Ramones did towards the end of their time. We settled for the 'It's Alive' tempo as it still held true to the songs' melodies but was fast enough to really rock." The band played many small pubs and festivals along the North Wales coast and there were many highlights. These included a concert supporting *Sandraiser*, a Jimi Hendrix/Rory Gallagher tribute, a packed pub for Gary's debut at his local in Bodelwyddan, and their biggest gig the *ParaFest*, the North Wales paragliding festival, with around 300 in the crowd.

Both Gary and Huw had seen The Ramones play live. The bassist saw them not in Wales but in England as he crossed the soft border which broadly follows the ancient boundary of Offa's Dyke. The concert was at the *Rock City Hall* in Nottingham on 20th October, 1987 and came after a turbulent period for The Ramones which had seen the group have three drummers in quick succession. By the summer of that year, Richie had quit the band. After hearing that the roadies were making the same salary as he was and then having his request for 10% of any merchandise money rejected by Johnny, he walked out. [302] His last gig was on August 12th at the *Jag* club in East Hampton, Long Island, New York. The departure of Richie after over four years on the drummer's stool put the band into turmoil. As Joy Taysom describes having already been forced to cancel two concerts at the New York *Ritz*, "the band were desperately aiming to avoid more cancellations." The call was made to Clem Burke who was a mainstay in the iconic group *Blondie*

and a friend of Joey's. With little rehearsal time, he was thrown straight into the dragon's den, taking the seat on two occasions at *The Living Room* in Providence in Rhode Island and the *City Gardens* in Trenton in New Jersey. Even Elvis Ramone, as he was coined, admitted that the first live show was a "disaster" adding that "it was the hardest work I ever did in a band." [303] The new drummer goes into further detail stating that "I was never Clemmy Ramone; I was Elvis Ramone. It was the second time I was asked to join them and I was glad to fill in but when it became obvious that Marky had cleaned himself up and wanted to be back in the band I think it was best thing for those guys. I'm sorry two of them are not around anymore. It was a very hard job. They didn't want to rehearse so it was kinda trial by fire. It's common knowledge now that Johnny and Joey didn't speak to one another for 17 years and all that acrimonious stuff was going on when I joined. Also Dee Dee was particularly out of his mind at the time in another way." [304] With the group realising almost immediately that Elvis' freer, less rigid style did not suit the needs of The Ramones and the necessity for someone more akin to playing 'double time on the high hat', a new solution was sought after. After another call, this time from Monte Melnick to ex-drummer Marc Bell, the drumming revolving door was in action once again. The stick man recites how he met Johnny at the *Daily Planet Rehearsal studios* and subsequently carried out an informal audition with the guitarist. "After 10 songs we wrapped it up" he recalls – alcohol free, Marky Ramone was back in the band. [305] Marky's first concert in his second spell with the group was on September 4th at *Rumrunner* in Oyster Bay in New York and he went on to play in each and every subsequent Ramones concert. Elvis' much criticised debut performance can in fact be heard on a bootleg and although the drumming is maybe 'looser' and not so "frenetically pounding" as one is used to with The Ramones, the ample condemnation of it being way too slow by many seems unfounded. Check out his performance, for instance, on the *Far Out* website.

The line-up reconfigurations may have caused long-term disorder in many a band but not The Ramones. Huw recollects that the 1987 Nottingham performance was "astonishing" remembering that it was "very, very loud, very, very fast and complete mayhem. It was fantastic. A wall of energy." Huw was keen to replicate this type of all action, non-stop show into his own live sets with the *CB Ramones*. Rehearsing in a converted dairy in Colwyn Bay, the bass man sets the scene. "We didn't wear wigs. We wore leather jackets, Ramones T-shirts, ripped jeans and sneakers but we were obsessed about getting the techniques right. Only downstrokes and instruments sounding as close as possible to the original. Effy even built his own Moserite guitar" he recalls. "It was an honour to play their music and feel part of a handful of tributes worldwide. Being able to shout '1,2,3,4!' was a real thrill." Gary saw The Ramones 10 times in total including performances in Germany, Holland, Belgium as well as in the UK. Interestingly the vocalist always looking for a little bit of a deal bought and sold Ramones shirts, with some fetching £200 one of which he traded to The Ramones museum located in Berlin. A quick search online will show *CB Ramones* in fine form. I would recommend the studio rehearsal of the linked masterpieces of "Havana Affair" and "Commando" which are as tight as sardines in a tin. If you want a flavour of them live, then check out their second gig and see them perform the likes of "Beat On The Brat", "The KKK Took My Baby Away" or their final tune of the evening "Pinhead", which although doesn't reach the heights of their practice session is still well watch scrutinising.

The *CB Ramones* played across North Wales for a few years. With its seaside resorts, sandy coastline, market towns, lakes, forests and even mountain ranges, make no mistake this must have been a hard gig for any punk tribute. Although they always went down well with their audiences, by 2021, they had pretty much done all they can do and the band disbanded in 2021. Despite this, founder member Huw Roberts wanted to continue to honour the band that he considers as "one of the most influential bands in Rock and Roll history both in playing style and fashion." Indeed, the bass player set up the *Facebook* group "Ramones Tributes worldwide" which continues to grow in both numbers and strength. Long may that continue.

Don Ramones
Puerto Rico

It may well surprise one or two people out there but in 1988 The Ramones flew to the Caribbean island of Puerto Rico to perform two concerts. The island is located around 1,000 miles southeast of Miami in Florida and approximately 50 miles east of the Dominican Republic and 40 miles west of the U.S Virgin Islands. Just over 3.2 million people reside in the country with the most populous city the capital, San Juan. The official languages are Spanish and English with the former being primarily spoken. Puerto Rico has a tropical climate with little seasonal variation and is typically sunny, hot and humid all year-round. Puerto Rico is described as an unincorporated territory of the United States with official Commonwealth status. Although the relationship with the USA has become politically controversial, the vast majority of Puerto Rican voters have continued to favour union with Washington, with a slightly greater number favouring the current commonwealth position rather than statehood. A small but persistent minority has advocated independence. [306]

After just touring the southern states of the United States, The Ramones finished in Miami in Florida and then headed further south. The band would next play two gigs on February 19th and 20th in Puerto Rico as part of an event incorporating the "World Surfing Titles" with the first show a private performance open to the surfers and the second open to the general public. The concerts were held in the coastal town of Aguadilla which is renowned for its miles of white sandy beaches and for the site of the U.S military *Ramey Airbase* which was where the '*fast four*' were billed. It must have been a strange sight to behold with not only the beaches crowded for the international tournament but also scores of people lining up to see four punks in the scorching heat take to the stage in their obligatory black leather jackets. One local remembers vividly the scene stating "The Ramones played where the running track is now, behind the Ramey gym. The shows were in the afternoon after the competitions" whilst also recalling that there were "at least 15,000 people there." Another fan recalls that "the heat was so unbearable that firefighters threw water from their hoses to relieve those that were present." [307] Neither concert had the set list recorded for posteriety but we do know that the gigs were aimed to promote the "Halfway To Sanity" album and would have in all probablility featured tracks such as "Bop 'Til You Drop", "Garden Of Serenity", "I Wanna Live" and "Weasel Face" which was accustomary around this time.

Originating from Isabela, a town just half an hour away from Aguadilla, one fan who was in the audience for that second show was guitarist Rick Deliz. Just a young 19 year old at the time, he remembers the concert with fondness stating "I was at the front and there was lots of *"moshing"* whilst nowadays ruefully looks back and reflects "it's incredible how The Ramones have influenced a generation without hardly ever getting any radio airplay." In 2009, Rick, who also plays in the band *Secret Agent*, decided that he wanted to form his own Ramones tribute not only because he "was a big fan but also because the songs were fun and easy to play." Rick and his friend Juan Carlos Del Valle who was also drummer for a *Beatles* tribute called *Jukebox,* invited their friends bassist Jacob Javier and front man Rambert

Cobian to join the arrangement. After initially playing under the designations of *Surfing Bird* and *Psycho Therapy*, the name of the group, *Don Ramones* was chosen by Rick. The connection may well be something fans in Europe will be unfamiliar with but as Rick explains it "is a take of Don Ramón, a character from the famous '70s Mexican TV sitcom *El Chavo Del Ocho*."

By 2012, there were a couple of changes within the band with Luis Roberto Gonzalez taking over as lead singer and Francisco Cairol on the bass guitar. Luis was previously the singer of *Voodoo Lounge*, a *Rolling Stones* cover, whilst Fran played guitar for *Jukebox* before switching instruments on to the four string for *Don Ramones*. In true punk style and long-established tradition, the boys decided to take stage names with all of them natural designations. The most recent quartet, for example, transformed into Rick, J C, Lou, and Fran Ramone respectively.

Don Ramones played many times in local clubs and bars around the island of Puerto Rico usually to audiences numbering between 50 to 100. These included establishments such as *Dom Pepe* in Mayaguez, *Dom Italian Lounge* in Cabo Rojo and *The Brewmasters Bar, Red Shield, The Handlebar* and *Super Bar* all in San Juan. The band also performed on a number of occasions in the town of Rincón at *Café 413, Hotel Bunger's Inn, The Skate Town* with *The Pool Bar Sushi* possibly being his favourite venue of them all due to its iconic setting with the stage set in front of a magnificent swimming pool. Rick loves the fact that just like The Ramones back in Aguadilla in 1988, his band gets their fans to '*mosh*' although of course on a somewhat different scale.

A look at *Don Ramones'* set list shows a nearly thrirty strong repertoire with most of our favourites included. Although the majority of the songs come from the self-titled debut "Ramones",

"Leave Home" and "Rocket To Russia", there are some picks from later albums too. Examples from the earlier material include "We're A Happy Family", "Gimme Gimme Shock Treatment", "Havana Affair" and the alluring "I Wanna Be Your Boyfriend" whilst if you enjoy the material from the 1980s then you will not be dissatisfied with the choices of "The KKK Took My Baby Away", "Pet Semetary", "Somebody Put Something In My Drink" and "Psycho Therapy".

Observing our tribute bands to see if they hit the right spot is an indispensible part of assembling this book and a search on social media shows just a couple of extracts from *Don Ramones'* past performances. My first port of call was to the band's *Facebook* page and one can immediately find a bundle of informtion on both The Ramones and the tribute. Rather oddly, however, a cover of "Rockaway Beach" was prominent but this was not performed by *Don Ramones* but instead by *Secret Agent,*

Rick's other project. Thankfully, "Chinese Rock", Dee Dee's *call to arms* for any junkie crazed raggamuffin, is on display live at *The Pool Bar* in Rincón in December 2018. Similarly, a look onto *Youtube,* reveals the classic "We're A Happy Family" from the *One Ten Thai* in Aguadilla back in April 2015. Both videos find the band in fine form, blazing out the two songs in a direct, no-nonsense punk aesthetic style.

Don Ramones have never officially called it a day but the band members are now touring pretty much constantly with their own projects so having the time for the tribute is logistically difficult. As Rick states though "if we get called to do a show we try to make it happen" so maybe Puerto Rican fans will get a chance to *'mosh'* again, sooner rather than later!

Remones
England

The Ramones had never been shy of performing at a festival. Not only would it be another useful payday but also would give the band the opportunity to gain exposure to a larger and more diverse crowd. In 1975, for instance, the band received positive reviews for their performance at the *Summer of Rock Festival* at *CBGBs* – an event which according to Johnny Ramone "made a big difference" to the group. "The festival went on for a week or so, six bands a night", the guitarist recalled. "*Rolling Stone* did a full page covering it. About three quarters of the page was on us, some on *the Talking Heads*, and the rest of the bands just got mentioned," he went on to add. In April 1976, the group performed in another New York celebration, this time at the *Easter Rock Festival* at *Max's Kansas City* whilst on Independence Day, 1977 they ventured outside the *Big Apple* to perform at the *Summerfest* in Milwaukee in Wisconsin. All told they performed in over 40 festivals throughout the world taking in countries such as Denmark, Switzerland, Sweden and Germany to name but a few. Not all festivals were a success, however, with Monte Melnick reciting how they were once showered with missiles at the *Canadian World Music Festival* at the *Toronto Exhibition Centre*. Additionally, some of the conditions that the concerts were performed in were less than ideal. Booking agent, John Giddings remembers that The Ramones were "disgusted" by some of the environmental conditions in Scandinavia described as "like going to hell" explaining that "you'd see these people sitting in these filthy fields in their own rubbish." [(308)]

One notable festival at which The Ramones performed in was in Reading in England. The town lies in the county of Berkshire around 50 miles from the centre of London. It is a home of a *red brick* university and is also famed for hosting an annual music event over the August bank holiday weekend at *Little John's Farm* on Richmond Avenue near Caversham Bridge. The history of the event is interesting - It is the longest-running popular festival held in the UK and was originally known as the *National Jazz Festival* which commenced in 1961. This event initially had a nomadic existence, moving between several sites until it found its permanent location in Reading in 1971. It was the first type of gathering to incorporate punk rock and new wave with the likes of *The Stranglers, Sham 69 and The Jam* all headlining. Other noteworthy acts who have played at the function include Alice Cooper, *Nirvana, Status Quo, The Stone Roses, The Prodigy* and *Beastie Boys*. In 1984 and 1985, there was a two-year hiatus because the local council designated the site for development and refused to grant licences for any alternative venues in the Reading area. Fortunately, in 1986 permission was given for fields adjacent to the original site to be used, and a line-up was put together at short notice.

The Ramones played at the festival on August 26th, 1988, sharing the bill with Iggy Pop on the first night of a three-day event. One music critic commented that "looking at the line-up, it is hard to believe that anyone would really have wanted to buy a weekend ticket. The strongest night was Friday, I'd have paid good money to see Iggy and The Ramones, and *The Godfathers* and *Fields Of The Nephilim* would have been good value too. But what sort of Iggy or Ramones' fan would have wanted anything to do with the Saturday offering?" [309] Indeed, a glance of the other acts on the programme does indicate a rather odd mix with the likes of *Meat Loaf, Starship* and *Bonnie Tyler* performing on the Saturday *and Squeeze, Deacon Blue* and *Hothouse Flowers* playing on the Sunday. Thankfully, someone from the crowd had the vision to video The Ramones' show that Friday evening although admittedly the quality of the film on *Youtube* leaves a lot to be desired. Nonetheless, it is well worth sounding out with a volley-fire of 29 tunes delivered like an artillery barrage in front of a hugely appreciate audience. Along with the usual favourites, some of the more interesting picks that night include "Needles and Pins", "Weasel Face", "Bop 'Til You Drop" and a masterful, speedy version of "Too Tough To Die".

A review of The Ramones' rota during that period, provides an indication of the band's frenetic programme. This was not part of a British tour – this was just a fleeting two-stop visit to Europe. Their previous gig was six days before at *The Ritz* in New York whilst after their show in Berkshire they would fly to Belgium for the *Pukkelpop* - another festival performance near the city of Hasselt. After this, they would make the return flight back across the Atlantic Ocean with a short break until their next show in New Jersey on September 13th. This relentless, strenuous and challenging schedule, I believe not only is a pointer why the dynamics of the group become so strained, but also a reason why performances were deemed less energetic and why for many the role of a Ramone during this period seemed more like employment than enjoyment.

One tribute which originates from Reading in Berkshire is *The Remones.* Formed in 2018 and still going strong today, the group consists of singer Nigel Millson-Crane, Bob Clarke on guitar, Charlie Alessandro on drums and his sister Sophie on bass. The band took up pseudonyms as a sign of concord with Nigee, Bobby, Charlee and Fifi the selected monikers and soon adopted the famous Ramones' eagle to re-enforce the link with the New York punk legends. The band members knew each other from the local music scene for a few years with Bobby playing with a well-established cover band called *Mini Scratch* and Charlee performing for the local original bands *Kill Committee* and *Almost Aliens*. Nigee describes how *The Remones* came about "we were at a local jam in The *Plough Pub* in Tilehurst one night and decided to try a Ramones song just to mix it up one evening and it went down a storm!" The singer goes on to add that "we were all huge fans anyway and we thought let's give it a go."

Photograph courtesy of Sam Cowlam

Since 2018 the bands have played the local bars and clubs around Reading and the surrounding area. Nigee cites a number of memorable gigs such as their first headliner at *The Sun Inn* in

Reading in September of that year or a number of shows at the *Purple Turtle,* also in the same town. The group are regulars at the *Facebar* supporting *The Pistols* in December 2021, *Totally Blondie* and *Pistols Expose* in October 2022 *along with The Sex Pissed Dolls* in November 2023. Out of Berkshire, *The Remones* paired up again with *Totally Blondie* to play a gig at the *Bosham Village Hall* in the summer of 2022 and crossed into Hertfordshire at *the Horns* in Watford to again support *The Pistols.* The front man explains that their typical set "generally follows 'It's Alive' although we mix it up depending on the gig with some additions such as "Pet Sematary", "Bonzo" and "Life's A Gas". Indeed, when describing the L.P, Nigee believes that it is "the definitive live album - The raw energy and power is phenomenal. It goes from zero to 150mph." When asked about the influence of the *'Fast Four',* the vocalist enthuses that "The Ramones were not punk, they were not rock, they were Ramones - a huge influence on nearly every guitar band since the mid '70s. You can hear Ramones influences in a vast array of bands even in 2024."

A scrutiny of all our bands is indispensable and pleasingly there are some opportunities to catch a sight of *The Remones* on social media. As good an induction as any, is a search on their own website at *www.remones.co.uk* or the band's *Facebook* home page. On the latter, along with gig announcements and general information you will find a fantastic version of "Rockaway Beach" and an even better rendition of "Teenage Lobotomy" with associated clips from the *Oakford Social Club* in Reading. Both tunes have that trademark fuzz tone guitar and thumping drums and I strongly urge readers go examine for oneself. A look on *Soundcloud* has further delights with "Pet Semetary", "I Wanna Be Sedated" "Blitzkrieg Bop" and a rather unique version of "Bonzo Goes To Bitburg" given exposure. With more gigs planned, the future for the Reading band looks rosy – indeed maybe, just maybe there could be a festival thrown in soon… Now wouldn't that be appropriate?!

Brain Drain
Greece

It was not until 1989 that The Ramones ventured to Greece, the historic country in south east Europe situated on the southern tip of the Balkan peninsula. Greece shares borders with Albania, North Macedonia, Bulgaria and Turkey and has the longest coastline in the Mediterranean Basin, featuring thousands of islands. The nation is probably best known as *the cradle of western civilisation* as it was hugely influential in ancient times. It is considered by many as the birthplace of democracy, philosophy, political science, literature and major scientific and mathematical principles as well as the source of the Olympic Games. Athens, its capital, retains landmarks which date back to 5th century B.C with probably the most famous feature being the Acropolis citadel which is located on a rocky outcrop above the city and contains several ancient buildings, the most renown, the Parthenon temple. Ancient Greece was the home of three of the greatest philosophers - Socrates, Plato and Aristotle along with two famed mathematicians Archimedes and Pythagoras. It was also the birthplace of the poet Homer who wrote the epics the Iliad and the Odyssey and is considered as one of the most influential authors in history.

The visit by The Ramones was surely long over-due as by this time they had already picked off most of western Europe and of course countries in the Pacific rim such as Japan, Australia and New Zealand along with Brazil and Argentina in South America.

The band played four nights on that first Greek tour but in just one venue - the choice was apt, however, as it was at the *Rodon* in Athens. The establishment was a rock and pop venue which opened in 1987 and ran for nearly 20 years until its closure in 2005. The 1,500-capacity venue was revamped into a fully equipped concert hall, following its life as a cinema. A number of famed artists performed at the site which included Iggy Pop, *The Triffids, Motörhead, Blondie, Sonic Youth* and *Blue Oyster Cult.* The club's very existence sparked an increase in the number of concerts offered in the ancient city and to their seriously deprived concert goers. The *Time Out* guide described the venue as "the oldest rock club in Athens (and for a long time the only one). The name alone brings tears to the eyes of the average Athenian concert goer." [310] The first Ramones gig in Greece took place on May 12th after an eight-leg tour of Italy whilst the next evening on the 13th saw the concert taped and has subsequently featured in the bootleg CD *"Blitzkrieg in Athens"*. Playing 32 tunes at breakneck speed, the record contains four tracks from their forthcoming album "Brain Drain" - "Don't Bust My Chops", "I Believe In Miracles", "Pet Sematary" and "Palisades Park". Released on May 23rd, "Brain Drain" was the first album to feature the re-stablished Marky on drums, the last to include Dee Dee on bass and also the final studio album released by Sire Records. The band performed at the *Rodon* for the next two nights until their flight back home to the States. It is also notable because the show on the 15th was the last performance to see Dee Dee on stage with the band in Europe.

Jimmy Markovich, sound technician for The Ramones, describes one of *the Rodon* concerts and paints a fascinating picture regarding what life could be like on the road. "There was a riot in Athens, Greece, once. We always played the same club, this tiny place where we'd do several nights in a row. First the people busted in and tore up the club before the show. Then, while we were playing, they let too many people in. Some gang tried to get in and when they were refused they broke down the door. When they got in and saw there was nowhere to go, there was a solid wall of people, they went back outside and started burning up cars and a bus stop. It was insanity. Those were the best times." [311] For those aficionados out there, The Ramones returned to Greece a further three occasions in 1992, 1993 and 1994 and including their inaugural visit they played in the country a total of 13 times. Their last gig in the country was on October 8th and featured local support act *Nightstalker* labelled as a 'stoner metal' band.

In 2014, a group of fans established The *Ramones Greek Fan Club* which organised parties, on-line discussions, concerts, exhibitions and charity events with the aim to keep The Ramones legacy going. One of those founder members was Johnny Afendras, who along with some other self-confessed Ramones maniacs decided that the next natural step was to set up their own cover band. Formed in 2015, the band took their name fittingly from "Brain Drain", the 11th studio L.P which coincided with their first tour of Greece. Although none of the line-up had seen The Ramones live, they were all members of the Greek music scene and had already gained experience in a number of bands such as *The Mr. Highway Band, Spring Shoe, Project Sacromonte, Small Chanter* and *4LT.* The quartet are all good friends and consists of Gregory Psaltakos as the vocalist, Antonis Kanaras on drums, Bill Karidis on bass as well as Johnny on guitar.

The group described the legacy of Ramones believing it remains "huge in many aspects of modern culture. Not just in punk but in music as a whole, in fashion and in the general attitude towards life and what anybody can do with his own goals and dreams." Johnny Afendras explains why they continue play the songs to this day stating that "we are trying, in our own way, for one simple but important thing – to keep The Ramones spirit and legacy alive. As C.J shouts at the end of ever solo performance 'Ramones Forever'!"

Although their favourite album was probably The Ramones debut, a typical set consists of about 40 songs covering every era and every album of the band's history. In order to keep fresh, the group tries not to play the same tracks every time but makes four to five tweaks per gig. In 2015 and 2016, the group helped organise two shows dedicated to The Ramones at the *Kyttaro Live Club* in Athens. In total, more than 25 of the best Greek bands participated, each playing three or four Ramones cuts apiece. With around 700 and 500 rapturous fans at each gig respectively, *Brain Drain* "headlined", performing at the end of each evening. I strongly recommend an excursion on to *Youtube* and an exploration of *"A night for The Ramones"* at *Kyttaro* where you can see some of the bands performing including *Brain Drain's rocky* take on the classics "Commando", "Surfin Bird", "Any Way You Want It", "We're A Happy Family" and closing the show inevitably with "Blitzkrieg Bop". It is certainly well worth a look and there is no doubt in my mind that if you fail to heed this advice, it would be somewhat of a *Greek tragedy*!

Commando Mexico

Although Mexico borders the United States of America to the south, it was not until 1989, that The Ramones crossed into their neighbouring nation. Mexico has been described as a land of extremes – with high mountains and deep canyons, sweeping deserts and dense rain forests. [312] Historically, it was famed for the Aztec people who ruled the area, until the Spanish conquistador, Hernán Cortés, took control of the country in the 16th century. Nowadays, it has the largest population of Spanish speakers in the world with nearly 130 million inhabitants with its largest metropolis, the capital Mexico City.

The first time, The Ramones performed in the country was not in the capital, however, it was in Tijuana. This city, is located in Baja California, on the north western Pacific coast and in close proximity to the border crossing with the USA. After playing in San Diego on June 22nd, it therefore made perfect sense to travel less than 20 miles southwards and cross the frontier into Mexico. The venue that night was at *Iguana's Nightclub,* a site that had a capacity of 1,000 and had only been formally opened on May 18th of the same year. Built by American entrepreneurs for $1.3 million, it provided a location which offered easy access to potential American day-trippers as well as Mexican music goers. John D'Agostino writing in the *Los Angeles Times* in 1991 described the scene "15 minutes away from San Diego, yet light-years away from parental supervision, *Iguanas* offers an ambience of almost anything goes, frontier neutrality that gives under-agers an intoxicating whiff of freedom." According to the *San Diego Union Tribune*, "the list of bands that played the venue as alternative music began swimming in the mainstream is the *definitive* list from that time: *Nirvana, Rage Against The Machine, Sonic Youth, Bad Religion, Screaming Trees, Nine Inch Nails, GWAR*" [313] so no wonder that The Ramones would be one of the first bands to take to the stage at this club. According to one regular, the atmosphere at *Iguanas* "was amazing and the bands would just feed off it." Sadly, the last concert performed at the venue was in 1994 with *Offspring* headlining [314] and after the club closed it became a disco named *Zool*. [315]

Like many of the concerts around that period, there is no definitive record of what The Ramones played that night but we can surmise that around 30 songs would have been discharged with around three to four picks from the most recent "Brain Drain" album. It is also worth putting the show into context – after the gig, founder member Dee Dee would perform just 10 more concerts before he quit the band.

The Ramones would not return again to Tijuana but would perform in the capital, Mexico City with *Da Brudders* playing two shows in September 1992 and a further two in the July of 1993. The metropolis is not just the most populous city on the North American continent with over 9.2 million people living there, but it is also famed for its location within the high Mexican central plateau at an altitude of 2,240 metres. In his autobiography, *Punk Rock Blitzkrieg*, Marky Ramone describes how the *thinner air,* associated with life a mile and a half above sea level, could affect performance although fortunately he felt that one's lungs acclimatised after the second day so it did not hinder his drumming. Marky also cites the sheer excitement that was generated by the local Latin fans with their quest to get a souvenir from the band. By this time, Marky would always sign a few pairs of his sticks and throw them out in between certain songs to the appreciative supporters. Indeed, the stick man felt that "we were no longer just a band. We were ambassadors." [316] There is no doubt that The Ramones developed a strong cult following in Mexico which includes a DIY museum in Mexico City called the *Ramones Casa Club*. In fact, according to journalist Reed Dunlea, the capital is "home to an obsessive Ramones fan base, and the museum is a haven for rockers in the neighbourhood, their families and die-hard fans who make the pilgrimage to the two-storey home-turned museum filled with records, photos, skateboards and other memorabilia. Alejandro "El Roko" Garrido, who runs the museum is no doubt why the New Yorkers were so popular in a country which had *a bad government and bad economy.* "The important thing is that The Ramones invented a style of music that makes you forget about that shit," he claimed. [317]

Based in Guadalajara, a city in western Mexico and the capital of the state Jalisco, another bunch of die-hard fans loved The Ramones so much that they decided to start their own tribute band. The initial line-up of 2016, saw Bigthor on the guitar, Martin Velasco as drummer, Checo playing bass and Yahir as vocalist. As is seen with many of our groups, all the bandmates took up the collective sir name of Ramone with the guitarist, for instance assuming the pseudonym of Bigthor Ramone. Some of the musicians had already gained experience in other local bands - Checo had played in *Xemican*, Yahir was previously in *Lacertilia* whilst Martin had performed in *Ligeros de Equipaje* and *Alpha*

Menos. For the second time in this book, we have seen the name of the band, originating from superlative track off the "Leave Home" L.P and the title of Johnny Ramone's autobiography with the lads choosing the designation as *Commando.* Compared to many of the tributes, the fellas have enjoyed a stable line-up although they did undertake one change in their cast with Doros taking over the stickman's duties in 2017 when Martin went to reside in Germany.

The band performed in a number of local bars with on average around 40 or so people in attendance but maybe their stand-out show was at the *Tianguis,* an open-air market cultural festival where over 200 people gathered to watch. Generally speaking, *Commando* performed a similar play-list each gig, with more emphasis and choices from the first three albums. However, there were some other picks selected to give their catalogue a broad and balanced feel with "I Wanna Be Sedated", "Psycho Therapy" and "Poison Heart" all played. Interestingly, the much-loved track from Joey's solo period "What A Wonderful

World" was another novel selection to give the set some variety. Probing social media for glimpses of the band, initially proved quite difficult with search engines continually directing you to the German *Commando* counterparts. However, eventually there was some success and for a brief foray, a good place to commence proceedings is with either "I Don't Care" or "Havana Affair". The latter song is live at *Desde el Cultu* and although being just a short extract from the concert, gives you an indication of the Mexican passion and spirit generated by the band. If you would like to see a whole concert of *Commando*, then track down the group live at the *Pulp* in Guadalajara. Here you will find the four lads in action for over 40 minutes with all the favourite songs such as "Rockaway Beach", "Sheena Is A Punk Rocker", "Now I Wanna Sniff Some Glue", "53rd and 3rd" and a superlative version of "Beat On The Brat" all blasted out.

Sadly, the band disbanded in 2020 with family and employment commitments getting in the way of their musical hobby. However, original drummer Martin cites a number of factors where The Ramones influence shaped future generations including "their intense energy, their fashion style and the fact that they helped start the punk movement." Maybe more importantly, however, was the encouragement "to be yourself" and get up and *just do it* - undoubtedly *Commando* was certainly a band who lived up to that.

The Ramoned
England

At face value, the show in Leicester on September 30th, 1989, should just have been another run-of-the-mill undistinguished gig. After all, the band had been playing for over 15 years all over the world and if ever a bunch of lads could be vindicated in saying *been there, done that and got the T-shirt* then this undoubtedly applied to The Ramones. However, the performance on that Saturday evening, heralded the start of a new era as it was the first concert that the band would play without founder member Dee Dee, arguably the most influential punk bassists of all time. It also signalled, of course, a new dawning as up stepped C.J Ramone, the man who stepped into the breach and go on to write his own chapter in the Ramones story.

The build up to Dee Dee's departure is well captured in his book *Poison Heart, Surviving The Ramones*. "However much I tried to hide my feelings, I knew pretty much I couldn't take it anymore," he said. "It was explained to me that The Ramones was my job – I had to do my job. But I felt let down, like I had to do all the work. I hated it. They expected me to write one song after another, and then have 10 people never say thank you. All they gave me was attitude." Dee Dee expands even more and specifically cites Johnny as the major contributory factor stating that the guitarist "was making too many musical decisions for someone who wasn't a songwriter" going on to describe that he hated recording the "Brain Drain" album and by this time "he dreaded being around them." By the time, the accompanying tour for the L.P reached California, Dee Dee was seriously ill, having weight problems and on anti-depressants. His last gig was in Santa Clara on July 5th at the *One Step Beyond* and after the flight back to New York, "packed a small bag and left, never to return." [318]

It is interesting to get the perspectives of others who were close to the bassist at the time. Johnny Ramone described his leaving as "the biggest blow in our career" believing that "he lost his mind." Johnny adds that by the end of his Ramone's tenure, Dee Dee had lost interest in playing the bass and had not even performed on the last three albums that he was credited on. "Worse than that", the guitarist recalled, "he wouldn't even move; he would just stand there and not even try", referring to the changes in his actions in their live shows. Although, he wasn't doing hard drugs during this period, Johnny felt he was getting "crazier and crazier" with the likely cause the combination of the band and his failing marriage. According to the guitarist, Dee Dee "would throw tantrums all the time" and looked "bloated" due to so many medications. It was at this time that he started getting into rap music something which "was everything we hated." Interestingly Johnny states that "I never thought of replacing him" and "I never wanted him to go. I'd always presumed Dee Dee was staying. We'd said we were in it together until the end." [319]

Mickey Leigh cites Dee Dee's departure due to Johnny's 'Gestapo-like' control over everything from their music to their haircuts as well as the changes that were going on in his personal life at that time. Furthermore, Mickey points out that there were also difficulties with the relationship between his brother Joey and the bassist. "Joey's alcoholism was getting ugly," said Dee Dee. "There was a double standard in the group. Even when I was totally straight, I was being constantly watched and criticised." According, to Mickey, this contradictory treatment was another aspect that bothered the bassist at the time. (320)

Marky Ramone remembers that on the flight back from the California tour, Dee Dee told the rest of the band that he was going to quit although they initially took it with a *pinch of salt* as he had been threatening this for the last few weeks. Moreover, he recalls that at this time, the bass player had just left his wife Vera and unwisely had taken himself off his medication. A few days later, Johnny called the drummer to inform him that Dee Dee was definitely quitting and they needed to have an emergency meeting. Marky recollects that the guitarist had a plan to move forward. "It was fine that he quit. Let him" with Johnny adding that The Ramones would find "a young Dee Dee without the drugs." Dee Dee would still write songs for the group and Marky agreed "we should continue as a band." (321)

The auditions for the replacement took place at *Studio Instrument Rentals* and according to Marky had at least 50 hopefuls taking a shot. The drummer recalls that one would-be replacement, the 24-year-old Christopher Joseph Ward, played "an okay version of Sedated" but was worried by his finger playing rather than use of a pick, downstroking strength and ability to play fast eighth notes. Marky also recalls that Chris came back for a second audition and was asked to play "Blitzkrieg Bop" and "Rock 'n' Roll High School" and got the job." (322) The biggest advocate of Chris, or C.J as he would be dubbed, was Johnny with the founder member of the band remembering that "I saw C.J and just said, 'he's the one'. I knew right away. He looked like Dee Dee, he played like Dee Dee...C.J was just out of the Marine Corps, so he was used to following orders. I knew he was going to be perfect. 'C.J, just look at the mirror in front of you as we're playing, and you do what I do. You stand the way I'm standing. You move forward when I move forward. You move back when I move back. Just follow what I'm doing'. I gave him a bunch of tapes of Dee Dee and told him, study these concerts and watch what he does." [323] Evidently, both Marky and Monte did not agree with Johnny's choice with the guitarist believing that they were being too technical and short-sighted. Joey, who was not present at the audition, went with Johnny's gut feeling which was unquestionably the correct decision.

From C.J's point of view, he initially went to the audition in the hopes of simply meeting the band. At that time, he was in the U.S Marines Corps and was home on unauthorised leave when he heard about the try-out. C.J recalls that soon after "I got a call back from Monte Melnick and I figured I had left a cord behind or something, but they wanted me to learn a few more songs and come back. It went on for a couple of weeks, but I had to return to get my discharge sorted. My first night in military custody I got a phone call from Johnny Ramone. He told me to do my time and when I got out I had a job. I spent a few weeks in custody before I got out. When I did, I spent five weeks learning 40 Ramones songs and did my first show in Leicester, England." [324] As C.J prepared for his first show, in the inevitable photo shoots, amusingly the new bassist worn a bandana. This was nothing to do with a fashion statement but to hide the fact that the prison barber had given him a military style skinhead haircut. [325]

Leicester is a city in the East Midlands of England with a population of around 368,000 people. It is located just over 40 miles from England's second city, Birmingham and approximately 100 miles north of the capital of London. His first show was at *Leicester's University Students Union* in the *Queens Hall* now described as *Rockandy* and fortunately the set list that evening was recorded. Maybe surprisingly, only three songs were chosen from the most recent album "Brain Drain" with "Don't Bust My Chops, "Pet Sematary" and "I Believe In Miracles" the selected tracks. C.J would have plenty of opportunity to blast out the "1, 2, 3, 4s" with the customary favourites such as "Gimme Gimme Shock Treatment", "Rockaway Beach" and "Beat On The Brat" all performed. In front of the unforgiven English punks it must have been a baptism of fire of fire for the new bassist and it is worth reading C.J's description of events in its entirety. "My first gig with them was in Leicester, England, on September 30th, 1989, on the "Brain Drain tour", he recalls. "It's like the first time you have sex; you don't know what the fuck you're doing, you just wanna get it over with. The intro starts, we walk out onstage and my mind goes, 'Ding!' Totally fucking blank. Everything we rehearsed goes right out the window. It's a packed show and immediately I'm getting spat on and hit with handfuls of coins in the face. I can hear them bouncing off my bass. I made some mistakes, but no train wrecks. The crowd was into it, but the people in front of me were just brutal. This girl gets up on her boyfriend's shoulders with a sign that says 'We Want Dee Dee.' I walked back to my amp, grabbed my water bottle and - blam! - blasted her right in the face. She falls off her boyfriend's shoulders and that was that. By the end of the night, the people in front of me were chanting, 'C.J, C.J!' We come back to do the encores and I'm covered in spit. I can smell it, so I whip my T-shirt off and we go out to do the encores. When we come offstage, Johnny tears into me. 'What the fuck's wrong with you? You see us taking our shirts off? Why'd ya take your shirt off?'

I'm, like, 'I was covered in spit.' He chewed me out for that, but that's how Johnny ran things. I was greener than green." [326] A quick forage on to *Youtube* will give listeners audio coverage of the show with Joey introducing their new bassist before the start of "Blitzkrieg Bop" and although I cannot confirm this, one of the first hand eye witness' comments states that C.J jumped in the pit after he played the final chord of the night.

Photograph courtesy of Linz Ramone

Based in Leicester, one man who loved The Ramones music so much and their "never say die attitude" was David Oliver, who in 2015 decided that he wanted to start his own tribute band. Calling upon two of his old friends, Steve and Richard, who he went to school with in Kidderminster, the life-long Ramones fans recruited Andrew to complete the quartet. Naming themselves *The Ramoned,* the lads, as in time honoured tradition, decided to take a collective surname with Davey

Ramoned on vocals, Stevie Ramoned taking on the guitar duties, Richey Ramoned playing bass and Andy Ramoned on the drummer's seat. By the end of 2016, Richey and Andy both left the group and a reformed line-up saw Ryan as drummer and ex-Shamones guitarist Andy Johnson switching instruments to become bass player A.J Ramoned.

Their first ever gig was at the *Secret Garden* in Kidderminster on 11th June, 2015 and although Dave cites all their performances as "memorable", when pushed to name a favourite, the singer points to the show at the *Caerphilly Working Men's Hall* in south Wales in December of the same year. Playing to a hugely appreciate audience, the *Ramoned* shared the stage that night with two other tributes on the same bill - *The Clashed* and *The Pistols*.

Although there were some choices from later albums, their live set concentrated mainly around the first three classic L.Ps, the self-titled "Ramones", "Leave Home" and "Rocket To Russia". A look at their repertoire, which generally consisted of around 20 songs or so, reveals some real crowd pleasers. On offer, for instance, one can find such classics as "Today Your Love Today The World", "I Don't Wanna Walk Around With You", "Suzy Is A Headbanger", "Sheena Is A Punk Rocker" and of course "Blitzkrieg Bop".

A look on social media will find a *Ramoned Facebook page* which not only highlights their own band but has extensive information about The Ramones too. Without question, my recommendation to all fans is to take at all the bands on offer and although there are not as many videos of the *Ramoned* as some other groups, there are a few glimpses. Check out, for instance live at *the Donkey* in Leicester from 2015 where you will find "Havana Affair" and "Commando" played back to back by their first line-up. At the same venue, you can also observe the group's second combination in November 2016. Starting off with the leather cladded, Stevie, Ryan and A.J blasting out the instrumental "Durango 95", Davey coolly strolls on to stage without a moment to lose before the call to arms of "Teenage Lobotomy". Initially it was slightly disconcerting to find the bassists and guitarist facing the opposing side than is the norm, but once you get over that, then there is no doubt that the group had a bundle of energy and were a tight-knit outfit with a great guitar sound.

Sadly, in 2020, after five years of performing, the band decided to call it a day with geographical and logistical reasons defining that it was no longer practical to play. Nonetheless, Davey strongly believes that part of the legacy of The Ramones is that they showed that "anyone could get up and play." Since their formation, he and the *Ramoned* have loved meeting fellow *Ramoniacs* at their own gigs. He has also met and performed along-side fellow tribute, the all-girl band *The Ramonas*. It has been a journey which he never would have missed.

Davey saw The Ramones no less than 16 times throughout their career. His most memorable recollection was undoubtedly a show in London at the famous *Lyceum Ballroom* on February 27th, 1985. After the show, he managed to meet the New Yorkers and got in to dressing room - an experience he describes as "priceless." Davey also shared the stage with C.J Ramone at the *Hairy Dog* in Derby in 2017 as part of the bassist's solo project and "American Beauty" tour. Indeed, the singer had the pleasure to give a rendition of his favourite tune "Havana Affair". Ironically, Derby is just 30 miles and a relatively short drive from where the *green* C.J started his amazing journey back in 1989 at that gig in Leicester.

Davey joins the stage with C.J: Photograph courtesy of Linz Ramone

The Cretins
Austria

It may astonish some readers that the first time, The Ramones performed in Austria was not until the November of 1990. Austria is a landlocked country, situated in central Europe and bounded by no less than eight nations sharing borders with Switzerland, Liechtenstein, Italy, Slovenia, Hungary, Slovakia, the Czech Republic and Germany. The official language of the country is German and Austria has an estimated population of nearly nine million people. Most of Austria is described as Alpine or sub-Alpine with heavily wooded mountains and hills cut by valleys of fast-flowing rivers. The country is drenched in history and is famed for being the heartland of the Habsburg monarchy, one of the most influential and long-lasting dynasties of Europe. Once the centre of power for the large Austro-Hungarian Empire, Austria was reduced to a small republic after its defeat in World War one. Indeed, the assassination of Archduke Franz Ferdinand, heir presumptive of the Austro-Hungarian throne in June 1914, has been described as the "powder keg" which lead to the bitter conflict up of the First World War. Following the Anschluss and annexation of the country by Nazi Germany in 1938 and subsequent occupation by the victorious allies, Austria's 1955 State Treaty declared the nation as "permanently neutral." However, since the Soviet Union's collapse, Austria has increasingly been involved in European affairs and joined the European Union in 1995 and the single monetary system four years later. Although not a member of NATO it did join the Partnership for Peace and participates in the Euro-Atlantic Partnership Council.

The Ramones' first concert in Austria was on November 21ˢᵗ at the *Bank-Austria Zelt* in Vienna. The group had just played a one-off show in Zurich in Switzerland and then headed eastwards towards Austria's capital city. Over the years a number of notable artists have performed at the venue which have included Iggy Pop, *New Model Army, Motörhead, Black Sabbath* and *Die Toten Hosen*. There is thankfully, a complete audio recording of the 31 tunes played that evening on *Youtube* and for those who are less acquainted with the group, perfectly depicts the band at the start of the '90s. The first stand out feature is that by now we have the tried and trusted start to all shows – "Durango 95", "Teenage Lobotomy", "Psycho Therapy", a brief 'welcoming' by Joey before they launch into "Blitzkrieg Bop". Secondly, compared to earlier highlighted concerts, for instance, an increased tempo is now truly noticeable. Using "Blitzkrieg Bop" as our exemplar and something which will be expanded upon later on in this book, one can track how The Ramones speeded up over the years. In 1975, during the performance in Arturo Vega's loft, for instance, the song clocked in at two minutes and 11 seconds, just a touch faster than the album pace. During this Austrian debut concert, however, the same song was being played in just one minute and 34 seconds – a reduction in time of an incredible 37 seconds. The third characteristic Ramones feature which can be just picked up is the introductory recording of "The Good, The Bad And The Ugly" which was played as the lads entered the stage. As an audience member, there was something quite enthralling when you heard this requisite tune with the realisation that *Da*

Brudders would be soon be performing. Similarly, one also is treated to the musical composition of the "Ecstasy of Gold" by Ennio Morricone which would accompany the New Yorkers as they left the stage. As a fan, this was the definitive but somewhat gloomy signal that they would not be back for another encore. It was also the first opportunity to find mates after the inevitable ferocious mosh pit had separated pogoing crazed friends. At the same time, it was the earliest chance to recover from the *onslaught* which was a Ramones concert – make no mistake your senses had been assaulted and recuperation time would be needed. Soon after, it was also a time to reflect on another superb, frenetic hour of pulsating fun and look forward in the hope that it wouldn't be too long before they toured again. Despite my reservations about the speed of the songs, overall the *Bank-Austria Zelt* concert undoubtedly stands the test of time – it even surprisingly has a flashback from the early days with two verses of "I Don't Wanna Go Down To The Basement" thrown in as the penultimate song of the night. It is well worth a listen, go check it out.

The next day, The Ramones played in Graz, Austria's second city which is just over 120 miles south of Vienna. The venue that evening was at *the Orpheum* which according to its own website appreciates "an almost legendary reputation amongst artists and fans worldwide" and enjoys "a classic theatre stage." The establishment, although renovated and technically brought up to date in 2016, still has the charm and décor of the traditional venue which was opened in 1899 and with a capacity of 1,310. [327] There were a few changes to the set list in comparison to the previous evening with two fewer songs performed overall – "Indian Giver" was played in Graz but "Basement", "Chinese Rock" and "California Sun" all discarded. To put into context, the band's hectic schedule, The Ramones immediately moved on to Zagreb in Yugoslavia where they performed on November 24th.

The group would visit Austria for a third and final time on October 12th, 1994. On this occasion they would play in the far north of the country in Linz which lies on perhaps Europe's most evocative river - the Danube. The venue that night was at *Posthof* which has housed a variety of genres of music such as rock, pop, reggae and jazz. There is no recorded set list that night but was part of the "Acid Eaters" tour so a number of cover songs would undoubtedly have been played. These would unquestionably have included "Have You Ever Seen The Rain?", "My Back Pages", "The Shape Of Things To Come" and "7 to 7 is" which were all prominent during this period. In all probability it would have also included "Cretin Hop" which was certainly on show in the November 1990 gigs too and it was this definitive tune which was used as the designation for our next tribute. *The Cretins* originate from Klagenfurt, a city in the southern region of Austria, near the border with Slovenia. Although the band only performed two shows on August 9th and September 5th in 2003, the very fact that a tribute was formed in a country where The Ramones rarely visited is testament to the significant influence the Americans have had. The group was a trio and consisted of Matthias Karlo on guitar and lead vocals, bassist Marco Perdacher and drum man Michael Kanduth. On stage, the lads took pennames simply being known as Matt C, Marc C and Mike C whilst two of the outfit had had previous experience with other bands. Matt for example had played guitar for *the Pinheads* and *the Beatbrats* and Marc had performed on the four string for *the Rotten Rooters*. Interestingly, guitarist Matt was fortunate enough to see The Ramones at *Posthof* in Linz as well in neighbouring Italy at the *Palasport* in Pordenone.

The group started in unusual circumstances. Drummer Mike wanted to play a Ramones cover set as his first show for his 18th birthday party and asked his close friends and fellow Ramones fans Matt and Marco to participate. Approximately 100 people attended the birthday bash with *the Cretins* opening up for another group, *The Incredible Staggers.* Around a month later they played their second and last show as a Ramones tribute at a small festival at a lake in the south of Austria with around 300 people in attendance. After the success of the two concerts, the lads decided to write original music. Mike declares the reason for their change in plan stating that "covering The Ramones was fun and we still throw in a cover in our set every once in a while, but we found it more challenging and exciting to create our own material and express our creativity and spirit, rather than being a tribute act."

Both gigs comprised of the same set list with 20 songs performed. To their credit, *the Cretins'* catalogue of songs was a hybrid of the new and the old and certainly delivered the goods. For those of you who enjoy the early material, the boys served up many of the *must-play* tunes such as "Sheena Is A Punk Rocker", "Blitzkrieg Bop", "Pinhead", "Rockaway Beach" and needless to say their *raison d'être* of "Cretin Hop". However, newer fans would also enjoy some of their mid and latter album picks with "Makin Monsters For My Friends", "I Don't Wanna Grow Up", "R.A.M.O.N.E.S" and "I Believe In Miracles" all, for instance, given an outing. Pleasingly, there were a couple of often neglected gems selected too – "I Wanna Be Your Boyfriend" and "Carbona Not Glue" both prime examples of overlooked triumphs. As a three-piece, the Cretins did not attempt to copy The Ramones so there were no wigs just ripped blue jeans and leather jackets worn. Mike recalls that "I did dye my hair black and get myself a Dee Dee haircut that I proudly wore from 2003-2004." The stick man also feels that The Ramones' influence is still apparent. "After our second show", he recalls, the band were motivated enough to "start writing our own material and continued under *The Cretins* name as a four piece until 2007, when we were legally forced to change the name by a German band. We became *DeeCracks* from then on and are still going strong, just celebrating out 20th anniversary in 2023." Indeed, after all this time, isn't it good that *these cretins are still hopping*? Go and investigate… your feet won't stop!

Chainsaw Eaters
Bosnia And Herzegovina

Although The Ramones never performed in Bosnia and Herzegovina, they did perform in Yugoslavia, a country located in south east and central Europe and an area often referred to as The Balkans. Translated as the "Land of the South Slavs", Yugoslavia was founded after the First World War in 1918 from territories previously owned by the Austrian-Hungarian Empire and existed until its break up in 1992. After the end of World War Two in 1945, a communist government under Josep Tito was established and by 1963, the country was renamed as the Socialist Federal Republic of Yugoslavia (SFRY). Whilst ostensibly a Communist state, the country broke away from the Soviet sphere of influence and adopted a more de-centralised and less repressive form of government compared to other East European states during the Cold War. The reasons for the break-up of the nation are varied ranging from the cultural and religious divisions between the diverse ethnic groups and a series of major political events which served as an independence drive within the various regions of the Republic. [328] After the fragmentation of the country, the six constituent republics became the sovereign states of Croatia, Slovenia, Montenegro, Serbia, North Macedonia along with Bosnia and Herzegovina whilst in 2008, Kosovo declared its liberation from Serbia and is now deemed to have partial independence.

Despite Johnny Ramone's loathing of anything remotely liberal let alone socialist, the commercial and financial lure of a new market would no doubt override any political high ground and after performing in Graz in Austria, The Ramones headed into Yugoslavia. Their first concert in the country was on November 24th 1990 in Zagreb in Croatia with the chosen venue, the *Dom Sportova* which translates to the "House of Sports". Built in 1972, it is a multi-purpose sports arena used for basketball, handball, volleyball and gymnastics but also doubles up as a concert-hall and has witnessed a number of celebrated artists over the years. These have included *The Rolling Stones, Queen, Dire Straits,* David Bowie and Paul McCartney to name but a few. The group performed 32 songs that night, including two encores. Maybe surprisingly there were only two tracks chosen from the most recent album "Brain Drain" - "I Believe in Miracles and "Pet Sematary" which would be the first L.P to re-feature drummer Marky and also the last to include renowned Dee Dee on bass. Some of the other picks that evening was the pugnacious "Animal Boy" and the seminal hardcore refrain "Wart Hog" along with the gemstones "Psycho Therapy", "Mama's Boy", "Somebody Put Something In My Drink" and the oh so catchy "I Wanna Live".

The next day the band would travel just under 90 miles into Slovenia and play in Ljubljana at the *Tivoli Hall*. Interestingly, the site was another multi-purpose indoor sports complex and amongst others has hosted table tennis, figure skating, weightlifting and ice hockey sporting competitions. Just like the *Dom Sportova,* it also doubled up as a music venue and the likes of Louis Armstrong, Cat Stevens, *Iron Maiden, Siouxsie and the Banshees, Green Day* and *The Sex Pistols* have all at one time or another played between its four walls. The Slovenian crowd were treated to exactly the same set as their Croatian counterparts except for whatever reason, the second encore did not occur and 29 songs therefore were played without the likes of "Do You Wanna Dance?", "California Sun" and "Judy Is A Punk". [329] To put their busy schedule into context, there would be no rest for the wicked. The next day, on November 26th they moved on to another country, this time performing in Milan in northern Italy.

By the time The Ramones returned to *Tivoli Hall* and *Dom Sportova* for further shows in the autumn of 1994, the political landscape had transformed and the band would no longer be touring officially to Yugoslavia but now the independent nations of Slovenia and Croatia. C.J was now on the four string and "Acid Eaters", the only album to be entirely composed of covers, was the order of the day. Although the renditions of "My Back Pages", "7 And 7 Is", "The Shape Of Things To Come" and "Have You Ever Seen The Rain?" were still top draw, for many Ramones fans there was too much emphasis on the remake rather than the original.

The '*fast four*' never did cross the border into Bosnia and Herzegovina but a group of musicians who loved punk rock, grew up with The Ramones and adored their songs were inspired enough to form their own tribute band. Heralding from Banjaluka, the second largest city in the country and the largest within the Republic of Srpska, the group originally consisted of singer David "Dejvi Ramone" Pećanac, Siniša "Sina Ramone" Blažić on guitar, Fedja "Fele Ramone" Stojaković as bassist and Srdjan "Srki Ramone" Banjac playing drums. At this stage in 2009, the band originally started under the name *Acid Eaters,* coined after that 13th studio album. However, when this dissolved a new band *Chainsaw Bop* kept the flame burning which included

Bojan "Robi Ramone" Tomić as guitarist. Recently, the first line-up has reformed and with the group reinforced by Bojan the lads decided to use a combination of the two designations – enter the new, exciting merged *Chainsaw Eaters* which hit the streets in the autumn of 2023.

Bojan cites a number of memorable *Chainsaw Bop* gigs particularly those in their home town of Banjaluka and also in the capital of Bosnia and Herzegovina in Sarajevo. Their set list is of particular interest to those of us who enjoy a few of the lesser exposed tracks and there is a healthy mix from the celebrated first three albums and those from later L.Ps. Maybe the selection of the more contemporary songs such as "The Crusher", "R.A.M.O.N.E.S", "Spiderman", "I Know Better Now", "I Don't Wanna Grow Up", "Tomorrow She Goes Away", "Zero Zero UFO", "Strength To Endure", and "She Talks To Rainbows" is systematic of the fact that The Ramones toured the region at the latter stages of their career.

As Bojan explains Chainsaw Eaters do not wear wigs or try to imitate The Ramones but instead "try to get the sound as right as possible." However, he has not ruled out the move towards a *'wigged tribute'* impersonation in the future and goes on to state that "we'll see if we can take that step as well." The guitarist has high hopes for the band aiming to continue to improve with ambitions that "one day our wish is to play outside our country and all over the world."

Although there is naturally no footage on social media of *Chainsaw Eaters,* the old *Chainsaw Bop* is readily available. One's immediate observation is the sight of an additional guitarist along with a bassist, does take some acclimatising to and will no doubt leave any Ramones nit-picker uneasy. However, once one gets over this, the medium paced songs such as the "Death Of Me" and "Poison Heart" from the *Omladinskog Zagovarannja Festival* in 2022 are well worth listening to. My personal favourite, however, is "Commando" from 2016 with the 'four rules' shouted out alternatively in true Ramones fashion.

Bojan feels that The Ramones "had and still have today, a great influence on the fans - they left something eternal in the hearts of people with their emotion, in their lyrics and with their melodies. We experience them together with the fans and when we play… we are one." With these sentiments, we look forward to see how *Chainsaw Eaters* develop with eager anticipation.

Mondo Bizarro
Brazil

"Mondo Bizarro" was recorded in the January and February of 1992 at *the Magic Shop* and *Baby Monster Studio* both in New York City. It was the 12th studio album by The Ramones and released on the 1st September and their first release for three years. On the one hand, the L.P signalled a return to the tried and trusted. Ed Stasium, for example, who had a long connection with The Ramones was asked to become the producer. On the other hand, however, there were significant changes. It was the first studio L.P, for instance, to feature C.J on the bass. It also saw their association with Sire Records/Warner Brothers come to an end and along with it, their bond with Seymour Stein. Stein, who had been instrumental when the band signed their first contract in January 1976, was president of the former company and vice president of the latter and described by Marky Ramone as "an uncle to us." (330) The chosen new record label was Radioactive Records which was owned by The Ramones manager Gary Kurfist and a situation that both Marky and C.J believed signalled a conflict of interest. In his autobiography, *Punk Rock Blitzkrieg*, the drummer posed the question "could we rely on Gary to push Gary?" (331) whilst in an interview with Mark Prindle, the bassist was far more critical of the decision not to explore other labels. "Brett Gurewitz of Epitaph Records was following us around, begging us to let him put out the next Ramones record. I mean, literally", C.J pointed out. "In Amsterdam, he came to see us and literally was begging Johnny and Joey to let him do it. And then we had Stormy Shepherd, I can't remember the name of her company, but she was booking everybody. All those bands - *Rancid, The Offspring.* She had an unbelievable roster of bands that she was booking." Instead, Johnny was insistent in signing for Radioactive Records, and when he challenged the founder member, C.J received a terse response. "When you have as many years in the business as I do, then you can make the decisions", the guitarist replied. C.J remembers that "at that point I realised it was completely pointless to try and discuss any business stuff with Johnny. So he signed with Gary Kurfirst, the record came out and sold about what Ramones records usually sold, and we went and toured the same shitty little clubs throughout the States that The Ramones did for most of their career." (332)

Three of the 13 tracks on the album were written by Dee Dee Ramone. According to the ex-bassist, "The Ramones management turned on me" referring for his need of money to pay for a lawyer to get him out of jail after being caught in possession of marijuana. "They took advantage of my bad luck streak, and strung me along to get material for a new Ramones album" he said, feeling that the band could have loaned him a few thousand dollars to help him out of prison in his time of need. The three tracks in question were certainly some of the best from the album with "Poison Heart", being chosen as a single and reaching number six on the *Billboard Modern Rock Tracks* chart. The slower than norm song became one of the live favourites during the last few years of their career and according to Dee Dee was autobiographical, written with all his *"heart and soul."* (333) Ironically, the other two songs penned by the punk icon, "Main Man" and "Strength To endure", were both given to his replacement, C.J Ramone to sing and to his credit, he did an outstanding job in the delivery. The new bass man remembers that at this time Joey didn't go to rehearsals and the ones he was sounding better on, were simply the ones that he sang on the albums. [334]

Unusually, two songs from the album were penned by Marky and both beckons the question why did the drummer not deliver more of these delights? "Anxiety" is a fever pitched, manic attack on one's senses whilst the "The Job That Ate My Brain" captures everybody who had an occupation that they loved in one sense but drove them a little crazy in another. Undoubtedly, the drummer had one eye on his own job when he lay down the words of that tune. [335] Two rocky numbers written by Joey deserve a mention. "Cabbies On Crack" will get you bouncing around as if your life depended on it, whilst "Heidi Is A Headcase", although never reaching the heights of a "Sheena", "Judy" or "Suzy" still warrants a listing in The Ramones female hall of fame. One of the vocalist's tracks "Censorshit", has an unfamiliar slant and was addressed to Tipper Gore, the wife of eventual Vice President, Al Gore. The song was about how the *Parents Music Resource Centre*, who Tipper was part of, wanted to put ratings on records. However, the riff is catchy and not dissimilar to Steve Jones' guitar sound on the infamous Sex pistols' "Holidays In The Sun".

Although, the album went gold in Brazil in 2001, it is hard to argue with Johnny's assessment of a "C Grade" of the L.P. Similarly, it is difficult to disagree with his rather ironic statement that "the songs are the weak spot on this album… We needed more Dee Dee songs on it." [336] C.J felt that "for 'Mondo Bizarro', they thought they were going to get there by making everything sound nice and it didn't pan out that way.

I thought it came out too slick-sounding." [337] Indeed, for punks like myself, nearly half of the tracks from the cut were as a tame as a sheep and the likes of "Touring", "Tomorrow She Goes Away", "I Won't Let It Happen" and the cover of "The Doors'" track "Take It As It Comes" tended to be fast forwarded on my C.D player. Interestingly, the name of the album derived from the Italian *'mondo bizzarro' or 'weird or bizarre world'* although The Ramones variation of the spelling of *'bizarro'* was taken from the title of a film. The L.P cover was a distorted image of the quartet and was the work of stalwart George DuBose whose psychedelic, LSD picture fitted in perfectly with the designation of the album. Additionally, to mask the appearance of three quarters of the ageing band was probably at the forefront of Johnny's mind although personally these types of semi-hidden photographs did nothing to enthuse us fans.

One tribute group who took their designation from the album, originate from Rio De Janeiro in Brazil. *Mondo Bizarro* was founded in 2014 by die-hard fan and school teacher, Felipe Rozza because "he was so passionate about his favourite band." Indeed, Felipe admits that "he becomes very emotional when watching Ramones videos", describing them as "his religion" and even "part of his extended family." "I miss them so much", Felipe pronounces and "wanted to honour them, showcasing to new generations, the band that changed rock 'n' roll." The first line-up started as a three piece with Felipe carrying out bass and lead vocal duties whilst Roger Rock was on the drums and Nikolas Zanette played guitar. Over the years there were a number of changes with the only constant, the ever present Felipe. Eventually, the group was extended to a quartet with Felipe solely singing and Leonardo Drummond picking up the bass duties.

The band's set list altered due to the variations in the group's line-up but tended to follow The Ramones "Loco Live" sequencing. This would see the instrumental track of "Durango 95" initially played, followed by "Teenage Lobotomy", "Psycho Therapy" all the way until "I Wanna Be Sedated". After this, there were minor adaptions with some of their favourite songs from "¡Adios Amigos!" and of course "Mondo Bizarro" being added. When asked about his most memorable gig, Felipe ruefully recalls a concert played in **São Gonçalo** in the Federal Unit of Rio De Janeiro which was notable for unfortunately all the wrong reasons. "We were promised a big festival", the bassist recalls, "but when we got there, it was totally amateurish. There was no stage and we had to play on the floor. Instead of a 40-minute set which we were promised, it was immediately cut and despite being asked to get off, we kept on performing. Eventually, as we sung 'Pet Semetary', they turned off the sound. It was quite funny as I flipped them, the middle finger!"

A look on to their *Youtube* channel, initially directs you to a super-fast rendition of the masterly "Pinhead". For those Ramones disciples who like their cover bands to look like the originals then you will, no doubt, find it somewhat problematic. The performance is shown as a three-piece rather than a quartet and there is no attempt to copy the New Yorkers by, for example, wearing wigs. Indeed, Felipe always felt that adorning themselves with a hairpiece not only looks "ridiculous" but was just not practical in a country which can get to near on 40 degrees Celsius. If you can be receptive to this, you will find songs which are played hard and fast with an abundance of energy and a stunning attack on your senses. Even more impressive, is the next link from 2017, which proved to be the last project the band carried out, where *Mondo Bizarro* play the whole of the first album live from their studio. Each and every song is delivered with a passion and expertise although my personal favourites have to be "Now I Wanna Sniff Some Glue", "Havana Affair" and the brutal "Loudmouth". Interestingly, drummer Roger Rock shouts the "1,2, 3, 4s" and aids with the backing vocals. The band can also be seen from a little earlier, as a four-piece performing "Pet Sematary" live with Felipe purely on vocals, Marcos playing guitar, Leo on bass and Erick on the skins.

Felipe saw The Ramones twice in 1994 and 1996 in Rio De Janeiro on the "Acid Eaters" and "Adios Amigos" tour. He remembers that everyone knew it was their last tour and it was a very emotional time for the passionate Brazilian fans. He also recalls that when they finished their set with "Beat On The Brat" he had tears in his eyes and he was not the only one as he saw "an extremely muscular, bare chested man with a Ramones logo tattoo, sitting on the floor and weeping as they left the stage."

When asked about The Ramones influence, Felipe feels that they came up with something new and changed rock 'n' roll for the better. Back in the '70s, at a time when the progressive rock bands were abandoning standard pop traditions in favour of a more instrumentation and compositional techniques with more technology harnessed for new sounds, The Ramones reverted to a back-to-basics live focus rather than music approached as a form of art from the studio. Felipe is genuinely shocked why the iconic group never became as famous as some bands such as *Nirvana* and still does not understand why *Da Brudders* fail to get the credit they deserve. For me, there is only one answer – we do live in a *bizarre world*.

Acid Eaters
Chile

Chile is located along the western coast of the southern cone of South America and shares borders with Peru to the north, Bolivia to the north east and Argentina to the east. The geographical dimensions of Chile are unique. It is one of the longest countries in the world stretching 2,672 miles from north to south whilst it is also one of the narrowest with an average width of only 112 miles and at its tightest point just 40 miles from east to west. [338] The *pencil-thin* country encompasses a remarkable variety of climates and landscapes and is also home to numerous beaches, fjords, deep sea channels, glaciers and icebergs - and the Atacama Desert - a virtually rainless plateau made up of salt basins and lava flows whilst the snow-capped Andes cover almost all of its eastern border. Generally lower, non-Andean ranges dissect Chile with the largest being the Cordillera de la Costa in the far south. Located along the Pacific Ring of Fire, the Andes includes over 600 volcanoes, within Chile alone, many of them active, and almost 10% have erupted, at least once. [339] At the southernmost tip of the country sits Cape Horn, the famous headline of the Tierra del Fuego which heralds the northern boundary of the Drake Passage and marks where the Atlantic and Pacific Oceans meet. Historically, by the 16th century, Spanish conquistadors began to colonize the region replacing Inca rule and the territory was a colony between 1540 and 1818, when it gained independence from Spain. In the 20th century, after a period of severe left-right political polarisation in the 1960s and 1970s, the country experienced a *coup d'etat* in 1973 by the military dictatorship of General Auguste Pinochet whose subsequent 17-year regime was responsible for many human rights violations. In 1990, Chile made a peaceful return to democracy and has since become one of the most economically and socially stable nations in South America. The population of Chile is 19.6 million with approximately 6.5 million people, living in the capital city of Santiago. It is located in the country's central valley and is also renowned for its altitude – most of the city lies between 1,640-2,133 above sea level. Santiago is situated within an hour's drive of both the Pacific Ocean and the Andes Mountains whilst the outskirts of the city are surrounded by vineyards. Founded in 1541 by the Spanish conquistador Pedro de Valdivia, the city is the financial and political centre of the country and is home of the nation's executive and judiciary branches.

The Ramones would visit Chile on two occasions and unsurprisingly the chosen hub for both concerts was in Santiago. The first concert was on September 13th, 1992 at the *Velódromo Estadio Nacional*, officially known as the *Sergio Tormen Méndez Velodrome*. The venue is a cycling stadium located in the Parque de la Ciudadanía in the municipality of Ñuñoa with a capacity for 7,500 people. Interestingly, the stadium has a notorious past as it was once used as an imprisonment, torture and execution facility under the Pinochet dictatorship. The unusual setting must have left an impressive with tour manager Monte Melnick as he cited it in his book *On The Road With The Ramones* recalling how the band played in the stadiums with "huge oval tracks in the middle of an arena." [340] In addition to the velodrome, the venue has a handball court, and several artistic shows and concerts have been held in its premises. Indeed, there have been plenty of top artists performing at the venue over the years. Examples include *Bon Jovi, Depeche Mode, Duran Duran, Metallica* and Peter Gabriel. From the 27 tunes on offer that night, none were selected from "Mondo Bizarro" which had been released just a couple of weeks prior to the gig, clearly suggesting that the lads were not quite ready to unleash those songs live. Some of the interesting choices off the 1989 previous "Brain Drain album" were "I Believe In Miracles", "Pet Sematary" and the often discarded little gem "Ignorance Is Bliss" whilst fans were also naturally treated to older songs such as "I Wanna Be Well", "I Wanna Be Sedated" and "Cretin Hop". For those fans who like to dig a little deeper explore the documentary entitled simply *"The Ramones Live in Chile, 13th September, 1992"* which has been posted on *Youtube* which shows interviews, some live footage of the show, the sound check and build up to the concert. It is well worth watching.

This would only be a transient visit with just one performance before moving on to play four shows in Buenos Aires in Argentina. However, they would return to Chile one further time on May 16th, 1994 when they played at a more traditional venue, the *Teatro Caupolicán*. Looking at this particular itinerary, highlights, the hectic schedule the band faced - the Santiago gig was in fact sandwiched between concerts in the Argentinian capital on the 14th and 18th of that month, and perhaps suggests why at this time of their career many have proposed that gigs seemed more like a job than enjoyment.

The *Teatro Caupolicán* is a theatre and music venue located on the San Diego street in Santiago and was first opened in 1936. Currently it is an important concert venue for popular Chilean and international artists, with a seating capacity of 4,500 and a total capacity of 5,400 including standing places. During its long history, it has hosted sporting, political, and cultural events. These have included operas, symphony orchestras, ballet, the Moscow circus, Holiday on ice, boxing bouts and basketball matches. As well as The Ramones, the *Teatro Caupolicán* has hosted such notable artists as Louis Armstrong, Duke Ellington, *Bill Haley and His Comets, the Electric Light Orchestra* and *Green Day*. The Ramones would perform 32 songs that night and as customary on the "Acid Eaters" tour would play unsurprisingly a number of covers including "Substitute", "My Back Pages" and "7 And 7 Is" made famous by *The Who,* Bob Dylan and *Love* respectively. Again, pleasingly, audio coverage of virtually the whole concert exists on social media and a search of *"Ramones en Chile (Teatro Monumental, Santiago, 16/05/1994)"* will do the trick.

The Ramones' influence, of course, is not solely confined to the limits of capital cities and their legacy spreads to places far and wide. One such place is Concepción, which lies just over 300 miles away from Santiago and in the south of the country. With a population of around 220,000 inhabitants, Concepción, has been described as he 'Chilean capital of rock' since numerous bands have started their careers from this city. Examples include *Los Tres, Los Bunkers* and *Emociones Clandestinas* so it is maybe of no surprise that our next Ramones tribute originate from this location. Formed in 2017, the name of the band was inspired by one of their favourite albums, the record that comprised solely of cover tracks - "Acid Eaters". The original line-up consisted of bassist Gustavo "El Warez" Carrasco, guitarist Lorenzo Martínez, front man Felipe "El Flaco" Morales and drummer Raul Gallardo. All of the band members had met through playing in previous tribute bands along with their own original musical projects with bass player Gustavo explaining that the lads formed *Acid Eaters* because of "the respect and admiration we felt for The Ramones." Over the years there have been some alterations in the band's set-up with Gastón Troncoso, for instance, succeeding Lorenzo as guitarist in 2022. In addition, *Acid Eaters* have experienced variations on the skins with Sebastian "Chocokrispis" Duran taking over on the drummer's seat between 2018-22 and he likewise being replaced by Billy Solar or "Billy Palito" as he was known after nearly two years. In 2024, original stick, man Raul Gallardo, returned to the helm and re-joined the Concepción group. The lads adopted Arturo Vega's celebrated insignia with a few adaptions – their own names were predictably sited around the periphery, the name *Acid Eaters* was placed on the ribbon and the coat of arms of the city - the Black Eagle upon a golden field - was positioned centre stage.

The band soon started to play in the main venues of Concepción with Gustavo pleasingly pointing out that they performed Ramones music "both for young audiences and old fans alike." The group also reached out to other regions of the country particularly as part of a variety of public events, including concerts, in the context of the "Social Outbreak" that occurred in Chile. This began in the autumn of 2019, triggered by a multitude of political and socioeconomic factors which led to widespread protests in the country. [341]

Acid Eaters' set naturally varies depending on the length of time allocated for their show but the band will always play the *classics* off the earlier albums such as "Rockaway Beach", "Sheena Is A Punk Rocker", "I Wanna Be Sedated" and "Blitzkrieg Bop". Some of the interesting picks off the more contemporary records include "Spiderman", "Bonzo Goes To Bitburg" and the mid-tempo tracks of "Poison Heart", "Pet Semetary" and "I Believe In Miracles".

Unlike some of our other tributes, postings on social media of the group from Chile are few and far between. However, a search on *Youtube* under *"Acid Eaters, Concepción"* does come up with a fantastic version of "Surfin' Bird" – the tune which was originally performed by the surf rock band, *The Trashmen* in 1963 and popularised by The Ramones on their "Rocket To Russia" L.P in 1977. Here you will find the band not trying to be *copycats* and not wearing wigs, for instance, but still producing a typical trademark, Ramones high energy rendition of the cover. What is abundantly clear is that both the band and the crazed audience feed off each other with both parties thoroughly enjoying their time at the show.

Although none of the band saw The Ramones in action, in recent years, *Acid Eaters,* have had the pleasure of seeing the surviving members perform in their solo projects. Gustavo explains that "we were able to enjoy Marky, have a beer with C.J and listen to Richie sing. Fortunately for us, they have travelled to our country and have given us part of the experience of seeing The Ramones play." What is also clear is that the lads from Chile believe that their influence "is indisputable" and that bands "could not understand current music without the foundations that were created by bands like Ramones all those years ago."

Gustavo acknowledges that *Acid Eaters* are one of the world's most southernmost Ramones cover bands. [342] Indeed, he believes this highlights the work of so many musicians who are passionate about the group and also highlights their legacy, indicating that geographical distance has been no barrier in keeping The Ramones name alive. The bass man passionately points out that "it is beautiful to think how these special people managed to do something so big that it has grown from Queens to Concepción. With a powerful heart, their music has been beating for more than 50 years and we will make sure it stays that way." Indeed, this book has been filled with people like Gustavo who ensure that The Ramones are not forgotten and to coin a title from "Acid Eaters" maybe *this is the shape of things to come.*

The Ramines
France

After their inaugural visit to France in the spring of 1977, The Ramones would perform in total over 30 gigs in the country and visit 19 different centres within the nation. Just on the 1993 "Mondo Bizarro" tour, for example, they played in Paris, Dijon, Grenoble, Toulouse, Bordeaux and Cabourg. The latter is a popular seaside resort with locals and tourists and is located in the Calvados department, region of Normandy and it is within this part of northern France where our next tribute is based. Normandy is laden with history – under 70 miles away from Cabourg, for instance, lies the beautiful city of Rouen, the prefecture of Normandy and once the capital of the Duchy until William the Conqueror moved his residence to Caen. Rouen, which lies on the River Seine is probably best known for the place of execution of Joan of Arc who was burnt at the stake in the city in 1431 for heresy and support of a return to French rule from the English. In more recent times, Normandy was famed for the location of the Allied landing operations on the 6th June, 1944, often referred to as D-Day which was the precursor to the liberation of France. Indeed, the beaches code-named *Utah, Omaha, Gold, Juno* and *Sword* where the Battle of Normandy took place are less than an hour's drive from the city of Cabourg.

The Ramones performed in Cabourg on February 23rd, 1993 at the *Hipperdrome*, located just over a mile from the seafront, in a building adjacent to the famous racecourse. The *'fast four'* played 32 songs that day which included two encores. Thankfully, there is nearly 30 minutes of footage on *Youtube* which gives real insight into the action that evening although in all honesty the film quality is not the greatest. What is immediately apparent from the video is the fans reaction and the excitement is palpable as the rammed, fist punching, heaving mosh pit sways to those celebrated tunes. As well as the usual favourites such as "Rockaway Beach", "I Wanna Be Well", "Beat On The Brat" and "Sheena" there were some more unusual picks which naturally featured during that tour to plug the latest album - "Main Main", "Censorshit", "Tomorrow She Goes Away", "Take It As It Comes" and "Poison Heart" were all given an airing.

One person who saw them that evening at the *Hipperdrome* was Philippe Inemer. Heralding from Rouen in Normandy, bassist Philippe was founder member of the tribute, *The Ramines,* which also included, drummer Daniel Lebailly along with guitarist and vocalist Philippe Nicholas who was instrumental in making the phone calls to start the three-piece band in 2002. As with many of our groups, the lads decided to take stage names with Philippe Inemer converting into his nickname Teddy, Daniel transforming into K Tambourg and Philippe Nicholas adapting his sir name to become Nicky. The three boys had experience in other bands. Nicky had previously played as a punk drummer since 1978 for many years in various groups such as *Acid Vicieux* and *Skin Korps* before moving on to the guitar with *Sid et les Vicieux.* Teddy had performed with the *Dogs* and *Dominique Laboubé* whilst he and K Tambourg had played together with the *Chainsaw* and *Vermines.* The band's name was a clever combination of the word Ramones and their own group, *Vermines* (Ram+ines) and as with many of our covers, in time honoured tradition amusingly adapted the famous eagle logo to include a guitar and bass rather than the baseball bat and apple branch.

Their first *Ramines* gig was on January 7th, 2003 and very quickly the Ramines played at the various Rouen clubs and bars such as *Brooklyn Café, Bateau Ivre, Kalif* and *Parc des Expositions.* The group experienced a number of line-up changes over the years. In 2004, Damiens took over on the drummer's stool and he in turn, two years later, was replaced by Eric Pinson aka Ricky, a mods-style drummer who had previously played in the '80s with *the Tweed.* In March 2007, a further and more radical change in the formation took place when during a *Ramines* concert at *La Grande Rotonde*, Nicolas Piolé took the mic for the first time with the group converting to the more conventional four-piece. Mickey, as he likes to be called, was guitarist for a number of groups since the '80s and was also vocalist with the *Flying Cadillac.* The last change to the line-up was in 2014 when Antoine Leblond took over from founder member Nicky on the guitar and took up the moniker as Tony for *The Ramines.* The group continued to perform until 2020 when the musicians decided to hang up their leather jackets and call time on the project.

The Ramines cite a number of favourite gigs over the course of the years. In 2009 and 2010, for instance, they performed in Spain on two, one-week mini tours. They have also crossed the French border eastwards, playing in Berlin in Germany and Brussels in Belgium. Other notable concerts include when they opened for *The Buzzcocks, Demented Are Go, Sick Of It All* and performed along-side the all-female British tribute, the *Ramonas.* Teddy also describes their shows on the *esplanade of the Museum of Modern Art* in the city of Paris and when they played every evening of a week in the *Shari-Vari Bar* with a different opening band as particularly memorable. Similarly, their performance in a cinema previewing the screening of the 2002 film *"Hey! Is Dee Dee at home?"* which was a documentary feature by Lech Kowalski about the life and times of the legendary bassist. To their credit, *The Ramines* produced three DVDs – two incorporate the renditions of "It's Alive" and "Loco Live" albums in their entirety whilst the third is a live set of 33 Ramones songs.

Without fail, I encourage all Ramones aficionados to take a look for themselves at all our tribute bands covered in this piece of research. Satisfyingly, there are numerous glimpses of *The Ramines* in action and maybe a great starting point is an unusual one when the band can be seen performing on the French TV show *Canal Plus.* Here you will see snippets of "Commando" and "Listen To My Heart" as well as a full interpretation of "Rockaway Beach" where the programme host and audience are *jigging away* as the quartet blast out the classic. Adorn in leathers, jeans and wigs, you cannot argue with Teddy's *raison d'être* when he states that "we wanted to get as close as possible to what we understood about The Ramones, in terms of music, state of mind, clothing, energy. We tried to sound as much like them on stage as possible, a lot of people in the audience told us it worked well." Alternatively, if you wish to view a rather more personal piece of footage of the band, then a search on *Youtube* for the sound check of "Judy Is A Punk" from the same TV programme shows *les hommes* without the hairpieces but with the same energy and vigour. If you wish to examine some live material, then maybe "Blitzkrieg Bop" at the *Betizfest* in Cambrai in 2017 will be to your liking or if you have a touch longer then there is nearly nine minutes of the boys in warp speed mode taken from an extract of the "Loco Live" DVD. Before you have time to draw breath, the lads have cruised through "Rockaway Beach". "Pet Semetary". "Don't Bust My Chops" "Palisades Park" with Teddy transforming from Dee Dee to C.J at his very best. There are many other fine examples of the band on social media and well worth searching up.

Not only did Teddy have the pleasure to watch the Ramones live in his home province in Normandy but also witnessed them in Paris and Ris-Orangis in France and amazingly four times abroad in New York City, London, Glasgow and Hasselt in Belgium. He is undoubtedly well-versed when asked the question about the Ramones legacy and impact. "The Ramones influenced all rock music over the last 40 years in so many means" the bass player points out - "The way they used the drums on their music, playing only a few chords, not doing guitar solos, singing comic-style lyrics, to have set lists without breaks, to not talk between songs, the way they wear their clothes. In short, the Ramones were unique, copied but never equalled." I am certainly not going to argue with those sentiments – The Ramones were the best, the elite of their class or maybe as a Frenchman would say the crème de la crème.

Acid Eaters
Brazil

Right from their first album and the self-titled "Ramones", the *'fast four'* had not been averse to carry out a cover – Jim Lee's "Let's Dance", originally recorded by Chris Montez in 1962 was the first to be given the *Ramone* treatment which usually involved an increase in pace and of course that buzzsaw guitar sound. As the band searched for that much coveted and sought after breakthrough, the remakes often took a more pragmatic and commercial slant. For example, Phil Spector's production of "Baby I Love You", first recorded by the *Ronettes* in 1963, gave The Ramones their biggest hit, peaking in the UK charts at number eight after remaining in the hit parade for nine weeks in 1980. It maybe was no real surprise, therefore, that as the band neared the end of their career, there was a release of an album solely of cover tunes. "Acid Eaters" was the 13th studio L.P recorded by the group and released on December 1st, 1993 by Radioactive Records. The record was produced by Scott Hackwith at the *Baby Monster Studio* and *Chung King Studios* both in New York City and was a tribute to some of The Ramones' favourite artists of the 1960s.

One of the highlights of the album, was undoubtedly *Creedence Clearwater Revival's* "Have You Ever Seen The Rain?" which became a popular live pick with The Ramones from 1994 onwards and was transformed, using typical Ramones style and tempo. Indeed, if you have not heard the original tunes, then it is well worth comparing all the versions such as another high spot, "7 And 7 Is". Marky comes into his own with his intense, continuous drum rolling and they certainly do credit to the song which was first performed by the eclectic and hugely innovative '60s band *"Love"*. Interestingly, during this track, The Ramones leave out the blues outro from the original which gives it a more punk feel. There are two songs, both sung by C.J - "My Back Pages" and "Journey To the Centre Of Mind" which exemplified how The Ramones can stamp their authority on a cover – the former is arguably better than Bob Dylan's folk creation whilst the latter at least did justice to the mind-blowing song by the psychedelic rock band *the Amber Dukes.* The third track which saw C.J on lead vocals was "The Shape Of Things To Come" which was originally released in 1968 by *Max Frost and the Troopers* was in golfing parlance, *par for the course.* This song, along with Joey's renditions of "I Can't Control Myself" and "Somebody To Love," were in all honesty nothing to write home about compared to past glories but at least was up to *scratch.* Undeniably, although the remakes did not compare quite as well to the originals, performed respectively by *the Troggs* and the latter song by *the Great Society* or particularly the one popularised by *Jefferson Airplane,* they were at any rate, easy on the ear and to continue the golfing analogy *hit the green.* If those tracks *made par* then the rest of the album was played via the rough, bunkers and trees with *bogies* sadly picked up all over the place. Indeed, surely the wrong club was taken out of the bag for the 1963 smash hit, "Surf City" by the duo *Jan and Dean* – with even Johnny Ramone admitting that the cover "fell short because we didn't do it in the right key" and that "Joey never rehearsed it with us, so it didn't come out right." (343) Even worse were the *duffs* of "Out Of Time", "When I Was Young" and "Can't Seem To Make You Mine" which all *dribbled* along miserably – no catchy hooks, just *hooks and slices*. By the time you get to "Substitute", which featured none other than Pete Townsend on backing vocals, it was none other than a complete *shank*. The classic tune by the *Who* where you would expect The Ramones to *tap in* for a *birdie* and be right on their *A Game* sounds more like it has been delivered by inexperienced *hackers*.

C.J Ramone felt that the album "should've been an EP, which it originally was intended to be." The bass player goes on to elaborate stating that "Johnny seemed to think that it made better sense to price it like a full CD. And, you know, finances were always a part of everything. So rather than it being six or seven pretty good songs, it turned into a whole lot of filler. And I don't think it was necessarily the choice of songs; it's just that not every song translates well to The Ramones style...But the problem is that the time period that they were going for -- that late '60s acid-pop stuff -- that's an odd period to try to choose songs from for The Ramones. Some of them, like I said, really worked out well. But the slower, poppier ones just didn't come off. They didn't come off very well. When we sat down at the end of it to listen to the final mix, I was just like, "Oh my God, I can't believe this is gonna come out." I was actually dreading its release. And anybody I knew that was a Ramones fan, I told them beforehand, "Prepare to be disappointed." (344)

Johnny Ramone felt Acid Eaters was "hit and miss, but overall I think we did a good job." From a fan's point of view, it seemed more like the band had run out of ideas and without the inspirational Dee Dee writing new material, the group needed to rely on covers to bridge a gap. Although the style of some of the songs without doubt questionable, his comment about the timing of the record is surely spot on. "We never could have done this album early in our career, because the songs would have had to be adapted to a strict Ramones style, like 'California Sun', the guitarist reflected." He also added that "one of the problems was that as we undertook this, we were getting all kinds of suggestions from everybody, and it was getting to be a pain in the ass…It's always hard to pick covers, and after all those years it was still hard to tell." [345]

One group who used the title of *"Acid Eaters"* as the name of their own tribute band originate from Porto Alegre in Brazil. The city is located in the south of the country with a population of just under 1.5 million inhabitants and was visited by The Ramones twice in 1991 and 1994, performing both times at the *Gigantinho*. The complex is a sports arena, located in the riverside Beira-Rio complex of Sport Club Internacional and was opened in 1973. [346] As well as hosting such events as Davis Cup tennis, it also doubles up as a music venue and has witnessed a number of famed artists over the years. These have included *The Jackson Five, Genesis, New Order, Red Hot Chili Peppers, Deep Purple* and *Green Day.*

Indeed, one fan who was at the show in 1994 at the *Gigantinho* was vocalist Douglas Wyse. He would have been fortunate to have observed 29 songs that evening with the likes of "Animal Boy", "Glad To See You Go", "Today Your Love, Tomorrow The World" and "Sheena Is A Punk Rocker" all logged as being played. [347] Douglas, along with three *old school* punk rock friends in 2012, got together and decided to play one tribute concert in their home town to honour the American punk rockers with the rest of the band comprising of Davi Pacote on guitar, Igor Pires on the bass and stick man Rogério Kiko Ribeiro.

Guitarist Davi explains why the band got together stating that The Ramones "were the biggest influence for all of us and what made us get to know each other in the first place." The show went down so well that the lads decided to book more concerts and would end up continuing to play for five more years. All the musicians had had experience in previous bands prior to starting up *Acid Eaters* and these included *Rotentix, Os Torto, Julio Igrejas, Tequila Baby* and *Os Thompsons.*

Photograph courtesy of Abstratti Produtora

The group performed approximately 50 concerts in total in around 20 towns and cities of southern Brazil. Of course, it is always difficult to talk about favourite concerts but when pressed Davi recalls that "we played regularly at festivals in *Bar*

Opinião in Porto Alegre with about 1,000 in attendance and these were probably the most memorable ones." As expected for a band with the designation taken from The Ramones' penultimate studio L.P, *Acid Eaters'* set list was very much based from the American's last shows of 1995-1996 focussing on the *Lollapalooza* tour. This would see all the albums covered with the likes of "I Believe In Miracles", "Pet Semetary" and "Teenage Lobotomy" all performed as well as some of their favourite picks from that self-titled 33 such as "Have You Ever Seen The Rain?" and "Substitute". Indeed, the guitarist goes into detail stating how they wanted to get it as close to the originals as possible. "We did our concerts like a play", Davi states. "We acted like The Ramones on their last tour. Same set, speed of the songs, T-shirts, hair, instruments and the speeches between songs." A look on to *Youtube* immediately confirms this, where you can witness extensive coverage of either their debut gig at the *Bar Opinião* in September 2012 or one from April 2013 where they opened for Paul Di'Anno, the ex-heavy metal singer for *Iron Maiden*. One's instantaneous gut reaction is how closely the boys resemble the originals from New York City. Douglas Wyse, is an absolute dead ringer for Joey. Tall, slim and levitating over the stage like a bird of prey. Doug's mannerisms and motions are incredibly akin to the front man from Forest Hills - Sloping on to the stage as "The Good, The Bad And The Ugly" was being trumpeted out with his hair flicked periodically, signalling maybe a touch of nerves rather than just the need to keep those flocks out of his doe like eyes. His mic stand was flaunted around like a lance in time with the beat whilst he not only sings the old favourites but even imitates Joey's *ad libs* at remarkably the same *pre-prepared moments* as the original. To Douglas' left, we have another clone.

Igor not only looks like the young C.J but plays like him too. Hair long, spiralling as his head spins, his bass is low, legs bent and wide whilst he bounces and jigs appropriately just like the young Ramone from days gone by. He, of course, accompanies Douglas suitably with backing vocals, screams the "1, 2, 3, 4s" and when called upon delivers such masterpieces as "Wart Hog" with an expertise just like days of yore. To the songster's right is Davi. He too, could be thrust in a police identity parade as he doubles up for Johnny. Scowling just like the downstroking maestro and complete with basin haircut wig, spread-eagled legs, he brandishes his guitar as if holding a *Sten gun*. Both guitarists move forwards and backwards in tandem as if attached to a piece of string which Davi controls just like the past masters. Although you can only see glimpses of drummer Rogério, you can certainly hear his presence with a pounding drum beat, incessant crashes and rhythmic high hat technique on offer. It goes without saying, that the four boys are adorn in clothes reminiscent of The Ramones – leather jackets, blue jeans, sneakers and comparable T-shirts. It is also noticeable, that the band are playing in front of a crowded, passionate audience who clearly loved what was being served up.

Their last concert was on May 13th 2017, ironically at the same venue as their debut – at *Bar Opinião* in Porto Alegre with Davi citing that "the group disbanded because they set out everything which they wished to achieve." There is no doubt that if you like your tribute band to look like the originals, sound like the originals and act like the originals, *copycat* style, then tune into this group, they will deliver the goods. Indeed, my biggest compliment to *Acid Eaters*, the band, is that they made more of a positive impact on me than "Acid Eaters", the album.

Photograph courtesy of Abstratti Produtora

Tommy And The Rockets
Denmark

The last occasion that The Ramones performed on Danish turf was at the *Midtfyns* on the 25th June, 1994. *Midtfyns* is a famous rock Festival which first took place in 1976 and continued until 2003 when falling ticket sales led to its closure. Thankfully the event was relaunched in 2019 with the focus now mainly on local and upcoming artists. The festival is held in Ringe which is a small town located on Funen, the third largest island in Denmark. Over the years, a number of famed performers have played at *Midtfyns* including Suzi Quatro, Joe Cocker, *Marllion, Simply Red*, Jethro Tull, *The Kinks*, Chuck Berry and Lou Reed. In 1994, The Ramones played on the Saturday – the third day of four and over the course of the festival it also saw the likes of Johnny Cash, *Rage Against the Machine*, *Whitesnake* and *Spin Doctors* take to the stage.

The Ramones played 29 songs that day which was part of their "Acid Eaters" tour. There were some great song choices which included the covers "7 And 7 Is", "Journey To The Centre Of My Mind" and "My Back Pages" along with a handful of their more contemporary original tracks such as "I Wanna Live", "Poison Heart" and "Strength To Endure". To compliment these, there were naturally the proven, time-tested favourites with "Listen To My Heart", "Commando" and Cretin Hop" just three examples from 11 tunes which were performed from the first three albums. Pleasingly, there is audio coverage of the concert on

Youtube which naturally starts off with the requisite introduction of "The Good, The Bad And The Ugly" and finishes with "We're A Happy Family" played at supersonic speed. Ennio Morricone's "The Ecstasy of Gold" can also be heard as the tape filters out and for all Ramones fans, it is possibly somewhat of a hidden gem and well worth searching up.

One person who was in the crowd at *Midtfyns* was Thomas Stubgaard and in 2016, he decided to create his own unique tribute to honour his favourite band – a group which he loved "since the age of 10 and still the best band to this day." Jokingly Thomas goes on to add that "I was born on the exact same day The Ramones released their debut album. Divine intervention some would say!" When reminiscing about the concert back in 1994, Thomas points out that "The Ramones couldn't do anything wrong in my eyes at that time (I was 18 years old and didn't know any better), but looking back in hindsight it wasn't all that great really. Don't get me wrong, it was amazing to see them, but since the mid '80s they started playing way too fast live. I wish I could've seen them at their peak in the late '70s/early '80s. A fun fact about the concert is that they were a replacement band! They were on their way back home across the Atlantic after having played in Finland when they got the call to replace *Blind Melon* who had cancelled. At one point during the concert Joey said something along the lines of 'We're The Ramones. We're not *Blind Melon*, thank God.' I wasn't even supposed to be at the festival and I only found out the same day they played when I heard an announcement on the local radio. I paid to get in for the entire day, but I only saw The Ramones and left again. I managed to catch one of C.J's picks. I had to almost fight the guy beside me who was hell-bent on getting it."

Thomas or Tommy as he likes to be called was born in Odense in Denmark and had played in a number of bands. These included *The Family Jewels* and *The Play-Offs* as guitarist and vocalist and *The Hitchcocks* as drummer and backing vocalist. Between 2012 to 2013, Tommy also played for *The Lingertones*, this time as singer and bass man. As can be seen, the versatile musician had fulfilled a number of roles and this ability to be a multi-instrumentalist was the basis of his distinctive tribute to The Ramones. His idea was to create a solo studio project where all vocals and all instruments were handled by himself apart for the occasional guest-musician. Initially, his first inkling was to call the project *Tommy and The Torpedoes*, but torpedoes was soon modified to the word 'rockets' because, as the musician points out "rockets are way cooler, a rocket can fly to the moon and back for Pete's sake!" The name Tommy is naturally used because his real name is Thomas and also refers to founder member Tamás Erdélyi with the Dane pointing out that it is "my own little homage to Tommy Ramone."

After starting the project in 2016, *Tommy and The Rockets* released a Ramones tribute album in 2018 called "I Wanna Be Covered". Two songs from each of the first four Ramones albums were picked, along with "Rock 'n' Roll High" School from "End of the Century". The venture was a joint release by five different labels with Rocket Launch Records (Denmark), Woimasointu (Finland), Monster Zero Records (Austria), KOTJ (Spain) Rocktopus Tea Party Records (Spain) all getting involved.

Tommy explains his choice of songs declaring that those first five albums "are the true classics" adding that there isn't a bad song on any of them. They're all perfect in their own way." Tommy, in my opinion, was wise to stay away from some of the more obvious picks such as "Pinhead", "Blitzkrieg Bop" and "I Wanna Be Sedated" and instead concentrated on some of the lesser known tunes. There are a number of links to check out Tommy's work including *Facebook, Bandcamp* and *Youtube* and I advise all fans to go and examine for yourselves. There's a real essence of the *Beach Boys* and if you like Ramones played in a melodic format and given a power-punk, rock 'n' roll feel, this will certainly be for you. Have a listen to tracks such as "Oh Oh I Love Her So", "Havana Affair" and my personal favourite of "I Can't Give You Anything" where Tommy even takes on a slight American twang which adds a cheery, finishing touch to the covers. The musician has not ruled out one day getting a band together and playing live gigs although maybe the next logical step for Tommy is to cover *his very own Rocket To Russia!*

Ramones Revival
The Czech Republic

In October, 1994, The Ramones performed for their one and only time within the Czech Republic. The country is located in Central Europe and is bordered by Austria to the south, Germany to the west, Poland to the north east and Slovakia to the south east. During the last 100 years or so, the nation has undergone many political changes. In 1918, for instance, when the country gained its independence after the First World War and the fall of the Austro-Hungarian Empire, the new name of Czechoslovakia was coined to reflect the union of the Czech and Slovak nations. After the Munich agreement of 1938, Hitler's Germany systematically took control of the Czech lands but following the fall of the Nazi regime, post-war Czechoslovakia became an Eastern Bloc communist state in 1948. In 1989, the *Velvet Revolution* ended Communist rule in the country and restored democracy. By the 31st December, 1992, the country of Czechoslovakia was peacefully dissolved with the country split into the constituent states of the Czech Republic and Slovakia and both becoming sovereign powers in their own right. In 1999 and 2004, the Czech Republic joined NATO and the European Union respectively with many politicians in the country hoping to adopt the single European currency in the near future. The capital and largest city of the nation is Prague which is located in the region of Bohemia and is the home to just over 1.3 million people. The city is traditionally one of the cultural and liveliest centres of central Europe which include a variety of music festivals. It was maybe expected, therefore, that it was chosen as a centre to host American's top punk rock icons, The Ramones.

After performing in Linz in Austria, the next day the band moved northwards to the Czech capital. The gig is Prague was held on October 13th at the *Lucerna Music Bar.* It is housed within the *Lucerna Palace,* an entertainment and shopping complex, in the new town quarter of the city. There have been a variety of musical talents which has graced the stage at the venue. Just a few of the examples include Louis Armstrong, *The Beach Boys,* Tina Turner, *Siouxsie And The Banshees* and Bob Dylan. This was part of the "Acid Eaters" tour and therefore a full range of tunes covering three decades of albums would have been on offer. From the '70s we would have seen the firm favourites of the likes of "Pinhead", "Listen To My Heart" and "Teenage Lobotomy", from the '80s "I Wanna Live", "Wart Hog" and "Somebody Put Something In My Drink" whilst from the '90s "My Back Pages", "The Shape Of Things To Come" and "Poison Heart" would have all got an outing. One fan who was at that show that evening, went into detail about what he saw that night and was quite brutal with some of his assessment. Although his comments are drawn from a social media platform, I do think that it is worth sharing particularly his remark about the band appearing as if it had become merely an occupation rather than exhibiting an enthusiasm or desire for performing. "Personally", he declares, "I was most pleased by 'Beat On The Brat' and then the ball lightning 'Psycho Therapy' from the record 'Subterranean Jungle' from 1983, played with a modern swing. I was curious if Johnny would at least for a moment forget about his "kilo" repertoire and play some solo. But mushrooms, mushrooms goldfish! The wall of sound remained intact. Joey was as I expected him to be. Purely static (sometimes some mic-stand gesture) with hair in his face because not many people are that ugly. He got a lot of relief when singing, where he replaced whole words with his 'yeahs' and 'oh yees'. I think he should use more of the vocal capabilities of bassist C.J Ramone, who pleasantly surprised me in 'Strength To Endure', for example. It's maybe a little shocking, but I liked him the most out of the band. He seems to be the only one who still enjoys it. For others, it's a job," he announces. [348] Whether one agrees with his comments or not, one thing for certain, is that the band had an exhausting rota. To get an idea about The Ramones hectic schedule, for instance, it is worth noting that after the visit to Prague they headed over 500 miles northwards again, this time to play in Arendonk in Belgium two days later on October 15th.

Our next tribute originates from Prague, the same city where the '*fast four*' played their one-off gig in the Czech Republic. The band was formed in 2009 and initially consisted of Jan "Stinky" Truhlář on vocals, guitarist Tomas "Warwin" Wawra, drummer Pavel "Sliva" Kopal and Pavel Skrleta on the bass. It was Jan's idea to call the band *Ramones Revival* and in fact he had thought about a name for a potential tribute way back in 2006, three years before their actual formation. Jan recalls that when he decided to take the plunge and start the band, he made "some telephone calls to the music world and within one hour *Ramones Revival* was born!" The front man started the group purely because of his love of The Ramones with Jan pointing out that "everybody knows that bands were influenced by Ramones - *Green Day, U2, Rammstein* etc but few people in our country knew The Ramones. I wanted to convey the most authentic experience possible, so that we and the audience can feel what it might have been like in the seventies. Because it's fucking amazing!" Over the years, the band's line up has remained pretty constant with only changes on the bass - Jan Melmer or Melmak as he liked to be called played in the band in 2010 and he in turn was replaced by Petr "Cecil" Sandera after five years in 2015.

Each of the band members play in their own groups which means that there is less time to practice and perform gigs for *Ramones Revival* than the artists would like. Nonetheless, the musicians manage to devote at least one or two sessions per month to the tribute. The band perform in the local bars and clubs around Prague and although Jan points out that "every gig was memorable" when pressed about his favourite gigs Jan cited either the 2018 outdoor festival known as *K2 Sokolák České Budějovice* where they performed to a thousand strong audience or one in 2016 to around 400 people. Here the singer laughs when he pronounces that "the atmosphere changed from a stupid disco to a wild, fun event where the crowd almost brought the club down!"

The band have three different set lists depending on the requirements of the venue – a short, medium and long repertoire although occasionally perform songs from the first to the last tracks on certain albums. Pleasingly, the singer believes that the group "are starting to get close to The Ramones' original sound" although he does not personally attempt to sound like Joey. "We try not to add anything of our own to the songs", Jan expresses. "Only the maximum possible energy!!! A concert is like an hour-long sprint digging with a pickaxe", he amusingly utters. The group wear wigs and leather jackets with the vocalist explaining that "we want to be in the gig like The Ramones – we are like actors in a punk circus – a theatre at full throttle!" Jan also talks about the complications in performing in his tribute stating that "unfortunately, it is difficult to find comparable equipment in the Czech Republic and it is very expensive for us."

There is satisfyingly video footage of the České Budějovice outdoor concert with five back to back tunes on offer. The first refrain, "R.A.M.O.N.E.S", shows bassist Cecil on lead vocals à la C.J for Lemmy Kilmister's unique reverence to the boys from Queens whilst subsequent songs switch to front man, Jan. What is clear is that all of the songs, "Blitzkrieg Bop", "Let's Dance" and "Today Your Love Tomorrow The World" are well acknowledged by a packed audience and indeed in one refrain, the mid-paced "Poison Heart", we see the band joined by an animated female member of the audience who shows her appreciation by dancing on the stage. Another great clip is from their first gig – check out *Ramones revajvi* and "Chainsaw" where the wigged quartet are as raw as red meat as they storm though that authoritative track in front of that famous Ramones logo. Alternatively, look into their first-rate promotional 2022 video which include a number of snippets from various songs such "Beat On The Brat", "Cretin Hop", "Sheena Is A Punk Rocker" and "I Wanna Be Your Boyfriend" – you will certainly be content.

When asked about The Ramones' impact, Jan feels that "their influence was undeniable effecting the United States, South America, Europe, Japan – the whole world. Not bad for a bunch of losers from New York! The front man goes on to add that "in the Czech Republic, we have a saying: There is strength in simplicity! The Ramones had it all whether it be strength, speed, opinion, the look, the style, the sound, inspiration, the choreography." The singer speaks with passion when he adds that "I hope The Ramones' legacy stays in everyone's hearts for as long as possible, so that the old fans can remember their youth and the young can see how music should be made. We are just intermediaries between the genius of The Ramones and the ears, eyes and hearts of the audience!" Finally, Jan reflects "that I have a dream that one evening there will be a big show with Japanese, British, French and all our tribute bands from across the globe coming together to celebrate." What an idea that is and what a way to start a proper *Ramones revival*!

Stalin
Uruguay

After performing five times in Brazil in the November of 1994, the band played in Uruguay on the 14th of that same month. As well as Brazil, the country shares borders with Argentina and has a coastline on the Atlantic Ocean to the south east. Uruguay was colonised by Europeans relatively late compared to its South American neighbours with the Spanish founding Montevideo as a military stronghold in the early 18th century. Independence was declared in 1825 and recognised in 1828, following a four-way struggle between Spain, Portugal and later Argentina and Brazil. In the twentieth century, an armed group of Marxist-Leninist urban guerrillas emerged in the 1960s, engaging in activities such as bank robberies, kidnapping and assassination, along with attempting to overthrow the government. This culminated in a *coup d'etat* and a period of repressive military rule between 1973-75 when the armed forces were asked to disband parliament. The population of the country is around 3.4 million with incredibly a third of the nation, 1.3 million living in the capital, Montevideo. It was naturally in this city where The Ramones played their one and only gig within Uruguayan territory.

The chosen venue that day was an indoor sporting arena. The *Palacio Peñarol Contador Gastón Guelfi*, commonly known as *Palacio Peñarol*, was originally opened in 1955 and is primarily used as a basketball venue. With an impressive seated capacity of 4,700 for matches, it has hosted the 2017 FIBA AmeriCup, the Championship that takes place every four years between national teams of the western hemisphere continents. The arena has been renovated between 2010-11 and since the closure of the *Cilindro Municipal* in 2010, it is the main indoor establishment of the country. A couple of the more interesting bands who had played at the venue include *Los Shakers*, a local rock band from the 1960s, who were heavily influenced by *The Beatles* and *Gene Loves Jezebel* who London Ramones fans will be familiar with having supported the New Yorkers on four consecutive nights at the *Lyceum ballroom* in February, 1985.

As part of the *Acid Chaos* tour, The Ramones would play 32 tunes that evening including two encores. Pleasingly, apart from "Durango 95" which was for some reason missed, there is a full audio coverage on *Youtube* of events that evening which I urge you to explore. Part of the set was devoted to the covers from the "Acid Eaters" album, with "My Back Pages", "The Shape Of Things To Come", "7 And 7 Is" and "Have You Ever Seen The Rain?" all delivered at the usual high tempo ferocity. Some of the other renditions that evening included "I Wanna Live", "I Believe in Miracles" and the hardcore "Wart Hog" with the latter roared out by C.J Ramone. Indeed, by this time, the band was giving the bassist more and more responsibility as a vocalist with no less than five allocated to him at the *Palacio Peñarol*. For aficionados, the gig is available as a C.D, "Live in Montevideo" as it was broadcasted on the Uruguayan radio station, *El Dorado*. Interestingly, after this concert, the band crossed the River Plate into bordering Argentina and played a further three gigs, their last concerts of 1994.

One group of lads who not only saw The Ramones play their one and only show in Uruguay but also quite literally had the best seats in the house were *Trotsky Vengarán,* a punk rock band heralding from Montevideo. To be more precise, they had the pleasure of supporting the '*fast four*' and were remarkably the opening act that night in November. The band were formed in 1991 and cite The Ramones as a major influence. In 1994, they released their first album, called "Salud, Dinero y Dinero" which translates to "Health, Money and Money" and since then they have released further records with an impressive discography as long as your arm. Hugo Diaz, the guitarist of *Trotsky Vengarán*, sets the scene regarding the evening when they opened for the New Yorkers. "It was absolutely forbidden for the supporting band to talk to The Ramones backstage", he remembers. "We were even told to go inside our dressing room and shut the door when they arrived at the venue. I don't think this order came directly from The Ramones, but from the production team, which was Argentinian. Argentinians are very particular and at that time we were an absolutely unknown for them, so it was easy for them to look down on us. Anyway, we never shut the door of our dressing room. Seeing them in the flesh was way too tempting. I remember them walking by us and saying "Hi" out of pure manners, and we just couldn't believe our eyes. They didn't seem very happy, the only one who didn't stay in their dressing room was C.J, and we managed to talk briefly to him. Afterwards we learned that they weren't on the best of terms, at least Johnny and Joey, and everything kind of clicked. We watched the show from the sound desk. It was amazing."

Hugo Diaz, also explains how this morphed into a Ramones spin off which included fellow *Trotsky* band mates, bassist Héctor Souto and drummer, Guillermo Perazzo. "We formed out of boredom", he says. "*Trotsky,* started to get a lot of attention in our country and around 2003, our singer had to move to Chile, but we managed to keep on working. The three of us rehearsed in Montevideo and once a month our singer would come to Uruguay and *Trotsky* would play three or four nights in a row. Meanwhile, we had to rehearse without our singer, and just for fun we started playing Ramones songs, as we all loved the band." Amusingly, they called the name of this new band *Stalin,* "as a joke, because *Stalin* was the one who ordered Leon Trotsky's murder", Hugo laughs, going on to add that the tribute "was our side project for 12 years between 2004 to 2016, and we would play small venues whilst our main band would gradually get more and more famous."

Stalin would mainly play songs from the three Ramones albums, but liked to rehearse different ones for every gig, even performing some of the songs from "Acid Eaters". Fascinatingly, just like many of our other tribute and cover acts, the group enjoyed the slightly slower speed of "It's Alive" than the much faster pace of The Ramones 1990s shows. The group even made an adaption of the famous Ramones logo which was based on the seal of the United States presidency but instead of the eagle the boys used the silhouette of *Trotsky's* logo - a cartoonish devil.

The group never attempted to look anything like the actual Ramones. "But", as Hugo points out "our stage persona is moulded after them. The way we stand, the height of our guitars, wearing jeans, T-shirts and leathers jackets. We dressed as we dress on stage with *Trotsky.* We liked to think of ourselves as competent punk rock musicians playing a bunch of songs we absolutely adore." When asked about his favourite *Stalin* show, Hugo fondly recalls one in particular. "We did our one and only live record in a basement at the club *Decibelios* in Montevideo packed with 150 drunks who would jump and stage dive on top of each other permanently", the guitarist recites. "The stage was small, is was pretty hot and we played as loud as fuck and all the songs came out pretty good. That was a great night." Indeed, a search on to the social media platform *Youtube* under the designation of *'Don't Talk To Commies'* reveals 24 numbers recorded by *Stalin* with a score of these Ramones classics. Take a listen to, for example, to "Chainsaw" which has those trademark fuzz tone guitars, characteristic blistering pace and the unusual but somehow pleasing *inaugural* correct pronunciation of the word *massacre* by singer Hugo! If you enjoy a more melodic Ramones tune, then you will undoubtedly love "Do You Wanna Dance?" which has a real rock 'n' roll flavour with drummer Guillermo taking over the singing duties. Perhaps my favourite, however, is their take on "Judy Is A Punk" – complete with the *oohs* and the *arghhs* and complimentary backing vocals, close your eyes and just for a minute one could be back in time at *CBGBs* – it's that good. There are even four non-Ramones songs thrown in - Johnny Thunders' "Born To Lose", Billy Idol's "Dancing With Myself", *The Clash's* "Clampdown" and the superb take on the *Sex Pistols'* "God Save The Queen". The audio is high quality and if it wasn't for the "1, 2, 3, 4s" and the occasional shout from the audience, you could quite easily think it was recorded in a studio.

By 2010, there were some changes in the line-up with Stalin enlarging to become a quartet - Juan Pablo Granito taking over the bass duties and Charly Rivero being added on guitar. There is no doubt that Trotsky and indeed Stalin are talented punk musicians. It is also refreshing that these boys are die-hard Ramones fans too. As well as the Montevideo gig, for instance, Hugo had no hesitation in journeying across the borders to neighbouring countries to watch the New Yorkers. One such gig, saw him travel to Buenos Aires in Argentina in 1994 to see the double delight of The Ramones and Motörhead. All in all, the guitarist states that "we tried to catch them every time they came to South America in '95 and '96 until they quit. I myself must have seen them live maybe four or five times." Two of the lads' experience, however, goes way beyond watching the group, covering their tunes and performing as a support slot. In 2006 and 2008, when Marky Ramone started touring by himself, Hugo and Héctor had the pleasure to play alongside the legendary drummer in his band for two shows in Montevideo. Hugo explains how they got the gig stating "that they had not only opened for The Ramones in '94 but also for *Marky & The Intruders* in '98. Both guitarists knew the tour manager who had worked with Marky so when the opportunity came, Hector and I were the best choice. They knew us, they knew we could play and also not be too star struck by Marky. We were also willing to do it just for the experience and form a good band for free. My favourite story was when I met Marky that first time. We had been given the set list of the tour in advance, so that we could rehearse the songs by ourselves, but anyway we were pretty nervous. When Marky came down for breakfast we introduced ourselves, and then he took us to our room and him, us and Sebastian, his singer, rehearsed all the songs. Our guitars were unplugged of course, and he drummed on a chair, wearing nothing but black sweatpants and in a very good mood. I remember thinking that I'd never thought you could pull out so many different sounds from just a chair, but he could. The second time we played with him it was in a Festival that also had *Trotsky* in the line-up. So we played with

Marky and then came a Colombian band and then us, so we were kind of headlining. It's amazing if you think about it, but in Uruguay we are more popular than our idols. People listen to *Trotsky* because it's part of a Uruguayan rock scene, not a punk rock scene, so maybe only 30-35% of our fans actually listen to The Ramones. That show was great, and after the last song backstage Marky hugged me. I was pretty surprised, and I was told 'he must have liked the way you played. I've never seen him hug anybody like that!'. Maybe he was sugar coating it, but I like to believe it!!" The guitarist has no hesitation when describing The Ramones' influence. "Without them there would be no modern rock at all" he articulates. "Every guy who ever grabbed a guitar from the '80s, without that much skill or prior knowledge would have not done so if it wasn't for The Ramones. We absolutely adore them."

Photograph courtesy of VivianaCondeVitureira

After playing around 35 to 40 gigs in total, in 2016, *Stalin* stopped performing with Hugo explaining that "it had always been a side project for us, something we did for fun. We started playing less and less, until we did only two or three gigs a year and eventually put it on standby. We may return in the future - no one knows." Indeed, maybe, we shall see a follow up live recording one day, which based on *the fifth rule*, will need to be called *'The Laws Of Uruguay!'*

The Cretins
Sweden

For any musician in a cover band, there cannot be too many better accolades than to gain acceptance or recognition from the original group. After all, in the vast majority of cases, these artists have performed their favourite songs for love not money, living out a dream and paying homage to their beloved heroes. Our next featured band, *The Cretins,* a Swedish tribute, had that honour bestowed upon them when they were acknowledged at the *Festivalområdet* in Skellefteå, on June 24th in 1995, the last ever performance by The Ramones on Swedish soil.

Skellefteå, is a city in the Västerbotten County of northern Sweden and is a venue for annual outdoor music festivals. These festivals are still going strong and according to their own website, the 2024 organisers expect between 90,000 to 100,000 visitors over the four-day event. [349] During the 1995 festival, as well as The Ramones, other groups to play that year were *Sator, Kent, Clawfinger, The Wannadies* and *Suede* whilst maybe the most well-known performer who has played at the show is Iggy Pop who took to the stage three years later in 1998. Interestingly, the band *Sator* tell the story where they bumped into The Ramones at the airport, initially were 'star struck' but eventually managed to get their autographs on the poster which can be seen on this page. Coming on just before midnight, The Ramones performed there as part of the "¡Adios Amigos!" tour with just a few tracks selected from that latest cut – "Cretin Family", "The Crusher" and "I Don't Wanna

Grow Up" along with "Spiderman" which would be included on the US version initial releases and various other subsequent albums. From the 32 songs on offer that night, old timers would have loved the fact that six tunes were selected from the 1976 debut L.P – "Beat On The Brat", "Today Your Love, Tomorrow The World", "53rd and 3rd", "Havana Affair", "I Don't Wanna Walk Around With You" and of course the punk anthem "Blitzkrieg Bop". It was just prior to the rendition of this song where Joey, as spokesperson for the New Yorkers, dedicated the song to *The Cretins* – surely the ultimate compliment for a tribute band.

The group were formed way back in 1985 and are still performing to this day. To put into context, their formation was at a time when Richie was still on drums and just a year after the release of The Ramones' eighth studio album, "Too Tough To Die". Just like *The Melones* from Germany, this means that the band have been in existence even longer than the New Yorkers were together and gives the band the honour of being the longest surviving Ramones tribute in this research. The origins of the band stem from Umeå, a city in the north east region of the country with a population of just over 130,000 making it the 13th largest in the nation. It is a university town and centre of education, technical and medical research and cited as one of Europe's fast growing cities. [350] The group was formed by guitarist Kenneth Bergdahl with the original line-up also including drummer André Lundström, Lars Oskarsson on the bass and Henrik Kjellberg as lead vocalist. As is often customary, the four lads took up the collective title of Ramone as a sign of uniformity with the adopted names of Kenny, Andy, Larry and Henry being taken up accordingly. It was Kenny who chose the group's moniker, *The Cretins,* stating that "I have been listening to The Ramones since 1978 and I wanted a Ramones related band name." The guitarist opted for one of those classic tracks off "Rocket To Russia", using the song 'Cretin Hop" as his inspiration.

Not only have *The Cretins* headlined their own festivals but they have also been the support act for punk bands such as *Dia Psalma* and the famous Swedish metal band *Meshuggah.* Indeed, although there have been so many favourite moments, when pushed Kenny cites a gig at Scharinska Villan in 1994 as possibly his favourite with "the audience going crazy and some stage diving taking place." Over the years they have adapted their set list with initially most songs from The Ramones' first three albums. Nowadays, however, they have added material from more contemporary albums, a few self-penned tunes and some cover songs from '60s bands as well. In 1994, the band released their eight-track CD entitled "Disturbed" which featured Ramones favourites – "Rockaway Beach", "I Wanna Be

Your Boyfriend", "Pet Semetary" and "Psycho Therapy" along with some non-Ramones tracks such as "Sweet Pea", "Sheila" and "I Don't Wanna Be Disturbed". In order to keep the band going, Kenny has had to recruit new members. One major change, for instance, occurred in the late '90s when the group was re-organised into a three-piece with Larry also taking over the singing responsibilities as well as playing on the bass. The present line-up includes Kenny, Larry and new drummer Jimmy Ågren who naturally took up the moniker of Jimmy Ramone.

Kenny looks back at some great Ramones memories and they are so rich that I will finish this narrative by relaying his own story in its entirety:

"I have personally seen The Ramones six times and the most memorable gigs are the first when I saw them in Roskilde, Denmark in 1985 and the last one in Skellefteå, Sweden in 1995. Both times I met all the band members and therefore those gigs are very special to me. Before the Skellefteå gig. I met them and talked for an hour. I gave them *The Cretins'* album, "Disturbed" and that's why they dedicated "Blitzkrieg bop". When *Marky Ramone and The Speed Kings* had a gig in Stockholm we picked them up at the airport and drove them to the hotel. Marky and me sat down in the lobby. We had a great and relaxed conversation and he signed a couple of records he played on before and after The Ramones (*Dust, Estus, Voidoids, Intruders, The Speed kings*). Later when we came to the venue, Marky rigged his own drums, I asked Nick Cooper from *The Speed Kings* if I could play a Ramones song with them. He gave me his guitar and we sat down and he wanted me to play some Ramones songs, and I did. Then he went to ask Marky if it was okay for me to play a song at the gig. Nick told him that I could play the songs really well so Marky said it was okay. When it was time for the encore Nick said: 'now we proudly present the mighty Kenny from *The Cretins*' and he gave me his guitar and we played the tune "Blitzkrieg Bop". It was such an unbelievably great feeling that I stood there and performed with Marky, I couldn't believe it! A few months later I received an e-mail from Nick who asked if I could drive their van on a short European tour. Sadly, I could not do that because of my work commitments. Later on *Marky and The Speed Kings* recorded a live single called "Rawk Over Scandinavia". I was asked to translate the song, "I Wanna Be Sedated" with Swedish lyrics. I did it and I was very honoured for that. It feels great to read on the record label that the music Ramones/lyrics have been credited to my name: Kenneth Bergdahl. Ramones has meant everything to me for my whole life. After all these years, it was a great honour personally as a huge fan since 1978 to hear Joey dedicate the song "Blitzkrieg Bop" to my band *The Cretins*, to have played live with Marky, written Swedish lyrics to one of the greatest Ramones songs, 'I Wanna Be Sedated'. Now I can die happy!"

Amigosunited
Poland

"¡Adios Amigos!" was the 14th and final studio album fashioned by The Ramones. It was released on July 18th, 1995 through Radioactive Records and recorded at Baby Monster Studios in New York City. It was produced by long-term friend Daniel Ray who had already collaborated on two previous albums "Half Way To Sanity" and "Brain Drain" as well as having co-written the songs "Daytime Dilemma (Dangers Of Love)" and "Pet Sematary" with Joey and Dee Dee respectively. Relations during this period within the band continued to be strained. Not just because of the long-term ongoing feud between Johnny and Joey but also because of the singer's deteriorating health having been diagnosed with Non-Hodgkin lymphoma.

The front cover of the album depicts two dinosaurs in sombreros with the prehistoric monsters related to the band members' age. Johnny Ramone by this time was "always trying to protect that we were getting older by using pictures that were darker or distorted. I was worried about the band looking old." Marky Ramone hated that cover simply saying "great album, terrible cover" [351] and to be fair it's hard to argue against the drummer's sentiments. For the back cover, the guitarist was very adamant about not having a photograph with the band facing the camera again due to their appearance describing the situation at the time as "some of us looked worse than others." The chosen image is iconic though, with the group facing a wall, hands tied with a firing squad ready to execute the New Yorkers although Johnny could not get permission to have the name of the record company on the backs of the executioners. [352] Photographer, George DuBose was given the task of making the scene as authentic as possible and reminisces that "I had to rent Springfield rifles and military sabres. I built a stucco wall. I put bullet holes in the wall, sand on the floor." [353] Fittingly, Monte Melnick gets in on the act and is also in the shoot dressed as a shirtless, sleeping Mexican just like some of those old western movies.

Despite leaving the band back in 1989, six of the L.Ps compositions were written by Dee Dee Ramone. Indeed, even on "Mondo Bizarro", the first album which featured C.J, the original bassist had already sold the publishing rights to "Poison Heart", "Main Man" and "Strength To endure" for a few thousand dollars so he could hire a lawyer to get out of jail for possession of pot. [354] It was refreshing and certainly becoming, to hear Dee Dee on the final album itself as he was allowed to sing the bridge section of the closing track "Born To Die In Berlin" in German with his voice uniquely recorded via a telephone link to the studio. [355] For many people, myself included, "¡Adios Amigos!" was a step up from the recent L.P releases although maybe surprisingly C.J was not overly impressed stating "I did not think it was a good record at all" [356] and maybe even more startling when you consider that the bass man was given four songs on lead vocals - "Makin Monsters For My Friends", "The Crusher", "Scattergun" and "Cretin Family". Other great picks included one of the few tunes written by Marky – the abrasive and ironic "Have A Nice Day" and C.J's "Got A Lot To Say" which highlights the band at its minimalistic best. The chosen single was a cover of Tom Waits "I Don't Wanna Grow Up", which peaked at number 30 on Billboard's Modern Rock Tracks. Maybe one of the most poignant songs of their career was saved to the last album - "Life's A Gas". Whether it was because of the realisation about Joey's health problems or maybe because of the awareness that the band was about to pack up but this moving song will surely bring a tear to even the most hardened punk. Although the track "R.A.M.O.N.E.S" was not on the original album and came out as a bonus on later editions, the tribute to our '*fast four*' originally recorded by the English heavy metal supremos *Motörhead,* is simply one of their finest. Overall, the album was a generally well received by both fans and critics alike and a decent swansong to bow out to.

One band who used this album as a moniker for their own designation is *"AmigosUnited".* The group originate from Bytom in Upper Silesia in Poland making them the first band in our review to herald from a country where The Ramones never visited. Nowadays, Poland is a unitary parliamentary democracy with a president and head of state and is currently a member of the European Union. In the '70s and '80s however, the country was very much aligned within the Warsaw Pact after the Soviet annexation of the country at the end of the Second World War. From 1989 through to 1991, Poland engaged in a democratic transition which would put an end to the communist ruling state and eventually saw the Polish people having free parliamentary elections.

Although The Ramones performed in Communist Yugoslavia, this nation had always distanced itself from the Soviet Union. Similarly, the lads from New York did play in the Czech Republic though this was in the autumn of 1994, nearly five years after the *Velvet Revolution* and the non-violent transition of power towards a liberal democracy. The Ramones, therefore never played behind the "Iron Curtain", a term coined by Sir Winston Churchill defining a notional barrier between the Soviet bloc and the western world. In his autobiography, Johnny Ramone, an unwavering Republican supporter and belligerent anti-socialist, talked about why the group never ventured into Eastern Europe. "We had offers, but I refused", he boldly stated. "I don't know if they could have made me an offer big enough to go. I just expected the place to be so horrible and disgusting and I felt I bad-mouthed Russia so much in the past, I was afraid they might know about that and do something. So I was a little worried about going there, and I just felt like it wasn't worth it. There were enough places for me to go and play." [357]

The fact that Ramones tributes have blossomed in places such as Poland is hugely significant as it highlights the fact that their legacy reaches far beyond the places they toured. *AmigosUnited* started rehearsing in January 2015 and was the *brainchild* of rhythm guitarist Winston Wolfe and bass player Tomek who wanted to start a group because The Ramones were one of their favourite bands. The line-up has seen many comings and goings with constant changes. Indeed, so far the band have played with 11 drummers, five guitarists, three male and six female vocalists. Some attended one rehearsal whilst some have stayed for longer. The current and more stable formation is unusually a five-piece which includes bassist Tomek, Janek on the drums, Winston on guitar and two singers, Kojot and Rudolf.

After many months of practising, *AmigosUnuted* were finally ready for their first gig which they played in July of 2016 opening with their favourite "Blitzkrieg Bop". Their collection of songs has expanded to around 30 tunes spanning right across The Ramones' history. Some of the less common picks include "Let's

Go", "Main Man", "Life's A Gas" and even a version of "Happy Birthday" which The Ramones presented on the TV show "*The Simpsons*". However, if you like those traditional live choices from the typical latter day sets, then you will not be disgruntled with the likes of "Wart Hog", "I Wanna Be Sedated", "Commando" and "Somebody Put Something In My Drink" all on offer. *AmigosUnited* have since played extensively but according to the band members a couple of performances really stand out. For example, in December 2016, they performed in a prison in front of an audience of some of Poland's most dangerous incarcerated prisoners with the inmates joining in unreservedly with the yells of "hey ho, let's go". In 2019, they also played a gig in the historic coalmine of *Zabytkowa Kopalnia* - maybe not a "Pet Semetary" as such but certainly 320 metres underground!

A look online reveals that the band are one of the most fascinating of all our tributes as you never know exactly what is in store - not merely due to the many line-up changes over the years and slight alterations in the arrangements of the tunes but also because of the variations in vocalists, both male and female. For instance, check out "I Believe In Miracles" and "Poison Heart" which are both rocky studio recordings with different vocalists. Ex-front man, Werner takes responsibility for the first track whilst guest songster Manu sings the latter tune. I was intrigued how the band would integrate the combination of a male and female singer at live gigs and in essence, *AmigosUnited* carry this out in a variety of ways, always *mixing it up*. On one occasion, back in 2017 in Trzciel, "I Wanna Be Sedated" is covered at the *Ramona Fest* purely with male vocals whilst at Warsaw and Zabrze in 2019, the set is performed with three guitarists and solely a female vocalist. Here you will find "Blitzkrieg Bop", "R.A.M.O.N.E.S" and naturally a completely different feel for "I Believe In My Miracles". I love their take on "Sheena Is A Punk Rocker" from June 2019 – starting with a slow almost *disco* first verse of the classic, ex-singer Anna suddenly blasts off into orbit at warp speed singing from the floor as opposed to the stage, whilst also periodically handing the mic to slam dancing fans. At *Klub Piekarnik,* in April 2023, there is an extremely interesting take and my personal favourite of "I Don't Care" which sees alternating vocals and the adapted line of 'she don't care' strangely but appropriately sung. At the same gig, there are back to back renditions of the album version of "Today Your Love Tomorrow The World" along with "You're Going To Kill That Girl" where Werner is somewhat more prominent but both vocalists take part. Again at *Klub Piekarnik,* you will find the crazed, screeching Kojot demanding to "Beat On The Brat" whilst the more melodic Werner enquires "what can you do?" –

it is definitely a distinctive play on the old ditty. "Havana Affair" is more orthodoxly sung whilst "Loudmouth" is acted out by both singers as if performed at the *Globe Theatre* rather than a club. Talking of "Loudmouth" there is an altered format played in the studio which has a thrash metal style and also well worth exploration. All in all, there are all sort of distinctions delivered by *AmigosUnuted* and their major strength is their uniqueness and their ability to keep the audience entertained with fans never knowing what to expect next.

When asked about the importance of The Ramones, bass player Tomec is quite philosophical about their legacy. They "did not know that they had initiated a musical revolution, the echoes of which can still be heard to this day", he states. "They are a band whose songs are liked by everyone: punks, Metalheads, rockers and hippies and of course, *AmigosUnuted!*" Maybe even more pertinent is the fact that the Polish group are still evolving and indeed moving from strength to strength performing Ramones songs to audiences which never had the opportunity to see the originals from *across the pond* from New York.

Rawones
Estonia

Estonia is located in Northern Europe and is bordered by the Gulf of Finland across from Finland to the north, by the Baltic Sea across from Sweden to the west, to the south by neighbouring Latvia and to the east by Russia. It is one of three countries which forms a geopolitical term described as the Baltic States with Latvia and Lithuania making up the trio. All three countries are now members of NATO and the European Union after a period of Soviet occupation after the Second World War. It was not until the introduction of *perestroika* by the Soviet government in 1987 which made open political activity again possible in countries such as Estonia which triggered an independence restoration. This process was later coined *The Singing Revolution* due to spontaneous mass evening singing demonstrations in Tallinn. In November 1988, a non-rigged multi-candidate election was held and by August 20th, 1991 Estonia declared independence with this being ratified by Soviet authorities on September 6th. The country is now a democratic unitary parliamentary republic but in the '70s and '80s, with The Ramones keeping an arm's length between themselves and countries from countries behind the "Iron Curtain", it meant that the band never ventured into any of the Baltic States. Estonia has a population of just under 1.4 million with the capital, Tallinn, the most populous city with around 454,000 living here. Tallinn is situated in north Estonia, on the Gulf of Finland and lies just 50 miles south of Helsinki in Finland.

When describing Tallinn's nightlife, one promotional website painted a great picture. "Estonians love to party," it states, "and despite being quite a small city, Tallinn is packed with bars, pubs and nightclubs." (358) It seems therefore quite consistent, therefore, that not only has Marky Ramone's *Blitzkrieg* played at the *Rock Café* in Tallinn in 2016, but also that a group of Tallinn devotees started their own Ramones tribute to the American punk innovators. Formed in 2004, the band were supposed to be a "one-off project" although ended up playing three shows that year. The quartet saw Mart Niineste on guitar, Peeter Tristan Valk as vocalist, Joel Berg on bass and Maik Grüner on the drums. The group was the inspiration of guitarist Mart who remembers that after he "saw a *Misfits'* tribute band in the autumn of 2003, he reached out to like-minded Ramones fans in order to recreate the sound of the *'fast four'*. He also simply says "The Ramones are gods" which pretty much sums up the passion that is a common theme throughout these narratives.

The band's designation was called *The Rawones* and was Joel's idea with the bass man simply turning the "M" upside down into a "W". As with many of our bands, the group took on pennames as a mark of their unity with the lads assuming the titles of Marty, Petey, J.B and Maik Rawone. The group had much experience with other bands. Petey, for instance, had played both bass and guitar for a variety of punk rock bands, Maik had played drums in the snowboard-metal band of *East Trading Wang* whilst J.B's band *Blind* had success in Estonia and have even toured the United States of America. Marty had played in several punk bands and later enjoyed success with the garage rock band *Les Diamants* and the impressively named new wave group *Chungin & The Strap-On Faggots*.

Their first gig took place on March 30th, 2004 at the *Von Krahl Theatre* in Tallinn. The band headlined in front of a full house of around 200 people and as guitar player Marty describes "it was a blast" with the set list simply consisting of the musician's favourite songs. The group even received a positive review from *Eesti Päevaleht*, a major Estonian daily newspaper. Their second show was also memorable and took place soon after in the spring of 2004. It was played at *Club Rockstars* in the capital city and was at an Estonian national football match 'after party'. On the bill that evening was *Butt Rock* band *Tanel Padar and The Sun,* who soon found fame a few months later as a mainstream Estonian band. Looking back, Marty remembers that first of all, singer Petey tried to use a wig to look like Joey but the rest of the lads "couldn't stop laughing so we gave it up and grew our own hair out instead."

Photograph courtesy of Sven Oeselg

Another one of the band's highlights was performing on Estonian television on the talk show "Kahvel". Marty pronounces how the group *blagged* their way onto the screen. When asked by the company to send some material in for scrutinising, he burned a C.D which was in fact the work of a different tribute. Thankfully, this was not checked and the Rawones were invited on the programme and performed snippets of "Blitzkrieg Bop" and "Cretin Hop" before bowing out to the tune of "I Wanna Be Sedated".

After their third gig at the *Club Illusion* in Tartu, the short-term project came to an end and the lads went their seperate ways. However, in 2016, Marty was asked to reform the band for a one-off show to mark the fortieth anniversary of the release of The Ramones debut album. Here the Estonian boys had the pleasure to perform the whole of that first album in its entirety adding a few other tunes such as "Sheena Is A Punk Rocker" in the encore. Three of *the Rawones* line-up were re-united with only the drumming position needing to be re-shuffled. Anneli Kadakas took up the responsibility of Anny Ramone and was well suited – the musician is a professional drummer and known for her time in the reggae band *Rasta Orchestra* along with the punk rock group *Vennaskond*.

A search on to *Youtube* delivers a few glimpses of the band in action. Unusually, the first two gives an insight to two sound checks and their preparation for a gig with "53rd and 3rd and "Rockaway Beach" both on offer. More relavent is a third clip where you can see some of the gig at *Rockstars* from May 2016 where *The Rawones* perform part of that Ramones debut album - The first six songs played in the same order as the L.P was cut: "Blitzkrieg Bop", "Beat On The Brat", "Judy Is A Punk", "I Wanna Be Your Boyfriend", "Chainsaw" and "Now I Wanna

Sniff Some Glue". Although the video footage is not of the highest quality with the stage lighting somewhat masking the musicians, what is unquestionable is the group's intense energy as they blast out the classics. Bassist J.B is twitchy and edgy, legs astride, head nodding à la Dee Dee whilst Marty propels the band onwards with his chainsaw guitar. Petey, tall and slim, adorning the trade mark sun glasses, stands sideways on, right foot forward, very much in the style of Joey. Behind those front three, drummer Anny is the linchpin with her meticulous, accurate, yet thumping drum pounding. My personal favourite, undoubtedly is "Judy" which is belted out in a style which would make *Da Brudders* proud – go have a look for oneself.

Despite *The Rawones* performing for just a brief period of time, the fact that the group carried a torch for the New Yorkers in Estonia is still worthy of intention. Just like the band, *AmigosUnited* from Poland, it is clear that The Ramones touched many people worldwide and in far more places than just those they toured.

I Wanna Be Sedated
England

To many British fans, February 3rd, 1996 was a bittersweet moment. On the one hand, supporters would be content that one could witness those boys from Forest Hills for one more occasion. On the other hand, however, enthusiasts were no doubt downcast due to the realisation that it was the last time The Ramones would play in *Old Blighty* and indeed the whole of the European continent. I am sure that there were many old punks at the gig, who would have cast their minds back two score years to the *Roundhouse* and recalled the night when they supported the *Flamin' Groovies* and inadvertently helped stimulate the UK punk scene in 1976. Personally, I remember looking back at some of my favourite Ramones moments of the past – the first time I saw them at the *Rainbow* in 1980 or my favourite all-time gig at the *Victoria Apollo* in 1981, coined as the *Midnight Madness* concert. All told they had performed over 30 times in London, over a century of gigs in England and nearly 130 times in the United Kingdom. This was undoubtedly an end of an era and they would certainly be missed.

The chosen venue for the last show in England was *Brixton Academy,* a grade II listed building. It was an old hunting ground for the '*fast four*' who had performed at the venue six times previously with one particularly memorable show in 1991 which saw *The Damned* co-headline. The location in South London has had a number of different designations over the years. Opening in 1929 at a cost of £250,000, it initially served as a place to watch movies and was originally known as the *Astoria Variety* cinema. In 1972, it was converted into a discotheque known as *"Sundown Centre"* but this was not a commercial success and swiftly closed. After a period where it was merely used as a storage facility, the venue was re-modelled in 1981 and re-opened as a rock venue under the moniker of *"Fair Deal"*. By 1983, it was sold and re-named *"Brixton Academy"* but by 2004 it had been re-branded again and known as *Carling Academy Brixton*. It is currently under the title of O_2 *Academy Brixton* but was sadly closed in December 2022 after two people died and others seriously injured following a crowd crush at the door. An array of top artists has performed at the venue which have included Deep Purple (which took the reins for the first night in 1983), *The Smiths, U2*, Madonna, Debby Harry, *The Clash, Kraftwork, The Buzzcocks, The Prodigy*, Bob Dylan, Amy Winehouse, Lady Gaga, *Motörhead, Blur, Coldplay, The Stranglers* and *Iron Maiden*.

There is thankfully an audio recording of that final British show. Although in all honestly the quality of the soundtrack is not the greatest, it does give you a flavour of that historic night. There were 35 songs were on offer with a mixture of old and new tunes. Of course, they played the established favourites of "Blitzkrieg Bop", "Beat On The Brat", "Rockaway Beach" and "Commando" but also performed some of the more contemporary tracks such as "I Don't Wanna Grow Up", "7 And 7 Is" and "Cretin Family". Their last song on English soil was "I Just Wanna Have Something To Do" with Joey Ramone poignantly leaving the stage to rapturous applause with the words "Hey, long live, England, thank you, adios amigos." It might interest some readers that the price of a ticket for that momentous Saturday evening was just £12.50 – money well spent for sure.

One person in the Brixton audience was Simon Sanett who described their performance that night as "absolutely amazing." In 2007, Simon and a group of like-minded Ramones fans from the Brixton area decided that they would form their own tribute with the drummer explaining why this came about. "Ramones are a classic band with a blistering live show and a huge back catalogue of tracks. They are no longer with us, so we wanted to give people a chance to experience The Ramones' sound live." Named after one of the American's most famed tunes, *I Wanna Be Sedated* - the band initially saw Dave Webster as vocalist, Sam Brown on bass, Phil Ross on the guitar along with stick man Simon. As with many of our tributes, the lads took on the collective stage name of Ramone with Dave having the nom de plume of Wonky, Sam taking up the psydonym of Sammy, Phil naturally transforming to Philly and Simon morphing into Razor. The group also used the famous Ramones eagle logo with one amusing adapation - the baseball bat was changed to a cricket bat as a subtle hint to their English heritage. Razor cites a number of personal favourite shows such as the launch of *CBGB* photo exhibition at *Proud Gallery* in Camden or the gig at the *Prince Albert* on New Year's Eve back both in 2009. In addition, he fondly remembers London's *Rock 'N' Roller's Roller Derby* half time show or the celebration for the Dutch Queen's Birthday festival in Den Helder, Holland both in 2010. The group play a typical Ramones set featuring all the classics such as "53rd and 3rd", "Californian Sun", "Judy Is A Punk" and "The KKK Took My Baby Away" with some more unusual picks thrown including "Danny Says" and "What A Wonderful World" to give their own distinctive, singular take. The band also carried out a cover of *The Clash's* classic "I Fought The Law" as well as "Baby I Love You" which was complemented by the addition of

Corinna Sanett on the violin, all so reminiscent of The Ramones' rendition back in 1980 on BBC's *Top of The Pops*.

The group had a line-up change in 2009 with Ed Sonsino or Eddy Ramone recruited as guitarist and he performed with the band until 2015 when the lads decided to call it a day because members wanted to concentrate on their original groups along with family commitments. The hiatus lasted for eight years but fortunately a new invigorated *I Wanna Be Sedated* emerged in 2023 with two of the originals Wonky and Razor coming out of 'retirement' and Matt Saywell-Burr and Dave Sharman added on bass and guitar respectively. Unsurprisingly, the two new lads took up pennames with Matty and DJ Ramone, the approved monikers.

A search on to the band's *Facebook* page will see a variety of footage of *Sedated* in action. Immediately, you observe the boys dressed like The Ramones with Razor explaining that "we try to look as close as the real thing as possible. We wear wigs, black leather jackets and Ramones style T-shirts!" The drummer goes on to add that "we love playing The Ramones songs and our goal is to have fun. If we are having fun, so do our audience. We don't take ourselves too seriously, how can we whilst wearing wigs on stage!?" The enjoyment factor is certainly apparent when checking out "Blitzkrieg Bop" at the *Rebel Inn* in Streatham, South London, for instance. Here you will find a bunch of fist punching, excitable fans clearly having a ball and one lucky member of the audience joining in on vocals on the stage. There is also on offer an interesting rendition of Rockaway Beach" which is played at an album tempo rather than at live warp speed whilst I love their version of "I Fought The Law" at the *Prince Albert* in Brixton with guitarist DJ excelling in the manner of Mick Jones of *The Clash*. Possibly my favourite, however, is the song which carries their name - "I Wanna Be Sedated". The group get absolutely the right blend between melody and the power of the buzzsaw guitars as lead singer Wonky and bassist Matty alternate the vocals declaring that maybe getting chemically knocked down is more preferable than boredom.

When asked about The Ramones influence, Razor feels that the New Yorkers "are *the* seminal punk rock band" and heavily influenced the punk rock scene of the '80s and '90s without getting the recognition or the accolade that they deserved during their lifetimes." He concludes that "Joe Strummer once said 'without The Ramones there would be no *Clash* and that is the reason why we play 'I Fought The Law'." You cannot really argue with his sentiments and my advice would be if you ever find yourself in South London with *nothing to do* or *nowhere to go,* there's no need for sedation - instead *get to the show* and check out this band!

Photograph courtesy of Karen Ward

Ramoncs Brazil

A second tribute group heralding from São Paulo in Brazil is *The Ramoncs*. Formed in 2021, the idea of starting the band stemmed from guitarist, Luciano Kaskinha who wanted to pay homage to The Ramones. He soon got on board a factory co-worker, drummer Vanderson Pavani, with vocalist Marcelo Santos and bass player Thiago Lima expressing an interest through advertisements on *Facebook* groups posted by Luciano. When Vanderson left the band in 2022, Thiago invited Lucas Rebouças, with whom he had already previously rehearsed in another project, to take over the drummer's seat. Lucas improved the band's rhythm section and also provided opportunities for shows in larger venues enabling more fans to watch the group. According to Thiago, "it wasn't difficult for the members to accept the invitation to join the project as The Ramones are everyone's favourite band." The name *The Ramoncs* was chosen by Luciano as soon as he founded the band. The idea was simply and to choose a name that immediately referred to the New Yorkers and that sounded similar, in a respectful punk rock way. A couple of the band members have had experience in other groups. Thiago Lima, for instance, plays bass in *The Divorce Factory* whilst Lucas plays drums in two other bands called *Wildrock* and *Severinos HC*.

Thiago was just 15 years old when he watched The Ramones in March 1996. This would, be the New Yorkers' last visit to Brazil with the group performing six times altogether in the country that tour – firstly in Rio de Janeiro then on to Mogi das Cruzes and Santo André before three shows in São Paulo with the finale in the country taking place on March 13th. The chosen venue was at the legendary, but since closed concert hall, the *Olympia*. Opened in 1988 until its closure in 2006, the site had a capacity for 5,000 people and one can only imagine the atmosphere as the '*fast four*' performed to a full-house, hysterical, frantic crowd. As well as The Ramones, a number of highly regarded artists have performed at the venue including David Bowie, Cyndi Lauper, Eric Clapton, Sting, *Deep Purple* and *Black Sabbath*. Although the tour was to help promote the "¡Adios Amigos!" album maybe surprisingly only three tracks, where selected for their live shows from this L.P, two of which were sung by C.J - "The Crusher" and "Cretin Family" plus the cover "I Don't Wanna Grow Up" crooned by Joey. Other interesting selections those nights included "SpiderMan", "My Back Pages", "Main Man" and "Have You Ever Seen The Rain?" whilst the old favourites such as "Rockaway Beach", "Teenage Lobotomy" and "Pinhead" were there too to give fans a balance of new and old.

There are a host of audio recordings and videos out there on *Youtube* demonstrating the passion of the Brazilian crowds not only in São Paulo during the 1996 tour but also previous gigs throughout the country in 1987, 1991, 1992 and 1994. To truly appreciate the esteem that the band were held in, it is well scrutinising and I am sure that first time viewers will no doubt be wholly surprised. Similarly, tune in to *the backstage interview* for *MTV Brazil* by Edgard Piccoli with Johnny Ramone at the *Olympia i*n 1996 where there is a discussion on the band's formation, early *CBGB* gigs, the London punk scene in 1976 and their imminent retirement. The guitarist will also discuss the love seen from Brazilian and Argentinian fans describing them as "the best two audiences in the world." [359]

Marky Ramone recounts the scenes in São Paulo stating that "the chants of "Hey Ho, Let's Go!" were even louder than we were used to. They started well before the show and continued well after the second and final encore. The fans spoke primarily Portuguese, but when it came to singing out the lyrics to "Sedated", "Sheena" and the "KKK" their English was great." [360] Another aspect which is emphasised in the videos and audio tapes is how the band speeded up over those years. This is indeed highlighted, again on *Youtube* by an excellent piece of investigatory work by *Heatseeker* who took "Blitzkrieg Bop" as an exemplar of the evolution of the band. The results were intriguing to say the least with the group initially clocking in at 176 bpm in 1975 during the performance in Arturo Vega's loft. By 1987, at the time of their first Brazilian gig, the tempo had increased to 240 bpm but by 1996 and the "¡Adios Amigos!" tour it had risen again to an incredible 252 bpm. [361] For me, this was to the detriment of the overall quality being produced and particularly hindered Joey's ability to sing. Although the gigs were always fantastic and there is no doubt that the band were the ultimate *well-oiled machine*, there was also the impression that by the end of their career the group were going through the motions to some degree.

There was an attempt to get the Ramones to play their final show in Brazil rather than having their last concert in Los Angeles. According to Marky, a major promoter from South America, who carried with him a petition containing thousands of signatures, offered the band $1 million to come back to

Brazil. Johnny and Marky wanted to do it but Joey didn't due to health reasons. (362) Johnny concurs affirming that "we had a chance to make more money than we did on that entire tour (Lollapalooza), for just three shows in South America" but Joey said "he was tired." Johnny admitted "that he got so tired of hearing from everybody about how fragile Joey was." (363) Mickey Leigh is most insightful about this period and asserts that Joey confided with his brother telling him that the Ramones were "pissed at him because they had an offer to go to South America for a lot of money. The Ramones had become like *The Beatles* in South America, but he didn't want to do this tour. I haven't been feeling just right, ya know?" Joey told him adding that "I just don't feel like I have the strength to do another tour like that, not right now, anyway." Mickey supported his brother's decision to put his health above the finances of the band and even though he did offer to do the concerts in a few months, Johnny wanted to do them immediately or not at all. (364)

The show at the *Olympia* was Thiago's first rock concert and he defines that day as a turning point in his life – "the day that changed everything" he says. It certainly gave him the inspiration to be part of that *Ramones Family* and be involved in a cover band. The bassist describes his experiences on stage. "As a rule, we are very successful in our presentations because everyone loves the Ramones", he says. "Sometimes people ask to come on stage to sing with us, other times fans who have never had the opportunity to see the Ramones live thank us for the experience. So, every show brings some special moment. But we can highlight two memorable concerts. In 2022, we played at a charity event for one of the most renowned motorcycle clubs in the state of São Paulo - *Maiados MC* - as the opening band for *365*, one of the most traditional and well-known bands on the Brazilian punk scene. In 2023 we had the debut of the new drummer, Lucas, at a punk rock festival organised at a place called *Cervejazul*, an underground club known for having supported the beginnings of several successful Brazilian punk and hardcore bands. In both concerts, together with the public, we managed to transform the venues into a kind of "local CBGB's", keeping the legacy of the Ramones alive."

The Ramoncs generally adapt the set list to the stage time they receive from the organisers. Therefore, the it can vary between 20 to 40 songs. In shorter sets the focus is on the best known songs mainly using "It's Alive" and "Loco Live" as a base. In the longer sets they cover songs from all the albums, as a way of paying respect to all eras and all the members of the band. As well as the landmark tunes, some of the often overlooked choices include "Strength To Endure", "Suzy Is A Headbanger", "Outsider", "Needles And Pins" and "I Don't Want You".

Thiago expands on how the group delivers the Ramones tunes "we don't do anything different in terms of visuals. What we do is often give ourselves room to be creative and try something different, adding backing vocals to some parts or changing the vocalist in others. As a tribute band, our main commitment is to the vibe that the Ramones' music can bring to all generations of rockers." A search on social media will find *The Ramoncs* in action and as always it is imperative to see if the band cuts the mustard yourself. The first song which pops up is "Glad To See You Go" and my first impressions was being taken aback by Lucas on the drums unusually being placed at the side of the stage as opposed to centrally and reminiscent of the Ramones' awkward performance of "Baby I Love You" on BBC's *Top of The Pops* back in 1980. At the same gig, there is an extract from "Have You Ever Seen The Rain?" which is very much suited to Marcelo's melodic vocals and my personal favourite of all the songs on offer. Similarly, the mid-tempo tracks of "I Believe In Miracles" and the rehearsal footage of "Bonzo Goes To Bitburg", "Beat On The Brat" and "I Just Want To Have Something To Do" shows the band at their best. Indeed, these rockier, intermediate, paced tunes with a steady cadence of drums and guitars undoubtedly seemed to fit their style. One thing is unquestionable is that the boys are having fun and this clearly rubs off on their audiences. Guitarist Luciano and bassist Thiago compel the band forward with their punchy, twangy guitar sound, Lucas holds it together with his booming, skin punching drumming whilst Marcelo is a compact, bundle of punk energy at the front. You certainly cannot fault the enthusiasm shown from any of the lads and there is no doubt that *The Ramoncs* are doing their bit to keep the Ramones' name thriving. Indeed, when Thiago was asked about the importance of the Americans' work over the years, the bass man did not hold back in his assessment. "The Ramones had, and still have, the power to influence music as a whole and help shape people's lifestyles. They are and will always be the main gateway to punk rock. Thousands of bands, known or not, and millions of people around the world, are what they are because of the Ramones. We, the *Ramoncs*, one of the main Brazilian tribute bands, are a living example of the immense success they had in South America, where the Ramones are like a religion. We proudly fulfil the mission of, night by night, chord by chord, keeping the legacy alive and vibrant."

Mondos Bizarros –
Ramones & Blondie Revival
United States Of America

The Ramones performed over 50 times in Texas with their last concert in the state taking place on the July 25th 1996 in Ferris at the *Old Fort Dallas*. Ferris is a small town located in Ellis County and lies around 20 miles south of Dallas. It thrived during the early post-war years earning the nicknames of "the Brick Capital of the Nation" and "The City that bricked the World" due to having four brick plants operating there in the 1950s. The concert was part of *Lollapalooza* – the annual travelling music festival. As well as the Ramones, there were a number of other bands on the bill that day with the likes of *Sponge, Melvins, Rancid, Devo, Soundgarden* and *Metallica* all performing, resulting in the boys from Queens playing fewer songs than the norm. The audience were still treated to 20 ripsnorters which included the tried and tested ditties of "Do You Wanna Dance?", "Sheena Is A Punk Rocker", "Rockaway Beach", "Wart Hog" and "Cretin Hop". [365]

One fan who was at that gig was Louis "Gino" LaVecchia who remembers seeing the Ramones in Ferris just before they quit "as a bitter sweet moment." He also points out that he "was bitter to see *Metallica* infiltrate the subculture and realise that the counter culture movement of Alternative Rock of the '70s, '80s and '90s was dead. Ramones were great, but I wish I had been up closer to see them, and of course had seen them when they were younger. I still, was absolutely impressed and liked them better than *Soundgarden* and *Metallica's* performances on the same day. Those two bands went on after dark, the premium spots in the festival line-up." Gino would go on to be instrumental in keeping the Ramones' name flourishing in Texas. In the August of 2015 the bass player put out an advertisement looking for like-minded musicians to form a Ramones tribute. He was initially joined by Chris Russell (aka Chris Zativah) on guitar, who was in a previous tribute band know as *Original Sedated* which was active between 2006-2012. In spite of the fact that Chris soon left, the band kept a link with the past naming themselves *Sedated -The World's Greatest Tribute to the Ramones* which was then soon modified to the name of *Sedated - A Celebration.* This would of course signify their mission statement – a salutation to the music of those punk giants from Queens. When the band broke up in October 2019, Gino continued to rehearse with Ralph Lopez on guitar and Brian Ivo "Cuban" Ascanio on drums, who since the age of 15 had played with his original punk band *The Scandals, TX.* The lads then brought in Joe Frascino in May 2020, who had played in *Original Sedated* as vocalist to complete the quartet and the new designation of *Mondos Bizarros* was chosen with their first gig in November of that year. It was Ralph who came up with the new moniker adding the "s" to make it different from the Ramones' twelfth studio album with Gino explaining that the name also takes into account the musicians' origins stating that "we're all Americans, born in the US, but also we're all of varying different mixes of Italian and Hispanic/Spanish heritages."

Mondos rehearse every week and to keep everything fresh, continually learn new songs and now incredibly have well over 150 tunes in their locker. They shake up the set lists all the time and never do the same show more than once or twice. Gino explains that "we borrow some of the style and music of their studio recordings and blend that with style of their live performances. We might cover some songs closer to the album version, while others sound more like it is off 'Loco Live' or 'It's Alive'". The group have started playing more of the complex Ramones tunes aiding by the fact that singer Joe Frascino was trained vocally in classical opera. Gino proudly points out that "we've done every song on the "Anthology" and "Mania" along with all songs in sequential order from the albums "Ramones", "Leave Home" and "Rocket to Russia". The bassist goes on to add that "some of the deeper cuts we play are "Tomorrow She Goes Away", "Mental Hell", a lot of songs off "Animal Boy", actually just all over their discography. We really enjoy doing "7 And 7 Is" from "Acid Eaters". We do any and all Ramones songs we want." Compared to other Ramones tributes, it is apparent that *Mondos* are certainly more Dee Dee-centric. By that I mean that there is more emphasis on those songs that Dee Dee fronted such as "Wart Hog", "Endless Vacation", "I Lost My Mind" and "Time Bomb" whilst the tribute is one of the few I have discovered who also perform "Born to Die in Berlin", the final track off the last album "¡Adios Amigos!". Gino even takes on the singing of the mid-section part in German just like Dee Dee Ramone did back in 1995. In addition, the group use more harmony from the vocals of the bass man than the Ramones did in live settings with the idea almost of a dual front-man band.

When looking back Gino cites a number of memorable gigs both with *Sedated* and *Mondos* such as in 2019, when they played the *Pyramid Club* in East Village of Manhatten, New York and met members of *the extended Ramones family* such as John

Holmstrom, David Erdelyi and film maker and photographer George Seminara. In the same year they played *The Texas Theatre* which interestingly is the same Dallas venue where Lee Harvey Oswald was captured after assassinating John F. Kennedy. "It is highly preserved", Gino states, adding that "I met C.J Ramone here and got to sit down and talk to him." *Sedated* also performed for a screening of *"Rock and Roll High School"* with the bass man able to hang out with guest, PJ Soles as she took part in the meet and greet and autograph session. Probably their most memorable show since performing as *Mondos Bizarros* was at the *Rubber Gloves*, a multi-venue complex which includes a college bar and rehearsal studio, in Denton, Texas which was particularly pleasing as the audience comprised of a wide range of ages, especially young adults who were interested in seeing what the Ramones might have been like to see live.

In January 2023, *Mondos Bizarros* decided to diversify to some extent and added a new member to their group in order for fans to experience the delights of another New York legendary band, *Blondie.* The new edition was Star Daniels, a vocalist and dancer who also works as a digital influencer and promoter of live music in the Dallas-Ft. Worth Metro area and she would take on the role of none other than Debbie Harry. The majority of the band's

set is still Ramones based with presently four songs sung by the *blonde bombshell*. At the start of the concerts, Star Daniels, aka Debbie Harry recites the famous *Blondie* show opener monologue before breaking into "Dreaming". Other tunes on offer are the *Blondie* tracks of "I'm on E", "Hanging on the Telephone" and "Rip Her to Shreds" whilst there is unsurprisingly a rendition of "Go Little Camaro Go" where Debbie of course guested on the 1987 Ramones album "Halfway To Sanity". Gino points out that although they may add one or two more of "Blondie's punkier" tunes such as "Will Anything Happen?" or "I Know But I Don't Know", it will always be "Ramones first."

There is pleasingly much footage of the band and a great first port of call is on *Youtube* with their concert in Lewisville, Texas in October, 2023. Here can you see *Mondos Bizarros* in full swing with both singers in action sending out the creative image of what a Debbie Harry and Ramones concert might just have been like all those years ago. You will find nearly 50 minutes of high energy fun with my personal picks some of the less famed beauts such as "She's The One", "Locket Love", "I'm Against It", "Somebody To Love" as well as "Go Little Camaro Go" which sees Star back on the stage. The video portrays the band in full Ramones battle dress complete with jeans, sneakers and leathers and with Ralph, Cuban and Joe all in wigs although Gino explains that the group *Mondos* "changes the look with every show. Sometimes we go natural hair. I had long hair, now I've cut it and used the wig a couple shows but eventually as my hair grows back I'll go to a short early Dee Dee hair style. Sometimes we dress as Zombies or dead Ramones in line with some of the Tales of the Ramones box set comics and music box set of the Ramones." A search onto their *Facebook* page will see a plethora of information and song links to some real pearls. Alternatively check out *Soundcloud*, for instance for "Somebody Put Something In My Drink", "Bop 'Til You Drop", "Commando" or "Blitzkrieg Bop" which were all recorded live at *Rubber Gloves* in Denton, Texas in January 2023. In all their tracks, there is that trademark bright, buzzsaw whirlwind guitar sound, a relentless, pounding bass and crashing but simplistic drumbeat but my biggest compliment is that the group radiate a fun-based energy which is exemplified by the two vocalists and picked up by the audience.

Today *Mondos Bizarros, Sedated Ultimate* and a reformed *Original Sedated* all perform in the Dallas – Ft Worth Metro area which has one of the US's most vibrant and robust tribute scenes in the country. It is apparent that the Ramones have shaped so many lives and it is people like Gino of *Mondos* who keep the New Yorker's legacy thriving. "My favourite band is the Ramones and my favourite bassist is Dee Dee Ramone", he utters. Gino's love of the band is without question and he additionally tells us that "I've read seven books by or about the Ramones. I'm presently reading Seymour Stein's autobiography *"Siren Song"*. I've studied them, spoken to many people that were around the Ramones including Vera Ramone. I think the Ramones influence is important enough that their legacy will grow and fame will be even greater in the future, à la Vincent Van Gogh. They were at a monumental period in popular rock music where everything had become very hippie and progressive, with a roots revival, punk rock simplicity…Something that gave R&R back to the masses and the DIY feel." The bass player points out that "music is everyone's passion in *Mondos Bizarros*. We do not practice weekly to be a Ramones band", he utters, "we practice weekly to enjoy a little vacation away from work, home and life. We are sincerely paying tribute to the Ramones, not trying to steal their identities, make money, or boost our own egos. We just think they are sorely needed, they have passed away, and we love the Ramones." Possibly the most gratifying aspect of any band, however, is the reaction of the audience with Gino revealing life as a tribute act. "We play shows that feature many young local punk bands because you know, the Ramones were seminal to the genre. They all kind of hang out after they play, to watch us. They're ready to make fun of us, put us down, then they watch us and tend to love us. It's a lot of fun, I feel like we are disciples in the religion of Ramones" he states. Indeed, there are so many fans out there who will certainly say amen to that.

Too Tough 2 Die
United States Of America

After 22 years, 14 studio albums and 2263 concerts, the Ramones performed their last concert on August 6th, 1996. For fans like myself, there had been an inevitability about their retirement for some time but it was somehow still hard to take. In February, however they had waved goodbye to England and indeed Europe, in March they had said adios to Brazil and Argentina in South America whilst by July they had joined the *Lollapalooza* tour with *Metallica* and *Soungarden,* bidding farewell to much of the United States. Despite the predictability of their cessation and in spite of the fact that no-one wanted them just to chug along as also-rans, the band had always been there in our formative years. In their black leather jackets, plimsolls, ripped jeans and bowl haircuts, they were a constant. After the curtain closed for that final time, would life be the same without them?

The chosen city for their final gig was in Los Angeles. L.A, as it is known, is in the state of California and the second most populous city in the United States of America with nearly 3.9 million residents living there. It is famed for its fabulous beaches, theme parks and TV, pop and film culture and maybe most notably the Hollywood attractions. The venue for the last show was at *The Palace* near the intersection of Hollyood and Vine Street. Opened in 1927 as the *Hollywood Playhouse,* the building has a capacity of 1,500 and designed in Spanish Baroque style. The site has had various designations over the years, namely the *Federal Theatre Project,* the *El Capitan Theatre,* the *Jerry Lewis Theatre,* the *Hollywood Palace* and is now known as the *Avalon Hollywood* or simply the *Avalon*. During the '70s and '80s, *the Palace* gained notoriety as the 'hottest' night club in the state with the likes of Prince, Madonna and *The Rolling Stones* seen frequenting the institution whilst some of the bands who performed there include *The Eurythmics, Culture Club, The Clash, Duran Duran, Madness* and *The Beastie Boys.* [366]

The show that night was videod and was released in 1997 through Eagle Rock Records under the title "We're Outta Here!" The concert was unusual as it had a number of guest performers such as Lemmy Kilmister from *Motörhead's* who played his "R.A.M.O.N.E.S" accolade, *Rancid* members Tim Armstrong and Lars Frederiksen performing on guitar for "53rd and 3rd", Ben Shepherd from *Soundgarden* did the same for "Chinese Rock" and *Pearl Jam's* Eddie Vedder sung with Joey for the Dave Clark cover "Any Way You Want It" for their very last tune. *Soundgarden's* Chris Cornell also acted as a MC to keep the crowd engaged for the encore whilst pleasingly, Dee Dee also featured solely on lead vocals but along-side C.J on bass, for his version of "Love Kills". Writer Veronica Kofman sums up the inclusion of the band's founder member at the show perfectly stating "it may not have been a perfect ending, but the circle was completed." [367] Fascinatingly, during the rendition of the song, Dee Dee appears that he forgets the words and eventually adlibbing "it's me, this is the way I am" although maybe, just maybe, he meant to create a little bit of mayhem knowing that he would upset the perfectionist Johnny. According to Mickey Leigh, "the atmosphere at the last performance was typically strained. The band displayed their usual dourness. They didn't appear to be celebrating their remarkably ground-breaking and illustrious career. It seemed more like they just wanted to get it over with. The big event was hugely uneventful and even anticlimactic, especially for the band members." Mickey also recalls that C.J felt it was kind of a fitting end with the bass man confessing "I didn't even say goodbye to anybody." Maybe Mickey's most significant comments were that Joey "was just glad when it was finally all over" and regarding the relationship of his singer towards Johnny recollecting the "most mutually passive-aggressive act of their whole career" was when they left and crisscrossed the stage as the singer and Johnny practically rammed into each other. [368] Marky also paints the picture about that last gig stating "backstage there were no good-byes and no pats on the back. We just went about our business in the dressing room. There was too much to say and no reason to try to say it. I thought ending with a tight, workmanlike set was very Ramones." [369] Johnny gives his version of events stating "I had blocked out the significance and the finality of it all." "I said nothing to the other guys; I just walked out. It was the way I lived my life." [370]

There seemed something strange about having the last show in Los Angeles rather than in New York where the band had grown up and was so closely associated with. According to Mickey Leigh the Californian choice was because Johnny had bought a house in L.A and insisted that it should be performed here. [371] However, rewind the clock and the Ramones had a close association with the *City of Angels*. Their first visit to the city was back in August 1976, a month after they had helped jump-start the punk movement in England. Just like their two gigs in London, they co-performed with the San Francisco rock band *Flamin' Groovies*. The venue that night was at the iconic *Roxy*, a nightclub on the Sunset Strip in West Hollywood. Two songs were recorded that evening - "California Sun" and "I Don't Wanna Walk Around With You" and these would give many fans their first indication of how good the Ramones were live as both would feature on a "B" side single release. Surprisingly, the "A" side would have different formats with "I Wanna Be Your Boyfriend" released in the USA whilst UK enthusiasts would collect "I Remember You".

The *Roxy* was also the setting for the live shots during the movie *"Rock 'n' Roll High School"* which was filmed on December 14th, 1978. For Johnny, who hated wasting time and hated any fuss the filming was "torture" with the band "sitting around all the time" which gave Dee Dee plenty of opportunity to party and get "high all the time." The guitarist goes into further detail describing the plot. "The concert scene took about 18 hours to film. They changed audiences three times. The morning audience got in free, the afternoon audience paid $2 and the night audience was $5. So extras had to pay. I felt bad because these kids had paid five bucks and we had played the same five songs over and over again, so when it was all over I said I wanted to play more songs, and we played a few more songs. Then they pulled the plug on us." Johnny also points out that the band only made a total of $5,000 for the film so whilst they shot the movie, they also performed some shows to pay the expenses. This included opening for heavy metal pioneers *Black Sabbath* which proved to be a disaster with an unappreciative audience booing the punks off stage. [372] The choice of the Ramones for a movie might seem rather odd and it was Allan Arkush who was paramount regarding the decision to hire the band. The film director was thinking about making a film with famous B-movie producer Roger Corman about *daydreaming in a high school.* Arkush had toyed with the title of the film as *Heavy Metal Kids* or *Disco High* and contemplated using the bands *Cheap Trick, Van Halen* or *Devo.* When someone mentioned the Ramones instead, Arkush had a change of heart, affirming. "It just so happens that Danny and Linda were in LA, and when I went and met with them their eyes lit up," the director states. "The Ramones in a Roger Corman movie - what could be more perfect? And they were trying to break them nationally and at that point punk rock had a real stigma. The fact that it was a comedy and was new wave was very appealing to them. Roger was easily convinced. Plus, they were cheap, so he was sold. So I went to New York to see them live. They played at *Hurrah's* with *Talking Heads.*" (373) With this 'audition' going well, they were signed up and travelled down to L.A. Much of the filming was carried out at the already closed Mount Carmel High School in Los Angeles which in the movie would convert to the *Vince Lombardi High School.* Known for their minimalistic music, the punk rockers would certainly have minimal speaking parts. Johnny delivered the words "we're not students, we're the Ramones", Joey declares "things sure have changed since we got kicked out of high school" whilst Dee Dee amusingly was given the line "Oh Boy, pizza." The film generally had positive reviews although personally it was a largely forgettable movie with the saving grace, the performance of PJ Soles as her role of Riff Randall. The film and soundtrack were released in August 1979 and the vinyl was complete with a medley of five live songs – "Blitzkrieg Bop", "Teenage Lobotomy", "California Sun", "Pinhead" and "She's The One" as well as "I Want You Around" and naturally the film title, "Rock 'n' Roll High School.

Other performers on the album include *The Paley Brothers, Devo,* Alice Cooper *and* Nick Lowe to name but a few.

The Ramones played just over 40 times all told in Los Angeles with a number of other memorable concerts within the city. At *The Whisky,* for instance, fortunate fans would see a double dose of delight with *Blondie* also performing whilst at the *Hollywood Palladium* and *California State University* at Northridge, those lovable speed merchants, *The Dickies* would be in support. L.A would also see the production of the much debated Phil Spector's "End Of The Century" album which was carried out in a variety of establishments such as *Gold Star, Salty Dog* and *Devonshire Sound Studios*. More poignantly, Los Angeles is the grave site of both Dee Dee and Johnny Ramone with both founder members laid to rest at the *Hollywood Forever Cemetery*. Please refer to appendix four for more details of the burial sites of all four founder members.

One musician who had seen the Ramones in Los Angeles in the '80s was drummer Nick Vale. Nick met bass player and vocalist George Hanna-Wilson at a punk show in 2016 and with the lads hitting it off straight away and due to their love of the Ramones and their love of playing, they decided to form a tribute band. The pair then started to look for guitar players and met Rich Maza on-line with the trio agreeing to focus mainly on '80s and '90s songs. Indeed, they particularly looked at the harder core and deep cuts because no-one else was doing this as far as they knew. Interestingly, George had already featured in a more traditional Ramones tribute called *Remones USA* as well as a bunch of other ventures including a hardcore punk group named *Family Members* which is still active. Nick plays in a punk band with his wife called *Ley Valentine* whilst Rich has also played in various projects. Their name derived from the eight studio album which was the much heralded L.P which leaned back towards a harder punk edge and the first to feature new drummer Richie. The boys just changed one part of its title to give some uniqueness with the "to" being replaced by "2" and saw the creation of *Too Tough 2 Die*. The fellas have played many shows but when pushed about the most notable, George sites "a couple of punk themed burlesque shows at a bar in Reseda, California called *Petie's Place* back in 2018. It was us and a bunch of burlesque dancers. A lot of fun. The dancers were great." He also goes on to add that "we've also played with a bunch of other tribute bands in the past. Tributes to *the Cramps, the Misfits, Social Distortion* and *the Cars*."

In terms of a set list, it is inspiring to find the boys take a different slant than the normal Ramones cover hit list. The bass man pronounces that "we did a lot of stuff from the Ritchie Ramone era. Tunes from "Too Tough To Die", "Animal Boy" and "Halfway To Sanity" albums. We'd sometimes throw a couple of more classic hits in there like "Commando" and "Cretin Hop"." In fact, refreshingly, this was the first cover band analysed in this book whose song catalogue had no mention of "Blitzkrieg Bop" or "Sheena Is A Punk Rocker". In their repertoire, amongst other tunes, one finds such nuggets as "Wart Hog", "Bop 'Til You Drop", "Cretin Family", "Endless Vacation" and the title tracks from the 33s "Animal Boy" and "Too Tough To Die". One of the features about observing our tributes is that every band have been somewhat different - each group has had its own unique identity. During the late 1970s and early '80s, a punk subculture known as hardcore grew with a faster and more aggressive feel than previous years. Its roots have been attributed to California with underground scenes, amongst other places springing up in cities such as San Francisco and Los Angeles. *Too Tough 2 Die* have that abrasive edge and they have taken Ramones' songs and given it a hardcore feel. A trip onto *Youtube* or their *Facebook* page gives various links to many of their songs. Those perfectionists who like their Ramones cover bands as a quartet rather than a three-piece will probably find it somewhat challenging but as soon as you get past the fact that there is no front-man as such, then *Too Tough* is an extremely thought-provoking take on the New Yorkers. George alludes to this when he states "we don't wear wigs or anything and we're a 3 piece. We're not gimmicky about it like some of the other tributes. Our tribute comes from playing the songs hard and fast and as close to the Ramones style as we could. We play downstrokes and no gaps between the songs." For a taster, check out "I'm Not Jesus" at the *Five Star Bar* in downtown Los Angeles which will immediately give you an impression of this band. Alternatively, "We're A Happy Family" at the *Liquid Zoo* in 2022 where they attack your sensibilities like a sledge hammer cracking a walnut. If you like your Ramones, Dee Dee driven *'Eat That Rat' style* as opposed to Joey's melodic "Baby I Love You" panache, then these may well be the *jewel in the crown* for you. For those who have more time to burn, then refer to the gig from Long Beach in 2018 which gives you over half an hour of uninterupted, primal, neolithic punk rock. The picks are probably "Who Wants The Airways", the punkiest interprtaion of "I Don't Want You" that I have ever heard, "Bonzo Goes To Bitburg", a superb interpretation of "Weasel Face" and my own personal favourite "Wart Hog" which includes drummer Nick on backing vocals. It is also great to see some audience participation with a guest singer pulled up to the stage, dressed in shirt and tie and giving his all for the timeless classic of "Pinhead".

Too Tough 2 Die are still active although they do not play as much these days because band members are busy with their own original musical projects. Whenever a good gig comes up though they will do it, still knowing all the songs "pretty well." I will leave the last words to George when he talks about the Ramones legacy. "They're one of the most influential bands of all time", the bassist points out. "They stripped rock 'n' roll down to it bare bones and basically created modern punk. Their style, look, humour, and attitude was so unique and cool. Tons of bands to this day still copy them but they were the best."

I Remember You

Accolades come in all shapes and guises. On March 18th, 2002, for instance, the Ramones were inducted into the "Rock and Roll Hall of Fame" at the annual ceremony at the Waldorf Astoria Hotel in New York City. On November 30th, 2003, a further honour was assigned when a block of East 2nd Street in New York City was officially renamed Joey Ramone Place. The campaign to name the street after Ramone sprang from the ground up following a celebratory birthday bash in his honour. The idea was first brought to life by a young fan, Maureen Wojciechowski, and was helped along by long-time friend and founder of *Punk* magazine, John Holstrom, and Ramones artist Arturo Vega. Interestingly, the sign has been pinched several times, making it the most stolen street sign in all of New York City. Each time it is replaced at a higher spot on the post and is now about 20 feet above street level. [374] In February 2011, some 15 years after they disbanded, the punk rock pioneers were finally presented with their first Grammy: A Lifetime Achievement Award. In an acceptance speech, Marky Ramone humbly pronounced "this is amazing, I never expected this. I'm sure Johnny, Joey and Dee Dee would never have expected this. I'm extremely honoured." [375]

Maybe, however, the greatest compliment that could be bestowed on a band, is not a physical award as such but something more intangible. Indeed, possibly the ultimate accolade is acknowledged when fellow musicians pay homage to you, when they *remember you* in their own unique way. This certainly is the case with the Ramones both at the *bargain bucket* end of the music spectrum and with some more famed groups with a plethora of performers writing about those lads from Forest Hills. For example, according to Uli Hesse's outstanding piece of research in 2020, there were 444 songs by artists that mentioned or referred to the Ramones in one way or another. The list he composed he states "started innocently enough in the summer of 2011" when he was commuting to work. "One morning", the Ramones fan remembers, "I noticed that my journey had begun and ended with a song from my iPod that namechecked the Ramones. One of those songs will have been familiar to a lot of people ("Ask Her For Adderall" by *The Hold Steady*), the other was fiendishly obscure ("Too Much Jazz" by *The Beat Angels*). I wondered how much of a coincidence that was. On the one hand, it all seemed rather unlikely. After all, how many bands devote songs to other bands in the first place? On the other hand, I knew there were a couple of additional recordings on my mobile device that explicitly mentioned the Bruddas, such as "As Long As I Can Listen" by *The Dubrovniks* (from Sydney) and *Sleater-Kinney's* "I Wanna Be Your Joey Ramone... So it wasn't totally outrageous that I had happened to hear two songs that paid homage to the Ramones while in shuffle mode. But how many such songs were there? I racked my brains, asked around, googled a bit and quickly came up with 25. That was so impressive, I felt, that I posted a *Facebook* note about my research. It immediately led to further suggestions from friends of mine and just a few months later I had compiled 100 tunes. At the time, I was in touch with someone who worked for a maverick culture website from England called *Sabotage Times*, now defunct, and they were happy to publish my list. Over the next three years, between early

2012 and March 2015, the collection steadily grew to 400 songs. Anybody who knows the band will realise while this was a good number to end the project on, not least because it was getting increasingly difficult to find additional songs… Still, every once in a while a new song would trickle in. Which is why five years later the list stood at 444." [376]

The catalogue Hesse comprised ranged from using the name *Ramones* in the title such as "Bad Ramones" by *the Graboids* or having key words in the song's heading like "I'm Lobotomised 'Cause Of You" by *the Riptides* or exhibiting significant associations such as "1-2-3-4" by *Jukebox Zeros*. There are also many tunes which mention the New Yorkers' names. Indeed, most of the band members have had refrains written about them. Examples include "Tommy Ramone" by *The Vapids*, "Joey Ramone Is One Of Us" by *Stinking Polecats*, "Johnny & Bo" by *The Dustaphonics*, "I Wanna Cut My Hair Like Marky Ramone" *by The Spazzys* and my personal favourite "I Wanna Be Like Dee Dee Ramone" by *The Parasites* or a cover of the same track by *The Accelerators*. Undoubtedly, the most famed song mentioning the *'fast four'* must be *Motörhead's* "R.A.M.O.N.E.S" which of course, was so loved by the boys from Queens, they performed the ditty themselves. Although I make no attempt to claim that these are the only tracks to mention the band, a list of these 444 tunes, has been published in appendix one at the back of this book.

Rather than produce their own songs to honour the Ramones, some groups have clearly loved the tunes so much that they wanted to recreate their own versions of the famed melodies. In fact, some bands have recorded albums in their entirety with Chicago's based *Screeching Weasel's* superb effort of the first album possibly the best of the bunch. Not only did the band reproduce all 14 tracks from the Ramones' 1976 debut L.P but they also mimicked the famous photo taken all those years ago by Roberta Bayley in Albert's Garden, situated in the Bowery in New York.

Another group to have complimented the lads from Forest Hills with their own take on an album is *The Queers,* a band from North Hampton in New Hampshire who recorded "Rocket To Russia" in 1994. Fascinatingly, their association with The Ramones extends beyond this - *The Queers* opened for The Ramones four times. Similarly, *The Huntingtons,* a punk band from Baltimore in Maryland, is heavily influenced by the New Yorkers and recorded two albums "Rocket To Ramonia" and "File Under The Ramones" in 1996 and 1999 respectively - both compilation albums of classic Ramones tracks. It is interesting to note that *The Huntingtons* have performed with Joey and two of the band have also toured with C.J Ramone.

Their influence in terms has not been constrained to the consigns of the United States either. *Shonen Knife,* the all-female pop-punk band formed in Japan released an album, "Osaka Ramones" with the cover taking its inspiration from the artwork from "Road To Ruin". Some of the tracks include "We Want The Airways", "Scattergun", "Sheena Is A Punk Rocker" and "Blitzkrieg Bop". The girls have also performed as a Ramones tribute under the name *Osaka Ramones.* In Norway, a short-lived spin off project from members of the *Yum Yums* and *the Kwyet Kings* called *The Tip Toppers* recorded the whole of "Subterranean Jungle" with artwork of the album cover akin to the famous metro photograph from the 1983 album. The recording was also mastered by record producer and friend of the Ramones, Daniel Rey. [377]

There have been numerous compilation albums over the years with a variety of bands performing. Maybe the most famous being "We're A Happy Family: A Tribute To The Ramones" which was produced by Rob Zombie and overseen by Johnny Ramone with the guitarist advising bands to make the songs their own. Indeed, one band who certainly did that was the *Red Hot Chilli Peppers* with their chilled, slow version of "Havana Affair" although my favourite pick from the album was *Green Day's* twisted "Outsider" with both versions, absolute punk gems. This would not be the Californian's band only association with The Ramones – they would also perform at the Ramones' "Rock and Roll Hall of Fame" induction, blasting through "Teenage Lobotomy", "Rockaway Beach" and "Blitzkrieg Bop". The fact that so many famed artists chose to take part is a measure of the high-esteem The Ramones was held internationally – *Kiss, U2, Rancid, The Pretenders, The Offspring*, Tom Waits, *Marilyn Manson*, Eddie Vedder and Zeke and *Metallica* were just some of the entertainers who performed on the record. Many of the songs were also released by the musicians in their own right and *Metallica* not only performed "53rd and 3rd" for this album but also recorded "Today Your Love Tomorrow The World", "Commando", "Now I Wanna Sniff Some Glue", "We're A Happy Family" and "Cretin Hop" for the "B" side of their "St. Anger" single as well. Undeniably, if you have never viewed their heavy metal take on the classics, then it is well worth checking out on *Youtube*. A further band who have a Ramones song posted on the social media platform is the *Dickies*. Their version of "Today Your Love Tomorrow The World" has the trademark helium fuelled vocals by Leonard Graves Phillips whilst guitarist Stan Lee citing the *'fast four'* as a "huge influence." (378)

Other more unusual compilation albums by various artists include "The Rockabilly Tribute To Ramones" and "Brats On The Beat" featuring '*kiddified*' - covers of classic Ramones songs. Again although there is no claim that this is a definitive list, a catalogue of Ramones cover records can be seen in appendix two and three which shows full albums and compilations.

Of course, it is not just those bands who cut Ramones' records who should be mentioned. The style of so many bands have The Ramones stamp all over them. Is there really a better way to pay reverence to another than try to emulate them with your own music? In the late '70s, for instance, Brian James of The Damned talked about the first Ramones album stating that 'we played it to death. We'd been listening to "Help!" and wondered what it would sound like Ramones-style. That's how our version of "Help!" became the B-side of "New Rose". We thought it would be a nice finger up to The Beatles.' Similarly, Pete Shelley of the Buzzcocks admitted "as soon as we heard the album, we ordered two copies on import, and soon we were doing our own version of "Judy Is A Punk". Listening to the Manchester outfit's debut L.P, "Music In A Different Kitchen" is trademark Ramones and Penetration singer, Pauline Murray agrees commenting that "it was the blueprint for punk: all barre chords, no solos, and no tracks over three minutes. The songs were fast, the drums were rattly, the bass plugged away on the root note, and the buzzsaw guitar was the sort that Buzzcocks and early Penetration would use." (379) John O'Neill, rhythm guitarist of the Northern Irish band, The Undertones points out that "we were huge Ramones fans. You can always hear that in the tunes, and some of the words too." (380) Just take a listen to their self-titled debut album and the likes of "Here Comes

The Summer", "I Know A Girl" or "Get Over You" to get a feel for the New Yorkers' influence. Likewise, if you love the Ramones, then you will have a soft spot for The Lurkers, the West London based band who were notable for being the first ever group on the Beggars Banquet Record label. Their debut studio album "Fulham Fallout" oozes Ramones with tracks such as "I Don't Need To Tell Her", "Go, Go, Go", "Ain't Got A Clue" and "Shadow" so reminiscent of the boys from the Bowery that they could have been lifted from "Leave Home". Arturo Bassick, long-serving member of the group declares that "the British punk scene would never have existed without the New York scene. The Ramones were the most important of all in starting it." [381] In terms of British bands, undoubtedly the most *Ramoney* I have witnessed or heard is *Erazerhead*. Heralding from the East End of London and dubbed as the "Cockney Ramones", the boys were famed for their live sets, "1, 2, 3, 4s" and original tunes that were continuation of Ramones themes and delivered with a confident swagger and flair. The underrated band produced some absolute masterpieces such as "Do The Geek", "Shellshock", "The KGB" but the pick of the bunch was probably "Next Stop (Germany)" which sounded like it was penned by Dee Dee himself.

Of course, it is not just in Britain where bands have wanted to sound or indeed look like The Ramones - their influence has been global. Nor has it been confined to bands from the late 1970s or early 1980s, there are so many contemporary groups who have clearly been inspired by the punk icons. It would be an impossibility to cite all the groups they have shaped – their impact has been too large but just taking Argentina as just one other exemplar, it becomes clear how immense their legacy is. Groups such as *2 minutos* and *Baggales* have those buzzsaw driving guitars and catchy hooks whilst check out *Sinfexis* and *Expulsados* who not only have a sound that is reminiscent of The Ramones but have undoubtedly attempted to look like "Da Brudders" too. All over the world, the message is clear - *we will remember you.*

Erazerhead

Whether The Ramones invented punk or not is up for debate. But what is clear, according to Scott McLaughlan is that the group "burst onto the scene and revolutionized rock and roll. Their short, punchy songs slammed the audience with relentless downstrokes, rapid-fire drums, and thumping bass lines. Combined with Joey's stirring vocals, The Ramones represented something entirely new. Clad in their iconic black leather jackets, ripped jeans, and battered sneakers, Johnny, Tommy, Joey, and Dee Dee changed the course of rock and roll history. The deadpan simplicity and upfront vocals of The Ramones spawned an entire genre. The iconic chant of Blitzkrieg Bop, "Hey, Ho! Let's Go!" signalled that The Ramones were a gang that anyone could join." [382] And join they did – ***The Cretin Family.***

All The Stuff And More: Volume 2

Appendix 1

https://www.shootfarken.com.au/444-songs-that-mention-ramones/ - Shoot Farken - (Uli Hesse) - 15/12/20

444 songs which mention the Ramones

001. "Adios Amigos" – Special Duties
002. "Adios Ramones" – The Miscounts
003. "Aí É Que Foi Tri" – Rotentix
004. "Alice Clair" – Pelebrói Não Sei?
005. "All Good Cretins" – Predator
006. "All I Want For Christmas" – The Malakas
007. "All My Favorite Ramones are Dead" – Jeff Dahl
008. "Alter" – Afro Kolektyw
009. "American Child" – The Stone Coyotes
010. "Apathisch Warten" – The Wohlstandskinder
011. "Around With You" – The Chromosomes
012. "Ask Her For Adderall" – The Hold Steady
013. "As Long As I Can Listen (to the Ramones)" – The Dubrovniks
014. "A Tribute" – Torment
015. "Audacity of Huge" – Simian Mobile Disco
016. "Audiobiographie" – Ferris MC

017. "Baby I Love You (But I Need Somebody to Talk to About the Ramones)" – The Transgressions

018. "Back In The Days" – Union Jack

019. "Bad Ramones" – The Graboids

020. "Ballad Of Joey Ramone" – Abortion Clinic

021. "Bárbara" – Bikini Hunters

022. "Bis Ans Ende Meiner Tage" – Mittendurch

023. "Bleed Betty Bleed" – 3D In Your Face

024. "Boonaraaa Girl" – The Reekys

025. "Booze-Up With Dee Dee Ramone" – Riccobellis

026. "Bortom Månen Och Mars" – Perssons Pack

027. "Boys In The Band" – Jinkx Monsoon

028. "Brad Boys" – Tronic

029. "BRB" – Dumbfoundead feat. Andrew Garcia

030. "B-Side Baby" – Adam Ant

031. "Buddies" – The Hard-Ons

032. "Buddy Holly Was The First Ramone" – Ultimate Power Duo

033. "Bye Bye Joey" – Airbags

034. Camisa do Ramones – Frost Rocks

035. "Can't Stop The Boy" – Blast Furnace

036. "Champion The Underdog" – Eureka Machines

037. "Charissa" – AM Taxi

038. "Chcę Być Taki Jak Ramones" – On Yer Bike

039. "Chinese Rocks" – The Heartbreakers

040. "Chiodo" – Gemello

041. "Cielo Estrellado" – Quebraditos

042. "Circles" – Fifteen

043. "Clockwork Ramone" – Hamburg Ramönes

044. "Clone A Ramone" – The Liabilities

045. "Cogido Por Los Güevos" – Reincidentes
046. "Cold Win" – Ghostpoet
047. "Country Song (NOFX Should Listen More Ramones)" – Gramofocas
048. "Dancing With Joey Ramone" – Amy Rigby
049. "D-A-M-E Darcy" – Rat Fink
050. "Dazont Ebet" – Tri Bleiz Die
051. "DD Don't Like Ska" – Voodoo Glow Skulls
052. "Dead Love" – Project Wyze
053. "D.E.A.D.R.A.M.O.N.E.S." – Modern Life Is War
054. "Debbie Loves Joey" – Helen Love
055. "Dee Dee" – Terrorgruppe
056. "Dee 9ee And Joey" – The Transistors
057. "Dee Dee In the Bathroom" – Idaho Rainys
058. "Dee Dee Ramone" – Henry Fiat's Open Sore
059. "Dee Dee's Dead" – Ramonez 77
060. "Dee Dee Taught Me How to Count" – Kepi Ghoulie
061. "Dee Dee Took The Subway" – The Badtown Boys
062. "Dee Dee Was A Murder Junkie" – Grayline
063. "Denim Guinness Boys" – Fat Tony & Tom Cruz
064. "Depressing Ramones" – Deadly Weapons
065. "Die Abrechnung" – StaatsPunkrott
066. "Disneyland" – Harlem
067. "Dive Down" – Schäffer The Darklord
068. "Do Da Snake" – Bad Karma Beckons
069. "Don't Let The Night Get You Down" – The Zatopeks
070. "Downtown Rockers" – Tom Tom Club
071. "Do Your Parents Know You're A Ramone?" – Acid Reflux
072. "Droppin' Like Flies" – The Real McKenzies
073. "Drowning" – Debeli Precjednik

074. "Ella Ya No Escucha Los Ramones" – Bam Bam Estás Muerto

075. "Elvis Lives And Carterbreakamerica" – Carter The Unstoppable Sex Machine

076. "End Of The Ramones" – Mr. T Experience

077. "En Voksen Mand I Ramones T-Shirt" – Peter H. Olesen

078. "Estilo" – Los Punsetes

079. "Even Babies Like The Ramones" – DeRita Sisters

080. "Everybody Is A Ramone" – Romeos

081. "Everybody Loves You (When You're Dead)" – Gallows

082. "Everything In Moderation (Especially Moderation)" – NOFX

083. "Everything You Hate" – Delay

084. "Everything You Took" – Lee Bains III & The Glory Fires

085. "Fall for Me" – Teenage Bottlerocket

086. "Festa Punk" – Os Replicantes

087. "Fiesta Ramone" – F.A.N.T.A.

088. "15 in '77" – Antidote

089. "For The Ramones" – Lester & The Landslide Ladies

090. "Frühstücksclub der Toten Dichter" – Prinz Pi

091. "Galaxy Ramone" – Redclouds

092. "Get It Ya Self" – Curren$y

093. "Getting Evil" – Damnation

094. "Gibi, Ramones e Motörhead" – Devotos De Nossa Senhora Aparecida

095. "Girl About Town" – Tullycraft

096. "God Bless The Ramones" – Patrick McGoran

097. "Gone Forever" – The Raveonettes

098. "Goodbye Joey" – The McRackins

099. "Goodbye Joey" – Sator

100. "Good Bye Ramones" – The Fialky

101. "Granola-Head" – The Queers

102. "Green Like The G Train, Green Like Sea Foam" – Aaron West And The Roaring Twenties
103. "Gutter Talk" – Backstreet Girls
104. "Hampton Beach" – The Riverdales
105. "Hangin' Out With The Ramones" – Highschool Dropouts
106. "Hari Karaoke" – Beach Bastards
107. "Hate The Disco" – The Driven
108. "Have You Seen Dee Dee Ramone" – Jesus H. Presley
109. "Hawaii Ramones" – The Sentiments
110. "He Looked A Lot Like Dee Dee Ramone" – Mouthguard
111. "Homenaje A Los Ramones" – Los Petersellers
112. "(I Am Your Ramone) Be My Ramona" – Sonic Dolls
113. "I Blame His Brother" – Lugless Booth
114. "I Can't Stop Listening To The Ramones" – The Quintessentials
115. "Ich Will Nicht So Enden Wie Die Ganzen Ramones" – Supernichts
116. "I Don't Live Well" – The Murderburgers
117. "I Don't Wanna Get Thin" – Blubberry Hellbellies
118. "I Don't Wanna Look Like No Ramone" – Latex Novelties
119. "I Feel Better When I Listen To The Ramones" – Flanders 72
120. "I Fell In Love With An Alien Girl" – The Crumbs
121. "If Not For The Ramones" – Inciting Riots
122. "I Just Wanna Be a Ramone" – Car Bomb Driver
123. "I Know a Girl Who Looks Like Joey Ramone" – Justin Owens
124. "I Like The Ramones" – The Mansfields
125. "I Love Her, And She Loves The Ramones" – The Havenots
126. "I Love Punk Rock" – The Fades
127. "I Love The Girl Who Love The Ramones" – The Spikeweed
128. "I'm A Ramone" – Punkroiber

129. "I'm Gonna Miss The Ramones" – The Bittersweets
130. "I'm Lobotomized 'Cause Of You" – The Riptides
131. "I'm Not A Kid Anymore" – Sloan
132. "I'm Not Ready To Love You Like I Do" – Sioen
133. "I Miss the Ramones" – Kung Fu Monkeys
134. "I Miss the Ramones" – Mommy Sez No
135. "Incredibly Cliched" – Rude Kids
136. "I Never Saw the Ramones" – The Young Rochelles
137. "Infatuated" – Jesus Honcho
138. "Inno No Senomar" – Me Wokkivihannekset
139. "Intro" – Kid Rock
140. "It's Up to You" – Chalk Farm
141. "I Wanna Be A Ramone" – The Daryls
142. "I Wanna Be A Ramone" – The Dinks
143. "I Wanna Be A Ramone" – Go Go Rays
144. "I Wanna Be A Ramone" – The Migraines
145. "I Wanna Be Like Dee Dee Ramone" – The Parasites
146. "I Wanna Be Your Joey Ramone" – Sleater-Kinney
147. "I Wanna Cut My Hair Like Marky Ramone" – The Spazzys
148. "I Wanna Go To A Ramones Show" – Durban Poison
149. "I Wanna See The Ramones" – The Dirty Scums
150. "(I Wanna Smoke A Bone With) Dee Dee Ramone" – Bad Karma
151. "I Was A High School Psychopath" – Screeching Weasel
152. "I Wish I Was A Ramone" – Candystore
153. "Jaqueta do Ramones" – Sukinho di 10
154. "Jaqueta Preta" – Fliperama
155. "Jeannie Hates The Ramones" – The Huntingtons
156. "Jeffrey's Gone" – Sixty-Nine Vette
157. "Joey" – Raimundos

158. "Joey And Dee Dee" – Kevin K
159. "Joey Had to Go" – The Hanson Brothers
160. "Joey Ja Dee Dee" – Häiriköt
161. "Joey, Johnny, Dee Dee & Marky (On Her Arm)" – The Hallingtons
162. "Joey Ramone" – 70-luvun Vihannekset
163. "Joey Ramone" – James Marshall Black
164. "Joey Ramone" – The Cascarinos
165. "Joey Ramone" – D.D.V.
166. "Joey Ramone" – Fattijons
167. "Joey Ramone" – Filibusters
168. "Joey Ramone" – Hände Weg Johnny!
169. "Joey Ramone" – Haggis
170. "Joey Ramone" – LifeSavers
171. "Joey Ramone" – The Voodoo Dollies
172. "Joey Ramone" – Wisdom In Chains
173. "Joey Ramone Boulevard" – Ricky-Bobby 1313
174. "Joey Ramone…" – Cornshafter
175. "Joey Ramone Is Dead" – Swastika Girls
176. "Joey Ramone Is One Of Us" – Stinking Polecats
177. "Joey Ramone's Dead" – Andersen Silva
178. "Joey Ramone" – Mason Zgoda
179. "Joey Ramone Street" – Raygun Cowboys
180. "Joey Ramone (Tributo)" – UHF
181. "Joey Ramone Way!" – Ghouls Against Boys
182. "Joey Ramone Won't Leave Me Alone" – Skintight Jaguars
183. "Joey's Outside" – Phoenix Thunderstone
184. "Joey's Radio" – Brant Bjork & The Operators
185. "Joey's Song" – Kitty Kowalski & The Manges
186. "Joey Went Home (Where the Good Boys Go)" – Psy-9

187. "Johnny & Bo" – The Dustaphonics
188. "Johnny And Dee Dee" – The Eastern Dark
189. "Johnny Doesn't Like The Ramones" – The Frampton Brothers
190. "Johnny Joey Dee Dee" – Fever Hut
191. "Johnny Ramone" – The Bobs
192. "Johnny Ramone" – Der Nino aus Wien
193. "Johnny Ramone" – Latte+
194. "Johnny Ramone" – Like Some Cat From Japan
195. "Johnny Ramone" – Los Mentas
196. "Johnny Ramone" – Santiago Delgado Y Los Runaway Lovers
197. "Johnny Ramone" – Scott Malyszka
198. "Johnny Ramone Syndrome" – The Latex Lovers!
199. "Johnny Ramone Was In A Fucken Good Band But He Was A Cunt" – Frenzal Rhomb
200. "Johnny Rides Shotgun" – Drivin' 'N' Cryin'
201. "Juerga" – Kaotika
202. "Just For Tonight" – Tim Armstrong
203. "Just Like Joey Ramone" – Groove End Road
204. "Just Like Johnny Ramone" – David Young & The Restless
205. "Kebab Spider" – Sleaford Mods
206. "Kill The Ramones" – Boris The Sprinkler
207. "Kött, Sås Och Potatis" – Massgrav
208. "La Fiesta Empezó" – Doble Fuerza
209. "La Machina Del Ziu Toni" – Davide Van De Sfroos
210. "Last Ramone" – Brutal Dildos
211. "Les Ramones & Les Heptones" – Steff Tej & Éjectés
212. "L'Etat C'est Moi" – Bonaparte
213. "Let's Rock and Roll" – The Yum Yums
214. "Liam Loves The Ramones" – Bus Stop Madonnas

215. "Lift Up Your Hood" – DMZ
216. "Light It Off (A Tribute to the Ramones)" – Osmium
217. "Like A Ramone" – High-School Motherfuckers
218. "Listening to the Ramones" – Dan Cortinovis
219. "Live And Die Rock And Roll" – Ray Wylie Hubbard
220. "Long Blonde" – The Long Blondes
221. "Long Time, No See" – Massy Ferguson
222. "Los Ramones" – Pistones
223. "Loud And Fast" – Supercharger
224. "Love And The Ramones" – The Hot Rod Honeys
225. "Lucia" – Zóna A
226. "Luxor Y Mohawk" – Las Ultrasonicas
227. "Made in NYC" – The Casualties
228. "Mama's Boy" – The Blue Van
229. "Marching Band" – Wiretree
230. "Marta No Es Una Punk" – Airbag
231. "Marzipan" – Monsters Of Liedermaching
232. "Matkalaulu" – Himanes
233. "Max's Kansas City" – Wayne County & The Electric Chairs
234. "Me And Stupid" – Rheostatics
235. "Medusa" – Dirty Heads
236. "Mere Pseud Mag Ed" – The Fall
237. "Miami Beach" – Lax'n'Busto
238. "M.I.L.F." – Judith Holofernes
239. "Milion Fałszywych Ramones" – Collina
240. "Mi Novia Punk" – Plagio
241. "Mi Ramone Favorito" – Vértigos
242. "Misery On A Mainline" – Clit 45
243. "Miss Argentina" – Iggy Pop
244. "Miss Intoxic Llega A La Disco" – Pánico

245. "M.O." – Mayer Hawthorne
246. "Morris, You Need a Leather Jacket" – Doped Dog
247. "Mother City" – Ginger
248. "My Baby's Got a Crush On Joey Ramone" – Rat Fink
249. "My Baby Stole My Ramones LPs" – Raggity Anne
250. "My Girlfriend Hates The Ramones" – The Creeps
251. "My Girlfriend Looks Like Joey Ramone" – Real Ramoneroonies
252. "My Grandpa Is Joey Ramone" – The Swoons
253. "My Little Dark" – Cercana Eternidad
254. "My Only Friend Is Dee Dee Ramone – The Manges
255. "My Other Guitar Is A Mosrite" – The Atoms
256. "My Punk Girl" – Pale Sunday
257. "Nancy Ramone" – Nancys Rubias
258. "Never Forget" – Goin' Places
259. "New York City" – Flashlight Brown
260. "New York Is Rockin'" – Curtis Stigers
261. "1975 (Joey Ramone)" – The Raving Knaves
262. "1983" – Janez Detd.
263. "1994" – After The Fall
264. "Noam Chomsky Versus The Ramones" – Milky Wimpshake
265. "No Disparó" – Anti-Sociales
266. "No Loot, No Booze, No Fun" – The Tossers
267. "No More Ramones" – Apocalypse Babys
268. "No Tienes Derecho A Llevar Una Camiseta De Ramones" – Trance
269. "Not Ugly Enough To Be A Ramone" – The Young Hasselhoffs
270. "Now I Wanna Listen To The Ramones" – Daggerplay
271. "NYLA" – The Weekend
272. "Oda The Ramones" – The Damrockers

273. "Ode To Ramones" – The Commandos
274. "Ode To The Ramones" – De Heideroosjes
275. "Oh Boy!" – The Dickies
276. "100 Discim" – HaShakranim
277. "1-2-3-4" – Jukebox Zeros
278. "Our Ramones" – The 99ers
279. "Pam Ain't No Punk Rocker" – The Overprivileged
280. "Pazza Dei Ramones" – I Monelli
281. "Pink Floyd Suck" – Belly-Button
282. "Plus One" – Coyote Shivers
283. "Pobre Corazón" – Embajada Boliviana
284. "Psychophant" – Krayolas
285. "Presentat-Arm" – Linea77
286. "Punk A Chien" – Les Fatals Picards
287. "Punk Is Dead, Deal With It" – Dick Fist
288. "Punk Pin Up" – Teasing Lulu
289. "Punkpolitie" – Kikkerspuug
290. "Punk Rock Christmas" – The Ravers
291. "Punk Rock Club RIP" – The Unlovables
292. "Punkrockgirl" – Die Ärzte
293. "Punk Rock Is Her Life" – Pyogenesis
294. "Punk Rock Janitor" – Tina Peel
295. "Punk Rock Uniform" – Karate High School
296. "Queen And Tequila" – The Mahones
297. "Qué hacer" – La Amenaza Amarilla
298. "Quero Meu Ingresso Pro Show Do Ramones" – Gritando HC
299. "Quiero Ser Un Ramones" – Dale Vuelta
300. "Ramona" – Las Ultrasónicas
301. "Ramone Control" – Gigantor
302. "R.A.M.O.N.E.S." – Motörhead

303. "Ramones" – Greenland Whalefishers
304. "Ramones" – Horsehead
305. "Ramones" – Hott Beat
306. "Ramones" – Japanische Kampfhörspiele
307. "Ramones" – Love A
308. "Ramones" – Roger Miret & The Disasters
309. "Ramones" – Mögel
310. "Ramones" – Odd Movers
311. "Ramones" – Pöbel & Gesocks
312. "Ramones Fever" – Paalmer
313. "Ramones For Yu" – Cómplices
314. "Ramones Girl" – Shock Treatment
315. "Ramones (Have Been Banished From Heaven)" – Romero's Nation
316. "Ramones Institutionalized Party" – Deadbeat Sinatra
317. "Ramones Ja Stravinsky" – Kollaa Kestää
318. "Ramonesland" – Adam Franklin
319. "Ramones Lovin' Girl" – Carter Peace Mission
320. "Ramones Majica" – Madresi
321. "Ramones Never Die" – Mudo
322. "Ramones No Bar Do Ico" – Reatores
323. "Ramones On My Stereo" – Tough
324. "Ramones Radio" – The Brewers
325. "Ramones Rock'n'Roll Radio, Let's Go" – Warrior Kids
326. "Ramones T-Shirt" – The Emersons
327. "Ramones T-Shirt" – The Hexstalls
328. "Ramones (We Don't Forget)" – Bulbulators
329. "Ramones Zombie Massacre" – The Renfields
330. "Readymade" – Red Hot Chili Peppers
331. "Remember The Ramones" – The Fleshtones

332. "Ripped Jeans" – Sneeze
333. "Rock'n'Roll Bullshit" – Government Issue
334. "Rock'n'Roll Can Rescue The World" – Electric Eel Shock
335. "Rock'n'Roller Girl" – Mooney Suzuki
336. "Rock'n'Roll Nerd" – Tim Minchin
337. "Rock'n'Roll Nursing Home" – Iron Prostate
338. "Rock Science" – Imperial State Electric
339. "Roxy" – Triumvirat
340. "Running Out Of Ramones" – Grover Kent
341. "Sandy" – The Maxies
342. "Santi Di Periferia" – Litfiba
343. "Schafter" – Pager Feat. Belmondo
344. "Schönen Gruß, Auf Wiedersehen" – Die Toten Hosen
345. "Seidl Doesn't Have All Ramones Albums" – Carbona
346. "741 Mph" – Pretentious Flamedogs
347. "Sexo, Algemas E Cinta-Liga" – Tequila Baby
348. "She's A Poser" – Teen Idols
349. "She's My Bitch" – The Supersuckers
350. "She's Ugly But She Likes The Ramones" – The Come Ons
351. "Shonen Knife" – Shonen Knife
352. "Shopping Revolution Reggae" – Visací Zámek
353. "Sin Titulo 5" – 3pecados
354. "Skateboard" – Beatnik Termites
355. "Sky Bleeds Red" – DieMonsterDie
356. "Sol Da Caparica" – Peste & Sida
357. "Son Of A Beach" – Venerea
358. "Sound Man" – Drapht
359. "Soundtrack Of My Life" – Born Cool
360. "Soy Más Ramone Que Tú!" – Maledukados
361. "Soy Un Ramone" – Fast Food

362. "Spacca I Dischi Dei Ramones" – I Vigliacchi
363. "Stars In Their Eyes" – Briskeby
364. "Supertramps And Superstars" – Simple Kid
365. "Sweet Disaster" – Dreamers
366. "Take Me To Manhattan" – The Disappeared
367. "Take That Tape" – Wicked
368. "Tarde De Sol" – Expulsados
369. "TCP" – The Boys
370. "Teenage Ramone" – Los Aarones
371. "Teenage Ramone" – The Monster Ones
372. "Teeth Only For You" – Say Hi
373. "Teresa" – All
374. "Te Vi (Dos)" – Shaila
375. "Thank You For The Ramones" – The 50 Kaitenz
376. "The Ballad Of Joey Ramone" – Spastic Panthers
377. "The Best Night Of Your Life" – Hello Saferide
378. "The Biggest Prick" – The Ashtones
379. "The CCC Took Joey Away" – The Dirtshakes
380. "The Chanukah Song, Part III" – Adam Sandler
381. "The Colour Of My Mind" – Red Fetish
382. "(The Day All The Girls In Philadephia Dressed Like) Ramones" – Howling Fantods
383. "The Day The Last Ramone Died" – The Coal Porters
384. "The Domino Effect" – The Blizzards
385. "The Ghost of Joey Ramone" – The Downrights
386. "The Girl With The Joey Ramone Tattoo" – The Surfin' Lungs
387. "The Mess" – Newtown Neurotics
388. "The Night That Joey Died" – wax.on wax.off
389. "The Other Improv" – Nirvana
390. "The Radio Is Trying To Kill Rock'n'Roll" – Colytons

391. "The Ramones" – Pinky Nackybal
392. "The Ramones And George Jones" – Heidi Howe
393. "The Ramones Are Dead" – The Playing Favorites
394. "The Ramones Saved My Life!" – La Massoneria Ramonica
395. "There's Only One Kind Of Rock'n'Roll" – 2*Sweet
396. "The Return of Jackie and Judy" – The Ramones
397. "The Sex Pistols & The Ramones (A Love Story)" – Gary Sunshine
398. "The Song Ramones The Same" – Bodyjar
399. "The Straight Mile" – Barton Carrol
400. "The Things That Dreams Are Made Of" – The Human League
401. "The Wrong Ramone" – The Monsignors
402. "Thin Ice (Don't You Ever Coz It Wouldn't Be Clever)" – The Crybabys
403. "This Is The First Night" – Anti-Flag
404. "This One's For Rock'n'Roll" – Hanoi Rocks
405. "Tommy Ramone" – The Vapids
406. "Tomorrow Tonight" – Jesse Malin
407. "Too Much Jazz" – The Beat Angels
408. "To The Ramones" – Dustin's Bar Mitzvah
409. "T-Shirt Van Metallica" – Fleddy Melculy
410. "29 x The Pain" – The Wildhearts
411. "Tyson Rock" – Punkreas
412. "Última Generación" – Porretas
413. "Uno Mas" – Los Delinquentes
414. "Vengan Juntos" – Tren Loco
415. "Vinyl Records" – Todd Snider
416. "Wake Up" – Abrasive Wheels
417. "Walk Away" – Barlow

418. "Weak Ass Shit" – R'N'R
419. "We All Wanted To Be Rocked By The Ramones" – Anna & The Psychomen
420. "We Are Rock'n'Roll" – The Hex Bombs
421. "We'll Miss You Joey Ramone" – TheGuillaTeens
422. "We Want Black Plastic Back" – Great Midori
423. "What If Punk Never Happened" – The King Blues
424. "What Would Joey Ramone do?" – The Creeping Ivies
425. "When the Flintstones (Met the Ramones)" – The Magic Sponge
426. "Where'd The Time Go?" – Michael Gaither
427. "White Trash" – Junior Senior
428. "Wutang Sucks" – The Bones
429. "Wir Hassen Die Ramones" – Lokalmatadore
430. "Wrongful Suspicion" – Rancid
431. "Wytrzepany Ze Styropianu" – Pidżama Porno
432. "Xerox Your Genitals, Not The Ramones" – The Ergs!
433. "Yes, I Miss the Ramones" – Johann Sebastian Punk
434. "Y No Cambiamos Ni Un Solo Minuto" – Benito Kamelas
435. "Yo Solo Quiero Ser Un Ramone" – Los Quebraditos
436. "You Are My Ramones" – New Pants
437. "You Can't Kill Joey Ramone" – Sloppy Seconds
438. "You Don't Like Rock'n'Roll" – Hunx And His Punx
439. "You Have Boarded" – Rogue Wave
440. "You'll Have Time" – William Shatner
441. "Your R.A.M.O.N.E.S. Cover Band Sucks" – Bad Drugs
442. "You Took My Life" – Triggerface
443. "Yo Queria a Los Ramones" – Miguel Costas
444. "Y Va A Quedar La Cagá" – Los Mox!

Appendix 2: Full Tribute Albums

1992   Ramones: Screeching Weasel
1994   Leave Home: The Vindictives
1994   Rocket To Russia: The Queers
1996   End Of The Century: Boris the Sprinkler
1997   It's Alive: Parasites
1997   Pleasant Dreams: Beatnik Termites
1998   Road to Ruin: The Mr. T Experience
1998   Too Tough to Die: Jon Cougar Concentration Camp
2000   Too Tough to Die: The McRackins
2001   Ramones Maniacs: Various
2004   Subterranean Jungle: Tip Toppers
2011   Halfway to Sanity: Kobanes
2019   Animal Boy: The New Rochelles
2021   Mondo Bizarro: K7s
2022   Leave Home: The Canceled Sitcoms

Appendix 3: Compilation / Other Albums

1987   Ramones (EP): Operation Ivy
1991   Gabba Gabba Hey: A Tribute to the Ramones: Various
1996   Rocket to Ramonia: The Huntingtons
1998   Blitzkrieg Over You: Various
1999   File Under Ramones: The Huntingtons
2001   Glue Sniffin' Shocker: Reload
2002   Strength to Endure: A Tribute to Ramones & Motörhead:
Riotgun. & Bullet Treatment
2002   The Song Ramones The Same: Various
2002   Ramones Forever: An International Tribute: Various

2003   We're a Happy Family: A Tribute to Ramones: Various

2004   Sniffin' Glue: A Las Vegas Tribute to the Ramones: Various

2005   Guitar Tribute to the Ramones: Various

2005   The Rockabilly Tribute to Ramones: Various

2005   Pan for Punks...A Steelpan Tribute to the Ramones: Tracy Thornton

2006   Brats on the Beat: Ramones for Kids: Various

2007   Rockabye Baby! Lullaby Renditions of the Ramones: Various

2008   Bossa n' Ramones: Various

2008   Rocket from Poland: Dumbs

2011   Osaka Ramones: Shonen Knife

2018   Songs in the Key of Joey: Aaron Stingray and the Brooklyn Apostles

Appendix 4: Details of burial sites

- Jeffrey Ross Hyman (aka Joey Ramone): New Mount Zion Cemetery, Lyndhouse, Bergen County, New Jersey, USA
- Douglas Glenn Colvin (aka Dee Dee Ramone): Hollywood Forever Cemetary – The Garden of Legends, Los Angeles, California, USA
- John William Cummings (aka Johnny Ramone): Hollywood Forever Cemetary – The Garden of Legends, Los Angeles, California, USA
- Tamás Erdélyi (aka Tommy Ramone): New Montefiore Cemetary, West Babylon, Suffolk County, New York, USA

Swallow My Pride - Why Is It Always This Way?

Post Script

The turn of the century saw the sad and untimely deaths of Joey and Johnny Ramone through cancer. In life, they co-founded arguably the most influential punk outfit the world has ever seen but had also sparred and fallen out over the affections of the same woman - Linda Danielle. This animosity led to the band members not speaking for years and since their deaths there has been no restoration in relations or reconciliation between the estranged families. Indeed, if anything the acrimony between Mickey Leigh (birth name Mitchel Hyman) and Linda Cummings, the representatives of the estates of Joey [383] and Johnny respectively, has deteriorated over the course of time. For example, after Linda had changed her surname to Ramone in 2014, five years later, the two settled a long-standing dispute over the use of that 'Ramone' title. It was alleged that Johnny's wife had illicitly used the designation on social media with an intention to also rename her Los Angeles home 'Ramone Ranch'. The arbitration resulted in Linda Cummings-Ramone being barred from renaming her home 'Ramone Ranch', though she was allowed to name it 'Johnny Ramone Ranch' or 'Linda Ramone Ranch' instead. Leigh was also barred from obstructing Linda's attempts to obtain trademarks for the names Johnny Ramone and Linda Ramone.

Arbitrator Bob Donnelly, who oversaw several of the disputes between Cummings-Ramone and Hyman, wrote in May 2019 in court papers that "it was unclear how much the band's name and music is worth today" going on to add that "their constant battles led to the 'tepid growth' of The Ramones brand. The lawyer stated that "Mickey Hyman and Linda Cummings-Ramone have been entrusted with the exceedingly important mission of preserving the legacy of The Ramones for its existing followers, and to grow this iconic brand to a new world-wide group of music fans. The only way those goals can be accomplished, in my estimation, is for there to be some radical changes made by Mickey, Linda, and their representatives." [384]

This advice was clearly not heeded. In January 2024, Johnny's widow, filed a lawsuit claiming that Leigh "covertly developed an unapproved and unauthorized Ramones-based biopic" based on his "one-sided recitation of the history of the Ramones" in relation to an upcoming film, starring Pete Davidson entitled "*I Slept With Joey Ramone*". Her objective was to receive in excess of $1 million in damages and for movie director, David Frey to be removed from his job. Specifically, according to her lawyers "Ms. Ramone objects to defendants' attempt to create a Ramones film without her involvement — not to be obstinate, but rather based on defendants' disregard for [Ramones] assets and their conduct and treatment of Ms. Ramone and her late husband" and "to permit defendants alone to tell the authoritative story of The Ramones would be an injustice to the band and its legacy." [385] In addition, she asserts that Joey's younger brother is cutting her out of the iconic punk band's merchandising deals and threatening to leak "compromising private footage" the singer once had of her, according to the lawsuit. Furthermore, Johnny's wife contends that Mickey Leigh just wants to push her out of Ramones Productions Inc., the company in charge of the band's work. In legal documents, her attorney's claim that "their main objective is to torment Ms. Ramone until she agrees to sell her interests in RPI. Regrettably, (they) appear willing to allow the band's legacy to decay, in order to benefit their own self-interest." The lawsuit goes on to add that instead of guarding the band's brand and helping to grow it by bringing in new fans, Hyman and David Frey have sabotaged business deals and "effectively shut down" Ramones Productions Inc. Lastly, the widow, who claims to have spent over $500,000 fighting the pair, maintains that the defendants "refuse to engage with The Ramones' record label, its social media creative agency, its merchandising partners, or its long-term business managers" while they "regularly create internecine disputes and unnecessary work that drains the company of funds." [386]

Mickey Leigh has since counter-sued, calling Linda's attempts to shut down a Netflix biopic "baseless and flimsy" rejecting her assertions, whilst also maintaining that she had already signed off on a biopic film several years ago. Lawyers for Joey's brother have stated that

"Ms. Cummings-Ramone's main purpose is to embarrass, harass, and destroy the integrity of Mr. Hyman, create an utterly false narrative about him, rewrite her role in the history of The Ramones, and win a popularity contest in which, in her mind, she takes over … the legacy of a band of which she never was a member and had nothing to do with creatively.

"She is driven by an alternate agenda, including her own fame and vanity, as well as a self-serving desire to obstruct projects and control RPI for reasons which conflict with her fiduciary duties and cause her to avoid any modicum of cooperation with Mr. Hyman." [387] Attorney Donna Tobin, asserted that "they look forward to being able to present the truth," and that "there is no sex tape and there has never been any threat by Mr. Hyman to 'leak' anything." [388]

Interestingly, Marky Ramone, who of course joined the band after the departure of Tommy Ramone in 1978 has stated that "between her and Mickey, I see Linda as the only one trying to grow The Ramones' legacy and trying to bring the band new opportunities and new fans. On the other hand, my experience with Mickey is that he spends too much time focused on harassing Linda and trying to benefit and bring attention to himself," the drummer wrote in an affidavit filed with Linda's case. [389] Additionally, comments on social media, have stated that C J Ramone has backed Johnny's widow rather than Mickey Leigh and Dave Frey to be in the best interests of working for developing the Ramones legacy. [390]

Raw emotions are usually very tense. Despite the years that have gone by since the deaths of their beloved ones, their sentiments are clearly still fresh, sharp and as one writer pointed out "sometimes to the point of being irrational." [391] Although it may be difficult for us fans to empathise with those who are close to the incidents that incited these emotions, we can only hope that sometime soon, some kind of compromise can take place which will further springboard The Ramones' heritage to existing and forthcoming enthusiasts. Rather than asking the question *why is it always this way* maybe a case of *swallowing pride* will one day come to pass. After all, I am absolutely convinced that the boys from Queens would have ultimately wanted the fullest possible exposure.

References

(1)   https://co-curate.ncl.ac.uk/resources/view/89823/: That Was the Year That Was - 1977 | Co-Curate (ncl.ac.uk)

(2)   Author's note: this probably refers to the nugget "I Don't Wanna Get Involved With You" which was never cut by The Ramones but was released by Dee Dee as a solo project by his band Inter-Celestial Light Commune.

(3)   Please Kill me – the uncensored oral history of punk – (McNeil & McCain) – 1996 – Abacus p265

(4)   The Ramones, Loud and Fast, (David Fricke) - 1999, Warner brothers

(5)   https://www.nytimes.com/2016/05/17/arts/music/tony-barrow-beatles-publicist-who-coined-the-term-fab-four-dies-at-80. html#:~:text=Tony%20Barrow% 2C%20who%20gave%20up, He%20was%2080.

(6)   https://www.roanrecords.co.uk/artists/ramoneS/

(7)   https:///www.thisdayinmusic.com/classic-albums/ramones/

(8)   Commando – (Johnny Ramone) – 2012 - Abrams p54

(9)   https://www.musicmusingsandsuch. com/musicmusingsandsuch/2021/4/10/ feature-beat-on-the-brat-the-ramones-eponymous-debut-at-forty-five

(10)   Commando – (Johnny Ramone) - 2012 - Abrams P. 57

(11)   Leave Home, Remastered album notes – 2001 - P 4

(12)   Rocket To Russia – Remastered album notes - 2001 – P4

(13)   https://.bbc.co.uk/music/reviews/rh28/ ramones, Rocket To Russia Review – (John Doran) – 2011

(14)   Road To Ruin Remastered album notes - 2001, P 4

(15)   Pleasant Dreams Remastered album notes – 2002 - P 4-5

(16)   Subterranean Jungle, Remastered album notes – 2002- P 13

(17)   Too tough to die, Remastered album notes – 2002 - P 4

(18)   Commando – (Johnny Ramone) - 2012 - Abrams P. 125

(19)   Commando – (Johnny Ramone) - 2012 - Abrams P. 90/91

(20)   https://www.grammy.com/news/2024-grammys-special-merit-awards-recipients-lifetime-achievement-award

(21)   I Slept With Joey Ramone – A Punk Rock Family Memoir – (Mickey Leigh with Legs McNeil) – 2009 – Touchstone p216

(22)   https://www.musicmusingsandsuch.com/musicmusingsandsuch/2021/4/10/feature-beat-on-the-brat-the-ramones-eponymous-debut-at-forty-five

(23)   The Encyclopedia of punk – (Cogan) 2008 - Sterling Publishing Co. P. 256

(24)   https://www.rrauction.com/landing/page/282-the-joey-ramone-collection

(25)   Punk. (Colegrave & Sullivan) - 2001 - Cassell & Co. P. 212

(26)   On the Road With The Ramones – (Melnick and Meyer) – 2007 - Music Sales Group – p39

(27)   https://www.allmusic.com/artist/joey-ramone-mm0000173487

(28)   Commando – (Johnny Ramone) – 2012 – Abrams- p40

(29)   Poison Heart – Surviving the Ramones - (Dee Dee Ramone with Veronica Kofman) –- SAF Publishing Ltd p21

(30)   On the Road With The Ramones – (Melnick and Meyer) – 2007 - Music Sales Group – p44

(31)   https://www.rollingstone.com/feature/the-curse-of-the-ramones-165741

(32)   Punk Rock Blitzkrieg Bop: My Life as a Ramone – (Mark Ramone with Rich Herschlag) - 2015 –Touchstone p19/20 and p31

(33)   I Know Better Now: My life before, during and after the Ramones – (Richie Ramone with Peter Aaron) – 2018 – Backbeat Books p 23

(34)   https://archive.blondie.net/clem_burke_iwaselvisramone.shtml

(35)   https://tidal.com/magazine/article/blondie-clem-burke/1-86367

(36)   https://www.protributebands.com/complete-history-of-tribute-bands/

(37)   https://www.saratogamountainamphitheater.com/events/get-the-led-out-tribute-band/

(38)   https://www.protributebands.com/complete-history-of-tribute-bands/

(39)   https://performingartistes.co.uk/artistes/bjornagain

(40)   https://www.protributebands.com/complete-history-of-tribute-bands/

(41)   https://www.worcesternews.co.uk/news/7491765.its-all-in-a-name-for-tribute

(42) https://allsmart.co.uk/tribute-bands/tribute-act-history/

(43) uk/tribute-bands/tribute-act-history/

(44) https://www.glastonbudget.org/band_type/tribute/

(45) https://www.protributebands.com/complete-history-of-tribute-bands/

(46) https://allsmart.co.uk/tribute-bands/tribute-act-history/

(47) https://expmag.com/2020/01/
      the-inevitable-rise-of-the-hologram-rock-concert/

(48) https://www.equinoxpub.com/home/send-clone

(49) https://www.protributebands.com/complete-history-of-tribute-bands/

(50) https://www.repeatfanzine.co.uk/interviews/The%20Shamones

(51) https://allsmart.co.uk/tribute-bands/tribute-act-history/

(52) https://www.musicradar.com/news/guitars/
      bon-jovi-sue-female-tribute-band-202490

(53) https://www.protributebands.com/complete-history-of-tribute-bands/

(54) Author's note – A ghost band is a legacy band that performs under
      the name of a deceased leader

(55) https://daily.jstor.org/how-tribute-bands-celebrate-music-history/

(56) https://www.protributebands.com/complete-history-of-tribute-bands/

(57) https://allsmart.co.uk/tribute-bands/tribute-act-history/

(58) https://www.saratogamountainamphitheater.com/events/
      get-the-led-out-tribute-band/

(59) https://allsmart.co.uk/tribute-bands/tribute-act-history/

(60) On the Road With The Ramones – (Melnick and Meyer) – 2007 -
      Music Sales Group p82 and p84

(61) https://www.cleveland.com/life-and-culture/g66l-
      2019/10/0a190b19ff3130/100-most-important-bands-since-the-
      beatles.html

(62) https://denimdudes.co/
      the-surprising-homoerotiv-roots-of-the-ramones-style/

(63) I Slept With Joey Ramone – A Punk Rock Family Memoir –
      (Mickey Leigh with Legs McNeil) – 2009 – Touchstone p397

(64) *www.faroutmagazine.co.uk – Look back at the Ramones' hilarious first
      ever press release - 25/7/20*

(65) Poison Heart – Surviving the Ramones - (Dee Dee Ramone with
      Veronica Kofman) – 1997 - SAF Publishing Ltd p29

(66) On the Road With The Ramones – (Melnick and Meyer) – 2007 -
      Music Sales Group – p20

(67) Commando – (Johnny Ramone) – 2012 – Abrams- p29-32

(68) Poison Heart – Surviving the Ramones - (Dee Dee Ramone with Veronica Kofman) – 1997 - SAF Publishing Ltd p36-37

(69) I Slept With Joey Ramone – A Punk Rock Family Memoir – (Mickey Leigh with Legs McNeil) – 2009 – Touchstone p67

(70) Commando – (Johnny Ramone) – 2012 - Abrams p40

(71) Poison Heart – Surviving the Ramones - (Dee Dee Ramone with Veronica Kofman) – 1997 - SAF Publishing Ltd p51

(72) Poison Heart – Surviving the Ramones - (Dee Dee Ramone with Veronica Kofman) – 1997 - SAF Publishing Ltd p21

(73) I Slept With Joey Ramone – A Punk Rock Family Memoir – (Mickey Leigh with Legs McNeil) – 2009 – Touchstone p104

(74) www.uncut.co.uk – The Story Of The Ramones: It was a nuthouse – we were the real deal – Peter Watts – 16/9/2016

(75) https://ultimateclassicrock.com/ramones-first-show/#:~:text=They%20actually%20played%20their%20first,handful%20of%20friends%20and%20assassocia – The Story Of The Ramones' First Show - Eduardo Rivadavia - 30/3/2016

(76) Please Kill me – the uncensored oral history of punk – (McNeil & McCain) – 1996 – Abacus p228

(77) On the Road With The Ramones – (Melnick and Meyer) – 2007 - Music Sales Group – p32

(78) On the Road With The Ramones – (Melnick and Meyer) – 2007 - Music Sales Group – p33

(79) Commando – (Johnny Ramone) – 2012 – Abrams- p42/3

(80) On the Road With The Ramones – (Melnick and Meyer) – 2007 - Music Sales Group – p48

(81) Poison Heart – Surviving the Ramones - (Dee Dee Ramone with Veronica Kofman) – 1997 - SAF Publishing Ltd p52/53

(82) Please Kill me – the uncensored oral history of punk – (McNeil & McCain) – 1996 – Abacus p251

(83) On the Road With The Ramones – (Melnick and Meyer) – 2007 - Music Sales Group – p52

(84) Commando – (Johnny Ramone) – 2012 - Abrams p50

(85) On the Road With The Ramones – (Melnick and Meyer) – 2007 - Music Sales Group – p284-288

(86) Please Kill me – the uncensored oral history of punk – (McNeil & McCain) – 1996 – Abacus p253

(87) I Slept With Joey Ramone – A Punk Rock Family Memoir – (Mickey Leigh with Legs McNeil) – 2009 – Touchstone p127

(88) Please Kill me – the uncensored oral history of punk – (McNeil & McCain) – 1996 – Abacus p259

(89) On the Road With The Ramones – (Melnick and Meyer) – 2007 - Music Sales Group – p85-86

(90) Commando – (Johnny Ramone) – 2012 - Abrams p49-51

(91) www.rollingstone.com – 10 things we learned from Godfather of Punk – Roc Doc: Danny Fields – By Jason Newman – 7/10/16

(92) On the Road With The Ramones – (Melnick and Meyer) – 2007 - Music Sales Group – p60

(93) Commando – (Johnny Ramone) – 2012 - Abrams p49-50

(94) www.faroutmagazine.co.uk – How Ramones recorded their iconic debut album – A. Starkey – 23/4/22

(95) England's Dreaming – (Savage) – 1991- Faber & Faber Ltd - p157

(96) If You Like The Ramones …. (Peter Aaron) – 2013 – Backbeat Books - p7

(97) Punk – (Colegrave & Sullivan) - 2001 - Cassell & Co. - p67

(98) I Slept With Joey Ramone – A Punk Rock Family Memoir – (Mickey Leigh with Legs McNeil) – 2009 – Touchstone p134

(99) Commando – (Johnny Ramone) – 2012 - Abrams - p54

(100) www.mrbeerys.com

(101) www.reddit.com – Club in Cambridge in the '70s – (GronamThe Ox) - 2017

(102) On the Road With The Ramones – (Melnick and Meyer) – 2007 - Music Sales Group – p73

(103) On the Road With The Ramones – (Melnick and Meyer) – 2007 - Music Sales Group – p82-84

(104) On the Road With The Ramones – (Melnick and Meyer) – 2007 - Music Sales Group – p75

(105) Please Kill me – the uncensored oral history of punk – (McNeil & McCain) – 1996 – Abacus p286

(106) www.timeout.com – The Roundhouse – 10/3/23

(107) Please Kill me – the uncensored oral history of punk – (McNeil & McCain) – 1996 – Abacus p287

(108) On the Road With The Ramones – (Melnick and Meyer) – 2007 - Music Sales Group – p75

(109) Poison Heart – Surviving the Ramones - (Dee Dee Ramone with Veronica Kofman) – 1997 - SAF Publishing Ltd p72

(110) www.udiscovermusic.com – Hey! Ho! Let's Go! Ramones debut at the Roundhouse, July 4, 1976 – (Tim Peacock) – 4/7/23

(111) www.squaremile.com – How the Ramones invented punk over two London gigs – Danny Fields – 25/5/18

(112) Please Kill me – the uncensored oral history of punk – (McNeil & McCain) – 1996 – Abacus p287-88

(113) https://www.loudersound.com/features/story-behind-the-song-blitzkrieg-bop-by-the-ramones

(114) http://www.thecollector.com/history-of-california/

(115) San Diego's five best concert venues you can no longer visit - The San Diego Union-Tribune (sandiegouniontribune.com)

(116) Cinema Treasures – The New Yorker – cinematreasures.org - 2010

(117) Punk Rock Blitzkrieg Bop: My Life as a Ramone – (Mark Ramone with Rich Herschlag) - 2015 –Touchstone p210

(118) On the Road With The Ramones – (Melnick and Meyer) – 2007 - Music Sales Group p144

(119) https://www.historichotels.org/us/hotels-resorts/fairmont-olympic-hotel/history.php

(120) https://www.seattletimes.com/entertainment/music/the-ramones-rattled-seattles-staid-olympic-hotel-exactly-40-years-ago

(121) www.setlist.fm – Ramones set list – March 6th 1977

(122) www.ramomsband.com

(123) www.ultimateclassicrock.com – 40 years ago: johnny Ramone nearly dies in a street fight – (Corey Irwin) – 13/8/23

(124) Commando – (Johnny Ramone) – 2012 – Abrams - p102

(125) www.meeting.zuerich.com – Volkshaus Zurich –

(126) On the Road With The Ramones – (Melnick and Meyer) – 2007 - Music Sales Group – p82

(127) I Slept With Joey Ramone – A Punk Rock Family Memoir – (Mickey Leigh with Legs McNeil) – 2009 – Touchstone p262

(128) I Know Better Now: My life before, during and after the Ramones – (Richie Ramone with Peter Aaron) – 2018 – Backbeat Books p 205-207

(129) Commando – (Johnny Ramone) – 2012 – Abrams - p158

(130) I Know Better Now: My life before, during and after the Ramones – (Richie Ramone with Peter Aaron) – 2018 – Backbeat Books p 202

(131) I Slept With Joey Ramone – A Punk Rock Family Memoir – (Mickey Leigh with Legs McNeil) – 2009 – Touchstone p261

(132) I Know Better Now: My life before, during and after the Ramones – (Richie Ramone with Peter Aaron) – 2018 – Backbeat Books p 208

(133) Commando – (Johnny Ramone) – 2012 – Abrams p70

(134) On the Road With The Ramones – (Melnick and Meyer) – 2007 -Music Sales Group - p79

(135) www.guestpectacular.com – Concerts at Auditoire Paul-Emile Janson

(136) www.setlist.fm – Ramones set list – May 2nd 1977

(137) I Know Better Now: My life before, during and after the Ramones – (Richie Ramone with Peter Aaron) – 2018 – Backbeat Books p199/199

(138) Punk Rock Blitzkrieg Bop: My Life as a Ramone – (Mark Ramone with Rich Herschlag) - 2015 –Touchstone p351

(139) Punk Rock Blitzkrieg Bop: My Life as a Ramone – (Mark Ramone with Rich Herschlag) - 2015 –Touchstone p154-6

(140) Poison Heart – Surviving the Ramones - (Dee Dee Ramone with Veronica Kofman) – 1997 - SAF Publishing Ltd p82

(141) On the Road With The Ramones – (Melnick and Meyer) – 2007 - Music Sales Group p82

(142) www.mvrdv.com – De Effenaar – 2018 – (Seb Paez)

(143) www.sandraschulman.medium.com – Ramones: Arturo Vega and the making of the logo Heard Round the World – (Sandra Hale Schulman) – 1/11/19

(144) www.songfacts.com

(145) https://peakd.com/@bengy/tasteem-f89e7d

(146) www.setlist.fm – Ramones set list – May 8th 1977

(147) https://www.spotgroningen.nl/de-oosterpoor

(148) On the Road With The Ramones – (Melnick and Meyer) – 2007 - Music Sales Group p78

(149) On the Road With The Ramones – (Melnick and Meyer) – 2007 - Music Sales Group p96

(150) www.faroutmagazine.co.uk – Why did Joey and Johnny Ramone hate each other? – (Arun Starkey) – 8/10/23

(151) Commando – (Johnny Ramone) – 2012 – Abrams - p96

(152) I Slept With Joey Ramone – A Punk Rock Family Memoir – (M. Leigh with Legs McNeil) – 2009 – Touchstone p214/5

(153) I Slept With Joey Ramone – A Punk Rock Family Memoir – (M. Leigh with Legs McNeil) – 2009 – Touchstone p230

(154) https://kulttuuritalo.fi/en/for-visitors/

(155) Commando – (Johnny Ramone) – 2012 - Abrams p115

(156) Punk Rock Blitzkrieg Bop: My Life as a Ramone (Mark Ramone with Rich Herschlag) - 2015 –Touchstone p144-145

(157) https://rippedandtorn.co.uk/now - (Jamie Havlin) – Now I Wanna Sniff Some Glue

(158) https://barrowland-ballroom.co.uk/about/

(159) https://www.rmg.co.uk/stories/topics/who-was-isambard-kingdom-brunel

(160) https://www.bristolpost.co.uk/news/history/hall-yesterdays-entire-history-colston-55500

(161) www.setlist.fm – Ramones set list – May 24th 1977

(162) https://punkgirldiaries.com/gabba-gabba-hey/

(163) On the Road With The Ramones – (Melnick and Meyer) – 2007 - Music Sales Group – p115

(164) https://www.oregonencyclopedia.org/articles/portland_paramount_theatre_arlene_schnitzer_concert_hall/ - The Portland Paramount Theatre/Arlene Schnitzer Concert Hall – (Joe Fitzgibbon) – 19/5/22

(165) I Know Better Now: My life before, during and after the Ramones – (Richie Ramone with Peter Aaron) – 2018 – Backbeat Books p120

(166) Punk Rock Blitzkrieg Bop: My Life as a Ramone (Mark Ramone with Rich Herschlag) 2015 –Touchstone p276

(167) I Know Better Now: My life before, during and after the Ramones – (Richie Ramone with Peter Aaron) – 2018 – Backbeat Books p 127-134

(168) I Know Better Now: My life before, during and after the Ramones – (Richie Ramone with Peter Aaron) – 2018 – Backbeat Books p136

(169) I Know Better Now: My life before, during and after the Ramones – (Richie Ramone with Peter Aaron) – 2018 – Backbeat Books p150

(170) www.vice.com – Remembering Arturo Vega, the 'Fifth Ramone' and My Former Roommate – (Jonah Bayer) – 7/5/2015

(171) Commando – (Johnny Ramone) – 2012 – Abrams - p72

(172) ww.stadiumjourney.com – A follow-up visit to the CFG Bank Arena in Baltimore – (Richard Smith) -28/3/2023

(173) www.venuesnow.com – Baltimore Reborn: CFG Bank Arena reimagined for concerts – (Wendy Pearl) – 17/4/2203

(174) www.loudersound.com – The story behind the song: The Ramones - Rockaway Beach – (Kris Needs) – 5/3/2018

(175) Author's note – Spahn Ranch was an established base for Charles Manson and his followers

(176) Rocket To Russia, Remastered album notes – (Legs McNeil) - 2001 - p5

(177) www.faroutmagazine.co.uk – Joey Ramone's favourite punk bands – (Aimee Ferrier) – 9/8/2023

(178) Ramones – "Rocket To Russia" Remaster Test Pressing LP/ From Producer Ed Stasium (recordmecca.com)

(179) Commando (Johnny Ramone) 2012 – Abrams p72

(180) Commando (Johnny Ramone) 2012 – Abrams p154

(181) Rocket To Russia, Remastered album notes – (Legs McNeil)
- 2001 – p4

(182) Rocket To Russia, Remastered album notes – (Legs McNeil)
- 2001 – p8

(183) I Slept With Joey Ramone – A Punk Rock Family Memoir – (Mickey Leigh with Legs McNeil) – 2009 – Touchstone p106

(184) www.songtell.com – meaning of I Wanna Be Well by the Ramones – 24/7/2023

(185) Commando (Johnny Ramone) 2012 – Abrams p153

(186) Rocket To Russia, Remastered album notes – (Legs McNeil)
- 2001 – p13

(187) www.scotsman.com – Memories of Edinburgh's most legendary gigs – By The Newsroom – 15/2/2017

(188) On the Road With The Ramones – (Melnick and Meyer) – 2007 - Music Sales Group P197

(189) https://pleasekillme.com/ramones-its-alive-by-ed-stasium/ - It's Alive! – The Ramones – Ed Stasium – 2/1/19

(190) https://pleasekillme.com/ramones-its-alive-by-ed-stasium/ - It's Alive! – The Ramones – Ed Stasium – 2/1/19

(191) https://colchesterartscentre.com/events/vinyl/ vinyl-sessions-the-ramones--its-alive

(192) www.superdeluxeedition.com - Ramones/Its Alive 40th anniversary – Ian Wade – 26/7/19

(193) https://pleasekillme.com/ramones-its-alive-by-ed-stasium/ - It's Alive! – The Ramones – Ed Stasium – 2/1/19

(194) http://www.markprindle.com/markyramone- Mark Prindle – 2008

(195) www.seconddisc.com – Review: Ramones, "It's Alive: 40th Anniversary Edition" – Joe Marchese – 24/10/19

(196) www.variety.com/lists/bests-live-albums-all-time-concerts/ -No concerts? Give these 50 live albums a listen – Amorosi, Aswad, Barker, Tangcay, Trakin and Willman – 6/9/2020

(197) www.allmusic.com – It's Alive Review – Mark Deming

(198) www.whatrecords.co.uk

(199) https://www.anrfactory.com/ramoanz-revived-rebellion-with-their-i-dont-wanna-go-down-to-the-basement-cover/

(200) www.theclio.com – Beacham Theatre, Orlando – (M. Ben & A Garcia) - 15/5/2017

(201) On the Road With The Ramones – (Melnick and Meyer) – 2007 - Music Sales Group p127

(202) www.sonicmoremusic.worldpress.com – The original art cover for Road to Ruin, featuring Tommy Ramone - 21/9/2014

(203) On the Road With The Ramones – (Melnick and Meyer) – 2007 - Music Sales Group – p127

(204) I Slept With Joey Ramone – A Punk Rock Family Memoir – (Mickey Leigh with Legs McNeil) – 2009 – Touchstone p173 and p183

(205) www.pitchfork.com/features/afterword/9456-ramones/ - Tommy Ramone – Evan Minsker 2014

(206) On the Road With The Ramones – (Melnick and Meyer) – 2007 - Music Sales Group – p127

(207) Poison Heart – Surviving the Ramones - (Dee Dee Ramone with Veronica Kofman) – 1997 - SAF Publishing Ltd p76

(208) On the Road With The Ramones – (Melnick and Meyer) – 2007 - Music Sales Group – p127

(209) Commando (Johnny Ramone) 2012 – Abrams p76

(210) On the Road With The Ramones – (Melnick and Meyer) – 2007 - Music Sales Group – p127/128

(211) Punk Rock Blitzkrieg Bop: My Life as a Ramone – (Mark Ramone with Rich Herschlag) - 2015 –Touchston p125/6

(212) On the Road With The Ramones – (Melnick and Meyer) – 2007 - Music Sales Group – p128

(213) Commando (Johnny Ramone) 2012 – Abrams p76/78

(214) On the Road With The Ramones – (Melnick and Meyer) – 2007 - Music Sales Group – p127-130

(215) www.gov.wales/welsh-language-wales-census-2021-html

(216) www.cardiff.ac.uk – The Great Hall

(217) www.setlist.fm – Ramones set list – Oct 3rd 1978

(218) ckiebadgersblog.blogspot.com/2011/03/1978-snips-ramones-and-chris-spedding.html

(219) https://www.repeatfanzine.co.uk/interviews/The%20Shamones.htm

(220) Author's note: Roman Jugg is keyboard player and guitarist who played for Victimize and The Damned

(221) https://www.repeatfanzine.co.uk/interviews/The%20Shamones.

(222) www.hamburg-ramones.de/about.html

(223) https://hopecollectiveireland.com - "The Ramones changed my life" Dublin's Music Champion: Eugene Connolly Interview Part 1 – (Michael Murphy) – 10/12/2017

(224) www.geocites.ws/pinheadireland/RAMIRE.htm – The Brudders were coming to town – (John O Sullivan)

(225) Poison Heart – Surviving the Ramones - (Dee Dee Ramone with Veronica Kofman) – 1997 - SAF Publishing Ltd p21-22

(226) On the Road With The Ramones – (Melnick and Meyer) – 2007 - Music Sales Group – p242

(227) On the Road With The Ramones – (Melnick and Meyer) – 2007 - Music Sales Group – p59

(228) Punk Rock Blitzkrieg Bop: My Life as a Ramone – (Mark Ramone with Rich Herschlag) - 2015 – Touchstone p149-151

(229) On the Road With The Ramones – (Melnick and Meyer) – 2007 - Music Sales Group – p234-5

(230) https://digitalfilmarchive.net/news/the-rolling-stones-remembering-charlie-watts-1248 The Rolling Stones: Remembering Charlie Watts - News - Northern Ireland Screen | Digital Film Archive

(231) https://www.loudersound.com/features/the-clash-in-belfast-riots

(232) https://www.spitrecords.co.uk/ramones.htm – Touring Bands: The Ramones – (Adrian Thrills) – NME - 30/9/1978

(233) https://www.mandelahall.com/about#:~:text=Mandela%20Hall%20is%20a%201000,international%20music%20and%20comedic%20talent

(234) https://breakingtunes.com/nomatter

(235) www.mybrightonandhove.org.uk – My Brighton: The award winning people's history of our city – (Richard J Szypulski) – 9/5/23

(236) www.setlist.fm – Ramones set list – May 7ᵗʰ 1986

(237) www.ramonesheaven.com – interview with Clare and Alex of AntiProduct – (Jari-Pekka Lattio-Ramone) – 2010

(238) Portsmouth Guildhall - Music Hall in Portsmouth, (visitportsmouth.co.uk

(239) Poison Heart – Surviving the Ramones - (Dee Dee Ramone with Veronica Kofman) –1997 - SAF Publishing Ltd p84

(240) Commando (Johnny Ramone) 2012 – Abrams p89

(241) Punk Rock Blitzkrieg Bop: My Life as a Ramone – (Mark Ramone with Rich Herschlag) - 2015 –Touchstone p238

(242) Author's note – Commando lyric: 3ʳᵈ Rule is – "Don't talk to Commies"

(243) www.torinoise80s.wordpress.com – "Ramones Live In Turin" - Torinoise '80 – 2016

(244) www.britannica.com – Iowa – (Rex D. Honey & Neil E. Salisbury) – 30/10/23

(245) https://thebigfootdiaries.blogspot.com/2013/06/1983-when-ramones-conquered-des-moines.html - 1983: When The Ramones Conquered Des Moines – 1/6/2013

(246) Commando – (Johnny Ramone) – 2012 - Abrams p157

(247) Subterranean Jungle, Remastered album notes – (Gil Kaufman) - 2002 - P5-7

(248) Punk Rock Blitzkrieg Bop: My Life as a Ramone (Mark Ramone with Rich Herschlag) 2015 –Touchstone p269

(249) Punk Rock Blitzkrieg Bop: My Life as a Ramone (Mark Ramone with Rich Herschlag) 2015 – p270-1

(250) Punk Rock Blitzkrieg Bop: My Life as a Ramone (Mark Ramone with Rich Herschlag) 2015 –Touchstone p230

(251) Commando (Johnny Ramone) - 2012 – Abrams - p115

(252) www.Ilikeyouroldstuff.com – Gabba Gabba we accept you – a love letter from down under to the Ramones – (by DL) – 20/7/2017

(253) www.capitoltheatre.com.au – About: Theatre History

(254) www.slq.gov.au – State Library Of Queensland – A Night at the Festival Hall with the Ramones (1980) – (Miles Sinnamon) - 18/6/2016

(255) wwwthemusic.com.au – The Ramones Have To Be The Band With The Worst Luck – (Steve Bell) 13/2/2015

(256) On the Road With The Ramones – (Melnick and Meyer) – 2007 - Music Sales Group P113

(257) www.eventfinda.co.nz/venue/logan-campbell-centre – The Logan Campbell Centre

(258) www.thespinoff.co.nz – Pop Culture – (Chris Schulz) – 24/6/21

(259) Punk Rock Blitzkrieg Bop: My Life as a Ramone (Mark Ramone with Rich Herschlag) 2015 –Touchstone p234/5

(260) Poison Heart – Surviving the Ramones - (Dee Dee Ramone with Veronica Kofman) – 1997 - SAF Publishing Ltd p126

(261) www.theculturetrip.com – The Dark History Behind Barcelona's Montjuïc Hill - (Tara Jessop) – 2019

(262) Punk Rock Blitzkrieg Bop: My Life as a Ramone (Mark Ramone with Rich Herschlag) - 2015 –Touchstone p342

(263) www.beyondthebarbs.wordpress.com – How OCD Killed Joey Ramone – (Cat Jones) – 2016

(264) On the Road With The Ramones – (Melnick and Meyer) – 2007 - Music Sales Group - P152

(265) Punk Rock Blitzkrieg Bop: My Life as a Ramone (Mark Ramone with Rich Herschlag) - 2015 –Touchstone p241

(266) https://osanosdanewwave.blogs.sapo.pt/tag/equator

(267) guestpectacular.com – concerts at Pavilhá **infant de Sagres**

(268) https://www.flickr.com/photos/lbeto/albums/72157602862886790/

(269) www.setlist.fm – Ramones set list – Nov 6th 1981 – Early Show

(270) On the Road With The Ramones – (Melnick and Meyer) – 2007 - Music Sales Group – p210

(271) Commando – (Johnny Ramone) – 2012 – Abrams - p156

(272) I Slept With Joey Ramone – A Punk Rock Family Memoir – (Mickey Leigh with Legs McNeil) – 2009 – Touchstone p216

(273) I Slept With Joey Ramone – A Punk Rock Family Memoir –
(Mickey Leigh with Legs McNeil) – 2009 – Touchstone p203-4

(274) I Slept With Joey Ramone – A Punk Rock Family Memoir – (M.
Leigh with Legs McNeil) – 2009 – Touchstone p241/2

(275) I Slept With Joey Ramone – A Punk Rock Family Memoir – (M.
Leigh with Legs McNeil) – 2009 – Touchstone p215

(276) I Know Better Now: My life before, during and after the Ramones –
(Richie Ramone with Peter Aaron) – 2018 – Backbeat Books p190

(277) Commando (Johnny Ramone) - 2012 – Abrams p157

(278) I Slept With Joey Ramone – A Punk Rock Family Memoir – (M.
Leigh with Legs McNeil) – 2009 – Touchstone p241

(279) I Slept With Joey Ramone – A Punk Rock Family Memoir – (M.
Leigh with Legs McNeil) – 2009 – Touchstone p242

(280) I Know Better Now: My life before, during and after the Ramones –
(Richie Ramone with Peter Aaron) – 2018 – Backbeat Books p188

(281) I Know Better Now: My life before, during and after the Ramones –
(Richie Ramone with Peter Aaron) – 2018 – Backbeat Books p187

(282) The long lineage of one-man bands – (Johnny Black) – Reverb.com
- 2018

(283) The Advocate – The Rise and Fall of the Arcadia – (Kriss Scott) -
Lakewood.advocatemag.com - 2023

(284) I Know Better Now: My life before, during and after the Ramones –
(Richie Ramone with Peter Aaron) – 2018 – Backbeat Books p217

(285) Commando (Johnny Ramone) 2012 – Abrams p123

(286) https://www.britannica.com/place/Sao-Paulo-Brazi

(287) www.accidentallywesanderson.com – Theatro Municipal de São Paulo

(288) I Know Better Now: My life before, during and after the Ramones –
(Richie Ramone with Peter Aaron) – 2018 – Backbeat Books p218

(289) Commando (Johnny Ramone) 2012 – Abrams p123-124

(290) Punk Rock Blitzkrieg Bop: My Life as a Ramone – (Mark Ramone
with Rich Herschlag) - 2015 –Touchstone p349

(291) https://www.britannica.com/place/Buenos-Aires

(292) On the Road With The Ramones – (Melnick and Meyer) – 2007 -
Music Sales Group – - p250

(293) Punk Rock Blitzkrieg Bop: My Life as a Ramone – (Mark Ramone
with Rich Herschlag) - 2015 – Touchstone p348 and 357

(294) I Know Better Now: My life before, during and after the Ramones – (Richie Ramone with Peter Aaron) – 2018 – Backbeat Books p 217/218

(295) On the Road With The Ramones – (Melnick and Meyer) – 2007 - Music Sales Group - p235

(296) Commando – (Johnny Ramone) – 2012 - Abrams p158-160

(297) I Know Better Now: My life before, during and after the Ramones – (Richie Ramone with Peter Aaron) – 2018 – Backbeat Books p220-24

(298) On the Road With The Ramones – (Melnick and Meyer) – 2007 - Music Sales Group – p214

(299) I Slept With Joey Ramone – A Punk Rock Family Memoir – (M. Leigh with Legs McNeil) – 2009 – Touchstone p268

(300) Commando – (Johnny Ramone) – 2012 – Abrams - p160

(301) Poison Heart – Surviving the Ramones - (Dee Dee Ramone with Veronica Kofman) – 1997 - SAF Publishing Ltd p121

(302) I Know Better Now: My life before, during and after the Ramones – Richie Ramone with Peter Aaron – 2018 – Backbeat Books p 235-239

(303) www.faroutmagazine.co.uk – Music – Remembering when Blondie's Clem Burk joined the Ramones for just 2 days – Joe Taysom - 2020

(304) https://archive.blondie.net/clem_burke_iwaselvisramone.shtml

(305) Punk Rock Blitzkrieg Bop: My Life as a Ramone (Mark Ramone with Rich Herschlag) 2015 –Touchstone

(306) www.britannica.com - Puerto Rico – (Thomas G Mathews, Kal Wagenheim, Olga J Wagenheim) - 3/11/23

(307) www.relojbomba.org – When the Ramones played P.R 20/9/2019

(308) On the Road With The Ramones – (Melnick and Meyer):2007 - Music Sales Group – p55, 70 & 241

(309) https://www.ukrockfestivals.com/reading-88.html

(310) Time Out Athens, Penguin Books, 2004

(311) On the Road With The Ramones – (Melnick and Meyer) – 2007 - Music Sales Group – p241

(312) www.kids.nationalgeographic.com – Mexico

(313) www.sandiegouniontribune.com – Short-lived Iguanas nightclub left a mark –(Matthew Hall) – 2/9/16

(314) www.concertarchives.org – Iguana's concert history

(315) www.reddit.com – 89-93, the golden time of TJ shows – 2019

(316) Punk Rock Blitzkrieg Bop: My Life as a Ramone – (Mark Ramone with Rich Herschlag) - 2015 –Touchstone p349-350

(317) www.splinternews.com – Hey Ho, let's Go (to the Ramones museum in Mexico City) – (Reed Dunlea) – 2/9/2015

(318) Poison Heart – Surviving the Ramones - (Dee Dee Ramone with Veronica Kofman) – 1997 - SAF Publishing Ltd p125-130

(319) Commando – (Johnny Ramone) – 2012 – Abrams - p110-111

(320) I Slept With Joey Ramone – A Punk Rock Family Memoir – (Mickey Leigh with Legs McNeil) – 2009 – Touchstone p276-277

(321) Punk Rock Blitzkrieg Bop: My Life as a Ramone – (Mark Ramone with Rich Herschlag) - 2015 –Touchston p330-31

(322) Punk Rock Blitzkrieg Bop: My Life as a Ramone – (Mark Ramone with Rich Herschlag) - 2015 –Touchston p334

(323) Commando – (Johnny Ramone) – 2012 – Abrams - p113

(324) www.undertheradar.co.nz – Interview C.J Ramone – 2/2/2015

(325) www.ramonesheaven.com – Interview with C.J Ramone – (Maggie St Thomas) – August 2001

(326) On the Road With The Ramones – (Melnick and Meyer) – 2007 - Music Sales Group – p232-233

(327) https://spielstaetten.buehnen-graz.com/grazer-spielstaetten/orpheum-graz/ - Orpheum Graz

(328) www.history.state.gov – Office of the Historian: The Break-Up of Yugoslavia, 1990-92

(329) www.setlist.fm – Ramones set list – Nov 25th 1990

(330) Punk Rock Blitzkrieg Bop: My Life as a Ramone (Mark Ramone with Rich Herschlag) - 2015 –Touchstone p343

(331) Punk Rock Blitzkrieg Bop: My Life as a Ramone (Mark Ramone with Rich Herschlag) - 2015 –Touchstone p344

(332) http://markprindle.com/cjramone-i.htm – C Jay Ramone – (Mark Prindle) – 2009

(333) Poison Heart – Surviving the Ramones - (Dee Dee Ramone with Veronica Kofman) – 1997 - SAF Publishing Ltd p143

(334) On the Road With The Ramones – (Melnick and Meyer) – 2007 - Music Sales Group – p217

(335) Punk Rock Blitzkrieg Bop: My Life as a Ramone (Mark Ramone with Rich Herschlag) - 2015 –Touchstone p344

(336) Commando (Johnny Ramone) - 2012 – Abrams p161

(337) On the Road With The Ramones – (Melnick and Meyer) – 2007 - Music Sales Group - p217

(338) https://www.gob.cl/en/ourcountry/#:~:text=Its%20shape%20is%20unique%3A%20it,sole%20exception%20of%20tropical%20weather.

(339) https://www.worldatlas.com/maps/chilE

(340) On the Road With The Ramones – (Melnick and Meyer) – 2007 - Music Sales Group – p250

(341) https://www.ncbi.nlm.nih.gov/pmc/articles/PMC10706229/#:~:text=In%20Chile%2C%20the%20%E2%80%9CSocial%20Outbreak,and%20residential%20areas%2C%20that%20lasted

(342) Author's note – the most southernmost tribute band found in this research was Der Ramoans of New Plymouth, New Zealand (39.05 degrees south as opposed to Concepción, Chile which has a latitude of 36.82 degrees south)

(343) Commando – Johnny Ramone – 2012 (Abrams) - p.161

(344) http://markprindle.com/cjramone-i.htm – C Jay Ramone – Mark Prindle – 2009

(345) Commando – Johnny Ramone – 2012 (Abrams) - p.161

(346) http://www.hypestudio.com.br/en/gigantinho

(347) www.setlist.fm – Ramones set list – November 9th 1994

(348) https://www.instagram.com/ramonestherapy/p/CxsuS0luLcU/?img_index=1

(349) https://www.summertime.nu - Skellefteå Summertime 2024 - Skellefteås största festivalområde

(350) https://www.visitsweden.com/where-to-go/northern-sweden/vasterbotten/umea/

(351) On the Road With The Ramones – (Melnick and Meyer) – 2007 - Music Sales Group P216

(352) Commando (Johnny Ramone) - 2012 – Abrams p162

(353) On the Road With The Ramones – (Melnick and Meyer) – 2007 - Music Sales Group P217

(354) Poison Heart – Surviving the Ramones - (Dee Dee Ramone with Veronica Kofman) – 1997 - SAF Publishing Ltd p143

(355) Punk Rock Blitzkrieg Bop: My Life as a Ramone – (Mark Ramone with Rich Herschlag) - 2015 –Touchstone p354

(356) http://markprindle.com/cjramone-i.htm – C Jay Ramone – (Mark Prindle) – 2009

(357) Commando (Johnny Ramone) - 2012 – Abrams p115

(358) https://chillisauce.com/stag/in-tallinn/post-f3645fdf94a8940fc95b3

(359) www.youtube.com/watch?v=2orignVS_co

(360) Punk Rock Blitzkrieg Bop: My Life as a Ramone – (Mark Ramone with Rich Herschlag) - 2015 –Touchstone p343

(361) www.youtube.com/watch?v=vFITxCm4XRU – Ramones: Blitzkrieg Bop Over The Years – 1975-96 – Heatseaker – 10/12/21

(362) Punk Rock Blitzkrieg Bop: My Life as a Ramone – (Mark Ramone with Rich Herschlag) - 2015 –Touchstone p361

(363) Commando – (Johnny Ramone) – 2012 – Abrams - p131-32

(364) I Slept With Joey Ramone – A Punk Rock Family Memoir – (M. Leigh with Legs McNeil) – 2009 – Touchstone p334/5

(365) tps://www.concertarchives.org/concerts/ lollapalooza-1996-203db94f-d2fe-4956-b20c-f6fa06e53c09

(366) www.avalonhollywood.com – History of the Avolon

(367) Poison Heart – Surviving the Ramones - (Dee Dee Ramone with Veronica Kofman) – 1997 - SAF Publishing Ltd p187

(368) I Slept With Joey Ramone – A Punk Rock Family Memoir – (M. Leigh with Legs McNeil) – 2009 – Touchstone p340

(369) Punk Rock Blitzkrieg Bop: My Life as a Ramone – (Mark Ramone with Rich Herschlag) - 2015 –Touchstone p360

(370) Commando – (Johnny Ramone) – 2012 – Abrams - p131

(371) I Slept With Joey Ramone – A Punk Rock Family Memoir – (M. Leigh with Legs McNeil) – 2009 – Touchstone p340

(372) Commando – (Johnny Ramone) – 2012 - Abrams - p83/84

(373) On the Road With The Ramones – (Melnick and Meyer) – 2007 - Music Sales Group – p200

(374) https://ultimateclassicrock. com/10-years-ago-joey-ramone-gets-a-street-named-after-him-in-nyc

(375) https://forums.macresource.com/read. php?1,1095230,1095696,quote=1

(376) https://www.shootfarken.com.au/444-songs-that-mention-ramones/ - Shoot Farken - (Uli Hesse) - 15/12/20

(377) https://www.juno.co.uk/products/tip-toppers-subterranean-jungle-vinyl/985910-01/

(378) https://glamadelaide.com.au/interview-lookout-australia-stan-lee-the-dickies-are-finally-coming/

(379) https://www.theguardian.com/music/2016/feb/02/forty-years-of-the-ramones-they-were-the-smartest-dumb-band-you-ever-heard

(380) https://www.loudersound.com/features/the-story-behind-the-song-teenage-kicks-by-the-undertones-1

(381) https://louderthanwar.com/an-interview-with-arturo-bassick-the-lurkers-999-punk-

(382) https://www.thecollector.com/did-the-ramones-invent-punk – Did The Ramones invent Punk? (Scott McLaughlan) – 18/12/2023

(383) Author's note: Joey Ramone left his 50% shares of Ramones Productions Inc. to his mother, Charlotte Lesher, with whom Cummings-Ramone said she had a good relationship. Hyman, inherited the shares from Lesher upon her death in 2007

(384) https://pagesix.com/2019/12/03/joey-ramones-brother-says-johnnys-widow-is-ruining-the-bands-legacy/

(385) https://www.nme.com/en_asia/news/music/joey-ramones-brother-hits-back-at-baseless-and-flimsy-biopic-lawsuit-3613602

(386) https://nypost.com/2024/01/27/metro/ramones-love-triangle-at-center-of-legal-dispute-over-bands-legacy/

(387) https://www.nme.com/en_asia/news/music/joey-ramones-brother-hits-back-at-baseless-and-flimsy-biopic-lawsuit-3613602

(388) https://nypost.com/2024/01/27/metro/ramones-love-triangle-at-center-of-legal-dispute-over-bands-legacy/

(389) https://nypost.com/2024/01/27/metro/ramones-love-triangle-at-center-of-legal-dispute-over-bands-legacy/

(390) https://www.facebook.com/groups/mickeyleighfans/

(391) https://www.septembercfawkes.com/2015/09/raw-vs-subdued-emotions-getting-them.html#:~:text=Raw%20emotions%20are%20usually%20very%20intense.%20They%27re%20fresh%2C,emotions%2C%20the%20more%20raw%20our%20emotions%20will%20be

The four original Ramones - Joey, Johnny, Dee Dee and Tommy can be seen performing at the Palladium, New York City on January 7th, 1978. Photo by Diana D'Amato, used with kind permission of the estate od Diana D'Amato, Thanks to Tom Ciorciari and Adam Greiss.

Thank you to

Beana Burns, Greg Simpson and *Ken Spearpoint*

for helping to fulfil a dream